B. Lee Cooper, PhD
Wayne S. Haney, BME

Rock Music in American Popular Culture: Rock 'n' Roll Resources

Pre-publication REVIEWS, COMMENTARIES, EVALUATIONS . . .

"*Rock Music in American Popular Culture* is an outstanding reference work that belongs in every university library. Cooper and Haney have assembled an intriguing collection of studies that will be of particular interest to popular culture scholars and to teachers in all fields who are interested in incorporating popular culture materials into their courses. The book's discographies and bibliography are especially strong."

Gary Burns, PhD
Associate Professor,
Communications Studies,
Northern Illinois University

More pre-publication
REVIEWS, COMMENTARIES, EVALUATIONS . . .

"*Rock Music in American Popular Culture: Rock 'n' Roll Resources* is a delight. A treasure-trove of 'trivia with a purpose,' this is a careful cataloging of the ephemera of popular culture, with an eye especially to those materials of interest to college and secondary-school teachers of American and cultural studies. Bibliographies and discographies are introduced with practical, sensible suggestions for working with the materials in a classroom setting. This book should be equally welcome for both classroom teachers and library acquisitions personnel, with whom Cooper and Haney plead for an expansive vision of what a research library is, what it can be, and what it *should* be. If you are a librarian, charged with the acquisition of popular culture resources on an ever-shrinking budget; or if you are a high-school, college, or university teacher interested in using the texts of culture–baseball cards and songs, mail-order catalogues, cartoons, record charts, board games–as an avenue into the burgeoning field of cultural studies, this text is required reading."

Kevin J. H. Dettmar, PhD
Assistant Professor of English,
Clemson University

"This eclectic guide to the resourcefulness of contemporary popular culture serves as a constant reminder about the richness and variousness of the common culture that binds us all together. For the serious teacher, this volume provides a wide-ranging look at the nature of contemporary culture while anchoring its observations in popular music. For it is in and through popular music that the culture reflects upon and comments on its own significance. From baseball songs to tunes about food, this volume catalogs our lyrical fascination with the details of everyday life. It also provides positive proof that no aspect of contemporary life is unrecorded in popular songs. The mass media transmit the human songs of everyday life in all of their humor, sadness, joy, and pain. B. Lee Cooper and Wayne S. Haney provide the student/teacher of contemporary culture with a seemingly endless supply of resources and sources. The rest is up to us!"

Michael T. Marsden, PhD
Dean of the College
of Arts and Sciences,
Northern Michigan University

More pre-publication
REVIEWS, COMMENTARIES, EVALUATIONS . . .

"This volume is just what librarians have been searching for as the one definitive resource tool to serve the research needs of their popular culture-seeking patrons. Cooper and Haney's collection of essays are as varied as the spectrum of popular culture, with subjects ranging from baseball cards and songs, to memorabilia and collectibles, to radio broadcasting.

The volume's strength, however, lies in the fact that it is a first-rate source for popular music research and teaching. Not only are the essays incisive and informational, but they also add the valuable component of otherwise-hard-to-obtain bibliographies and discographies. These music articles feature in-depth treatises on bootleg recordings, Christmas carols, food, nursery rhymes, record popularity charts, rock 'n' roll legends, and TV- and film-related music. This book belongs in every public, high-school, and university library!"

William L. Schurk, MSLS
Professor and Sound Recordings Archivist, Bowling Green State University

"Lee Cooper and Wayne Haney have blended a rich mix of essays that will open our eyes to the opportunities that popular culture provides for learning about the American people and the United States. The bibliographies and discographies alone make this book worth the price. The authors have focused on familiar but sometimes forgotten popular culture resources and provided in one volume materials that will benefit historians, history and social studies educators, and librarians."

Stephen Kneeshaw, PhD
Professor of History, College of the Ozarks

"In their book *Rock Music in American Popular Culture: Rock 'n' Roll Resources*, B. Lee Cooper and Wayne S. Haney make an invaluable contribution to our understanding of the critical role popular culture plays in the social construction of reality and vice versa; that is, how everyday experiences give rise to the creation, construction, development, and perpetuation of popular culture. This book is a godsend to music educators, for it will enable music teachers to reach their students on common ground. Lucidly written,

More pre-publication
REVIEWS, COMMENTARIES, EVALUATIONS . . .

the format and style render the content ready for use without spending the traditional time necessary for analysis and lesson plans. The authors use a style that spares teachers the time-consuming chore of writing goals, objectives, and teaching strategies.

Teachers, professors, and students of African-American studies, American studies, social studies, music education, and popular culture will find the text an indispensable resource or reference tool. The text is seminal in its coverage of the full gamut of popular culture, ranging from the use of baseball cards, popular music, radio programs, TV programs, and international studies. Well-documented sources used by the authors are clearly identified for others to reference. Information on the superstars of rock will be of particular interest to persons ranging from teenagers to middle-agers."

Warren C. Swindell, PhD
Director and Professor
of African-American Studies,
Indiana State University

"To paraphrase Alan Jay Lerner: 'Thank heaven for B. Lee Cooper (and, in this case, Wayne S. Haney).' Anyone who is engaged in research and scholarship in the area of Popular Culture knows Professor Cooper's work and is eternally grateful for his indispensable spade work in the area. The publication of Haworth's *Rock Music in American Popular Culture: Rock 'n' Roll Resources* is cause for continued thanks.

Ranging from baseball cards to Christmas carols to food to commercial catalogs, Cooper and Haney have assembled a collection of 25 essays devoted to popular culture subjects. Each essay provides succinct background on the subject, some sort of classroom project or exercise, and, of course, a wonderful bibliography.

What a wonderful resource for elementary, secondary, and college teachers! For instance, the entry on baseball cards focuses on using the cards to learn more about integration of African-Americans into the sport and, by extension, into other

More pre-publication
REVIEWS, COMMENTARIES, EVALUATIONS . . .

areas of the culture at large. As always with Professor Cooper's work, one of the greatest values of this volume lies in the bibliographies assembled for the different entries. Meticulously culled from a wide range of sources, they will certainly help scholars expedite their own research and will open up new sources of information for teachers at all levels.

Rock Music in American Popular Culture is a book that will be almost indispensable in any school library. Informational, insightful, comprehensive, useful and, dare I say it, fun, it is a book that will inform, engage, and challenge readers who care about education and culture."

Timothy E. Scheurer, PhD
Professor of Humanities,
Franklin University

Harrington Park Press
An Imprint of The Haworth Press, Inc.

NOTES FOR PROFESSIONAL LIBRARIANS AND LIBRARY USERS

This is an original book title published by Harrington Park Press, an imprint of The Haworth Press, Inc. Unless otherwise noted in specific chapters with attribution, materials in this book have not been previously published elsewhere in any format or language.

CONSERVATION AND PRESERVATION NOTES

The paper used in this publication meets the minimum requirements of American National Standard for Information Sciences–Permanence of Paper for Printed Material, ANSI Z39.48-1984.

Rock Music in American Popular Culture

Rock 'n' Roll Resources

HAWORTH Popular Culture
Frank W. Hoffmann, PhD and William G. Bailey, MA
Senior Editors

New, Recent, and Forthcoming Titles:

Arts & Entertainment Fads by Frank W. Hoffmann and William G. Bailey

Sports & Recreation Fads by Frank W. Hoffmann and William G. Bailey

Mind & Society Fads by Frank W. Hoffmann and William G. Bailey

Fashion & Merchandising Fads by Frank W. Hoffmann and William G. Bailey

Chocolate Fads, Folklore, and Fantasies: 1000+ Chunks of Chocolate Information by Linda K. Fuller

The Popular Song Reader: A Sampler of Well-Known Twentieth-Century Songs by William Studwell

Rock Music in American Popular Culture: Rock 'n' Roll Resources by B. Lee Cooper and Wayne S. Haney

Rock Music in American Popular Culture

Rock 'n' Roll Resources

B. Lee Cooper, PhD
Wayne S. Haney, BME

Harrington Park Press
An Imprint of The Haworth Press, Inc.
New York • London • Norwood (Australia)

Published by

Harrington Park Press, an imprint of The Haworth Press, Inc., 10 Alice Street, Binghamton, NY 13904-1580

Library of Congress Cataloging-in-Publication Data

Cooper, B. Lee.
Rock music in American popular culture : rock 'n' roll resources / B. Lee Cooper, Wayne S. Haney.
p. cm.
Includes bibliographical references and index.
ISBN 1-56023-853-4 (acid-free paper).
1. Rock music–United States–History and criticism. 2. United States–Popular culture–History–20th century. 3. Music and society. I. Haney, Wayne S. II. Title.
ML3534.C663 1994
781.66 '0973–dc20 93-15554
CIP

To the founders and sustainers
of the Popular Culture Movement
in the United States and throughout the world:

Ray B. Browne
Pat Browne

ABOUT THE AUTHORS

B. Lee Cooper, PhD, is Provost and Vice President for Academic Affairs and Professor of History at The College of Great Falls in Montana. His previous publications include *Images of American Society in Popular Music* (1982), *The Popular Music Handbook* (1984), *The Literature of Rock II* (1986) with Frank W. Hoffmann, *A Resource Guide to Themes in Contemporary American Song Lyrics, 1950-1985* (1986), and *Popular Music Perspectives: Ideas, Themes, and Patterns in Contemporary Lyrics* (1991).

Wayne S. Haney, BME, is vicar of Holy Cross Church in Weare, New Hampshire. Formerly Associate Director of the Academic Resource Center at Olivet College, Father Haney is an organist and computer specialist who has co-authored *Response Recordings: An Answer Song Discography, 1950-1990* (1990) and *Rockabilly: A Bibliographic Resource Guide* (1990) with B. Lee Cooper.

CONTENTS

Acknowledgements

The genius of Sigmund Freud was that he could look at a few drops of water and envision the sweeping currents, unimagined depths, and pounding waves of an entire ocean. Similar perception can be attributed to Ray B. Browne. This teacher, scholar, and founder of both the Popular Culture Association and the American Culture Association is dauntless in his defense of examining ideas and materials from everyday life. This book is dedicated to Professor Browne and his energetic, affable, well-organized spouse, Pat. If Ray Browne is the theoretical fount of the popular culture movement, then Pat Browne is its most profound and prominent propagandist. She has served as managing editor for The Popular Press at Bowling Green State University for nearly two decades. She has been instrumental in publishing hundreds of significant scholarly monographs and anthologies, plus an array of quarterly journals including the *Journal of Popular Culture, Popular Music and Society*, and the *Journal of American Culture.*

This study reinforces and illustrates many of the principles articulated by Ray Browne over the past four decades. Yet none of the essays contained in this volume are his. The ideas about popular culture that he loosed in academia are currently so dominant that they have become intellectual "givens" in the geometry of contemporary cultural research. Interdisciplinary investigations of baseball cards, commercial music catalogs, dance crazes, folk songs, food, nursery rhymes, radio broadcasters, record charts, regional history, science fiction, sports heroes, and work experiences fit neatly under the broad umbrella of popular culture study. An anthology examining this variety of topics would have been unthinkable before Ray Browne identified the humanistic web of ideas, imagery, and history that links these seemingly disparate items of American life.

This volume views a variety of popular culture resources through the prism of modern music. Most of the authors represented in the text are lyric analysts, rock bibliographers, subject classification experts, and discographers. The essays compiled here differ markedly in style, structure, and length. Book reviews and record lists are combined with detailed historical studies and biographies to demonstrate a grand sense of literary mix. Transcriptions of radio programs and descriptions of board games are also included. Both critical and laudatory observations abound throughout the text. The alphabetical chapter format permits the reader to easily identify and then explore particular items of popular culture interest. Extensive book lists within each chapter and a lengthy bibliography at the end of the volume offer additional sources for future inquiries.

Beyond Ray and Pat Browne, the individual who contributed most significantly to formulating this anthology is William L. Schurk. As the Sound Recordings Archivist in the William T. Jerome Library at Bowling Green State University, Schurk has been an indefatigable ally in uncovering rare recorded resources, in supplying helpful commentaries from books and periodicals, and in suggesting off-the-wall ideas for new research avenues. He has been a chauffeur, an innkeeper, a guide to urban centers, and a selfless friend to popular music fans, students, librarians, teaching colleagues, and research scholars since 1967. His contributions to this volume are too numerous to mention.

Writers rely upon friends, colleagues, and professional acquaintances for ideas, assistance, stimulation, criticism, and companionship during various stages of scholarly production. While reviewing their superb books, articles, and conference papers, we have encountered and benefitted from the efforts of several exceptional thinkers: Mark Booth, Gary Burns, Ronald Butchart, George O. Carney, Norm Cohen, R. Serge Denisoff, Howard A. DeWitt, Allen Ellis, Colin Escott, Reebee Garofalo, Steve Gelfand, Archie Green, Charles Gritzner, Peter Hesbacher, Frank W. Hoffmann, David Horn, Hugo Keesing, Stephen Kneeshaw, David Leaf, John Litevich, Dennis Loren, J. Fred MacDonald, Jon McAuliffe, Hugh Mooney, Russel B. Nye, David Pichaske, George Plasketes, Lawrence Redd, Jerome Rodnitzky, Lucy Rollin, Roger B. Rollin, Timothy Scheurer, Fred E. H. Schroeder, Tom Schultheiss, Larry Stidom, Warren Swindell, Joel Whitburn, Brett Williams, and Morgan Wright. Through record collecting and correspondence concerning audiotapes, we have also established beneficial contacts with many shrewd, helpful persons: James A. Creeth, David A. "Radio/TV Dave" Milberg, Frank Scott, and Chas "Dr. Rock" White.

Finally, our activities as college teachers and academic administrators have enabled us to develop a cadre of professional friendships that were sustaining and supportive during the inevitable research doldrums: Sue Ayotte, Stuart and Teresa Blacklaw, David Boyd, Donna and Terry Brummett, Roger C. Buese, Dolores Chapman, Neil and Karen Clark, Barbara Cunningham, Colby Currier, Norma Curtis, Cynthia Eller, Charles and Jane Erickson, Shirley Erickson, Vicki Gallas, Frederick Gilliard, Susan Gray, Eric and Priscilla Hagen, Lee Harrier, Jerrilyn Holcomb, Jare Klein, Damon Lee, Laura Maas, David Malcolm, Don and Zella Morris, Jack and Anne Patterson, Stuart Parsell, Roland Patzer, Kevin Rabineau, Todd and Connie Reynolds, Kenn Robbins, Donald and Sue Rowe (and Jessi, too), Mary Schroth, Linda Jo Scott, Jeff and Rande Smith, Reginald Smith, Steen and Jane Spove (and young Steen, too), John and Linda Sukovich, Arthur Sunleaf, Paul Sutherland, David Thomas, Todd Trevorrow, Stewart Tubbs, Don and Louise Tuski, Donald Walker, Gary Wertheimer, James Wilson, Dirk G. Wood, and, especially, library historian/popular culture scholar Wayne A. Wiegand.

Authors also benefit from the loving, uncritical support of wives, children, parents, and other relatives. This indispensable sustenance was provided by Jill E. Cooper, Michael L. Cooper, Laura E. Cooper, Julie A. Cooper, Nicholas Cooper, Kathleen M. Cooper, Charles A. Cooper, Patty Jo Cooper, Larry W. Cooper, Angie Cooper, Dustin Cooper, Leon Haney, Marian Haney, Mary Haney, Herbert Jones, Judy Jones, Carol Moore, Harry Moore, and David Osmycki.

The final type of support that made this study possible was financial. Two agencies provided generous economic assistance. We wish to thank the Division of Fellowships and Seminars of the National Endowment for the Humanities (NEH) for awarding B. Lee Cooper a "Travel to Collections" Grant during 1985. We also acknowledge similar research funding for Professor Cooper provided by the Grants Committee and Board of Directors of the Association for Recorded Sound Collections (ARSC) in 1990 and again in 1992. This special financial support permitted lengthy periods of research access to both literary and audio materials housed at the Sound Recordings Archive in The Jerome Library at Bowling Green State University.

B. Lee Cooper and Wayne S. Haney

Introduction

> Academic library collection development has an inertia of its own which is aided and abetted by the academic librarian's preconceived predilections, conservative training, and book-oriented practical experience. Add to this the tacit (if not conscious) support of an academically conservative, culturally elitist faculty on most campuses, and one can readily see the reason why popular culture proponents receive little support from academic librarians in building collections of popular culture materials.
>
> *–Wayne A. Wiegand*[1]

Effective library service should be guided by two fundamental principles. First, the general educational interests of contemporary men and women are inner-directed. Although undeniably influenced by public schooling, churches, and other socializing agencies, individual learning pursuits warrant access to an unrestricted store of information. Second, libraries ought to provide the broadest spectrum of materials to encourage the public to perceive the library as a reasonable and reliable source for all information needs.

In Western society, learning has moved forward along an educational path bounded by two contrasting philosophies about each citizen's capacity to improve his or her own knowledge. Those who *knew* what should be learned established rigidly prescriptive instructional systems which attempted to ensure that only "proper"

A portion of this commentary was originally prepared by B. Lee Cooper for presentation at the 1980 Annual Convention of the American Library Association in New York City under the title "Providing Information Services for Young Adults: The Popular Culture Challenge for Librarians." Reprint permission granted by the author.

items of information would be available for human consumption. This paternalistic prior censorship allegedly spawned such social benefits as religious purity, political stability, and social continuity. On the other hand, those who believed that no single body of knowledge was absolutely indispensable to humanity's development championed varying forms of individualistic intellectual anarchy as an educational tonic to cure existing social and political ills. Theoretically, the result of fostering uncoerced thought patterns would be a more humanistic orientation toward community life.

Somewhere between these two philosophical extremes, librarianship has emerged during the past century as an independently functioning educational profession. Dedication to the expansion of personal intellectual horizons, rather than to the perpetuation of any single learning orthodoxy, is the cornerstone of information services in a free society. Most librarians consider both political censorship and intellectual anarchy equally detrimental to personal development. Librarians are champions of accumulating, organizing, preserving, and circulating all forms of information. They are neither value-free nor propagandistic, but remain firmly committed to the principle that all materials required to foster reflective thought and generate effective decision making must be readily available to all patrons.

Librarians are freelance academicians. They owe primary allegiance to managing information from all academic disciplines that will further the pursuit of individual learning and personal satisfaction. The link between librarianship and popular culture exists in the changing interest profiles and thought patterns of contemporary Americans. It is undeniable that "new" information resources are constantly sought by individuals and groups of students, scholars, housewives, businesspeople, and others. They make ever-broadening requests for information about subjects related to television, science fiction, motion pictures, comic books, and popular music. Librarians must be prepared to provide assistance to persons making inquiries about popular culture topics–yet, by training, they are often ill-equipped to cope with information needs in such nontraditional resource areas.[2]

Ignoring the precise, technical language of either formal learning theories or psychological modes of perception, we can depict the mind of a contemporary citizen as a combination of factual and fictional orbits. For the sake of discussion, these two orbits can be separated by definition; however, they invariably function concurrently. The factual portion of this dual mental model is informed by a variety of readily identifiable sources. Among these are: current and historical events, reference books, weekly news magazines, newspapers, radio news, television reports, and documentary films. Obviously, the sources within this factual realm are not isolated. They interact to reinforce, clarify, enlarge upon, and define individual understanding of ideas and events.

The other half of this perceptual model is the fictional realm. This area is also informed by a series of commonly available information sources that include: fictional tales, historical novels, satirical magazines, comic books, popular songs, science fiction stories, radio and television shows, and motion pictures. As in the case of the factual realm, there is duplication and interaction among images in each of these fictional items.

The ideas illustrated in Figures 1 and 2 are neither new nor startling. But if we are to conceive and deal constructively with the fundamental challenge of popular culture information to traditional librarianship, it is necessary to highlight those information resources that affect contemporary thought. On any major social or political issue, there is immediate integration among factual and fictional materials (see Figure 3). Popular culture is dominated by the resulting interactions of elements from within *each* realm. What happens to a viewer's thought patterns when documentary films of the Persian Gulf War are mixed with WTBS reruns of John Wayne's World War II motion pictures? How about when historical monographs and biographies of Henry Ford's automobile empire are combined with historical novels about the social, sexual, and political exploits of Detroit's automotive executive classes? Or when radio and television news reports of Los Angeles police racism occur adjacent to lilly-white daytime soap operas, black-oriented situation comedies, and evening dramas about salt-and-pepper police patrol teams? One might wish to assert that everyone knows the difference between fact and fiction. But this is only partially true. What is certain, though, is that modern people *learn* from each realm. And the interactions of fact and fantasy found in movie

FIGURE 1

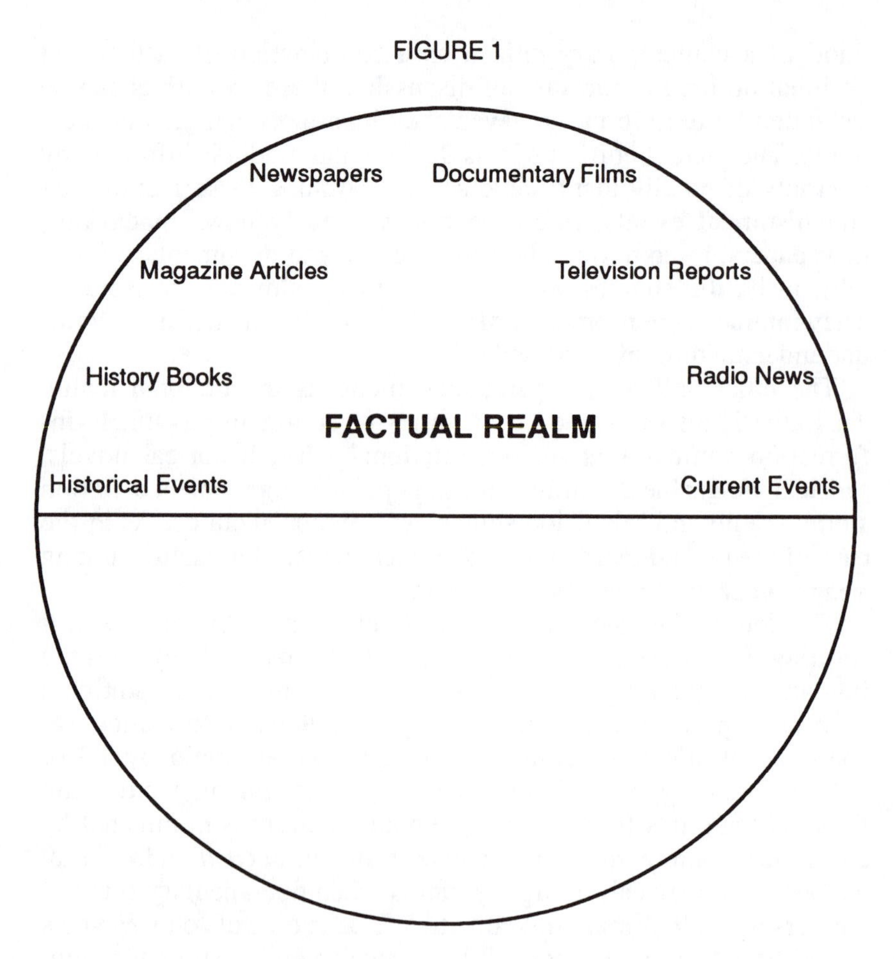

reviews, political cartoons, popular songs, speculation fiction, and other forms of fact/fiction combinations illustrate the mind's magnificent capability to assimilate information from all sorts of literary, auditory, and visual formats.

Providing information services with popular culture resources should be conceived as a dual concept relating to functional design in resource acquisition and to anticipated client needs. These two elements must correlate to a high degree if the public–real and potential library patrons–is to be satisfied. Increasing public interest

FIGURE 2

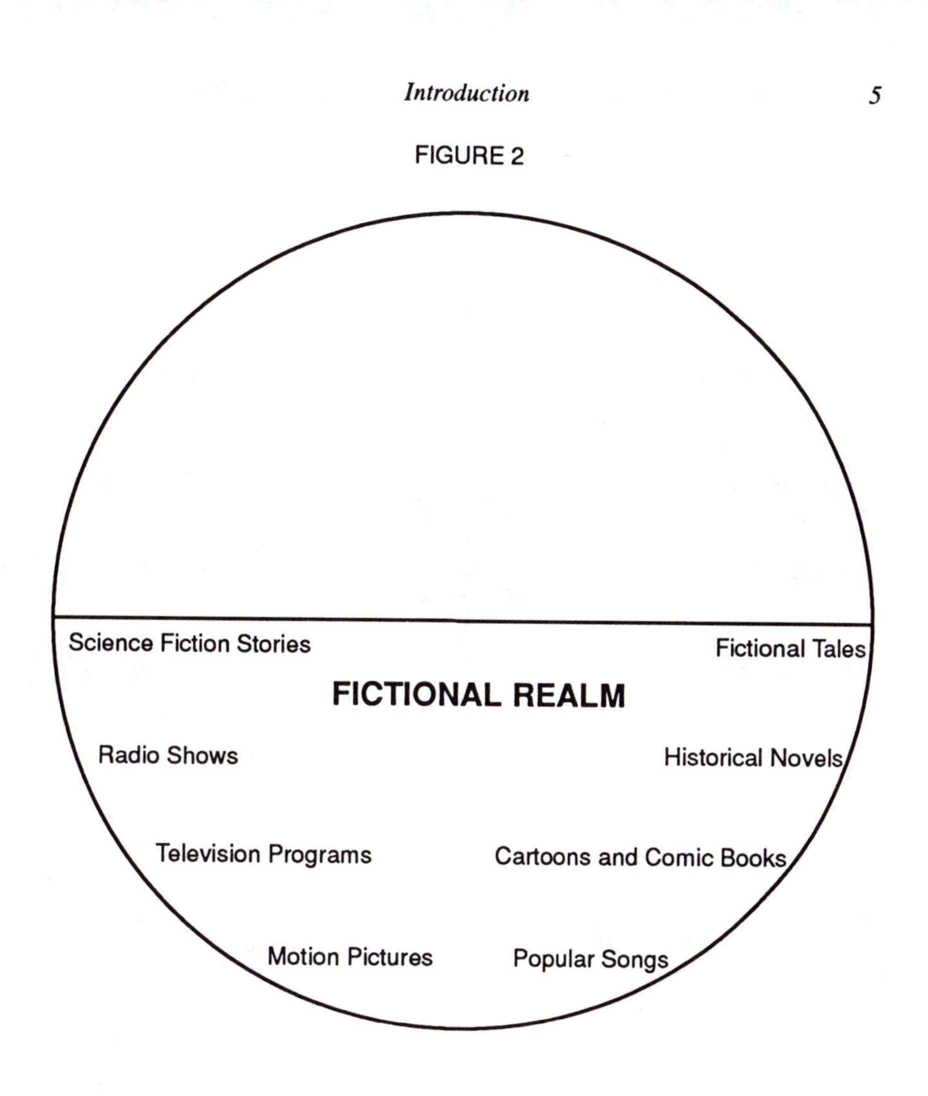

in popular culture materials dictates that librarians assemble accumulation and delivery systems that are specifically designed to meet these needs. Undeniably, the new kinds of information being requested–an issue of *Fantasy and Science Fiction*, a videotape of a recently televised program, recordings of a series of protest songs, a copy of a Marvel comic book, or an anthology of speculative writings about the American Tricentennial–are extremely challenging. Rather than adapting to this growing demand for nontraditional materials, some librarians might be tempted to argue that, since

FIGURE 3

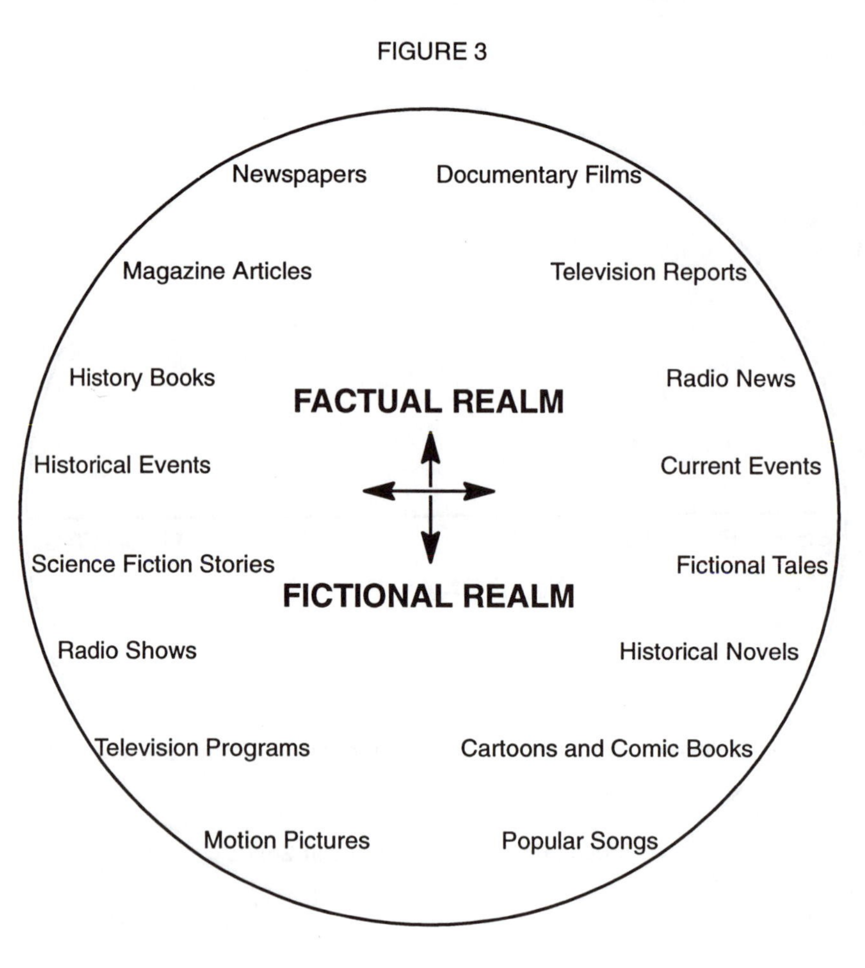

better and more conveniently packaged cultural resources are becoming more costly to acquire, current library collections should not be diluted at this time by adding socially questionable, "faddish" popular culture items. Yet such a purchasing stance denies the fundamental premise that underlies a democratic information services philosophy. Those items desired and utilized by a public that the library is attempting to serve should guide its acquisitions policy.

Librarians have an obligation to help people establish their own perspectives on life, especially during an age when reliance on the authority of tradition has been replaced by rampant public skepticism. This is certainly not a new quest. What is new, though, is the availability of such widely varied types of intellectual stimuli. The human mind is a marvelous instrument. It constructs reality in individualistic patterns from a multiplicity of external materials and specific experiences. As a major source of general information service, the library should be responsive to all forms, stages, and reasons for intellectual development. It is logical for a student patron to shift her requests from a play by William Shakespeare to a recording by Bob Dylan, or to seek materials comparing Henry David Thoreau's nineteenth-century tract on *Civil Disobedience* with either Martin Luther King's "Letter from a Birmingham Jail" or Muhammed Ali's refusal to participate in the Vietnam War. Neither time nor resources are static in an authentic learning environment.

If librarians are to succeed in providing present and potential patrons with comprehensive information services, they must collect and circulate popular culture materials. It is regrettable that so few libraries can currently be cited as models for offering such services or resources. The ideas that shape future generations will continue to be spawned through the interaction of both traditional and nontraditional learning materials. Neither culture censors nor academic anarchists offer suitable keys to unlock intellectual doors to visions of alternative futures. Librarians are obligated to assist individuals in their never-ending search for self-knowledge and social truth. It is a prized position, even though it may lack requisite compensation in terms of both financial reward and social recognition. The need for competent, flexible, energetic, creative thinkers in library work is greater today than ever before.[3]

NOTES

1. Wayne A. Wiegand, "The Academic Library's Responsibility to the Resource Needs of the Popular Culture Community," in *Twentieth-Century Popular Culture in Museums and Libraries*, ed. Fred E. H. Schroeder (Bowling Green: Bowling Green State University Popular Press, 1981), pp. 195-196.

2. Ray B. Browne, "Libraries at the Crossroads: A Perspective on Libraries and Culture," *Drexel Library Quarterly* XVI (July 1980): pp. 12-23; B. Lee

Cooper, "William L. Schurk–Audio Center Director: A Close Encounter with a Librarian of a Different Kind," and "An Opening Day Collection of Popular Recordings: Searching for Discographic Standards," in *Twentieth-Century Popular Culture in Museums and Libraries*, ed. Fred E. H. Schroeder (Bowling Green: Bowling Green University, 1981), pp. 210-225 and 228-255; Gordon Stevenson, "The Wayward Scholar: Resources and Research in Popular Culture," *Library Trends* 25 (April 1977): pp. 779-818, and "Popular Culture and the Public Library," in *Advances in Librarianship–Volume VII*, eds. Melvin J. Voit and Michael H. Harris (New York: Academic, 1977), pp. 177-229; Wayne A. Wiegand, "Taste Cultures and Librarians: A Position Paper," *Drexel Library Quarterly* XVI (July 1980): pp. 1-11.

3. B. Lee Cooper, "Information Services, Popular Culture, and the Librarian: *Promoting a Contemporary Learning Perspective*," *Drexel Library Quarterly* XVI (July 1980): pp. 24-42, and "Foreword," in *Popular Culture and Libraries*, comp. Frank W. Hoffmann (Hamden: Library Professional/Shoe String, 1984), pp. vii-xv. Also see Allen Ellis (comp.), "Popular Culture and Acquisitions," *The Acquisitions Librarian*, No. 8 (1992), pp. 1-146.

Chapter 1

Baseball Songs

Social studies teachers have been encouraged to use baseball materials[1] and popular song lyrics[2] to stimulate students to investigate contemporary American culture. Heeding the directive of cultural historian Jacques Barzun, a few classroom instructors have tested the hypothesis that whoever wishes to discover the heart and mind of America must learn baseball. But how can baseball be translated into historical personalities, social and economic issues, humor, and other cultural dimensions? Utilizing popular recordings that feature baseball imagery is an innovative way to introduce students to the pluralistic nature of American life. The following chapter outlines a variety of themes that combine baseball history and sporting metaphors with the lyrical poetry and rocking rhythms of popular recordings.

BASEBALL POPULARITY IN THE U.S.

Baseball is America's national game. It is also the sports repository of many of the nation's ideals, legends, and social conflicts.[3] Daily and weekly newspapers chronicle the exploits of major-league players from spring training through the World Series, with vivid game descriptions, statistical box scores, and serious journal-

---

This study by B. Lee Cooper and Donald E. Walker was originally published under the title "Baseball, Popular Music, and Twentieth-Century American History," *Social Studies* LXXXI (May-June 1990): pp. 120-124. The authors acknowledged the assistance of William L. Schurk in assembling the essay. Reprint permission has been granted by The Helen Dwight Reid Educational Foundation for Heldref Publications at 4000 Albemarle Street, N.W., Washington, D.C. 20016.

istic analyses. Fans listen to regional radio broadcasts, watch nationally televised games, and attend ballgames to cheer their summer heroes. From Babe Ruth, Walter Johnson, and Ty Cobb to Willie Mays, Mickey Mantle, and Stan Musial, the early twentieth century focused on famous baseball players as larger-than-life figures.[4] Even in 1988, the spectacular pitching feats of Orel Hersheiser and the clutch-hitting theatrics of Kirk Gibson set new standards for national admiration.

Although baseball is a sport to be played, observed, analyzed, and loved by individuals, it is also a subject of mass-media interest.[5] Several weekly and monthly magazines focus on player achievements and team performance–some examples are *The Sporting News*, *Baseball Digest*, and *Sports Illustrated*. The motion picture industry has also endeavored to capture the vitality of both major- and minor-league play. In earlier times, films like *Pride of the Yankees* (1942), *It Happens Every Spring* (1949), and *Fear Strikes Out* (1957) embodied the nation's fascination with baseball heroes. More recently, multiplex theaters have featured *The Natural* (1984), *Bull Durham* (1988), *Eight Men Out* (1988), and *Field of Dreams* (1989). Media attention on particular individuals or toward any sporting activity inevitably feeds public interest. Sometimes media moguls even attempt to promote popular support for a previously unrecognized athletic hero or a little-known sporting event. But acknowledging the sustained American interest in baseball, the national media usually reflects and reinforces public perceptions.

BASEBALL IMAGES IN POPULAR SONGS

American enthusiasm for baseball is undeniable. Similarly, interest in popular music is remarkably high. Some writers have asserted that the alliance between baseball and song is natural, productive, and highly popular.[6] This conventional wisdom seems reasonable. Consider the lament by Simon and Garfunkel in "Mrs. Robinson" (1968): "Where have you gone, Joe DiMaggio? A nation turns its lonely eyes to you." Or ponder John Fogerty's impassioned plea to play "Centerfield" (1985). Other contemporary songs echoing baseball themes include Bruce Springsteen's "Glory Days" (1985), Meatloaf's "Paradise by the Dashboard Light" (1978), and The

Intruders' "(Love is Like a) Baseball Game" (1968). Writers who champion the link between popular song and baseball note three primary reasons for the sport's thematic popularity: (1) baseball is celebrated as a contest of wills in a well-defined game; (2) baseball provides a showcase for national heroes and fabled athletic achievements; and (3) baseball is a useful metaphor for both dating and sex.[7]

The aforementioned popular recordings are only the tip of the baseball-song iceberg. Although not always heard on Top 40 playlists, there are numerous audio commentaries that social studies teachers can successfully adapt for instructional purposes. For instance, the concept of death at an early age is presented in "Roberto's Gone" (1973) and "Playing Catch with the Babe" (1979). Interest in the option of examining the biographies of Roberto Clemente, Pittsburgh Pirate All-Star outfielder and international humanitarian, or Thurman Munson, Yankee catcher and flying enthusiast, can be sparked by listening to such audio eulogies. Similarly, the cultural values of equality of opportunity and fair play can be clearly illustrated while discussing recordings about major-league integration during the late 1940s–"Doby at the Bat" (1948), "The Robbie-Doby Boogie" (1948), and "Doby's Boogie" (1949). Some students will be amazed to discover that Cleveland's Larry Doby was as heroic as Brooklyn's Jackie Robinson in his role as the American League's first black player. Finally, the negative reactions of fans–to shifts in baseball franchises from the East Coast to the West Coast, to extended losing streaks by local ball clubs, to player strikes, and to greedy baseball owners–are also featured on records.

TEACHING WITH BASEBALL THEMES

Classroom teachers should recognize that there are a variety of persistent lyrical themes that link baseball and American culture. Analyzing these themes can help students to conceptualize social change, cultural values, and heroic individual achievements. The remainder of this chapter outlines nine specific baseball themes depicted in songs. Featured under each theme are numerous recordings designed to stimulate discussions and debates. This information serves to illustrate baseball perspectives on twentieth-century American society through commercial recordings that feature baseball heroes, historical references, social themes, and baseball metaphors. Each theme is preceded by a brief introductory statement discussing relationships between lyrical baseball content and the broader concerns of cultural context.

Racial Integration of Major League Baseball Teams[8]

Between 1947 and 1959, major-league baseball was enriched by the contributions of black players such as Jackie Robinson of the Brooklyn Dodgers, Larry Doby of the Cleveland Indians, and Willie Mays of the New York Giants. Many popular songs celebrated both the practice of integrating major-league teams and the individual achievements of gifted black athletes. These songs include:

- "Did You See Jackie Robinson Hit that Ball?"
  (Decca 24675)
  Buddy Johnson and His Orchestra (1949)

- "Doby at the Bat"
  (Abbey 3016)
  Fatman Humphries (1948)

- "Doby's Boogie"
  (Derby 713)
  Freddie Mitchell (1949)

- "New Baseball Boogie"
  (Savoy 5561)
  Brownie McGhee (1948)

- "The Robbie-Doby Boogie"
  (Savoy 5550)
  Brownie McGhee (1948)

- "Say Hey! (A Tribute to Willie Mays)"
  (Apollo 460)
  The Nite Riders (1954)

- "Say Hey, Willie Mays"
  (Coral 61238)
  Johnny Long (1954)

International Variety Among Major-League Baseball Players

Beyond the integration of black ballplayers on major-league teams, the dominance of ethnic and Latin American hitters and pitchers–especially Los Angeles Dodger pitcher Fernando Valenzuela and Pittsburgh Pirate outfielder Roberto Clemente–has been lauded on several contemporary records:

- "The Ballad of Roberto Clemente"
  (BBB 233)
  Paul New (1973)

- "El Cielo Es Azul"
  (Loose Leaf 103)
  The Sketch (1982)

- "Fernando"
  (Horn 10)
  Stanley Ralph Ross (1981)

- "Go Fernando"
  (Kelly 101)
  Carmen Moreno (1981)

- "Polish Baseball Power"
  (Mishawaka 1702)
  Sig Sakowica (1970)

- "Tony, The Killer, and Carew"
  (Lifesong 45114)
  Terry Cashman (1982)

- "Viva Fernando"
  (Domain 1019)
  The Gene Page Orchestra (1981)

Major Events in Baseball History

From such heroic achievements as New York Yankee pitcher Don Larsen's "Perfect Game" in the 1956 World Series to Joe

DiMaggio's 56-game hitting streak in 1941 to the farcical tale of Kansas City Royal George Brett's pine-tar bat incident to the interruption of the 1981 baseball season by a prolonged players' strike, records have chronicled both large and small events of America's national pastime:

- "After Thirty-Nine Years"
  (Phonograph 002)
  John Frigo (1984)

- "The Ballad of Don Larsen"
  (TNT 9010)
  Red River Dave (1956)

- "Cooperstown (The Town Where Baseball Lives)"
  (Lifesong 45117)
  Terry Cashman (1982)

- "Joltin' Joe DiMaggio"
  (Columbia 38544)
  Les Brown and His Orchestra featuring Betty Bonney (1941)

- "Pine Tar Wars"
  (AFR 4233)
  C. W. McCall (1983)

- "The Summer There Was No Baseball"
  (Home Run)
  Randy Haspel (1981)

- "That Last Home Run"
  (Spoonfull)
  Willie Dixon's Chicago Blues All-Stars (1973)

Hall of Fame Baseball Heroes

Nearly 200 legendary major-league heroes are enshrined in the Baseball Hall of Fame in Cooperstown, New York. The lifetime achievements of these players range from more than 300 victories for pitchers to numerous batting averages, runs batted in, and home-run titles for hitters. From Babe Ruth of the New York Yankees to Johnny Bench of the Cincinnati Reds, the giants of the game have been heralded on vinyl:

- "Babe Ruth"
  (Tower 142)
  The Arrows, featuring Davie Allan (1965)

- "The Ballad of Satchel Paige (Don't Look Back)"
  (Cain and Able 3118)
  Raynola Smith (1982)

- "Did You See Jackie Robinson Hit that Ball?"
  (RCA Victor 47-2990)
  Count Basie and His Orchestra (1949)

- "Homerun Willie"
  (Warner Brothers 8445)
  Larry Hosford (1977)

- "Joltin' Joe DiMaggio"
  (Bluebird 11316)
  Bob Chester and His Orchestra (1941)

- "The Man Called Bench"
  (High Spiral 287)
  Cliff Adams (1983)

- "Move Over Babe (Here Comes Henry)"
  (Karen 714)
  Bill Slayback (1973)

- "Say Hey (The Willie Mays Song)"
  (Epic 9066)
  The Treniers (1954)

- "Seasons in the Sun (A Tribute to Mickey Mantle)"
  (Metrostar 45853)
  Terry Cashman (1985)

- "Thanks Mister Banks"
  (Barking Gecko 10655)
  Roger Bain (1979)

- "Warren Spahn"
  (Armada 104)
  The Blackholes (1979)

- "Willie (Stargell)"
  (Love 2019)
  Al Perry (1980)

- "Yaz's Last at Bat"
  (Lincoln 003)
  John Lincoln Wright and The Designated Hitters (1985)

Eulogies Acknowledging the Passing of Great Ballplayers

Whether depicting Babe Ruth at the end of his life–he died of cancer at age 53–or agonizing over Roberto Clemente being killed in a plane crash at the pinacle of his playing career, records eulogizing great players are valuable oral testimonies:

- "Baladas de Roberto Clemente"
  (BBB 233)
  Paul New (1973)

- "Clemente Lande"
  (Nu-Sound 1024)
  Jim Wheeler (1973)

- "Playing Catch with the Babe"
  (Thurman 82579)
  Jess DeMaine (1979)

- "Roberto's Gone"
  (Ace of Hearts 0476)
  Jim Owen (1973)

- "Safe at Home (A Tribute to Babe Ruth)"
  (Flint 1788)
  Tex Fletcher (1948)

- "Song of Roberto"
  (Chatham 10)
  Mario Martinelli (1973)

Nicknames Applied to Major-League Ballplayers[9]

George Herman Ruth is "Babe," James Hunter is "Catfish," and Joe DiMaggio is "The Yankee Clipper." A variety of major leaguers are known to fans by nicknames. Recorded salutes to such baseball stars often use such monikers to attract the attention of listeners and to describe the achievements or playing styles of specific players:

- "The Bambino, The Clipper, and The Mick"
  (Lifesong 45097)
  Terry Cashman (1982)

- "Catfish"
  (A&M SP 4574)
  Joe Cocker (1976)

- "The Catfish Kid (The Ballad of Jim Hunter)"
  (Moon 6021)
  Big Tom White (1976)

- "Charlie Hustle"
  (Nu-Sound 1030)
  Jim Wheeler (1974)

- "Hammering Hank"
  (Clintone 012)
  The Blast Furnace Band and The Grapevine Singers (1973)

- "Stan The Man"
  (Norman 543)
  Marty Bronson (1963)

- "Yankee Clipper"
  (RCA Victor 3552)
  Charlie Ventura and His Orchestra (1949)

Political, Social, and Psychological Commentaries Utilizing Baseball Terminology

The proliferation of baseball terms illustrates the power of athletic images, ideas, and attitudes that permeate American society. The lyrical question "Where have you gone, Joe DiMaggio?" has immense cultural meaning not only for Mrs. Robinson but also for the entire generation of the forties and fifties:

- "Bobby the Bomber"
  (Columbia A 2587)
  Byron G. Harlon (1918)

- "Centerfield"
  (Warner Brothers 29053)
  John Fogerty (1985)

- "Feel So Bad"
  (Checker 1162)
  Little Milton (1967)

- "Glory Days"
  (Columbia 04924)
  Bruce Springsteen (1985)

- "(I Used To Be a) Brooklyn Dodger"
  (Lifesong 1785)
  Dion (1978)

- "Let's Keep The Dodgers in Brooklyn"
  (Coral 61840)
  Phil Foster (1957)

- "Mrs. Robinson"
  (Columbia 44511)
  Simon and Garfunkel (1968)

- "The Old Ball Game"
  (Real Good 1002)
  King Hannibal (1984)

Descriptions of Romantic Relationships Utilizing Baseball Terminology and Metaphors

Singers and songwriters often portray the game of love in sporting terms: a suitor tries to get to "first base" with a young lady; a man "strikes out" when asking a pretty girl for a date; a rejected lover feels like a "ball game on a rainy day"; and a playboy always hopes to "score" with a date. The substitution of baseball terms and the use of baseball metaphors for courtship jargon is a sign of the power of the sport in American culture:

- "The Ball Game"
  (Specialty 855)
  Wynona Carr (1953)

- "Baseball Baby"
  (Deluxe 6167)
  Johnny Darling (1958)

- "Baseball Blues"
  (Island 1202)
  Claire Hamill (1972)

- "Brown-Eyed Handsome Man"
  (Chess 1635)
  Chuck Berry (1956)

- "Feel So Bad"
  (ABC/TRC 11308)
  Ray Charles (1971)

- "He Knocked Me Right Out of the Box"
  (Columbia 44162)
  Little Jimmy Dickens (1967)

- "Home Run"
  (Bull Dog 103)
  Chance Halladay (1960)

- "A Long Run Home"
  (Reel Dreams 1002)
  Rick Cerone (1981)

- "Love Is Bigger than Baseball"
  (Capricorn 0033)
  Dexter Redding (1973)

- "(Love Is Like a) Baseball Game"
  (Gamble 217)
  The Intruders (1968)

- "The National Pastime"
  (RCA 4078)
  Gary Buck (1972)

- "Our National Pastime"
  (Epic 11117)
  Rupert Holmes (1974)

- "Paradise by the Dashboard Light"
  (Epic 50588)
  Meat Loaf (1978)

- "Play Me or Trade Me"
  (Elektra 47247)
  Mel Tillis and Nancy Sinatra (1981)

- "The Rookie of the Year"
  (G.C. 609)
  Jimmy Piersall and The Three Heartbreakers (1960)

- "Zanzibar"
  (Columbia PC 35609)
  Billy Joel (1978)

Comic Commentaries Featuring Baseball Terminology and Themes

Humor and baseball are a natural combination. Records feature laments to the helpless, hapless Chicago Cubs, parodies of classic baseball situations, and off-the-wall tributes to sports fanatics:

- "Baseball Card Lover"
  (Rhino 004)
  Ritchie Ray (1977)

- "Base Ball Papa"
  (Blue 126)
  Billy Mitchell (1951)

- "The Bases Were Loaded"
  (Capitol 1060)
  Sugar Chile Robinson (1950)

- "Blasted in the Bleachers"
  (Major League Records 4502)
  Howie Newman (1960)

- "Casey (The Pride of Them All)"
  (Capitol 249)
  Jerry Colonna (1946)

- "Daddy Played First Base"
  (RCA 9866)
  Homer and Jethro (1970)

- "D-O-D-G-E-R-S Song (Oh, Really? No, O'Malley)"
  (Reprise 1368)
  Danny Kaye (1962)

- "A Dying Cub Fan's Last Request"
  (Red Pajamas 1001)
  Steve Goodman (1981)

- "Eleven Months and Ten More Days"
  (Columbia 15572)
  Vernon Dalhart (1929)

- "The First Baseball Game"
  (Capitol 15096)
  Johnny Mercer (1947)

- "I Hate Baseball"
  (Dore 974)
  A. Player and The Zanies (1981)

- "I Like Baseball"
  (Pro America)
  The New Marines (1980)

- "Myti Kaysi at the Bat"
  (Reprise 1370)
  Danny Kaye (1962)

- "Nishimoto at the Bat"
  (Capitol 2516)
  Harry Kari and His Six Saki Sippers (Date Unknown)

- "The Philadelphia Fillies"
  (United Artists 50802)
  Del Reeves (1971)

- "Reggie for Christmas"
  (Reel Dreams 1005)
  Hozay Smith and The Hammerheads (1982)

- "Swat Mulligan (Clobber that Ball)"
  (Columbia 41637)
  Ernie Sheldon (1960)

- "Take Me Out to the Ball Game"
  (Clean Cuts 902)
  Bruce Springstone (1982)

- "The Umpire Is a Most Unhappy Man"
  (Signature 15122)
  Ray Block and His Military Band (1947)

- "Will You Be Ready (at the Plate When Jesus Throws the Ball)?"
  (Oink 3801)
  Elmo and Patsy (1980)

CONCLUSION

One must note that the statistics of baseball, the lore of the game, and even those wonderful old baseball cards are often more reliable factual commentators on America's national pastime than commercial recordings. Nevertheless, baseball is a reasonable metaphor for The Intruders, a wonderful source of comic nostalgia for Cub fan Steve Goodman, and a convenient repository (especially prior to 1960) for untarnished sports stars and larger-than-life heroes. Popular records can serve as valuable reminders of how truly influential baseball is in American culture.[10]

For social studies teachers, baseball recordings are treasure troves. The lyrical Joe DiMaggio is not merely a contemporary TV personality selling Mr. Coffee products; he is an Italian-American whose legendary batting skills helped sustain the Yankee dynasty during the 1930s and 1940s. He is also the fleet-footed, smooth-fielding "Yankee Clipper" whose loyalty, integrity, and dedication to traditional American values elevated him to the status of cultural hero during the 1950s and 1960s. Whether vocally lauded as "Joltin' Joe DiMaggio" in 1941, hailed as the immortal "Yankee Clipper" in 1949, remembered as a source of cultural stability in "Mrs. Robinson" in 1968, or immortalized as part of the Yankee baseball tradition of "The Bambino, The Clipper, and The Mick" in 1982, popular recordings have chronicled the life and legend of DiMaggio with uncanny historical accuracy.

Other baseball stars have accomplished feats, created personas, and become legends in modern America. Jackie Robinson's grace under pressure while integrating the Brooklyn Dodgers in 1947 is heralded again and again in lyrics and nonfiction. The song "Did You See Jackie Robinson Hit that Ball?" (1949) also praised the professional performance of black ballplayers Satchel Paige, Roy Campanella, Larry Doby, and Don Newcombe. But the black Americans who followed Jackie Robinson into mainstream American social and economic life constituted the real story behind Brooklyn Dodger owner Branch Rickey's brave 1947 experiment in racial integration. The internationalization of American baseball, with the influx of Hispanic players from Central and South America, is also clearly communicated in recordings. "The Ballad of Roberto Clemente" (1973) and numerous other lyrical paeans to pitcher Fernando Valenzuela illustrate the same kind of ethnic pride that boosted so many Irish, Italian, Polish, and Jewish athletes throughout baseball history.

Finally, many songs utilize baseball heroes–both historic and fictional–to deliver social messages. Bruce Springsteen's aging pitcher longs for the "Glory Days" (1985) when he could sling his speedball past hitters; he is unable to adjust to the more difficult challenges of middle age. Unfortunately, alcohol appears to be the ex-pitcher's nostalgic crutch. Joe Cocker lauds the fabled major-league career of pitcher Jim Hunter in "Catfish" (1976). Yet the theme of his tune is strictly materialistic. Hunter, in verse after verse, is called "the million-dollar man," the hero in alligator boots who escaped from his Oakland A's contract to become a wealthy member of the New York Yankees. Other aspects of dark humor, personal anxiety, and unwillingness to face either the aging process or inevitable social change are featured in John Fogerty's "Centerfield" (1985), Dion's "(I Used To Be a) Brooklyn Dodger" (1978), Simon and Garfunkel's "Mrs. Robinson" (1968), and Steve Goodman's "A Dying Cub Fan's Last Request" (1981). The challenge for a teacher is to encourage students to listen carefully for these non-baseball secondary themes and implied problems.

NOTES

1. David Quentin Voight, *America Through Baseball* (Chicago: Nelson-Hall, 1976); Murry R. Nelson, "Baseball Cards in the Classroom," *Social Education* SLV (May 1981): pp. 364-366; and John D. Wells and James K. Skipper, Jr., "The Songs of Summer: A Sociological Study of Songs About Baseball and the Play Element in Culture," *Popular Music and Society* XII (Spring 1988): pp. 25-35.

2. B. Lee Cooper, *Images of American Society in Popular Music* (Chicago: Nelson-Hall, 1982) and *A Resource Guide to Themes in Contemporary American Song Lyrics, 1950-1985* (Westport: Greenwood, 1986); B. Lee Cooper and Donald E. Walker, "Teaching American History Through Major-League Baseball and

Popular Music: A Resource Guide," *International Journal of Instructional Media* XVII (1990): pp. 83-87.

3. Angus G. Garger III, *Baseball Legends: The Greatest Players, Best Games, and Magical Moments–Then and Now* (New York: Gallery, 1988); Donald Honig, *The World Series: An Illustrated History from 1903 to the Present* (New York: Crown, 1986); Lowell Reidenbaugh, *Baseball's Hall of Fame–Cooperstown: Where the Legends Live Forever* (New York: Arlington, 1988).

4. Leverett T. Smith Jr., "Ty Cobb, Babe Ruth, and the Changing Image of the Athletic Hero," in *Heroes of Popular Culture*, ed. Ray B. Browne, Marshall Fishwick, and Michael T. Marsden. (Bowling Green: Bowling Green University, 1972), pp. 73-85.

5. David Ansen, "Baseball Diamonds Are Forever," *Newsweek* CXIII (April 1989): pp. 72-73; James Mote, *Everything Baseball* (New York: Prentice Hall, 1989).

6. Paul Richman, "Baseball's Greatest Hits!" *Sports Collectors Digest* (August 1982): pp. 94-95ff; Joseph Petrarca, comp., "Baseball Sheet Music," *Sheet Music Exchange* III, No. 5 (October 1985): pp. 9-15; Michael G. Corenthal, " 'Casey at the Bat': 1909 and 1929 Records," *Goldmine* No. 149 (April 1986): p. 83.

7. Wells and Skipper.

8. Glen Macnow, "Baseball Far from Color-Blind: Blacks Remain Scarce on Bench, in Boardroom," *Detroit Free Press*, (21 September 1986), pp. 1E, 4E, 5E.

9. James K. Skipper, Jr., "The Sociological Significance of Nicknames: The Case of Baseball Players," *Journal of Sport Behavior* VII (1984): pp. 28-33, and "Nicknames, Folk Heroes, and Assimilation: Black League Baseball Players, 1884-1950," *Journal of Sport Behavior* VIII (1985): pp. 100-114.

10. Gerard O'Connor, "Where Have You Gone Joe DiMaggio?" in *Heroes of Popular Culture*, eds. Ray B. Browne, Marshall Fishwick, and Michael T. Marsden (Bowling Green: Bowling Green University, 1972), pp. 87-99; Dr. Demento, "Sportsman As Music Makers: From Dugouts to Discs," *Wax Paper* II, No. 8 (July 1977): pp. 11-13; and Jim Schottlekottle, "Terry Cashman Scores Hit After Hit As Big League Baseball's Balladist," *Sports Illustrated* LXII (April 1985): p. 8.

Chapter 2

Biographical Studies

DARYL HALL AND JOHN OATES

Daryl Hall/John Oates: Dangerous Dances–The Authorized Biography, by Nick Tosches, with Daryl Hall and John Oates. New York: St. Martin's Press, 1985. Illustrated. 144 pp.

Dangerous Dances is a peculiar literary beast. Although book-length in pages, this study is so crammed with photographs, drawings, sketches, cartoons, and other visual images that the literary commentary almost seems to be of secondary importance. The book is additionally complicated by being both a biography and an autobiography. Daryl Hall and John Oates are listed as co-authors, and it is reported that much factual and attitudinal information contained in the work has been drawn directly from their personal diaries and art pads. However, anyone familiar with the fascinating writing of Nick Tosches–*Country* (1977), *Hellfire* (1982), and *Unsung Heroes of Rock 'n' Roll* (1984)–will immediately recognize his wildly potent phrasing and disjunctive approach to casting musical figures as reflections of the social disorientation of contemporary American life. This book is undeniably a trick bag.

The structural format of *Dangerous Dances* is chronological. Hall and Oates are depicted from their bicycle-pumping childhoods to their current guitar-thumping stardom. Much emphasis is placed

---

These reviews by B. Lee Cooper originally appeared in the following periodicals: "Hall and Oates," *Popular Music and Society,* XI (Winter 1987): pp. 101-103; "Rick Nelson," *Popular Music and Society,* XIII (Winter 1989): pp. 77-82; and "Little Richard," *Record Profile Magazine,* No. 10 (July/August 1985): pp. 56-57. Reprint permission has been granted by the author and The Popular Press.

on the influences of rhythm 'n' blues music, black styles of dress and dance, and isolation from mainstream, middle-class society in both men's lives. Much is also mentioned about the speculative investment of the music industry in Hall and Oates, Inc. and the astronomical wealth gained by two "po' boys" who can generate popular hot licks. Tosches is no idealist. He has always been candid about musicians playing for *both* love (artistry, creativity, and personal communication) and money (materialism, sex, and power). Although this study doesn't reach any startling conclusions about talent, motivation, or success, it does render a solid statement about the value of persistence and perseverance in the contemporary rock music industry.

Beyond childhood romances, bar-band learning experiences, and on-again/off-again fame achieved by Hall and Oates, the reader is bombarded by a single sales theme: fans want "the beat." This implies that perfection in producing marketable dance music translates into financial success. Yet one senses that more ought to be said about Hall and Oates than the stereotypical *American Bandstand* epithet: "It's got a good beat; we can dance to it!" Songs like "Maneater" are especially entertaining and haunting for their *total* sound–the initial hook, the ever-lively beat, and the presence of controlled audio tension throughout the number. Strangely, Tosches accepts lots of diary and sketch-pad information, but he is apparently reluctant to analyze the two performers through their lyrical concoctions. Why? Do Hall and Oates consider their lyrics to be trash? I think not. This omission is the most serious flaw in *Dangerous Dances.*

Hall and Oates are presently, and unexpectedly, rich. Tosches laughs with them about this circumstance. But beyond material wealth, there lies the question of professional stature, a place in musical history. From a strictly quantitative perspective (*Billboard* chart listings and annual income), this dynamic duo has surpassed every other twosome, including The Everly Brothers, The Carpenters, Simon and Garfunkel, and The Captain and Tennille. But are Hall and Oates only popularizers of a new beat in the same vein as The Righteous Brothers, who introduced 1960s white audiences to tunes originally created by Don and Dewey and other black R&B performers? Are they destined to become eternal nostalgia figures like Don and Phil Everly? Are they soulful innovators like Sam and Dave? Are they a dynamic stage act like Ike and Tina Turner? This book doesn't confront these issues, because very few comparisons are ventured. This situation is particularly difficult to understand, since Hall and Oates are constantly identified as rock 'n' soul artists who owe their musical heritage to black sounds of the 1950s and 1960s.

It would be a disservice to Tosches in general, and to *Dangerous Dances* in particular, to leave the impression that this brief study isn't valuable. Some of the writing is pulsating, perceptive, and prophetic. Examples of Tosches' blazing rhetoric include the following two observations:

> It was, indeed, the dawn of the new musical age. Rock 'n' roll had once been the domain of blessed idiot savants who howled unaware of their own powers, ignorant as to the nature of their own magic. Now, spontaneity and raw emotion were being structured by craft, and thus carried to their fullest. The meaning of modern music was becoming similar to that of poetry: vivid feeling, passion, tempered and heightened by the technical skills of art. Magic and technology were meeting at their farthest points. (p. 132)

> It was their life's blood. It always had been, they knew: it always would be. Awake, they breathed music. They went to sleep enwrapped in it. They literally dreamed music, and woke mornings with those dreams. Unconsciously and consciously, in daywork and dreamwork, they existed in waves, ever more marvelous and consummately wrought waves of music. (p. 122)

How fascinating it would have been to allow Hall and Oates to analyze their 1981 hit "You Make My Dreams" in conjunction with Tosches' previous description. Without such linkage, however, the total impact of this study is less than complete. It feels rushed into print. It lacks a sense of necessary reflection, of critical judgment, or of broad analysis. Hopefully, Tosches will take another shot at Hall and Oates in a future study about white singers with black musical roots.

Dangerous Dances is a quick, lean profile. No bibliography or discography is provided; no chronology is attached; no song lyrics are assembled. This book, however, will probably be the best study available on the chart-topping Hall and Oates for several years. It will please fans, and hopefully spark more in-depth study on this popular duo.

RICKY NELSON

The Ricky Nelson Story, by John Stafford and Iain Young. Folkestone, England: Finbarr International, 1988. Illustrated. 268 pp.

There are "two" Rick Nelsons. Their biographies are identical: Rick Nelson and Eric Hilliard Nelson were born in Teaneck, New Jersey, on May 8, 1940, and died near DeKalb, Texas, on December 31, 1985. Their careers are also parallel in every facet: both performed as child actors along with an older brother, David, and their parents on the radio and television series *The Adventures of Ozzie and Harriet*. Both recorded successfully for the Verve, Imperial, and Decca labels during the fifties, sixties, and seventies, producing numerous hit singles ("Travelin' Man," "Hello Mary Lou," "Fools Rush In," and "Garden Party") and several popular albums. Both made appearances on television variety shows, at rock 'n' roll revival concerts, and on tours with The Stone Canyon Band. And both married Kristen Harmon.

Anyone familiar with Alfred Hitchcock's *Psycho* has already thought of the word to describe such forms of personality duality–"schizophrenia." Ironically, the personalities of the two Rick Nelsons are neither disintegrated nor psychotic. The duality of the Nelson character stems from polarized perceptions projected by music critics. The two personas–let's call one "Ricky" and the other "Rick"–have been the subjects of critical scrutiny since 1957. The result of this journalistic process has been the creation of two distinct public personalities.

Ricky

Ricky Nelson is an unprincipled, essentially no-talent, media-launched kid who managed to survive in the rock-music world thanks to his television residuals, his chameleon-like skills at copying the singing styles and songs of a variety of first-rate performers, his handsome face and Mr. Clean lifestyle, and his luck in reviving nostalgic feelings among his audiences. Numerous rock journalists and record critics created and circulated this image of the narcissistic Ricky. Note the following illustrations:

> Film and television were both a useful source for people who already had large numbers of admirers. Tab Hunter, Sal Mineo, and Ricky Nelson were the most successful of such media-derived performers in the early rock 'n' roll years.
>
> –Charlie Gillett (1972)

> Even Ricky Nelson took his sneer, his stance, and a large part of his repertoire from Elvis Presley.
>
> –Peter Guralnick (1980)

> More youthful-looking than Pat Boone and with less of a voice, [Ricky Nelson] served the same function as Boone and, later, The Beatles. The kids loved him but the parents did not hate him, as they did [Elvis] Presley. His brand of R 'n' R was distinctly white and embodied a juvenile sweetness that made his records a bridge between young and adult listeners.
>
> –Arnold Shaw (1974)

> The only way [Ricky Nelson] could begin to approach the rockabilly sound was through the hot guitar runs of James Burton, his Louisiana-born lead guitarist.
>
> –Peter Guralnick (1980)

> Most of what [Ricky Nelson] sang was covered material, or golden oldie hits from years gone by. Lately, he has been developing into a folk-rock artist along the same lines as Dion DiMucci and other retreads.
>
> –Dan and Nancy Tudor (1979)

The image of Ricky Nelson is clear. His career as a rock musician has been a totally fabricated, though commercially successful, junket. Ricky belongs eternally to screaming teenage girls, along with the likes of Tommy Sands, Bobby Vee, Frankie Avalon, Paul Anka, Bobby Vinton, Sal Mineo, and Pat Boone. At best, he was a physically attractive copycat-Elvis surrogate who somehow lucked out by securing support from two top-flight guitarists: James Burton (lead) and Joe Osborne (base). At worst, he was . . . just horrible.

Rick

Rick Nelson, the acclaimed counterpart of the much-maligned Ricky, was never hailed as the second Elvis Presley. No one should be. But many journalists were quick to separate his strong, independent performing style from the talentless pretty boys who dominated the pop-music scene between 1958 and 1963. Rather than being just another teenage idol, Rick was perceived not only as a talented adolescent artist but also as a developing, evolving rock professional. Los Angeles is a long way, both geographically and sociologically, from Nashville, Memphis, New Orleans, and Chicago. It's even further from Tupelo, Mississippi, and Ferriday, Louisiana. The Deep South blues and country music that inspired Elvis Presley, Jerry Lee Lewis, Carl Perkins, and dozens of other white rock 'n' rollers simply wasn't a part of Rick's childhood. However, throughout his career, he had searched for creative musical roots, experimented with new singing styles, and attempted to broaden his own performing perspectives. He matured gracefully. What is more interesting is the fact that his music broadened from his personalized 1950s rock 'n' roll tunes to include a sizable country repertoire, several fine Bob Dylan songs ("She Belongs to Me"), some great rockabilly standards ("Mystery Train" and "That's All Right Mamma"), and an extensive number of personally composed songs. It is through his development as a songwriter that Rick most clearly demonstrated his evolution as a significant rock personality.

The journalists who have praised Rick (and elected to ignore Ricky) tend to view the *Ozzie and Harriet* years as diamond-in-the-rough times for Rick. Their comments speak for themselves:

> Because he first appeared on television's *Ozzie and Harriet* and began his rock 'n' roll career in the same place, [Rick] Nelson has been unjustly underrated. In fact, he was a first-

rate rock singer–if not a great one; he was at least leagues superior to the Bobby Vee/Fabian/Paul Anka finger-pop axis.

–Dave Marsh (1979)

Rick was always better than his rep, true enough . . . Nelson's specialty was consistent, low-key excitement.

–Robert Christgau (1972)

Rick Nelson, who had a string of rockabilly-flavored pop-rock hits between 1957 and 1964, counts as the first true pioneer of Los Angeles country rock.

–John Rockwell (1980)

Rick Nelson has done an admirable job in keeping up with the rapid changes in rock, making a fairly successful transition from Ricky to Rick, while still keeping a style that was distinctively Nelson.

–Charlie Burton (1971)

This high praise of Rick, contrasted with the castigation of Ricky, is peculiar. Which of the two Nelsons is real?

Ricky vs. Rick

Rock journalists tend to write from the limited perspective of personal ideals, hopes, and dreams. Their views are rarely objective. They frequently take freeze-frame events–a single song, one album, or a major concert appearance–and extrapolate boundless meaning about an artist. This is not an indictment; it is an accurate description of a literary trade that faces tight publication deadlines and a volatile audience that craves subjectivity and firm black-and-white judgments. The Ricky-vs.-Rick schizophrenia is typical, though perhaps more extreme, of journalistic images related to hundreds of other popular musicians. Think of the divergent comments that have appeared in print about Bob Dylan, Elvis Presley, Mick Jagger, Madonna, Prince, and others throughout their careers.

The case for Rick Nelson deserves to be closed on a positive point. The longevity of his career, his creativity as a songwriter

("Garden Party"), his devotion to contemporary music, the breadth of his popularity as a radio, television, recording, and concert star, his experimentation with various musical genres, and his national recognition cannot be downplayed. Although his isn't the Johnny B. Goode story of the poor boy from humble roots who made good, he was undeniably a self-made man as a rock star. In 1980, Greg Shaw managed to constructively synthesize the two Rick Nelsons:

> Of all the Hollywood teen idols, only one can be said to have any claim to lasting importance–Ricky Nelson. At first glance, he seems like all the rest: a cute face, seen on TV every week, making records and trying to pretend he's Elvis. But Nelson was different; in addition to his moody sex appeal and television sinecure, he also happened to have real talent. He was a fine singer whose personal taste ran to raw rockabilly and blues, and whose band, featuring the brilliant guitarist James Burton, was one of the best in all rock and roll. His records were exceptionally tough and exciting, largely free of intrusive orchestration and studio gimmickry, and his material, whether covers of obscure rockers like "Shirley Lee" or originals written for him by the likes of ex-rockabilly Johnny Burnette or R&B veteran Baker Knight, was on the whole superb.

Conclusion

John Stafford, assisted by researcher Iain Young, has produced a detailed chronicle entitled *The Ricky Nelson Story.* The author is unequivocally partisan. Yet this study transcends the polarized perspectives that have haunted Rick Nelson's historic image. One suspects that the tragic death of the biographer's hero on December 31, 1985, sparked the desire to collect years of interviews, memorabilia, and facts, and to present a full case in writing. Whatever the stimuli, Stafford presents a cogent, balanced, firm argument that Rick Nelson was one of America's key rockabilly/country/pop music figures.

The material featured in *The Ricky Nelson Story* reveals information provided in the very best rock biographies, in both breadth and detail. Photographs abound. There are candid family shots, formal publicity photos, reproductions of magazine covers, newspaper articles, concert posters, and picture after picture of sheet music, 45-r.p.m. record sleeves, E.P. and longplay album covers, and even picture discs. Beyond these visual treats, an amazingly thorough U.S. and International discography has also been assembled. Each album listing provides individual song titles, the record producer and the arranger, the date of release, and the names of individual band members. This detail is not uncommon in the realm of discographic research, but Stafford's clarity of presentation is. For Rick Nelson researchers, these photographs and record lists alone are worth the price of the entire book.

Stafford's text challenges the Ricky-vs.-Rick dichotomy at every opportunity. Where he can, the author explains how a rich, urban, non-religious television star can be motivated to pursue the same musical paths as poor, rural, fundamentalist truck drivers and cotton pickers. It's hard to imagine Rick Nelson as Carl Perkins–but that was Rick's dream. In areas where facts were unobtainable or strongly conflicting opinions could not be resolved, Stafford simply reports these complex situations. He invariably sides with the best image for his hero, but he nonetheless gives his readers all sides of each Nelson-related issue. Finally, it is amazing to note how many of Rick Nelson's friends, professional colleagues, and family members contributed personal interviews to Stafford's study. From Ozzie and Harriet to Kristen and Tracy to James Burton and John Boylan to Rick Nelson himself, the text vibrates with on-the-scene comments from 1957 to 1985.

The shortcomings of the work are few, but they are significant. The author is so personally involved in telling this story that he continually interjects unnecessary sidebar statements or silly comments. His fact-filled prose is at times labored, but the strict chronological format of the text keeps him solidly on track throughout the book. The most serious flaw, especially given the exceptional discography, is the failure to present documentation of all interviews or provide a compilation of both articles and books consulted. This oversight obviously saves pages, but it reduces the scholarly credibility of the study.

This book is valuable because it investigates several unique angles related to a pop star's professional evolution. Why did Rick Nelson avoid those gospel and rhythm 'n' blues songs that served

Elvis Presley so well throughout his career? Why was Rick unable to develop a more distinctive, animated stage persona? How did Rick continually attract high-quality back-up artists? How much career-modeling for Rick was drawn from the successes and failures of Col. Tom Parker's handling of Presley? Finally, does financial security stimulate or inhibit artistic creativity? The fact that Stafford confronts these topics (even though he doesn't totally resolve any of them) makes his biographical effort valuable.

The value of *The Ricky Nelson Story* is not just academic. It is also worthwhile reading for 1950s rock 'n' roll fans, and it is a model format for those wishing to trace the year-by-year uncertainty of a career in popular music. What's more, it is a tonic to those who have endured several decades of conflicting Ricky-vs.-Rick analyses.

RICK NELSON REFERENCE SOURCES

Callahan, Mike, Bud Buschardt, and Steve Goddard. "Rick Nelson." No. 51 (August 1980): pp. 17-20.

Dodds, Harry. "Ricky Nelson–The Story of a Teenage Idol: Part One, 1940-1958." *Now Dig This.* No. 45 (December 1986): pp. 18-22.

Dodds, Harry. "Ricky Nelson–The Story of a Teenage Idol: Part Two, 1959-1965." *Now Dig This.* No. 46 (January 1987): pp. 10-13.

Dodds, Harry. "Ricky Nelson–The Story of a Teenage Idol: Part Three, 1966-1972." *Now Dig This.* No. 47 (February 1987): pp. 8-11.

Dodds, Harry. "Ricky Nelson–The Story of a Teenage Idol: Part Four, 1973-1985." *Now Dig This.* No. 48 (March 1987): pp. 25-28.

Fricke, David. "Ricky: TV's Teen Dream Knew How to Rock." *Rolling Stone.* No. 467 (February 13, 1986): pp. 16-19.

Givens, Ben. "Spotlight on Rick Nelson." *Rockin' 50s.* No. 18 (June 1989): pp. 9-15.

Grein, Paul. "Rick Nelson: TV's First Rock Star." *Billboard.* XCVIII (January 11, 1986): p. 6.

Hardy, Phil. "From Ricky to Rick: Twenty Years of Nelson Examined." *Let It Rock.* No. 29 (May 1975): pp. 25-27.

Hardy, Phil. "Small-Screen Rocker." *The History of Rock.* No. 16 (1982): pp. 302-305.

Jones, Peter. "The Rick Nelson Story." *Record Collector.* No. 14 (October 1980): pp. 44-48.

King, Stephen. "Hello Mary Lou, Goodbye Rick." *Spin.* II (April 1986): pp. 24-25.

Leigh, Spencer. "Rick Nelson." *Record Collector.* No. 78 (February 1986): pp. 17-23.

Newcombe, Jim. "Believe What You Say: An Interview with Ricky Nelson." *Now Dig This.* No. 34 (January 1986): pp. 6-9.
Obrecht, Jas. "Rick Nelson." *Guitar Player.* XV (September 1981): pp. 16-18.
Rice, Tim. *Rick Nelson: A Travelin' Man.* Preston, England: Rick Nelson International Commemorative Society, 1987.
Selvin, Joel. *Ricky Nelson: Idol for a Generation.* Chicago: Contemporary Books, 1990.
Skok, Neil. "Rick Nelson: The Lost Years, 1966-1972." *Blue Suede News.* No. 19 (1992): pp. 15-16.
Stafford, John. "Rockin' Ricky Nelson." *Now Dig This.* No. 32 (November 1985): pp. 18-21.
Tamarkin, Jeff. "Rick Nelson: Pioneer Rock 'n' Roll Teen Idol." *Goldmine.* No. 145 (February 14, 1986): pp. 14-16, 76-78.
Whitall, Susan. "Rick Nelson Wasn't Rock's Poor Little Fool." *Detroit* [Michigan] *News.* (September 5, 1990): p. 3H.

LITTLE RICHARD

The Life and Times of Little Richard: The Quasar of Rock, by Charles White. New York: Harmony Books, 1984. Illustrated. 269 pp.

British sociologist Simon Frith is a fan, commentator, and analyst of rock music and musicians.[1] In 1983, he reviewed 16 books about a variety of singers and songwriters. His perceptive commentary, entitled "Rock Biography: Essay Review" in *Popular Music 3: Producers and Markets* (Cambridge University Press, 1983), began with a quotation by the late *Rolling Stone* columnist Lester Bangs: "I have always believed that rock 'n' roll comes down to myth. There are no 'facts'" (p. 271). Following this anti-historical observation, Frith diagnosed numerous factual, stylistic, and structural flaws inherent in most "teenybopper biographies." Rather than condemning the entire literary genre, the sociologist-turned-literary critic identified two outstanding works of rock biography. Frith praised Nick Tosches' *Hellfire: The Jerry Lee Lewis Story* (Dell Publishing, 1982) as one of the best books he had encountered in the realm of music biography:

> Tosches immersed himself so deeply in Jerry Lee Lewis' history, in its mesh of fundamentalist fervour and dogged materi-

> alism, in its knot of racial, sexual, family appetites and guilt, that his writing has its own rock 'n' roll rhythm: southern cadences familiar from William Faulkner or Flannery O'Connor became flashy, vulgar, naive. Tosches gets inside Lewis' imagery, understands that his music (in its aggressive petulance, its equation of rhythm and sexuality) articulated desires that could not even be thought otherwise. Country boys in the 1950s had no cultural tools except music. They did not read, they hardly spoke, they were not yet all-American consumers. In showing how rock 'n' roll became Lewis' way of dealing with his own life, Tosches shows how the music had a power, carried a meaning, for adolescents everywhere. (pp. 275-276)

Beyond the culture-immersion approach of Tosches, Frith was also attracted by the scholarly biography *Sing a Sad Song: The Life of Hank Williams* (University of Illinois Press, 1981), penned by Roger Williams. Concerning this study, Frith comments, it "combines all the approaches I have been discussing: as a fan, Williams begins from his own responses to the music; as a journalist, he talked to as many people as he could, tried to pin down what really happened, explored the relationship between the man and the myths; as a critic, he situates his star, analyzes his musical, commercial, and social conditions of production" (p. 276). After explaining his preferences for the works of Tosches and Williams, Frith concluded his lengthy review with a thoughtful analysis of the complex world of rock stars, popular culture, and biographers:

> The problem seems to be that in dealing with rock lives we are dealing with ciphers that signify commercial calculations, audience expectations, vested interests, as well as individual experience. A good rock biography would treat the myth at the heart of the life (and not just the life at the heart of the myth), and this task, to celebrate, expose and use a myth all at once, is not easily done in the chronological confines of a biography. . . . What the stars themselves think, why they make their musical moves, seems less important than what everyone else thinks about them. I suppose that is the point. In rock biographies we see not the stars at work but the star-makers, the fans and journalists and critics through whose mediations musical

lives are continually being defined and measured and made meaningful. (pp. 276-277)

Few rock biographers are as meticulous, as devoted, as well-prepared, or as tenacious in their desire to allow their subjects to reveal themselves as Charles White. Under the media-induced pseudonym "Dr. Rock," this British-based chiropodist spends his leisure hours exploring the lives and listening to the lyrics of rock 'n' roll personalities. During the past two decades, White has interviewed numerous popular-music personalities (Professor Longhair, Jerry Lee Lewis, Chuck Berry, and Bo Diddley, just to name a few); attended rock concerts; written record reviews; created and taught courses on modern music ("The Development of Rock 'n' Roll" at Scarborough Technical College); conducted television programs ("My Show" for BBC-1 North TV in February 1983); appeared regularly on radio talk shows (particularly Tim Jibson's "Paul Hunsley Electric Wireless Show" on BBC Radio Humberside and Stuart Colman's "Echoes" on BBC Radio London); drafted liner notes for Charly record albums; contributed articles to rock journals (including *Now Dig This* and *Let It Rock*); collected more than 30,000 records; and established, along with Jamie "Dr. Elvis" Pearson, the Rock 'n' Roll Museum at the Olympia Centre in Scarborough.[2] All of White's accumulated knowledge and previous biographical inquiries–on figures ranging from Mick Jagger and Chuck Berry to King Curtis and Clyde McPhatter–surface in *The Life and Times of Little Richard*. The results are astounding.

The October 1984 release of Harmony Books' Little Richard biography was preceded by several years of pre-publication commentary. An initial announcement appeared on the album cover of a 1980 Charly Records reissue of 16 Little Richard tunes. The liner notes for *The Georgia Peach* (CR 30190) stated, "A book, *The Little Richard Story*, will be published on the 1st of January 1981. An in-depth look at Richard's extraordinary career. Co-authored by Chas. 'Dr. Rock' White and John Garodkin . . ." The date was premature by more than 1,000 days, and along the way, the Danish discographer Garodkin apparently lost interest in the literary project.

In the December 1983/January 1984 issue of Detroit's short-lived *Record Profile Magazine* (No. 3), a speculative essay about the nature and extent of White's study appeared in the article "Dr. Rock on Little Richard: Speculating on a Long-Awaited Biography," by B. Lee Cooper. Listing 45 specific questions about the singer's career, the skeptical author challenged White to produce a truly revealing biography on the rock 'n' roll giant (pp. 21-22, 25). Next, the formal pre-release machinery of an American publishing house began to crank up. Harmony Books produced a glossy-covered, 32-page illustrated booklet designed to tease and please retailers. *Rolling Stone* printed an inflammatory excerpt (under the title "Tooty, Fruity") from the forthcoming text in July (No. 426), followed in August (No. 427) by a brief commentary entitled "Introduction," by soul-music specialist Gerri Hirshey. The magazine's September 13, 1984, "Letters to the Editor" (No. 430) waxed enthusiastic about White's yet-to-be-released work, even though the excerpt had been extremely brief. Finally, *Time* magazine music critic Jay Cocks' pre-publication review, "Dancing in the Outer Darkness: Two Nifty Books Tap the Tangled Roots of Rock," (CXXIV, September 1984) praised White for having "the good sense to go off-mike when the major talent is in the room" and for allowing Little Richard to send readers "reeling" with his accounts of his childhood sexual pranks and raucous recording and performing career. Cocks sums up *The Life and Times of Little Richard* by labeling it "the woolliest, funniest, funkiest rock memoir ever" (p. 70).

What kind of book provokes this much interest from rock fans, scholars, and critics? Could the pre-publication hype, along with 50,000-copy first-run print plans of the New York publishers, be ill-founded? Not at all. Charles White has done more to accurately depict Little Richard Penniman's life than even Simon Frith would expect. By allowing Little Richard to conjure his own version of the past, by encouraging this frantic star's friends, fans, and music contemporaries to comment on his achievements and shortcomings, and by noting how Richard defied the tenets of his times through his bizarre behavior, White has made the "myth at the heart of life" actually breathe. Little Richard's candid comments are sometimes distasteful, occasionally unbelievable, but always fascinating. Tensions between his spirituality and sexuality are mammoth. Music–characterized as satanic rock and godly gospel–is the unifying thread in Richard's being. Even Richard's hilarious anti-homosexual dictums are couched in traditional gospel-preaching parodies: "God made Adam and Eve. Not Adam and Steve!" Such absurd statements illustrate the inner contradiction of a schizophrenic lifestyle that combines fundamentalist religion, guilt, fear, redemption, and personal salvation with lengthy periods of debauchery, orgy, voyeurism, homosexuality, drugs, and lust.

White initiates his study with hyperbolic zeal. Little Richard "has always been treated as a way-out demento, beyond ordinary comprehension or serious analysis," he notes in his preface. Why does Little Richard hold a special place in American musical history? First, White explains, he demolished established popular musical structures with songs like "Tutti Frutti," "Long Tall Sally," "Ready Teddy," "Lucille," and "Good Golly Miss Molly." Almost single-handedly, he laid the rhythmic foundation of rock 'n' roll. Second, he brought the races together in a common admiration for his music. Third, he twice discarded superstardom for the Church, typifying the continuing conflict between sacred and secular music that dogged him throughout his career. Fourth, he survived several decades of life on the wild side when others–from his close friends Sam Cooke, Jimi Hendrix, and Otis Redding to distant acquaintances like Janis Joplin and Jim Morrison–died prematurely. Fifth, the performing skill of Richard is described as "a special magnetism, bringing his audience together in one entity" and tapping some "mystical source of mental power that is only accessible to great preachers and shamans." White concludes his introductory observations by declaring:

> This is the story of a unique and dualistic psyche, an uncontrollable genius whose influence on western culture is incalculable, but whose personal life has been tormented by outrageous and freakist sexuality and a hunger for public adulation. As a totally new phenomenon in the 1950s, he caught every stigma and label that the press could lay on a man. Yet at the same time, Richard's desire to be a minister of God and a prophet of peace among the races epitomizes man's crucial struggle–the battle between the good and the evil that exists in all of us. (p. v-vi)

White's text is organized chronologically, but it is written in a fast-paced, pastiche style. Little Richard's memories of his activities are reported directly, with the author's own corrections, adaptations, and interpretations added for clarification. Throughout the literary dialogue, White inserts a wealth of commentary from former band members, personal friends, and fellow rock stars–including producer Robert A. "Bumps" Blackwell, composer John Marascalco and drummer Chuck Connors (from Richard's early label, Specialty Records), John Lennon, Jimi Hendrix, Smokey Robinson, Paul McCartney, Keith Richards, David Bowie, and Paul Simon. The stories of head-to-head concert clashes between Richard and Jerry Lee Lewis and between Richard and Ike and Tina Turner are magnificent in detail, varied in perspective, and packed with verve. Finally, White concludes his book with a record collector's dream section. With the assistance of Bob Hyde, he presents a complete "Sessionography" of Richard's recordings (pp. 223-246), and a full "Discography and Filmography" (pp. 247-255). Fully indexed and well-illustrated, with both candid and commercial snapshots, *The Life and Times of Little Richard* is a magnificent example of oral history.

White's biography–released almost 30 years after Richard's "Tutti Frutti" (Specialty 561) first hit *Billboard*'s rhythm-and-blues charts–raises more than a few questions. If Little Richard was quintessential as a founder, innovator, communicator, and influence in contemporary music, why had so little been published about him prior to this date?[3] Perhaps Richard himself has stymied most attempts to produce an authentic, thorough biography. Like a bucking bronco, too wild to tame, Richard's mercurial lifestyle has defied rational interpretation, scholarly investigation, and serious analysis. But the knowledgeable, tenacious White would not be denied. Like his fellow British scholars Simon Frith, Charlie Gillett,[4] and Stuart Colman,[5] he is determined to inform his American cousins about their musical heritage. His biography is obviously a labor of love. Yet it is also a tribute to White's sense of style that the volume tells Little Richard's story in the wild man's own words. No one who reads this book will ever again consider the rise of rock music without thinking of Little Richard.

NOTES

1. Among Simon Frith's most noteworthy examinations of music are (with Ian Hoare, Tony Cummings, and Clive Anderson) *The Soul Book* (New York: Dell Publishing, 1976); *The Sociology of Rock* (London: Constable Books, 1978); *Sound Effects: Youth, Leisure, and the Politics of Rock 'n' Roll* (New York: Pantheon Books, 1981); "Popular Music, 1950-1980," in *Making Music: The Guide to Writing, Performing, and Recording*, ed. George Martin (London: Pan Books, 1983), pp. 17-48.

2. Ian Key, "Dr. Rock Turns the Clock Back to the Golden Age of Elvis, Haley, Fats and All That Jazz," (publication date unknown); Dorothy Weirs, "Roll On, Dr. Rock: For Chas the Music Never Died," *The Northern Echo*, August 4, 1979, p. 1; "BBC Radio Humberside," *BBC Radio Times*, (September 26 - October 2, 1981): p. 84; "The Dr. Rock Show," *Scarborough Evening News*, January 17, 1983, p. 1.

3. Stuart Colman, "Little Richard: Back to the Church," in *They Kept on Rockin': The Giants of Rock 'n' Roll* (Poole, Dorset, England: Blandford Press, 1982), pp. 129-131; B. Lee Cooper, "Jerry Lee Lewis and Little Richard: Career Parallels in the Lives of the Court Jesters of Rock 'n' Roll," *Music World and Record Digest* No. 46 (May 1979): p. 6; Peter Doggett, "Little Richard," *Record Collector* XXV (September 1981): pp. 20-25; Howard Elson, "Little Richard," in *Early Rockers* (New York: Proteus Books, 1982), pp. 90-99; John Garodkin, comp., *Little Richard Special: King of Rock 'n' Roll* (Denmark: Danish Rock 'n' Roll Society, 1975); Langdon Winner, "Little Richard," in *The Rolling Stone Illustrated History of Rock and Roll*, ed. Jim Miller, 2nd ed. (New York: Random House/Rolling Stone Press Book, 1980), pp. 48-53.

4. Charlie Gillett, *The Sound of the City: The Rise of Rock and Roll* (New York: Outerbridge and Dienstfrey, 1970), and *Making Tracks: Atlantic Records and the Growth of a Multi-Billion Dollar Industry* (New York: E.P. Dutton, 1974).

5. Stuart Colman, *They Kept on Rockin': The Giants of Rock 'n' Roll* (Poole, Dorset, England: Blandford, 1982).

Chapter 3

Bootleg Records

THE BEATLES

You Can't Do That! Beatles Bootlegs and Novelty Records, 1963-1980, by Charles Reinhart. Ann Arbor: Pierian Press, 1981. Illustrated. 411 pp.

Charles Reinhart has assembled a unique discography of Beatles music. This 1981 work complements *All Together Now: The First Complete Beatles Discography, 1961-1975* (1975) and *The Beatles Again* (1977) compiled by Harry Castleman and Walter J. Podrazik. While these two earlier books surveyed the entire output of commercial recordings by John Lennon, Paul McCartney, George Harrison, and Ringo Starr, Reinhart's text examines only "underground" discs–bootlegs, pirates, and counterfeits–along with an array of novelty songs related to the Beatles. It is hardly surprising that this well-organized, highly specialized discography has been issued from Ann Arbor's Pierian Press. This publishing house seems dedicated to producing the best research resources possible on popular music in general, and on Beatles' music in particular, through its Rock and Roll Reference Series. Reinhart's book, volume five in this Pierian series, is a gem.

"Beatles bootlegging is big business," declares the author of *You Can't Do That!* Reinhart explains that the Beatles' overwhelming popularity–plus the fact that they produced so much noncommer-

---

These reviews by B. Lee Cooper originally appeared in the following periodicals: "Beatles," *Record Profile Magazine* No. 5 (July 1984): pp. 58-59 and "Elvis Presley," *Record Profile Magazine* No. 5 (May 1984): pp. 75-76. Reprint permission has been granted by the author.

cially released music (via live concert performances, radio broadcasts, TV and film appearances, and studio practice sessions)–has prompted the emergence of an immense, though uncoordinated, network of illegal record production. Although pirated and counterfeit materials, defined as "unauthorized repackagings of standard commercial albums," are discussed briefly, the author focuses his study on bootleg releases. Any disc that is "the creation of unauthorized recordings not from pre-existent ones, but from unauthorized taping of live performances or radio and TV broadcasts, or by utilization of stolen tapes from unreleased sessions" is regarded as a bootleg (p. 396).

Reinhart examines 834 Beatle bootleg albums. These recordings are divided into six unequal sections by artist (e.g., Beatles, Harrison, Lennon, Lennon/McCartney, McCartney/Wings, and Starr); each entry features the album title, record label and number, the songs presented, the dates and sources of each cut, and other bootleg discs featuring the same music. The author also presents more than 50 counterfeit Beatles records and nearly 400 novelty songs related to the Liverpool quartet. Reinhart offers detailed indexes–personal names, songs and album titles, labels, and topics–for all of the recordings he examines. As if this monumental assemblage wasn't sufficient, Pierian Press publisher Tom Schultheiss also contributes as a coda an authoritative 16-page historical profile entitled "Everything You Always Wanted to Know About Bootlegs, But Were Too Busy Collecting Them to Ask."

Beyond the stellar research featured in *You Can't Do That!*, there is a strange, humorous undercurrent of fear throughout the text. The topic seems to spawn it. Reinhart himself uses his introduction to stress the illegality and generally poor recording quality of all bootleg releases. Wally Podrazik's brief foreword questions the value of examining noncommercial discs and warns the author, "Your job has only begun Charlie! Wait until the lists of corrections, objections, additions, and discrepancies begin to arrive . . ." (p. xiv). Even publisher Schultheiss comments, "Charlie Reinhart's staggering discography of bootlegged, pirated, and counterfeited Beatles' recordings will doubtless epitomize to some a totally wrong-headed misapplication of research energies because, for them, it will represent merely a consecration of the illicit, the illegal, the ephemeral, and the trivial" (p. 395). Despite all of these stated concerns, Reinhart's study is as structurally superb as it is valuable. No serious student of the Beatles, or of popular culture, the recording industry, copyright law, economics, or the mass media should fail to consult this fine study. It sets the structural benchmark for all future examinations of noncommercial recordings.

ELVIS PRESLEY

Jailhouse Rock: The Bootleg Records of Elvis Presley, 1970-1983, by Lee Cotten and Howard A. DeWitt. Ann Arbor: Pierian Press, 1983. Illustrated. 367 pp.

The Pierian Press continues to expand its Rock and Roll Reference Series with the publication of Volume 8, *Jailhouse Rock.* This discographic study, authored by retail record dealer and Presleyana collector Lee Cotten and rock historian and biographer Howard A. DeWitt, provides a wealth of information on a rarely researched topic. The majority of the text (pp. 1-286) consists of magnificently detailed identifications of individual Elvis bootleg albums. Arranged alphabetically by title, the authors provide as much of the following information as possible about each bootleg recording: (1) the name of the "Record Company"; (2) the record number; (3) the date of release; (4) the country of origin; (5) the song titles included on each side of the record; (6) the source(s) of the performance(s); (7) a photograph of the front of the album cover; (8) a detailed description of the record packaging; (9) descriptive and evaluative commentary about the songs performed; and (10) a summary of the album in terms of technical audio quality, packaging attractiveness, and the value of the music on the disc within the total scope of Presley's commercially recorded output.

Beyond the main discography section, *Jailhouse Rock* contains a chronological guide to the most often bootlegged Elvis Presley performances (from the KWKH "Louisiana Hayride" show of October 16, 1954, to the Indianapolis Concert of June 26, 1977); an alphabetized "Song Title Index for Bootlegged Albums, EPs, and Singles"; a list of records of Elvis' "Interviews and Press Conferences"; selected examples of "Overseas Pirated-Releases of Elvis'

Albums''; a number of "Bootlegged Novelty Albums About Elvis''; a complete bootleg "Label Index''; and much more on the personalities mentioned on the recordings and bootlegged cassette tapes, super-8 films, and even videotapes. Cotten and DeWitt have provided everything imaginable.

Every Elvis Presley fan, record collector, discographer, and rock 'n' roll song buff will want to secure a copy of this fact-laden bootleg encyclopedia. But who else should read this rather esoteric book? Cotten and DeWitt provide answers to this question in their lengthy, cogent introduction. With remarkable objectivity, they argue that the emergence of bootleg recording practices were actually fan responses (starting with Frank Sinatra, The Beatles, and The Rolling Stones prior to the post-1970s Presley flood) to the unwillingness of the U.S. recording industry to tape and release concert performances by their contracted artists. Similarly, frequent examples of industry censorship of lyrics referring to sexual relations, drugs, and other controversial topics forced many popular concert songs to be withheld from national release. The rabid enthusiasm of music fans, combined with the post-1970 explosion in high-quality audio recording technology, spawned a nationwide copyright infringement binge that has lasted for more than a decade. For Elvis, as well as other performers, bootlegging activities included not only unauthorized taping of concert performances but also making or stealing recordings of pre- and post-concert jam sessions, studio outtakes and false starts, home strumming sessions, and tapes of other demo tapes. For some, bootleggers were counterculture Robin Hoods–stealing vinyl from the rich (RCA, Capitol, and Columbia) and sharing it with the poor (the record-hungry fans of Elvis, The Beatles, and Bob Dylan). Cotten and DeWitt note that this oversimplification ignores the meaning of copyright law, glosses over middlemen's profits, forgets the problems of bootleg forgeries and fraud, and generally overlooks a dozen other negative implications of the so-called Rock 'n' Roll Liberation Front activities. The authors carefully describe this complex organizational dilemma and then invite lawyers, sociologists, business executives, historians, and persons concerned about contemporary ethics to examine the multimillion-dollar bootleg phenomenon in American society. The authors don't lionize bootleggers–but they don't condemn them out of hand, either. They note, with conviction and justification, that the RCA Corporation has treated Elvis fans and Presley historians with disdain for decades. Cotten and DeWitt add that only after bootleg-style packaging and song arrangements had taught RCA executives something about "creative" album construction did such innovative commercial items as the Elvis *Legendary Performer* series and the multi-disc *Elvis Aron Presley* album appear.

Jailhouse Rock is a significant contribution to the study of American popular culture. It examines contemporary life (1970-1983) from varying perspectives of economics, law, sociology, and psychology. Using a dual popularity yardstick–for a person and a particular style of music–the authors have thoughtfully probed the responsiveness of a contemporary marketing enterprise to expressed public interest. Ironically, the authors discovered that the supply-and-demand system is sometimes ignored by corporate recording giants. This encourages unscrupulous entrepreneurs to use illegal tactics to provide popular vinyl goods that are restricted from the public as a result of complicated business contracts, censorship, and unenforceable copyright laws.

Cotten and DeWitt have written a fine scholarly book. Popular culture researchers, Elvis Presley fans, record company executives, bootleg album collectors, and record store owners should study the text carefully. The commentary should also be examined by media moguls, disc jockeys, corporate businesspersons, lawyers, and recording industry personnel. For general readers, the 200 bootleg album photographs alone are worth the price of admission.

REFERENCES

Albertson, Chris. "Benign Piracy." *Stereo Review.* XLV (October 1980): p. 60.

Anderson, Burnett. "Supreme Court Rules on Bootleg Shipments." *Goldmine.* No. 132 (August 16, 1985): p. 89.

Anderson, Burnett. "The RIAA: Are They Out to Throw the Switch on Collectors?" *Goldmine.* No. 210 (August 13, 1988): pp. 8, 20, 79.

Anderson, Burnett. "Counterfeits, Bootlegs, the Law and You," *Goldmine.* No. 257 (June 1, 1990): pp. 6-7.

Angus, Robert. "Pirates, Prima Donnas, and Plain Wrappers." *High Fidelity.* (December 1976): pp. 76-81.

Berkenstadt, James. "Bootlegs vs. Capitol Records: The Continuing Battle Over the Beatle Vaults." *Goldmine.* No. 77 (October 1982): p. 16.

"Bootlegs, Pirates, and Counterfeits: Why Is it Illegal to Manufacture and Sell Some Records by Top Artists," *Record Collector.* No. 149 (January 1992): pp. 30-32.

Cody, John. "Beach Boys Bootlegs: A Consumer's Guide." *Goldmine.* No. 257 (June 1, 1990): pp. 34-36, 98.

Cuscuna, Michael. "The Art of Bootlegging." *Down Beat.* L (September 1983): p. 64.

Dawson, Michael P. "Great White Wonders and Swingin' Pigs: The Bootleg as Collectible." *Goldmine.* No. 262 (August 10, 1990): p. 40.

Denisoff, R. Serge. "The Record Liberation Front: Bootlegging," in *Solid Gold: The Popular Record Industry* (New Brunswick, New Jersey: Transaction Books, 1975): pp. 356-376.

Elliott, Brad. "Defining 'Bootleg' and Springsteen Issues." *Goldmine.* No. 125 (May 10, 1985): pp. 30, 80.

Fripp, Robert. "Bootlegging, Royalties, and the Moment." *Musician.* No. 32 (April 1981): p. 28.

Frith, Simon. "Copyright and the Music Business." *Popular Music.* VII (January 1988): pp. 57-75.

Gart, Galen. "Booting the Blues: Record Piracy in the Late 1940s." *Goldmine.* No. 165 (November 21, 1986): pp. 28-29.

Melton, Gary Warren. "An Examination of the Bootleg Record Industry and its Impact upon Popular Music Consumption." *Tracking: Popular Music Studies.* IV (Winter 1991): pp. 16-25.

Morthland, John and Jerry Hopkins. "Bootleg: The Rock and Roll Liberation Front?" *Rolling Stone.* No. 51 (February 7, 1970): pp. 1, 6-7.

Reinhart, Charles. "Beatles Bootleg Update: Reviews of Recent CD and LP Releases." *Goldmine.* No. 295 (November 15, 1991): pp. 34-47.

"Special Report: Bootleggers–Rock Robin Hoods or Commie Threat?" *Bomp!* No. 21 (March 1979): pp. 22-23.

Walters, Art. "Bootlegging: Plague or Service?" *Record Exchanger.* No. 4 (August-September 1970): pp. 6-7.

Wile, Raymond R. "Record Piracy: The Attempts of the Sound Recording Industry to Protect Itself Against Unauthorized Copying, 1890-1978." *ARSC Journal.* XVII (1985): pp. 18-40.

Chapter 4

Christmas Carols

American historians have been using oral testimony for research, writing, and teaching purposes for decades. However, most social studies classes continue to focus on written reports about wars, presidents, and isolated social and economic events. This chapter suggests that students of contemporary American society can gain significant educational insights by investigating one major recurring cultural event–Christmas–to determine how personal, commercial, religious, and artistic activities influence public thinking. Clearly, singular facts must take a back seat to sweeping judgments about behavioral trends in such investigations. But sociologists and psychologists should not be the only teachers to sail into uncharted, subjective waters. Historians owe it to their students and to themselves to speculate on the nature and meaning of popular cultural events.

CHRISTMAS SONGS

Christmas comes but once a year. But it comes *every* year. Nevertheless, few social studies teachers perceive learning opportunities in holiday songs that dominate their students' lives each December. Traditional Christmas carols reflect the gospel stories of the birth of Jesus Christ in Bethlehem. Thus, comparisons of biblical commen-

---

This study by B. Lee Cooper is an expanded version of "Christmas Songs: Audio Barometers of Tradition and Social Change in America, 1950-1987," *Social Studies*, LXXIX (November-December 1988), pp. 278-280. Reprinted with permission of The Helen Dwight Reid Educational Foundation for Heldref Publications at 4000 Albemarle Street, N.W., Washington, D.C. 20016.

taries, historical recitations, and lyrical depictions are always possible. Some history teachers worry, though, that the study of Christmas songs may infringe upon the beliefs of students raised in Jewish, Muslim, or other religious traditions. They also worry that observations from Christian fundamentalist youngsters might clash with ideas presented by less conservative Christians. For these reasons, most high schools and colleges treat the Christmas season strictly as a time of social ritual, with an assembly, a December convocation, a few traditional carols sung in music classes, and a two-week vacation.

There is great potential, however, in the study of Christmas songs. Approached objectively, tunes of the Yuletide season can provide valuable illustrations of historical information, cultural borrowing, and social change. Presented in this context, both Christian and non-Christian students can benefit from examining oral history resources of the holiday season.

History teachers should introduce the investigation of Christmas songs by noting the wide variety of holiday tunes that are played on radios, heard in downtown department stores, and broadcast throughout shopping malls. The initial instructional goal should be to stimulate students to acknowledge that Christmas songs can really be quite different in sound, in lyric, and in meaning. Once the preliminary issues of rhythm, orchestration, instrumentation, vocal quality, and artists have been discussed, the classroom analysis should shift toward the varying Christmas messages being related. This latter activity will allow history instructors to involve students in vigorous, creative cultural analysis.

In order to structure discussions of Christmas-song content, a teacher should ask students to examine the following format. Most students believe that all Yuletide songs can be divided into two clear-cut categories: traditional or nontraditional. Once they begin to explore this simple dichotomy in detail, though, the class will note that the content of Christmas songs must be classified along more complex lines than the simple, bipolar traditional/nontraditional system. Lyrics fall into another dual system of sacred/secular themes. "Adeste Fideles" bids the faithful to come to Bethlehem to adore the King of Angels; it presents a clearly sacred message. In contrast, "Please Come Home for Christmas" beckons a wandering loved one to return to a lonely partner by December 25th (or by December 31st at the very latest), illustrating a secular holiday-season concern. Key terms in this sacred-versus-secular identification system are:

Sacred Images	Secular Images
Holy Night	holiday
Jesus Christ	Santa Claus
Emmanuel	St. Nicholas
Blessed Child	little children
Mary and Joseph	Currier and Ives
cradle	sleigh
straw in a manger	Christmas tree
lambs	reindeer
oxen and asses	Dasher, Dancer, Prancer, Vixen, Comet, Cupid, Donner, Blitzen, and Rudolph
cattle lowing	chestnuts roasting
harps of gold	tin horns and toy drums
blessed angels singing	carolers rejoicing
Three Kings	Alvin, Theodore, and Simon (The Chipmunks)
gifts of gold, frankincense, and myrrh	skates, sleds, and other presents
heaven and nature sing	bells on bobtail ring
good tidings	cup of cheer

In order to provide adequate recorded options for the four fields of analytical concern–traditional, nontraditional, sacred, and secular–the following lists may be used.

Traditional Christmas Recordings

Sacred Songs

1. "Adeste Fideles"
   by Bing Crosby (1960)
2. "Ave Maria"
   by Perry Como (1950)
3. "Silent Night"
   by Bing Crosby (1957)
4. "Silent Night, Holy Night"
   by Mahalia Jackson (1962)
5. "Silent Night (Christmas Hymn)"
   by Sister Rosetta Tharpe (1949)
6. "Silent Night (Sleep in Heavenly Peace)"
   by Barbara Streisand (1966)

Secular Tunes

1. "Christmas Song"
   by Nat King Cole (1946)
2. "I'll Be Home for Christmas"
   by Bing Crosby (1943)
3. "Jingle Bell Rock"
   by Bobby Helms (1957)
4. "Jingle Bells"
   by Perry Como (1957)
5. "Rockin' Around the Christmas Tree"
   by Brenda Lee (1960)
6. "Rudolph the Red-Nosed Reindeer"
   by Gene Autry (1949)
7. "Silver Bells"
   by Earl Grant (1967)
8. "White Christmas"
   by Bing Crosby (1942)
9. "Winter Wonderland"
   by Perry Como (1952)

Nontraditional Christmas Recordings

Sacred Songs

1. "Child of God" by Bobby Darin (1960)
2. "Do You Hear What I Hear?" by Bing Crosby (1963)
3. "Go Tell It on the Mountain" by Mahalia Jackson (1962)
4. "Little Drummer Boy" by The Harry Simeone Chorale (1958)
5. "Little Drummer Boy" by Moonlion (1975)
6. "Little Drummer Boy/ Peace on Earth" by David Bowie and Bing Crosby (1982)
7. "Mary's Boy Child" by Harry Belafonte (1956)
8. "Mary's Boy Child/ Oh My Lord" by Bony M (1978)
9. "What Child Is This?" by The Brothers Four (1962)

Secular Tunes

1. "Blue Christmas" by Elvis Presley (1957)
2. "The Chipmunk Song" by The Chipmunks (1958)
3. "Do They Know It's Christmas?" by Band Aid (1984)
4. "Donde Esta Santa Claus?" by Augie Rios (1958)
5. "Grandma Got Run Over By a Reindeer" by Elmo 'n' Patsy (1981)
6. "Green Chritma" by Stan Freberg (1958)
7. "Please Come Home for Christmas" by The Eagles (1978)
8. "Run Rudolph Run" by Chuck Berry (1958)
9. "Santa Claus Is Comin' to Town" by Bruce Springsteen (1985)

What can students learn by categorizing Christmas songs? Many things. First, church hymns and carols such as "Silent Night" are staples on numerous Christmas albums. Second, songs that deal peripherally with the Bethlehem story have become traditional Christmas favorites over the past four decades because of their special meanings to families and loved ones during the holiday period. Clearly, Bing Crosby's "White Christmas," Nat King Cole's "The Christmas Song," Earl Grant's "Silver Bells," and Dolly Parton's "Winter Wonderland/Sleigh Ride" are illustrations of this phenomenon. Third, there are no racist or sexist barriers for recording artists who produce highly popular Christmas recordings. Similarly, few religious or ethnic barriers exist, as illustrated by the hit recordings of "Silent Night (Sleep in Heavenly Peace)" by Barbra Streisand and "Donde Esta Santa Claus?" by Augie Rios. Fourth, a category of contemporary sacred Christmas tunes can be identified, with The Harry Simeone Chorale's "Little Drummer Boy" as the primary illustration. Fifth, the commercialism of Christmas and the materialism of the entire world is challenged in several recordings, especially in Stan Freberg's "Green Chritma" and Band Aid's "Do They Know It's Christmas?" Sixth, a variety of holiday heroes and singing creatures have become synonymous with the modern Yuletide season: "The Chipmunks" featuring Theodore, Simon, and Alvin; "Rudolph, the Red-Nosed Reindeer"; and "Frosty the Snowman." Seventh, the adaptation of traditional Christmas symbols into secular activities is demonstrated in Bobby Helms' "Jingle Bell Rock," Elvis Presley's "Blue Christmas," and Brenda Lee's "Rockin' Around the Christmas Tree." Eighth, comedy and humor are central features in a variety of Christmas recordings, such as Elmo 'n' Patsy's "Grandma Got Run Over by a Reindeer" and The Singing Dogs' barking rendition of "Jingle Bells." Finally, teachers and students alike will note that disagreements are inevitable as to whether or not songs like "Jingle Bell Rock," "Merry Christmas Darling," or "Please Come Home for Christmas" should be placed in either traditional/secular or nontraditional/secular categories. At this point, the issues of social change and public perception can be discussed, since "Frosty" and "Rudolph," today regarded as traditional Christmas figures, were strictly nontraditional, novelty characters during the 1950s.

In order to highlight the evolution of Christmas recordings, a broad survey of varying thematic images should accompany the initial bipolar sacred/secular design. Students need to recognize that the five decades since 1940 have yielded many different types of holiday-season songs. More importantly, as observers of social change, they need to explore the effects of shifting thematic images.

IMITATIONS OF YULETIDE SUCCESS

If imitation is the sincerest form of flattery, then performers such as Bing Crosby and The Harry Simeone Chorale should feel extremely honored. The following lists show how many different novice singers and established recording stars elected to release new versions of previously recorded Yuletide standards.

1. "White Christmas" (Decca 18429)
   by Bing Crosby (1942). Also recorded by:
   a. Frank Sinatra–Columbia 36756 (1944)
   b. Jo Stafford–Capitol 319 (1946)
   c. Perry Como–RCA Victor 1970 (1947)
   d. The Ravens–National 9062 (1949)
   e. Mantovani–London 1280 (1952)
   f. Clyde McPhatter and The Drifters–Atlantic 1048 (1954)

2. "The Little Drummer Boy" (20th Century Fox 121)
   by The Harry Simeone Chorale (1958). Also recorded by:
   a. Johnny Cash–Columbia 41481 (1959)
   b. The Jack Halloran Singers–Dot 16275 (1961)
   c. The Pipe and Drums of The Military Band of The Royal Scots Dragoon Guards–RCA 0709 (1972)
   d. Moonlion–P.I.P. 6513 (1972)
   e. Bob Seger and The Silver Bullet Band–A&M 3911 (1987)

These groupings of songs, provided for student examination, are structured strictly according to thematic variation. Historians can locate clue after clue about the nature of American culture through these popular recordings. Lines of evidence will not be singular or definitive, of course; the truth will be complex, contradictory, and obscured by various other concerns. As students begin to recognize the blend of ideas, myths, values, and humor that undergird the nature of all human institutions, they will also begin to appreciate the difficulty of defining "culture" (especially their own) with clarity and ease. Ideally, some of their ethnocentric assumptions will totter and fall. The enjoyment of listening to known audio commodities–contemporary Christmas records–with enlightened, perceptive ears will stimulate students to become better, more critical thinkers in history classes and other disciplines as well.

The following topics offer an appropriate cross section of themes that can be presented for classroom study.

IMAGES OF SANTA CLAUS

Whether Father Christmas, St. Nicholas, Santa Claus, or whatever else the Jolly Old Elf is called, this mythical character is central to the cultural definition of Christmas in the United States. The descriptions of St. Nick usually illustrate the goals of people who sing or listen to the popular lyrics. Thus, Santa becomes a fancy dancer, a loving father, a source of material goods, an international agent of peace and good will, or the personification of the Christmas spirit. The following songs typify such characteristics:

- "Boogie Woogie Santa Claus"
  (Exclusive 75X)
  by Mable Scott (1948)

- "C.B. Santa"
  (A&M 1887)
  by Homemade Theatre (1976)

- "Donde Esta Santa Claus?"
  (Metro 20010)
  by Augie Rios (1958)

- "Here Comes Santa Claus (Down Santa Claus Lane)"
  (Columbia 20377)
  by Gene Autry (1950)
- "I Believe in Father Christmas"
  (Atlantic 3305)
  by Greg Lake (1975)
- "I Saw Mommy Kissing Santa Claus"
  (RCA Victor 5067)
  by Spike Jones (1952)
- "Little Saint Nick"
  (Capitol 5096)
  by The Beach Boys (1963)
- "The Man with All the Toys"
  (Capitol 5312)
  by The Beach Boys (1964)
- "Mr. Santa Claus"
  (Fortune 550)
  by Nathaniel Mayer (1962)
- "Santa Baby"
  (RCA Victor 5502)
  by Eartha Kitt (1953)
- "Santa Claus Is Comin' to Town"
  (Decca 23281)
  by The Andrews Sisters (1947)
- "Santa Claus Is Watching You"
  (Mercury 72058)
  by Ray Stevens (1962)

NON-CHRISTMAS HOLIDAY SONGS

The Yuletide season is notable for its diversity of Christmas tunes, with lyrical commentaries ranging from sacred images to secular materialism. But how can the popularity of holiday recordings that refer neither to Jesus Christ nor to Santa Claus be explained? These songs include:

- "Baby It's Cold Outside"
  (ABC-Paramount 10298)
  by Ray Charles and Betty Carter (1962)

- "Frosty the Snowman"
  (Capitol 1203)
  by Nat King Cole, with The Pussy Cats (1951)

- "Jingle Bells"
  (RCA EPA 9201)
  by Perry Como (1957)

- "Let It Snow! Let It Snow! Let It Snow!"
  (Decca 18741)
  by Connie Boswell (1946)

- "Sleigh Ride"
  (Decca 9-28463)
  by Bing Crosby (1953)

UNUSUAL YULETIDE CHARACTERS

Christmas stories often highlight the roles of animals as symbols of innocence, kindness, and simplicity. The manger scene in Bethlehem emphasizes docile cattle and sheep, while the Santa Claus myth features sleeping mice and soaring reindeer. Why do contemporary recording artists often introduce unusual Yuletide characters in their Christmas tunes? These songs might be helpful in answering that question:

- "The Chipmunk Song"
  (Liberty 55168)
  by The Chipmunks (1958)

- "Frosty the Snowman"
  (Columbia 38907)
  by Gene Autry (1951)

- "The Happy Reindeer"
  (Capitol 4300)
  by Dancer, Prancer, and Nervous (1959)

- "Rudolph the Red-Nosed Reindeer"
  (Columbia 38610)
  by Gene Autry (1949)

- "Snoopy's Christmas"
  (Laurie 3416)
  by The Royal Guardsmen (1968)

SOCIAL COMMENTARY IN CHRISTMAS SONGS

It is not uncommon for contemporary performers such as Bruce Springsteen, Pink Floyd, Stevie Wonder, or Midnight Oil to pursue social commentaries in their lyrics. However, it is rare to encounter political or social criticism in holiday recordings. The following artists deliberately used Christmas songs to communicate their public-policy concerns:

- "Dear Mr. Jesus"
  (PowerVision 8607)
  by PowerSource (1987)

- "Do They Know It's Christmas?"
  (Columbia 04749)
  by Band Aid (1984)

- "Green Chritma"
  (Capitol 4097)
  by Stan Freberg (1958)

- "Happy Xmas (War Is Over)"
  (Apple 1842)
  by John and Yoko and The Plastic Ono Band (1971)

- "Pretty Paper"
  (Monument 830)
  by Rob Orbison (1963)

- "7 O'Clock News/Silent Night"
  (Columbia CL 2563)
  by Simon and Garfunkel (1966)

CHILDREN'S PERSPECTIVES ON CHRISTMAS

Whether focusing on a newborn babe in the manger as viewed by "The Little Drummer Boy" or bemoaning the fact that a youngster who is nothing but bad gets "Nuttin' for Christmas," Yuletide recordings often take on a child's perspective to encapsulate the nature and meaning of the December holiday. In the following songs, what individual values and cultural ideas emerge from children's images of Christmas?

- "All I Want for Christmas (Is My Two Front Teeth)"
  (RCA Victor 3177)
  by Spike Jones (1948)

- "I Saw Mommy Kissing Santa Claus"
  (Columbia 39871)
  by Jimmy Boyd (1952)

- "I'm Gonna Lasso Santa Claus"
  (Decca 9-30107)
  by Brenda Lee (1956)

- "Little Becky's Christmas Wish"
  (Warner Brothers 7154)
  by Becky Lamb (1967)

- "The Little Drummer Boy"
  (20th Century Fox 121)
  by The Harry Simeone Chorale (1958)

- "(I'm Getting) Nuttin' for Christmas"
  (MGM 12092)
  by Barry Gordon (1955)

YULETIDE PARODY TUNES AND SEQUEL SONGS

Why have performers like Allan Sherman, Stan Freberg, and David Seville used traditional Christmas songs as sources of comic parody or as initial resources for sequel tunes? These songs, followed by their sequels, may provide some insight:

- "Rudolph the Red-Nosed Reindeer"
  (Columbia 38610)
  by Gene Autry (1949)

  - "Run Rudolph Run"
    (Chess 1714)
    by Chuck Berry (1958)

  - "Rudolph the Red-Nosed Reindeer"
    (Liberty 55289)
    by The Chipmunks with David Seville (1960)

- "Happy Happy Birthday Baby"
  (Checker 872)
  by The Tune Weavers (1957)

  - "Merry Merry Christmas Baby"
    (Dot 16166)
    by Dodie Stevens (1960)

- "Jingle Bells"
  (RCA EPA 920)
  by Perry Como (1957)

  - "Yingle Bells"
    (Capitol 781)
    by Yogi Yorgesson (1949)

- "Twistin' Bells"
  (Canadian American 120)
  by Santo and Johnny (1960)

- "Jingle Bells"
  (RCA PB 10129)
  by The Singing Dogs (1975)

- "Jingle Bells (Laughing All the Way)"
  (Warner Brothers 49877)
  by St. Nick (1981)

• "The Twelve Days of Christmas"
(Decca 25585)
by Burl Ives (1962)

- "The Twelve Gifts of Christmas"
  (Warner Brothers 5406)
  by Allan Sherman (1963)

• "Mr. Sandman"
(Cadence 1247)
by The Chordettes (1954)

- "Mr. Santa"
  (Coral 61539)
  by Dorothy Collins (1955)

HOLIDAY LONELINESS

Joyous memories of holiday vacations, of family get-togethers, and of special times with a loved one dominate traditional Christmas songs. However, sociologists and psychologists have frequently noted the emotional stress encountered by individuals who find themselves alone on December 25th. The following Yuletide lyrics depict these feelings of isolation:

• "Blue Christmas"
(RCA 447-0647)
by Elvis Presley (1957)

- "Christmas Will Be Just Another Day"
  (Decca 31688)
  by Brenda Lee (1964)

- "(It's Gonna Be a) Lonely Christmas"
  (Jubilee 5001)
  by The Orioles (1948)

- "Just a Lonely Christmas"
  (Chance 1150)
  by The Moonglows (1953)

- "Lonesome Christmas"
  (Swing Time 242)
  by Lowell Fulson (1950)

- "Please Come Home for Christmas"
  (Asylum 45555)
  by The Eagles (1978)

- "What Do the Lonely Do at Christmas?"
  (Stax 3215)
  by The Emotions (1973)

SEXUALLY SUGGESTIVE YULETIDE SONGS

Whether sacred or secular, Christmas songs are generally wholesome, family-oriented tales emphasizing manger scenes, babes in toyland, or a red-clad elf guiding eight tiny reindeer. But there are a few sexually suggestive Christmas tunes that seem totally out of character with "Silent Night" and "The Christmas Song." Why would artists release such atypical recordings during the Christmas season?

- "Baby It's Cold Outside"
  (ABC-Paramount 10298)
  by Ray Charles and Betty Carter (1962)

- "Back Door Santa"
  (Atlantic 2576)
  by Clarence Carter (1968)

- "I'll Be Your Santa, Baby"
  (Stax 187)
  by Rufus Thomas (1973)

- "Let It Snow! Let It Snow! Let It Snow!"
  (Decca 18741)
  by Connie Boswell (1946)

- "Merry Christmas Baby"
  (Chess 1711)
  by Chuck Berry (1958)

- "Santa Claus Is Back in Town"
  (RCA 447-0647)
  by Elvis Presley (1957)

- "Santa Claus Wants Some Lovin'"
  (Stax 234)
  by Albert King (1974)

BIZARRE HUMOR IN CHRISTMAS SONGS

Although the humorous childhood perspectives presented in "I Saw Mommy Kissing Santa Claus" and "All I Want for Christmas (Is My Two Front Teeth)" are lighthearted extensions of youthful holiday concerns, the Yuletide season is also punctuated by unconventional recordings about vampires, wookies, and creatures from outer space. How do such bizarre tales capture the attention and interest of a record-buying public in the midst of religious worship and holiday shopping?

- "Christmas Dragnet (Parts 1 and 2)"
  (Capitol 2671)
  by Stan Freberg (1953)

- "Grandma Got Run Over by a Reindeer"
  (Soundwaves 4658)
  by Elmo 'n' Patsy (1981)

- "Merry Christmas in the N.F.L."
  (Handshake 5308)
  by Willis "The Guard" and Vigorish (1980)

- "Monster's Holiday"
  (Garpax 44171)
  by Bobby "Boris" Pickett and The Crypt Kickers (1962)

- "Santa and the Satellite (Parts 1 and 2)"
  (Luniverse 107)
  by Buchanan and Goodman (1957)

- "Santa and the Touchables"
  (Rori 701)
  by Dickie Goodman (1961)

- "What Can You Get a Wookie for Christmas
  (When He Already Owns a Comb?)"
  (RSO 1058)
  by The Star Wars Intergalactic Droid Choir
  and Chorale (1980)

RESOURCES FOR TEACHERS

Although teachers should invite classroom contributions of recorded resources to demonstrate the breadth of Christmas song content, an album discography is provided below. Instructors may use songs from these recent Christmas anthologies to supplement the inevitably random student contributions. Beyond these albums, the Sound Recordings Archive at Bowling Green State University in Bowling Green, Ohio, is available to educators to secure taped illustrations of specific holiday songs. Finally, a bibliography of recently published books and articles on Christmas as a social occasion, a religious event, and a musical festival is attached. With some thought and practice, the carols and Yuletide tunes played in future Decembers will become vital teaching tools–as well as audio signals announcing the always-welcome Christmas recess.

Selected Discography of Albums Featuring Traditional Christmas Hymns, Yuletide Novelty Tunes, and Other Holiday-Season Songs

Album Title and Record Number	Date of Release	Recording Artists Featured on the Album
Christmas Comedy Classics (Capitol SL 9306)	1985	Mel Blanc, Stan Freberg, The Chipmunks, Yogi Yorgesson, and others
Christmas Is . . . Memorable Songs Of Christmas by Great Artists of Our Time (Columbia P11417)	1972	Frank Sinatra, The Carpenters, Bing Crosby, The Mills Brothers, Julie Andrews, Patti Page, and others
Christmas Rap (Profile Pro 1247)	1987	Run-D.M.C., Sweet Tee, Dana Dane, The Showboys, Disco 4, and others
Christmas Rock Album (Priority SL 9465)	1986	Billy Squier, Queen, The Kinks, Dave Edmunds, Elvin Bishop, Elton John, and others
Cool Yule: A Collection of Rockin' Stocking Stuffers (Rhino RNLP 70073)	1986	Chuck Berry, The Drifters, Ike and Tina Turner, Clarence Carter, James Brown, Jack Scott, and others

Album Title and Record Number	Date of Release	Recording Artists Featured on the Album
Cool Yule–Volume 2: A Collection of Rockin' Stocking Stuffers (Rhino RNLP 70193)	1988	Johnny Preston, The Sonics, Huey Smith and The Clowns, Garry "U.S." Bonds, and others
Dr. Demento's The Greatest Novelty Records of All Time: Volume VI–Christmas (Rhino RNLP 825)	1985	Spike Jones, Allan Sherman, Tom Lehrer, Elmo 'n' Patsy, Cheech and Chong, and others
It's Christmas Time Again (Stax MPS 8519)	1982	Little Johnny Taylor, Rufus Thomas, Albert King, The Staple Singers, Isaac Hayes, and others
The Little Drummer Boy (Kapp 3450)	1966	The Harry Simeone Chorale
Mr. Santa's Boogie (Savoy SJL 1157)	1985	The Ravens, Little Esther Phillips, Big Mabelle, Charlie Parker, and others
Phil Spector's Christmas Album (Apple SW 3400)	1972	Darlene Love, The Ronettes, The Crystals, and others
Rhythm 'n' Blues Christmas (United Artists UA/LA 654-R)	1976	Baby Washington, The Five Keys, B.B. King, Amos Milburn, Lowell Fulson, and others

Album Title and Record Number	Date of Release	Recording Artists Featured on the Album
Rockin' Christmas The 50s (Rhino RNLP 066)	1984	The Penguins, Bobby Helms, The Moonglows, Marvin and Johnny, Ron Holden, and others
Rockin' Christmas The 60s (Rhino RNLP 067)	1984	Santo and Johnny, The Turtles, Aretha Franklin, The Wailers, Bobby "Boris" Pickett and The Crypt Kickers, and others
Rockin' Little Christmas (MCA 25084)	1986	Brenda Lee, Dodie Stevens, The Surfaris, Chuck Berry, and others
Soul Christmas (Atco SD 269)	1968	King Curtis, Otis Redding, Carla Thomas, Solomon Burke, William Bell, and others
The Stash Christmas Album: 16 Blues And Jazz Classics (Stash ST 125)	1985	Fats Waller, Louis Armstrong, Ella Fitzgerald, Benny Goodman, Paul Whiteman, and others
A Very Special Christmas (A&M SP 3911)	1987	The Pointer Sisters, Eurythmics, Whitney Houston, John Cougar Mellencamp, Sting, U2, Madonna, Bon Jovi, Stevie Nicks, Bryan Adams, Bruce Springsteen, Bob Seger, and others

REFERENCES

Almost Slim. "Christmas Classics." *Wavelength* 26 (December 1982): pp. 21-22

Almost Slim. "Christmas on Wax." *Wavelength* 38 (December 1983): p. 17.

Almost Slim. "Rock 'n' Roll Banned for Christmas." *Wavelength* 3 (December 1980): p. 14.

Bailey, Mike. "Collectible Christmas Albums." *Goldmine* 193 (December 18, 1987): pp. 12-16.

Barnett, James H. *The American Christmas: A Study in National Culture*. New York: Macmillan, 1954.

Beachley, Chris. "Beach Music in 1988." *DISCoveries* II (January 1989): pp. 80-81.

Belk, Russell W. "A Child's Christmas in America: Santa Claus as Deity, Consumption as Religion." *Journal of American Culture* X (Spring 1987): pp. 89-100.

Callahan, Mile. "Phil Spector, Christmas, and the Stereo Wall of Sound." *Goldmine* 55 (December 1980): pp. 174-175.

Canale, Larry. "Christmas Compact Disc Reviews." In *Digital Audio's Guide to Compact Discs*. New York: Bantam, 1986.

"Christmas Past." *Music World* 83 (March 1981): p. 38.

"Christmas Recording Reviews." *Goldmine* 273 (January 11, 1991): pp. 129-131.

Colby, J. M., and A. W. Purdue. *The Making of the Modern Christmas*. Athens: University of Georgia, 1986.

Cooper, B. Lee. "Christmas Songs: Audio Barometers of Religious Tradition and Social Change in America, 1950-1987." *The Social Studies* LXXIX (November/December 1988): pp. 278-280.

Cooper, B. Lee. "Do You Hear What I Hear: Christmas Recordings as Audio Symbols of Religious Tradition and Social Change in Contemporary America." *International Journal of Media* XVI, No. 3 (1989): pp. 265-270.

Dr. Demento. "Santa and the Hot 100: The History of Holiday Hit-Making." *Waxpaper* II, No. 11 (October 28, 1977): pp. 18-20, 36.

Doggett, Peter. "Rockin' Around the Christmas Tree!" *Record Collector* 28 (December 1981): pp. 44-51.

Elrod, Bruce. "In Country Music: A New Discovery and Some Holiday Chestnuts." *DISCoveries* II (January 1989): pp. 94-95.

Flanagan, Bill. "Making *A Very Special Special Christmas*: Behind Jimmy Iovin's All-Star Charity Album." *Musician* 109 (November 1987): pp. 72-73.

Fumar, Vincent. "Please Come Home for Christmas . . . and Bring the Turntable." *Wavelength* 38 (December 1983): p. 16.

George, B. "Christmas in the Caribbean." *Goldmine* 325 (December 25, 1992): pp. 26-30, 106.

Grein, Paul. "'Grandma' Runs Over Bing in Holiday Race: Adams, Springsteen Join Ranks of Yule Chartmakers." *Billboard* XCVII (December 21, 1985): p. 57.

Harker, Dave. "The Average Popular Song." In *One for the Money: Politics and Popular Song*. London: Hutchinson, 1980.

"Hit Song's Lyrics Lament Child Abuse." *The Battle Creek [Michigan] Enquirer* (December 1988): p. 1B.

Langstaff, Nancy, and John Langstaff, comps. *The Christmas Revels Songbook: Carols, Processionals, Rounds, Ritual, and Children's Songs*. Boston: D. R. Godine, 1985.

Lewisohn, Mark. "The Beatles' Christmas Records." *Record Collector* 112 (December 1988): pp. 11-15.

McAuliffe, Jon. "Christmas Collectibles." *Music World* 80 (December 1980): pp. 6-12.

McGee, David. "A Collector's Guide to Rock and Soul Christmas LPs." *The Record* (December 1981): p. 23.

Milberg, David A., ed. "Christmas Music." In *All Music Guide*, compiled by Michael Erlewine and Scott Bultman. San Francisco: Miller Freeman, Inc., 1992.

Milberg, David A., comp. "Radio/TV Dave's Rock 'n' Roll Christmas: The Ultimate Collection of Christmas Hits and Novelty Tunes." (This is a 1988 mimeographed list of audio-cassette recordings featuring original versions of songs performed over the past 48 years.)

Moonoogian, George A. "Merry Christmas Baby." *Record Exchanger* V (1978): pp. 12-19.

Moonoogian, George A. "Remember When?" *Goldmine* 31 (December 1978): p. 12.

Morthland, John. "Christmas." *Wavelength* 62 (December 1985): p. 28.

Munn, Bob. "Popular Christmas Music: A Collector's Guide." *Goldmine* 115 (December 21, 1984): pp. 60-62.

"1985 Christmas Hits." *Billboard* XCVII (December 21, 1985): p. 57.

"Oh Come All Ye Faithful Record Buyers." *Wavelength* 50 (December 1984): pp. 31-33.

Oksanen, Dave. "The Elvis Presley Christmas Records." *Music World* 80 (December 1980): pp. 39-43.

Osborne, Jerry P. "It's Beginning to Look a Lot Like Christmas." In *Our Best to You–From Record Digest*. Prescott: Record Digest, 1979.

Pattillo, Craig W. *Christmas on Record: Best-Selling Christmas Singles and Albums of the Past 40 Years*. Portland: Braimar, 1983.

Pimper, Steve. "A Slix Pix Christmas!" *DISCoveries* II (January 1989): pp. 100-101.

Radel, Cliff. "In Tune for Christmas." *Lansing [Michigan] State Journal* (December 13, 1992): pp. 1F, 3F.

Rosen, Mark. "Rockin' Around the Christmas Tree: A Rock and Roll Christmas Wrap-up." *Goldmine* 271 (December 14, 1990): p. 56ff.

Russell, Wayne. "Rockin' Around the Christmas Tree." *Now Dig This* 69 (December 1988): pp. 4-7.

Scaramuzzo, Gene. "Everywhere It's Christmas." *Wavelength* 110 (December 1989): pp. 17-18.

Scoppa, Jordan. "Picture This." *Music World* 80 (December 1980): pp. 28-35.

Sherwood, Lydia. "The Chipmunks Chatter–A Talk with Ross Bagdasarian, Jr." *Goldmine* 79 (December 1982): pp. 16-18, 23.

Stidom, Larry. "Izatso?" *Goldmine* 31 (December 1978): p. 31.

Stierle, Wayne. "A Real Rock and Roll Christmas (Or, How To Get Along Without Motown and Phil Spector and Still Have Some Super Holiday Music)." *DISCoveries* II (December 1989): pp. 120-122.

Studwell, William E. *Christmas Carols: A Reference Guide*. New York: Garland Publishing, Inc., 1985.

Tamarkin, Jeff. "1987's Christmas Albums." *Goldmine* 193 (December 18, 1987): p. 16.

Whitburn, Joel, comp. "Christmas." In *Top Pop Albums, 1955-1985*. Menomonee Falls: Record Research, 1991.

Whitburn, Joel, comp. "Christmas Singles, 1955-1990." In *The Pop Singles Annual, 1955-1990*. Menomonee Falls: Record Research, 1991.

Williams, Richard. "And So This Is Christmas: 'I Know Something About Christmas Records, Y' Know . . .'" In *Out of His Head: The Sound of Phil Spector*. New York: Outerbridge and Lazard, 1972.

Chapter 5

Commercial Catalogs

DOWN HOME MUSIC, INC.

Scott, Frank, Alan Scheflin, Nancy Noenning et al., comps. *Country Music Catalog 1981–Including Western Swing, Steel Guitar, and Cowboy Songs*. El Cerrito: Down Home Music, 1981. Illustrated. 40 pp.

Scott, Frank, Nancy Noenning et al., comps. *Blues Catalog 1982*. El Cerrito: Down Home Music, 1983. Illustrated. 64 pp.

Scott, Frank, Laurie Tsubouchi, Nancy Noenning et al., comps. *Vintage Rock 'n' Roll Catalog 1983*. El Cerrito: Down Home Music, 1983. Illustrated. 96 pp.

Frank Scott is a contemporary music curator and the general manager of a very distinctive record store in El Cerrito, California. Down Home Music, Inc., is much more than a typical pop-album reserve. Scott and the store's co-owner, Chris Strachwitz, are respected experts in the specialized recording fields of blues, vintage rock 'n' roll, folk, jazz, ethnic/international, country, old-timey, and bluegrass music. They stock not only American releases but also imported albums from British, European, and Japanese companies. The total inventory of Down Home Music numbers over 15,000 albums. The advertising and sales market for these recordings

---

This review by B. Lee Cooper originally appeared in *Record Profile Magazine* 5 (May 1984): pp. 74-75. Reprint permission has been granted by the author. Down Home Music, Inc. recently changed its name to Roots and Rhythm. It is located at 6921 Stockton Avenue in El Cerrito, California 94530.

stretches far beyond the San Francisco Bay area, thanks to the international distribution (free of charge, amazingly) of a monthly mail-order newsletter. In addition to these newsletters, Scott and his employees have compiled three unique music catalogs. These distinctive publications–focusing on recent album releases in country music, the blues, and vintage rock 'n' roll–are unabashedly commercial in purpose. Yet, they are fascinating, fact-filled resources that should be of interest and value to anyone interested in modern music.

Country Music Catalog 1981 contains citations on 1,200 different record albums by both major (Roy Acuff, Eddy Arnold, Chet Atkins, Moe Bandy, Bobby Bare, and others) and minor (Eddie Adcock, Phil Baugh, Norton Buffalo, and others) country and bluegrass performers since 1945. Artists from the fields of Western swing (Asleep at the Wheel, Bob Wills and The Original Texas Playboys), steel guitar (Noel Boggs, Roy Wiggins), and cowboy songs (Gene Autry, Sons of the Pioneers) are also represented. The alphabetically organized citations feature the performer's full name, a brief biographical description, and a list of currently-in-print American and foreign albums, including titles and record-company numbers. For most album entries, special notations are also provided that list the historical roots of the songs (e.g., "1955-1957 recordings with good notes"); the reissue status of the album ("Japanese reissue of a long unavailable U.S. album"); and brief critical commentaries ("great tribute").

The *Blues Catalog 1982* follows the same alphabetical format as the previous country-music publication. The 2,000 albums listed include discs by artists ranging from Johnny Ace, Dave Alexander, and Luther Allison to Jimmy Witherspoon, Jimmy Yancey, and Mighty Joe Young. Beyond the initial 45-page section, this catalog provides additional listings of anthology albums–"Pre-War Blues Collections" (seven pages) and "Gospel Music" (four pages). There is also a brief list of contemporary books and magazines covering various black-music topics.

The *Vintage Rock 'n' Roll Catalog 1983* is the largest, most detailed publication in this series. There are 1,500 different albums listed in such categories as "Rockabilly and '50s Rock 'n' Roll" (24 pages), "Rhythm 'n' Blues and Vintage Soul" (11 pages),

"Vocal Groups and Doo-Wop" (11 pages), "Surf Music and Instrumentals" (3 pages), and "Rockabilly Revival and European Artists" (5 pages). Among the artists featured are Chuck Berry, Eddie Cochran, Elvis Presley, Otis Redding, The Drifters, The Five Keys, The Ronettes, Duane Eddy, The Blasters, Shakin' Stevens, and many, many others. In addition to these alphabetized artist listings, this catalog contains 19 pages of anthology albums ("Collections by Label") arranged by recording companies. Beyond this, there is an unbelievably extensive alphabetical list of *all* performers ("Collections by Artist") featured in the anthologies. This 21-page section is remarkable in both scope and detail–including such specific entries as "Hardrock Gunter: 4 Tracks on White Label 8814, and 1 Track Each on Bopcat 400 and MCA (UK) MCF 3035."

The publication of these three Down Home music catalogs illustrates the successful marriage of musical expertise and computer programming. The dazzling array of record-related facts featured in these paperback volumes was organized by Peter Malden through a high-tech system previously unavailable to (and, currently, little understood by) most music salespeople. The achievement of Frank Scott and his Down Home colleagues, as stated earlier, constitutes far more than just a simple marketing venture. Along with Joel Whitburn's books of *Billboard* data statistics, the fine encyclopedias produced by Sheldon Harris (*Blues Who's Who*) and Irwin Stambler (*Encyclopedia of Pop, Rock, and Soul*), the insightful biographies of Jerry Hopkins (*Elvis: The Final Years*) and Howard DeWitt (*Chuck Berry: Rock 'n' Roll Music*), and the expansive discographical studies of Terry Hounsome and Tim Chambre (*Rock Record*) and Ray Topping (*New Orleans Rhythm and Blues Record Label Listings*), the three Down Home catalogs are sure indications that research of and scholarship into contemporary music is reaching new heights.

As Central Michigan University Librarian and music bibliophile David Ginsburg is so fond of repeating, the "serious study" of modern music is inevitably linked to the devoted accumulation activities of amateur pop-music enthusiasts. The splendid isolation of academic resource collections like Bowling Green State University's Sound Recordings Archive foretells little for increased scholarly understanding of post-1950s music. The failure of other educational institutions to turn their financial resources and academic resource expertise toward collecting, cataloging, housing, and circulating audio resources illustrates that day-to-day collecting of music's vinyl voices remains largely an idiosyncratic individual pursuit. Down Home Music's catalogs facilitate such private collecting. The hope for future knowledge about doo-wop, R&B, and rock 'n' roll music is the self-motivated work of current record collectors. The lament of discographic specialist Gordon Stevenson that we are in danger of losing the collective consciousness of black musicians from the 1920s to the 1940s continues to be a valid fear throughout the next four decades with respect to formal teaching, learning, and saving of audio resources by most educational repositories.

Thanks to perceived advertising and marketing necessity, the musical interest and expertise of two record-store owners, the availability and appropriate application of computer technology in the creation of a complex album-listing system, and the growing number of worldwide contemporary music collectors, a set of remarkable album catalogs are now in print. They're inexpensive. They're authoritative. They're marvelously fact-filled. The real beneficiaries of these catalogs, however, will probably be music archivists in the decades beyond 2000 A.D. By then, the names John Lennon, Buddy Holly, B. B. King, and Hank Williams will carry "historical validity" rather than just popularity.

Chapter 6

Exported Recordings

> One unforeseen side-effect of the BBC's great wartime use of records was growing public exposure to American popular music; few records were issued in Britain during the war because of the shortage in raw materials, so the BBC came to rely extensively on imported American discs. But American musical influence was most profoundly felt through the presence of U.S. troops in the country . . . and the programmes of the Armed Forces Network (AFN). Maurice Gorham recalled that when the AFN began in 1943, it was the preordained programme for the bobby-soxers, with its American comedy, American swing, and entire freedom from restrictions. . . Although Gorham, for one, thought that the popularity and influence of AFN were exaggerated, British popular culture as a whole did undergo an insidious "Americanization" as the war progressed.
>
> –Stephen Barnard
> *On the Radio: Music Radio in Britain* (1989)

Popular music served as a vehicle of cultural imperialism between the United States and Great Britain from 1943 until 1967. During this period, each country took a turn at dominating the

---

This essay was developed by Laura E. Cooper and B. Lee Cooper. It was presented as "The Pendulum of Cultural Imperialism: Popular Music Interchanges Between the United States and Great Britain, 1943-1967" at the annual meeting of the Midwest Popular Cultural Association in Toledo, Ohio, in October 1990. Reprint permission has been granted by the authors.

other's popular-record industry. From 1943 to 1963, British popular-music culture was dictated by American business interests and artistic styles. This hegemony was established through U.S. wartime and post-war military presence in Europe, by American trade activities in numerous English seaports, and because of Great Britain's inability to generate indigenous musical innovations. In 1964, the dominance was abruptly reversed when British recording artists exported their own, "new" style (which was, ironically, derived from America's own rock 'n' roll roots). Each country so completely dominated the other with its unique popular-music artistry over the 24-year period that few alternative commercial recording styles mounted viable competition, thus creating the situation of cultural imperialism.

SETTING THE STAGE: 1943-1953

Popular culture consists of a society's radio shows, motion pictures, television programs, literature, and music. It reflects the values and ideologies of a particular group, at a particular time. The American influence on Europe's popular culture was felt as early as the 1920s and 1930s, and the U.S. was considered to be synonymous with diversity, innovation, and vitality. American popular culture was admired and emulated by much of the British public because of its advanced stylistic and technological capabilities in both film and music. One German film director characterized U.S. overseas influence by declaring, "The Americans colonized our subconscious."[1]

American and British popular cultures were forced together during World War II. The presence of United States troops on U.K. soil precipitated direct contact and interchange. Also, because the United States served as the chief funding source for Britain's post-war economy, continuing U.S. involvement and influence was inevitable. Beyond the United Kingdom, many Europeans received a large dose of American values and beliefs during the 1940s. Americans left a popular-culture legacy throughout western Europe. Additionally, soldiers remaining in Britain under NATO agreements further contributed to the spread of American culture by importing pop records and other reminders of home. The availability of American cultural artifacts stimulated their popularity.[2]

Great Britain had an advantage over the rest of Europe in the acquisition of American music because of its many port cities. Liverpool, for example, received a steady flow of new American music from both commercial traders and the numerous U.S. seamen who journeyed across the Atlantic. Liverpool also hosted an American airbase at Burtonwood, in addition to being actively involved in the Atlantic trade routes. The late Beatle John Lennon described his birthplace by saying, "It's where the sailors would come home with blues records from America. There is the biggest country-and-western following in England in Liverpool, beside London . . ."[3] Obviously, the port cities throughout the U.K. emerged as the centers of Britain's growing popular-music scene.

The British airwaves, usually in a controlled state of institutional inflexibility, opened up during and after World War II to broadcast programs featuring American music. Exposure to American recordings–via the Armed Forces Network (AFN), Radio Luxembourg from the Continent, and even controlled exposure through the British Broadcasting Corporation (BBC)–introduced U.K. listeners to the latest U.S. musical trends. Although the presence of American cultural artifacts through channels of international trade made it relatively easy for American musical styles to assert themselves, it was Great Britain's lack of innovative radio programming and the BBC's stodgy commitment to classical and dance-band music that created a growing desire among youthful British listeners for new, more exciting musical entertainment. Great Britain's domestic pop format included traditional jazz and skiffle, which is a guitar-centered version of traditional folk sounds. Each of these styles resembled earlier forms of American music; they were undeniably illustrations of early-1950s popular-music influences.[4]

HEARING THE PIPER: 1954-1963

During the mid-1950s, BBC administrators did not feel that rock 'n' roll recordings should occupy too much public airtime. Consequently, popular music was relegated to only 22 hours of airplay per week. This limited public exposure created a type of underground music audience that sought access to more and more American music. Local dance clubs became showcases for both U.S.-recorded and domestically produced American music. Disc jockeys and amateur local bands played the new American rock hits brought to Britain by the U.S. military or by British seamen at local seaports.[5]

In 1954, Bill Haley and the Comets burst onto the British music scene with "Rock Around the Clock." This song was so popular that it remained on the British charts for 17 weeks in 1955 and then returned again in 1956 for 11 more weeks.[6] The fact that this one American rock tune could dominate the British charts for so long indicated the desire of young English record buyers for American rock 'n' roll. Accompanying the celebration of rock music was the emergence of the Teddy Boy. Teddy Boys were British teens who associated themselves directly with the new style of American music. They were readily identified by their slicked hair, slim-legged pants, and full jackets. The favorite hangout of the typical Teddy Boy was the local coffee shop. They represented an overt, active form of protest against "older tradition." Not unexpectedly, they were viewed by much of British society as negative counterparts of the raucous American rock 'n' roll. Rock music was encouraging a British subculture to promote itself, thus counteracting the formal resistance to this "new" music by the BBC. The Teddy Boy was rock music personified. Ironically, the rebellious Teddy Boy phenomenon receded with the growing acceptance of rock music in Great Britain.[7]

In 1958, Elvis Presley reached number one on Britain's record charts with "Jailhouse Rock." The Presley style was viewed as the prime example of the fusion of rhythm and blues with country music. His early hits were classic rock. His success in Britain was attributed to his unique "Americanness." That is, Presley's "Latin good looks" and "cowboy speech and manner" typified the American diversity that so greatly appealed to the British. Presley set a visual standard for many British rock musicians.[8]

American rock became an economic and artistic force to contend with. Great Britain, however, found no reasonable domestic alternative to combat this new form of cultural imperialism. Thus, direct imitation emerged. Television shows and artists similar to those in America presented subdued styles of rock music. Bill Fury, Marty

Wilde, Johnny Gentle, Dickie Pride, and Tommy Steele were a few British performers marketed in the Elvis mold.[9] It is interesting to note how Tommy Steele's professional life mirrored Elvis Presley's. From his initial career in rock music, he diversified to include television performances and, later, movie roles. His career track was manipulated by his manager, John Kennedy. Unlike Presley, though, Steele never achieved superstardom. His performing zeal eventually faded as a result of his disillusionment with the overbearing control of his strong-willed agent.[10]

Britain further attempted to reduce the desire for American rock by creating television programs that showcased the latest American hits performed by British bands. These shows included *Oh Boy, Juke Box Jury,* and *6.5 Special.* They were extremely popular. In addition to TV shows, two new music-oriented British publications emerged, *Melody Maker* and *New Musical Express.*[11] But American music was an unstoppable force, and it overwhelmed British popular culture. It embedded itself into British youth who demanded greater availability of American recorded products. To compete with rock 'n' roll's popularity, British music agents promoted more and more imitations of the imported art form. By 1958, American rock 'n' roll had become an important element of British culture and music. The United States had unconsciously become culturally imperialistic over Great Britain by stifling domestic creativity and by redirecting the U.K.'s conservative popular-music industry.

By the late 1950s and early 1960s, many British groups had internalized American popular music sounds and had begun to develop their own unique styles. Two groups, The Beatles and The Rolling Stones, emerged as successful British bands that drew strongly from rock, blues, and rhythm-and-blues roots. The change in the U.K. rock-music scene became apparent even in the early 1960s when Great Britain–the island that had seemingly been devoid of any pop-music creativity–suddenly began generating its own domestic music culture. America unexpectedly found itself in Britain's place, being unable to create a more original music product. The so-called Golden Age of Rock was dead, and for the first time, American rock music seemed to lack vitality.[12] Rock music's initial heroes were fading: Buddy Holly was dead; Chuck Berry was in prison; Jerry Lee Lewis was struggling with public relations problems; Little Richard had gone into a religious mode; and Elvis Presley had joined the military. American music had become a "teenage wasteland" filled with plastic teen idols.[13] However, the early rock style that was dying in the States was being adapted and internalized by new British "beat" bands. In truth, beat bands softened the energetic rock 'n' roll like so many white American musicians had softened gritty rhythm-and-blues music. This artistically dry period for American musicians proved to be a very creative period for working-class British youth who were rapidly formulating their own sounds.

Pirate radio broadcasting also grew during the early 1960s, providing the British public with even more American music on which to shape their style. Pirate stations like Radio Veronica and Radio Caroline, to name just two, served as alternatives to the conservative BBC and had their popularity reinforced by high profits and private backing.[14] Throughout the 1959-to-1963 period, British popular music expanded and flourished. In 1956, John Lennon and Paul McCartney had begun playing together in a group called The Quarrymen, and by 1958 George Harrison had joined the group. These three Liverpool natives were influenced almost entirely by American music.[15] Their beat band went through various name and member changes before finally emerging as The Beatles. John Lennon had formed The Quarrymen in a very poor, tough, but cosmopolitan port city. The Liverpool setting provided ready access to U.S., German, and other international music markets. This exposure to diverse cultures was a significant element in The Beatles' aesthetic inspiration. The melting pot of ideas, rhythms, and recorded performances was a goldmine to Lennon in particular, who consciously observed the cultural spectrum offered by the dynamic port city.[16]

Lennon and McCartney, who epitomized the rebellious Teddy Boy image, performed covers of many popular American rock 'n' roll hits. Elvis Presley had become a primary figure in Britain when "Heartbreak Hotel" was released in 1956; other American artists, especially Little Richard and Chuck Berry, also exerted significant musical influence on the two future Beatles. The Quarrymen distributed formal visiting cards describing themselves as "Country and Western, Rock 'n' Roll, and Skiffle performers."[17] This wide variety of musical styles illustrated the diverse experiences the youthful Liverpool-based band was absorbing.

The Beatles, in 1959 called The Silver Beatles, frequented many of Liverpool's beat clubs, especially The Cavern and The Crack. In these clubs, their performances earned them a small cult following. Their faithful fans were most impressed at the group's mastery of the singing styles of their American heroes, Elvis Presley and Little Richard. But 1960 became a low point in the careers of the struggling young musicians, who found themselves without a drummer and unsatisfied with the Liverpool club scene. It was during this bleak time that the group became The Beatles, a name derived from yet another of their American rock heroes, Buddy Holly and The Crickets. They decided to depart for Hamburg, West Germany. Reluctantly, John Lennon and Stu Sutcliffe left art school; Paul McCartney discontinued his teacher training; and George Harrison, who encountered no opposition from either family or friends about leaving the country, headed to Germany to seek a new audience. Their major problem, the lack of a drummer, was solved when Pete Best joined the group. The two-month Hamburg tour began with the band finally complete.[18]

The Kaiserkeller, a popular rock 'n' roll club in the German port city, was the site of the early Beatles' Hamburg performances. The Beatles played American rock hits hour after hour. Achieving musical success was of great importance to the group since they had all sacrificed college and jobs for this venture. The Hamburg experience, while full of personal, legal, and financial adversity, aided immeasurably in the development of The Beatles. The group's reflection on the Hamburg activities is captured in Paul McCartney's observation, "We had a long time to work it out and make all the mistakes in Hamburg with almost no one watching."[19] Their following grew, and during 1961 they adopted their characteristic floppy, banged hairstyles, acquired under the guidance of their future business manager Brian Epstein. The final shift in the group's line-up was the dismissal of Pete Best and the addition of drummer Ringo Starr.

On October 11, 1962, "Love Me Do" by The Beatles appeared on the British pop record charts.[20] Within weeks, the Liverpool beat group controlled the British pop-music scene, a prophetic national trend that they would repeat on the international music stage. Lonnie Donegan, a British skiffle group leader, reacted to the quartet's blitzkrieg popularity by noting, "A strange bedlam was taking over which had nothing to do with anything we had previously known."[21] The idea of British rock had never been accepted in the U.S., especially during the early sixties, when many Americans had become disillusioned with early rock 'n' roll music. The British felt that Americans were seemingly "kicking the rock habit."[22] The irony of the 1964-65 emergence of British rock in the States was the fact that rock 'n' roll, a black-derived American art form, would be revived via young white performers from Great Britain. The Beatles exposed many teenage Americans to an unknown subculture by reflecting the image of American black music from across the Atlantic, thus providing many Americans with their initial exposure to black music. Of course, black artists understood exactly what was happening. The 1953-57 cover era was being repeated. The Beatles, along with other artists of the so-called British Invasion, "sanitized" soul music. They made rhythm and blues commercially acceptable.[23]

REVERSING THE TREND: 1964-1967

The year 1964 proved to be a particularly appropriate time for the emergence of English beat music. Not only had the U.S. experienced a music dry spell, but America's youth had also lost a popular political idol in John F. Kennedy. A new charismatic focus was needed. Also by 1964, 17-year-olds constituted the single largest age group in the U.S., a prime target for the commercial distribution of the new British rock product.[24] The emergent British music phenomenon was tagged "Beatlemania." Both British and American publications accurately described the early sixties beat music as "a weird new kind of music that makes rock 'n' roll seem tame by comparison."[25] One American critic accurately charged that The Beatles playing the "Mersey Sound" is like "1956 American rock bouncing back at us."[26] Yet The Beatles successfully emerged as an American sound melded with European fashion. It should never be forgotten that Tommy Steele, Lonnie Donegan, Bill Fury, and Cliff Richard had, on previous occasions, unsuccessfully attempted to make an American impact. This faulty track record left many

American record companies suspicious of the long-term financial success of Beatlemania. Finally, the American music industry became convinced that The Beatles were marketable.

An all-out advertising campaign was launched to literally force The Beatles onto an unsuspecting U.S. public.[27] By February of 1964, The Beatles were scheduled to tour America, bringing their new music style to such diverse venues as Carnegie Hall and *The Ed Sullivan Show.* Radio stations continuously plugged their imminent arrival. Capitol Records distributed newsletters, stickers, and open-ended interview tapes that allowed U.S. disc jockeys to conduct seemingly live interviews with the Liverpool group. As a result of this no-holds-barred Beatles publicity barrage, their song "I Want To Hold Your Hand" became the fastest-selling release in Capitol Records' history.[28]

British beat music infiltrated U.S. popular culture in the form of four mop-headed boys from Liverpool who had been inspired by the American rhythm 'n' blues/rock 'n' roll subculture. Their dress and grooming challenged the clothing styles of conventional U.S. males, just as their R&B-based music differed greatly from the current pop styles of Frankie Avalon, Fabian, Bobby Vinton, and Bobby Vee. Yet they were stealing the hearts and dollars of the United States music culture. Achieving popularity in the United States was an impossible dream come true for The Beatles. Their generation had grown up under American influence as a result of World War II; the presence of U.S. popular culture had created an irresistible mystique. America was the home of their heroes. Preceding their arrival in the U.S., The Beatles frequently commented about their expectations:

> "They've got everything there. What do they want us for?"
>
> "We were only coming over to buy LPs!"
>
> "Rock 'n' roll music was a purely American invention. Who could possibly care about some English imitation?"

These statements illustrated their deep-seated opinions that the U.S. possessed a "self-satisfied egocentricity." These same tongue-in-cheek statements also shrouded genuine fears of unfavorable comparisons. But The Beatles yearned to experience the magic of

America, and they sought formal approval of their music. The Beatles were so set on conquering the United States that anything less than great success would have been a letdown.[29]

The huge advertising campaign paid off. The Beatles achieved complete fan idolatry, sold out concerts, staged an extremely successful Ed Sullivan performance, and won complete domination of the *Billboard* singles chart. The Beatles occupied the top five positions on the singles chart and the top two positions on the LP chart.[30] The Fab Four also enjoyed great financial success from the vast quantities of Beatle paraphernalia. Along with other souvenirs, their fashion style–consisting of the Beatle haircut, the collarless jacket, and the 2 1/2" heel boot–fostered commercial gain. The Beatles had infiltrated American popular culture; in essence, they dramatically turned the tables on the U.S., which had dominated both popular dress and music in Great Britain for two decades.[31]

While enjoying great popularity, The Beatles also encountered opposition. Conservative evangelist Billy Graham claimed they were "symptoms of the uncertainty of times" and only "a passing phase." Others contended that a conspiracy of rock music was being launched to destroy the country through the lyrical glorification of sex and delinquency. Another writer claimed that Beatlemania was a communist plot to make a generation of American youth mentally ill and psychologically unstable. The Beatles, displaying their usual cynical wit, responded: "We're the world's number one capitalists."[32]

One California record-store owner opposed the British rock 'n' rollers, claiming that they were only imitating American rhythm-and-blues artists and thus violating the artistic standards required for their work visas. He asserted that international performers must demonstrate works of distinguishable merit or unduplicated uniqueness. He stated that an influx of British performers would put small, independent American record labels and song publishers out of business. This same retailer also noted the official British practice of limiting U.S. records in England so that British cover recordings could be released.[33] This plea for protectionism went unheeded. The pendulum had already swung too far. The British Invasion was beginning.

In America, where music culture was a way of life among youth, kids discarded their Bermuda shorts and stopped going to the barber.

After The Beatles' initial visit, record sales rose dramatically and radio stations featured more and more British rock music. American record companies reacted to Fab Four success by scouring Liverpool clubs and dance halls in search of new Beatles-like groups. The new British bands that emerged included Herman's Hermits, The Searchers, Gerry and The Pacemakers, and The Kinks. American groups were also influenced by the British Invasion. Great Britain ruled the American airwaves.[34] As one author noted in 1964, "the advent of The Beatles shattered the steady day-to-day domination of made-in-America music. From here on it's expected that a significant ration of U.S. best sellers will be of foreign origin."[35]

Internationally, The Beatles had given rock music credibility. They also established writing and performing as interdependent art forms. This self-contained approach, successfully practiced on a smaller scale by Carl Perkins, Chuck Berry, and Buddy Holly, de-industrialized the music industry by demonstrating that rock artists could compose their own songs without assistance from assembly line writers.[36] The greatest overall effect, though, was the diversity of British beat music and its cultural impact. One writer observed, "The Beatles set the stage for the British Invasion with their unprecedented record sales and media appeal. They laid the groundwork for the April appearance of The Rolling Stones."[37] Mick Jagger and Keith Richards continued the irony of reinterpreting American culture.

The Rolling Stones, a London-based group, were influenced both by The Beatles and by black American artists like Chuck Berry, Jimmy Reed, Slim Harpo, and Bo Diddley.[38] While both The Beatles and The Rolling Stones were individually important factors in the mid-sixties British Invasion, they projected very different images. The Rolling Stones were viewed as a raucous group of devils that struck fear into the hearts of adults. The Stones adamantly proclaimed they were not merely a beat music band, but rather a black-oriented rhythm-and-blues band. Brian Jones elaborated: "We haven't adapted our music from a watered-down music like American rock 'n' roll. We've adapted our music directly from the early black blues forms."[39] Music rooted in social adversity and the virtually ignored black subculture served as The Rolling Stones' inspiration. The Stones considered themselves "Rebels *with* a cause . . . the cause of rhythm and blues." They were determined not to be sanitized or commercialized by the recording industry. These rebellious qualities were admired by their youthful audience. The Stones were the antithesis of The Beatles, who had rapidly gained a significant level of parental approval in the U.S. Either for publicity purposes or in reality, The Stones fostered the outsider image. Their hair was long and shaggy; they were a white band mastering forbidden black-based rhythms. This rebelliousness created a strong cult following. To be a Rolling Stone was to partake of a secret vice.[40]

An early Rolling Stones' American hit was "King Bee," a tune originally recorded by American bluesman Slim Harpo. While The Beatles were politely saying "I Want To Hold Your Hand," The Rolling Stones were suggestively singing, "I'm a king bee, baby, buzzing 'round your hive . . . Let me come inside." *Vogue* magazine described the Rolling Stones as "more terrifying than The Beatles." The Stones introduced their white audience to blues music, a music many Americans had ignored when it was originally performed in the fifties by domestic black artists.[41] The Stones stunned *The Ed Sullivan Show* and *The Hollywood Palace* with their rebellious style. They received as much negative publicity as The Beatles had received positive publicity. This controversial British rock group further established the new British foothold on the international pop-music scene.

CONCLUSION

The Beatles and The Rolling Stones, while performing different types of music, both relied heavily on the exported songs and performing styles of American artists. They had successfully integrated and adapted American models into their own music.[42] The irony of the British Invasion of the mid-sixties was that it represented the simultaneous triumph and demise of American dominance over U.K. popular-music culture. The period of one-sided cultural imperialism (1943-1963) had ended. An intervening time of adjustment (1964-1966) allowed an inordinately large number of British bands to test their commercial wings in the States. Yet the era of British dominance was destined to be brief, though undeniably significant. The Beatles and The Rolling Stones–schooled by Chuck Berry, Howlin' Wolf, Marvin Gaye, Bo Diddley, Carl Perkins, and others–

graduated into their own world of imagery, instrumental experimentation, lyric structuring, and rhythm manipulation. Many critics echoed in awe the observation of Jeff Greenfield: "The Beatles were a powerful influence in music and popular culture. Their success resulted from ever-changing style; they were always moving."[43]

Great Britain was still not completely free of American musical influence. By 1967, though, with the release of the *Sgt. Pepper's Lonely Hearts Club Band* album, the group that had won the hearts of America and Great Britain had identified its own independent musical style. The album also ended the era of rock as an adolescent phenomenon. The Beatles helped make rock the music of an entire international generation. One critic acknowledged the creative brilliance of the album by saying: "Sgt. Pepper isn't in the line of continuous development; rather it is an astounding accomplishment for which no one could have been wholly prepared, and it therefore substantially enlarges and modifies all the work that preceded it."[44]

The Beatles no longer needed to borrow American rock styles. They, like many other British bands (including The Rolling Stones and The Who), had developed into unique, visible rock 'n' roll artists. The American cultural imperialism that began in 1943 had ended. The rebounding British cultural imperialism of 1964-1966 waned after *Sgt. Pepper*. The commercial resurgence of American recording companies (Motown, Stax, and Atlantic) and the explosion of soul music (Wilson Pickett, Aretha Franklin, Sam and Dave, Otis Redding, The Temptations, and hundreds of others) generated the pendulum swing back to the center. Although the future would bring new invading artists from Ireland, Wales, England, and Australia, there would be no total chart dominance by either the U.S. or the U.K. The two nations found equilibrium in their popular music interchanges after 1968.

NOTES

1. Simon Frith, *Sound Effects: Youth, Leisure, and the Politics of Rock* (New York: Pantheon, 1981), pp. 39-57. For a more global view of cultural imperialism, see C. W. E. Bigsby, ed., *Superculture: American Popular Culture and Europe* (Bowling Green: Bowling Green University, 1975). The musical perspective on cultural imperialism has been detailed in Laura E. Cooper and B. Lee Cooper, "Exploring Cultural Imperialism: Bibliographic Resources for Teaching About

American Domination, British Adaptation, and the Rock Music Interchange, 1950-1967," *International Journal of Instructional Media* XVII (1990): pp. 167-177 and in Humphrey A. Regis, "Calypso, Reggae, and Cultural Imperialism by Reexportation," *Popular Musica and Society,* XII (Spring 1988), pp. 63-73.

2. Iain Chambers, *Urban Rhythms: Pop Music and Popular Culture* (New York: St. Martin's, 1985), pp. 18-49. For a general history of post-war England, see Arthur Marwick, *British Society Since 1945* (New York: Penguin, 1982), pp. 1-113.

3. Dave Harker, *One for the Money: Politics and Popular Song* (London: Hutchinson, 1980), p. 83. For a detailed analysis of British population distribution, trade arteries, and transportation facilities linking urban centers during the 1945-1960 period, see Bernard Reines, "United Kingdom," in *Europe–Worldmark Encyclopedia of the Nations*, ed. Louis Barron (New York: Harper & Row, 1963), pp. 305-328. For more specific studies about Liverpool, see Edward Lucie-Smith, ed., *The Liverpool Scene* (Garden City: Doubleday, 1968) and David Bacon and Norman Maslov, *The Beatles' England: There Are Places I'll Remember* (San Francisco: 910 Press, 1982).

4. Chambers, *Urban Rhythms*, pp. 44-49; Asa Briggs, *The BBC: The First Fifty Years* (Oxford: Oxford University, 1985); Tom Burns, *The BBC: Public Institution and Private World* (New York: Holmes and Meier, 1977); Richard Nichols, *Radio Luxembourg: The Station of the Stars* (London: Comet Books, 1983); and Phil Silverman, "Irish Biographer Says U.S. Armed Forces Radio Sparked His Lifelong Obsession with Little Richard and Rock Music," *Record Collector Monthly,* No. 34 (February-March 1986), pp. 1, 10-12.

5. Harry Castleman and Walter J. Podrazik, *The Beatles Again!* (Ann Arbor: Pierian, 1977), pp. 227-233; Stephen Barnard, *On the Radio: Music Radio in Britain* (Milton Keynes: Open University, 1988), pp. 17-49; Stephen Barnard, "Saturday Night Out," *The History of Rock,* No. 31 (1982), pp. 618-620; Eric Dunsdon, "Juke Box Memories," *Now Dig This*, No. 77 (August 1989), pp. 14-15; Marcus Gray, *London's Rock Landmarks: The A-Z Guide to London's Rock Geography* (London: Omnibus Books, 1985); Alistair Griffin, *On the Scene at the Cavern* (London: Hamish Hamilton, 1964); Brian Innes, "Clubs and Coffee Bars: Where Britain's Teenagers Found the New Music," *The History of Rock*, No. 7 (1982), pp. 132-134; Spencer Leigh, *Let's Go Down to the Cavern: The Story of Liverpool's Merseybeat* (London: Vermilion, 1984); John Pidgeon, "Blues in the Basement," *The History of Rock*, No. 30 (1982), pp. 598-600; Alan Thompson, "Hail! Hail! Rock 'n' Roll!" *Now Dig This*. No. 67 (October 1988), pp. 24-25; Jurgen Vollmer, *Rock 'n' Roll Times: The Style and Spirit of the Early Beatles and Their First Fans* (Woodstock: Overlook, 1983); and Chris Woodford, "Boppin' the Blues in Newcastle!" *Now Dig This*, No. 77 (August 1989), p. 23.

6. Harker, pp. 68-69; also see Jo and Tim Rice, Paul Gambaccini, and Mike Read, comps., *The Guinness Book of British Hit Singles*, second edition (Enfield, Middlesex: Guinness Superlatives, 1979), p. 104 and Clive Solomon, comp., *Record Hits: The British Top 50 Charts, 1954-1976* (London: Omnibus, 1977), p. 71.

7. Chambers, pp. 22-39; Michael Watts, "The Call and Response of Popular Music: The Impact of American Pop Music in Europe," in *Superculture*, ed.

C. W. E. Bigsby (1975), pp. 123-139; Richard Barnes, Johnny Moke, and Jan McVeigh, comps., *Mods!* (London: Eel Pie, 1979); Peter Everett, *You'll Never Be 16 Again: An Illustrated History of the British Teenager* (London: BBC Books, 1986); Robert Freeman, *Yesterday: The Beatles, 1963-1965* (New York: Holt, Rinehart, and Winston, 1983); Stuart Hall and Tony Jefferson, eds., *Resistance Through Rituals: Youth Subcultures in Post-War Britain* (London: Hutchinson Books, 1976); Grace Hechinger and Fred W. Hechinger, *Teenage Tyranny* (London: Duckworth, 1964); Dan O'Sullivan, *The Youth Culture* (London: Methuen Educational, 1974); Crispian Steele-Perkins and Richard Smith, comps., *The Teds* (London: Traveling Light Photography, 1979); and David P. Szatmary, "The Mods vs. The Rockers and the British Invasion of America," in *Rockin' in Time: A Social History of Rock and Roll* (Englewood Cliffs: Prentice-Hall, 1987), pp. 78-106.

8. Chambers, pp. 36-37; Rice et al., pp. 175-177; Solomon, pp. 116-118; and John Towson, comp., *Elvis U.K.: The Ultimate Guide to Elvis Presley's British Record Releases, 1956-1986* (Poole, Dorset: Blandford, 1987).

9. Watts, p. 130; Steve Aynsley, "British Rock 'n' Roll, 1956-1962," *Now Dig This*, No. 15 (June 1984), pp. 15-17; Brian Bird, *Skiffle* (London: Robert Hale, 1958); Ashley Brown, "The U.K. Rocks–Rock 'n' Roll Hit the Shores of Great Britain Like a Tidal Wave: Music Was Never the Same Again," *The History of Rock*, No. 7 (1982), pp. 121-123; Bob Brunning, *Blues: The British Connection* (Poole, Dorset: Blandford, 1986); Stuart Colman, *They Kept on Rockin': The Giants of Rock 'n' Roll* (Poole, Dorset: Blandford, 1982); Karl Dallas, "Lonnie Donegan and Skiffle: Was Skiffle the Start of British Rock?" *The History of Rock*, No. 7 (1982), pp. 124-128; Pete Frame, "British Pop, 1955-1979," *Trouser Press*, X (June 1983), pp. 30-31; Michael Heatley, "Lonnie Donegan: The First British Invader?" *Goldmine*, No. 174 (March 27, 1987), pp. 18, 87; Paul Pelletier, "Lonnie Donegan," *Record Collector*, No. 32 (April 1982), pp. 26-32; and Dave Waite, "Lonnie Donegan," *Record Collector*, No. 93 (May 1987), pp. 31-34.

10. Harker, pp. 70-71. For examinations of non-performing rock managers in pre-Beatles Britain, see Spencer Leigh, "Larry Parnes," *Record Collector*, No. 122 (October 1989), pp. 86-88; John Repsch, *The Legendary Joe Meek* (London: Woodford House, 1989); and Chris Woodford, "The Passing Of Parnes," *Now Dig This*, No. 78 (September 1989), p. 30.

11. Chambers, pp. 33-41; Kevin Howlett, *The Beatles at the Beeb, 1962-1965: The Story of Their Radio Career* (London: BBC, 1982); Mark Paytress, "The Rolling Stones at the BBC," *Record Collector*, No. 117 (May 1989), pp. 3-8; and Howard A. DeWitt, "Will The Beatles Please Go Away?" "*Melody Maker* Reacts to the New Music, and "*The New Musical Express* and the Beatles," in *The Beatles: Untold Tales* (Fremont: Horizon Books, 1985), pp. 183-225.

12. Bob Kinder, "Teen Idols and Rock-and-Roll Screamers (1959-1963)," in *The Best of the First: The Early Days of Rock and Roll* (Chicago: Adams, 1986), pp. 69-117; Jean-Charles Marion, "Death Valley Days of Rock, 1959-1963," *Record Exchanger*, V (1977), p. 15; and Jeff Tamarkin, "In Defense of Rock's Wimp Years," *Goldmine*, No. 81 (February 1983), p. 3.

13. Greg Shaw, "The Teen Idols," in *The Rolling Stone Illustrated History of Rock and Roll*, revised edition, ed. Jim Miller (New York: Random House, 1980), pp. 96-100; Ed Ward, Geoffrey Stokes, and Ken Tucker, *Rock of Ages: The Rolling Stone History of Rock and Roll* (New York: Summit Books, 1986), pp. 165-246.

14. Harker, pp. 79-80; Paul Harris, *When Pirates Ruled the Waves* (Aberdeen: Impulse Publications, 1968); John Hind and Stephen Mosco, *Rebel Radio: The Full Story of British Pirate Radio* (London: Pluto, 1985); Stuart Henry and Mike Von Joel, *Pirate Radio: Then and Now* (Poole, Dorset: Blandford, 1984); and Steve Jones, "Making Waves: Pirate Radio and Popular Music," *OneTwoThree-Four: A Rock 'n' Roll Quarterly*, No. 7 (Winter 1989), pp. 55-67.

15. Roy Carr and Tony Tyler, *The Beatles: An Illustrated Record*, revised edition (New York: Harmony Books, 1978), p. 25; Howard A. DeWitt, "Early Beatle Performances, 1956-1963," in *The Beatles: Untold Tales* (1985), pp. 227-249; Wilfrid Mellers, *The Music of the Beatles: Twilight of the Gods* (New York: Schirmer Books, 1975), pp. 23-43; Terence J. O'Grady, "Early Influences and Recordings," in *The Beatles: A Musical Evolution* (Boston: Twayne, 1983), pp. 7-20; and Tom Schultheiss, comp., *The Beatles–A Day in the Life: The Day-by-Day Diary, 1960-1970* (New York: Quick Fox, 1981), pp. 1-150.

16. DeWitt, pp. 1-125; Greil Marcus, "The Beatles," in *The Rolling Stone Illustrated History of Rock and Roll*, revised edition, pp. 177-189.

17. Phillip Norman, *Shout! The Beatles in Their Generation* (London: Elm Tree Books, 1982), p. 26.

18. Norman, p. 77; Dewitt, pp. 1-74; and Gareth L. Pawloski, *How They Became The Beatles: A Definitive History of the Early Years, 1960-1964* (New York: E. P. Dutton, 1989).

19. John Lahr, "The Beatles Considered," *New Republic*, (December 2, 1981), p. 20.

20. Rice et al., p. 21.

21. Chambers, p. 50.

22. Nicholas Schaffner, *The British Invasion* (New York: McGraw-Hill, 1983), p. 4.

23. Allan Fotherington, "Telling the Children How It Was," *MacLean's*, XXVII (February 27, 1989), p. 27; Harry Castleman and Walter Podrazik, "The Beatles from Others," in *All Together Now: The First Complete Beatles Discography, 1961-1975* (New York: Ballantine Books, 1975), pp. 226-242; Harry Castleman and Walter Podrazik, "The Beatles from Others," in *The Beatles Again!* (1977), pp. 77-83; and B. Lee Cooper, "The Black Roots of Popular Music," in *Images of American Society in Popular Music* (Chicago: Nelson-Hall, 1982), pp. 111-123.

24. Peter McCabe and Robert D. Schonfeld, *Apple to the Core: The Unmaking of the Beatles* (New York: Simon and Schuster, 1972), p. 48; Vance Packard, "Building the Beatle Image," in *The Beatles Reader*, ed. Charles P. Neises (Ann Arbor: Pierian, 1984), pp. 11-13; and Ray Coleman, *The Man Who Made the Beatles: An Intimate Biography of Brian Epstein* (New York: McGraw-Hill, 1989).

25. Chambers, pp. 50-83; Ray Coleman, "1964: The Year of The Beatles," *Melody Maker*, XXXIX (December 19, 1964), pp. 2-3ff; Evan Davis, "The Psycho-

logical Characteristics of Beatle Mania," *Journal of the History of Ideas*, XXX (April-June 1969), pp. 273-280; June Price, "The Beatles' Arrival: Mania in the Media," *Goldmine*, No. 224 (February 24, 1989), pp. 8, 93; A. J. S. Rayl and Curt Gunther, *Beatles '64: A Hard Day's Night in America* (Garden City: Doubleday, 1989), p. 1-233; Rich Sutton, "Beatlemania Revisited: A Look Back," *Song Hits*, No. 220 (June 1984), pp. 18-19; and A. J. W. Taylor, "Beatlemania–A Study of Adolescent Enthusiasm," *British Journal of Social and Clinical Psychology*, V (September 1966), pp. 81-88.

26. Alfred G. Aronowitz, "Yeah! Yeah! Yeah! Music's Gold Bugs: The Beatles," *Saturday Evening Post*, CCXXXVII (March 21, 1964), pp. 30-35; Castleman and Podrazik, *The Beatles Again!*, pp. 77-83; and B. Lee Cooper, "Popular Music and the Computer," in *Images of American Society in Popular Music* (1982), pp. 88-96.

27. Chambers, pp. 50-83.

28. Schaffner, *The British Invasion*, pp. 4-5.

29. Paul Theroux, "Why We Loved The Beatles," *Rolling Stone*, (February 16, 1984), p. 21.

30. Joel Whitburn, comp., *Top Pop Singles, 1955-1986* (Menomonee Falls: Record Research, 1987), pp. 38-39.

31. Schaffner, pp. 3-53; Jeff Augsburger, Marty Eck, and Rick Rann, *The Beatles Memorabilia Price Guide* (Elburn: Branyan, 1988); and Jerry Osborne, Perry Cox, and Joe Lindsay, *Official Price Guide to Memorabilia of Elvis Presley and The Beatles* (New York: Ballantine Books, 1988); for surveys of the British Invasion years, see Harold Bronson, ed. Michael Ochs, *Rock Explosion: The British Invasion in Photos, 1962-1967* (Santa Monica: Rhino, 1984); Alan Clayson, *Call up the Groups: The Golden Age of British Beat, 1962-1967* (Poole, Dorset: Blandford, 1985); Colin Cross, with Paul Kendall and Mick Farren, comps., *Encyclopedia of British Beat Groups and Solo Artists of the Sixties* (London: Omnibus, 1980); Peter Doggett, "The British Invasion," *Record Collector*, No. 114 (February 1989), pp. 19-22; and Charles Webb, "The British Invasion, 1964: A Chronology," *Goldmine*, No. 98 (April 27, 1984), pp. 36-44.

32. The most interesting overview analysis of the rock conspiracy issue is in Linda Martin and Kerr Segrave, *Anti-Rock: The Opposition to Rock 'n' Roll* (Hamden: Archon Books, 1988), pp. 111-184. For specific attacks, see Phillip Abbott Luce, "The Great Rock Conspiracy: Are The Beatles Termites?" *National Review*, XXI (September 23, 1969), pp. 959, 973; and David A. Noebel, *Communism, Hypnotism, and The Beatles: An Analysis of the Communist Use of Music* (Tulsa: Christian Crusade Publications, 1965), pp. 1-26.

33. "U.K. Rock 'n' Rollers Are Called Copycats," *Billboard*, LXXVIII (June 19, 1965), p. 12; "Beatles' Success in U.S. a Trend for the British?" *Variety*, CCXXXIII (February 5, 1964), p. 46; H. Schoenfeld, "Britannia Rules Airwaves: Beatles Stir Home Carbons," *Variety*, CCXXXIII (February 12, 1964), p. 63; "U.S. Rocks and Reels from Beatles' Invasion," *Billboard*, LXXVI (February 15, 1964), pp. 1ff; R. Watkins, "Rocking Redcoats Are Coming: Beatles Lead Massive Drive," *Variety*, CCXXXIII (February 19, 1964), pp. 1ff; and Ian Dove,

"January 1–March 31, 1964: 90 Days that Shook the Industry," *Billboard* LXXXI (December 27, 1969), p. 126.

34. Joel Whitburn, comp., *Pop Annual, 1955-1982* (Menomonee Falls: Record Research, 1983), pp. 150-187.

35. Schoenfeld, p. 63. For a thoughtful analysis of the internationalization of the recording industry, see Alan Wells, "The British Invasion of American Popular Music: What Is It and Who Pays?" *Popular Music and Society,* XI (1987), pp. 65-78; and Harker, pp. 87-145.

36. Chris Difford, "To Be as Good," *Rolling Stone*, (February 16, 1984), p. 59. Also see William J. Dowlding, *Beatlesongs* (New York: Simon and Schuster, 1989); William McKeen, *The Beatles: A Bio-Bibliography* (Westport: Greenwood, 1989); and Tim Tiley, *Tell Me Why: A Beatles Commentary* (New York: Alfred A. Knopf, 1988).

37. Dove, p. 126. For an overview of the Mick Jagger and Keith Richard songwriting team, see David Dalton, *The Rolling Stones: The First Twenty Years* (New York: Alfred A. Knopf, 1981).

38. Chambers, pp. 65-75; Alan Beckett, "The Stones," *New Left Review,* XLVII (January-February 1968), pp. 24-29; Roy Carr, *The Rolling Stones–An Illustrated Record* (New York: Harmony Books, 1976), pp. 18-19; David Dalton, ed., *The Rolling Stones: An Unauthorized Biography in Words and Photographs* (New York: Quick Fox, 1979), pp. 15-47; John M. Hellmann, Jr., "'I'm a Monkey': The Influence of the Black American Blues Argot on the Rolling Stones," *Journal of American Folklore*, LXXXVI (October-December 1973), pp. 367-373; and John D. Wells, "Me and the Devil Blues: A Study of Robert Johnson and the Music of the Rolling Stones," *Popular Music and Society,* IX (1983), pp. 17-24.

39. Schaffner, *The British Invasion*, p. 56.

40. Frith, p. 70-71.

41. Phillip Norman, *The Stones* (London: Elm Tree Books, 1984), p. 106; Schaffner, *The British Invasion*, pp. 54-93; and Robert Christgau, "The Rolling Stones," in *The Rolling Stones Illustrated History of Rock and Roll*, revised edition, pp. 190-200.

42. For an extended discussion on musical adaptation based on recorded songs, see David Hatch and Stephen Millward, *From Blues to Rock: An Analytical History of Pop Music* (Manchester: Manchester University, 1987), pp. 1-179.

43. Jeff Greenfield, "They Changed Rock, Which Changed the Culture, Which Changed Us," *New York Times Magazine*, (February 16, 1975), p. 12.

44. Richard Poirier, "Learning from The Beatles," *Partison Review,* XXXIV (Fall 1967), p. 526. For commentaries on the *Sgt. Pepper* album, see Peter Doggett, "*Sgt. Pepper*–The Album," *Record Collector,* No. 94 (June 1987), pp. 3-6; David R. Pichaske, "Sustained Performances: *Sgt. Pepper's Lonely Hearts Club Band,*" in *The Beatles Reader*, pp. 59-62; Charles Reinhart, "*Sgt. Pepper's Lonely Hearts Club Band:* It's 20 Years Later Now . . . And Still a Landmark," *Goldmine*, No. 182 (July 17, 1987), pp. 18-20; and Derek Taylor, *It Was Twenty Years Ago Today* (New York: Simon and Schuster, 1987).

Chapter 7

Family Businesses

MICHAEL JACKSON

Sequins and Shades: The Michael Jackson Reference Guide. Compiled by Carol D. Terry. Ann Arbor: Popular Culture, Ink., 1987. Illustrated, 507 pp.

Few rock performers merit literary attention. Fewer still warrant either bibliographic guides or discographic compilations. Michael Jackson, the singer/composer from Gary, Indiana, is the exception to both rules. A conglomerate-directing millionaire, an internationally acclaimed stage performer, and a prolific, talented recording artist, Jackson has established artistic and commercial standards that defy comparison. Since the 1968 release of the first recording by The Jackson 5 for Steeltown Records through the end of The Jacksons' "Victory Tour" and the 1984 release of the *Victory* album, Michael and his brothers have sold more than 100 million records. But it is as an individual artist that Jackson has received public accolades in clusters. During the 1984 Grammy ceremonies, for instance, he won eight awards: Album of the Year (*Thriller*); Record of the Year ("Beat It"); Producer of the Year (*Thriller*); Best Male Rock Performance ("Beat It"); Best New R&B Song ("Billie Jean"); Best Children's Album (*E.T.*); Best Male R&B Performance ("Billie Jean"); and Best Male Pop Performance (*Thriller*). Michael's humanitarian efforts–in conjunction with Lionel Richie and Quincy Jones–on the 1985 "We Are the World" project illustrated a philanthropic streak that complements his entre-

---

These reviews by B. Lee Cooper originally appeared in *Michigan Academician* XXII (Summer 1990): pp. 303-306. Reprint permission has been granted by the author.

preneurial drive. This young man is a music-industry force to be examined, pondered, and admired.

Sequins and Shades is a 500-page tribute to a popular-music colossus. Compiler Carol D. Terry acknowledges that her work is an in-process report, rather than the final chapter on this enigmatic young star. She notes that between 1988 and 1989, Michael Jackson was scheduled to issue two new albums, publish his autobiography, and launch a wealth of new commercial ventures. *Sequins and Shades* offers popular-culture researchers, record collectors, and M.J. fans access to all literary, vinyl, and historical information available on the personal life and professional career of Jackson up to December 10, 1986.

This reference guide is divided into five unequal sections. A bibliography (pp. 1-69) featuring citations from more than 1,000 different sources (books, magazine and newspaper articles, film and record reviews) dealing with The Jackson 5, The Jacksons, and Michael Jackson solo begins the study. This is followed by a day-to-day chronology (pp. 71-184) containing record release dates, concert appearances, birthdays and weddings, press conferences, record and video chartings, and recording sessions. The huge discography section (pp. 185-333) provides full details on more than 650 individual recordings (all released in the United States and Great Britain). This is followed by an alphabetical listing (pp. 335-357) of every song that Michael Jackson has been associated with, either as a composer, group member, soloist, backup vocalist, producer, or arranger. The final section of the guide features six indexes (pp. 359-507) organized by author, title, subject, date, publication, and record number; it also covers information from each of the previous four sections. *Sequins and Shades* is a truly remarkable work that will undoubtedly remain the key resource for the examination of Michael Jackson's early career for years to come.

MOTOWN

Heat Wave: The Motown Fact Book. Compiled by David Bianco. Ann Arbor: Pierian, 1988. Illustrated. 524 pp.

The Motown Recording Corporation means many things to many people. It is a triumphant black enterprise, the fulfillment of a rags-to-riches American dream, a continuing soap opera (complete with excesses of family love and personal tragedy), and the fountainhead of both distinctive soul music and legendary performing stars. The breadth of Motown's contribution to American popular culture makes each of these images valid and worthy of scholarly investigation. *Heat Wave: The Motown Fact Book* is designed to provide not only a general historical and biographical overview of the Motown family but also an in-depth discographic survey of the company's prodigious vinyl production between 1959 and 1987. Those seeking to trace the career of Motown artists, to chronicle the company's sale successes, or to explore popular music during the decades of the '60s, '70s and '80s should seek the assistance of Bianco's resource.

Heat Wave is structured into eight sections. Part I features brief biographies of corporation founder Berry Gordy Jr. and more than 90 of Motown's brightest recording stars. Part II offers a chronology from November 28, 1929, Gordy's birthdate, through December 1, 1987, when a Michigan State Historical Marker was placed in front of the original Hitsville Building at 2648 West Grand Boulevard in downtown Detroit. Part III alphabetically lists, and provides brief descriptions of, the American and British labels (from Anna, Black Forum, and Blaze to Week, Workshop Jazz, and Yesteryear) on which Motown recordings were issued. Part IV presents a mammoth U.S. discography of Motown singles and albums, while Part V features a United Kingdom Motown discography. Parts VI and VII provide indexes arranged by singer or group name, by song or album title, by date of release, and by record numbers for all U.S. and British Motown releases. Finally, Part VIII is an appendix of five Motown-related label discographies (Anna, Golden World, Harvey, Ric-Tic, and Tri-Phi). The text is liberally peppered with handsome black-and-white publicity photos and private shots of Motown's composers and artists, as well as reproductions of 45-rpm record labels.

In the foreword to *Heat Wave*, publisher Tom Schultheiss speculates that Motown intended to be–and became–a wellspring of American music. This was not simply blues or rhythm 'n' blues performed by black artists being accepted by white audiences; it was, in Schultheiss' words, "music without color." This thumbnail description does not connote a lack of artistic integrity, the presence of weakened rhythm patterns, or a blandness of vocal presentation. It accurately defines the marketing genius of Gordy and his Motown producers in creating an immensely effective crossover sound produced by young, attractive, talented artists. Why didn't other black-owned record companies translate their music into this kind of mainstream fiscal bonanza? If the commonly asserted charge that the Motown sound was strictly formula-driven is true, why didn't Specialty, Vee-Jay, or other labels produce batches of million-selling discs to sustain themselves? Several writers, including Peter Benjaminson, Ashley Brown and Michael Heatley, Nelson George, J. Randy Taraborrelli, and Don Waller, have begun to explore these questions. But a comparative examination of the marketing strategy of Atlantic, Chess, Stax, Volt, and other prominent black labels has yet to be printed. Bianco's rich discographic compilation might help to stimulate such a study.

Beyond financial success, the songwriting and performing achievements of Motown's talented stable of stars warrants serious examination. Superficial biographical studies on Stevie Wonder, Diana Ross, and Marvin Gaye have yet to scratch the surface in terms of illuminating the roots of their distinctive contributions to Motown magic. *Heat Wave* issues a biographical challenge. The Motown composing corps (Nicholas Ashford and Valerie Simpson, Brian Holland, Lamont Dozier, and Eddie Holland, Norman Whitfield, Lionel Richie, and William "Smokey" Robinson) and singing stylists (The Four Tops, Gladys Knight and The Pips, The Supremes, The Temptations, and Stevie Wonder) are oral-history subjects that are deserving of serious popular-culture analysis.

Bianco's superb study calls attention to Detroit's majestic contribution to popular music. Without James Brown, Otis Redding, Wilson Pickett, Aretha Franklin, and other flagship black artists, Berry Gordy Jr. created the monster music corporation of the 1960s. The *Heat Wave* text describes the nature of the expanding commercial phenomenon as follows:

> As Motown became a successful record company, Berry Gordy's vision expanded to include other entertainment outlets. It was the company's intention to pursue opportunities in

film, television, and the theater. West Coast offices were established as early as 1966, and in 1972 the company fully relocated to Los Angeles from Detroit. . . . In 1973, the magazine *Black Enterprise* recognized Motown as the #1 black-owned or managed business. In less than fifteen years, Motown had grown from a Detroit-based record company specializing in R&B hits to a full-fledged entertainment corporation. (p. 7)

Thus Bianco describes the musical equivalent of the Brooklyn Dodgers fleeing from Ebbets Field to Chavez Ravine. But, unlike the "bums from Brooklyn," Motown was already the fence-busting champion of the recording industry. Motown stars Michael Jackson, Stevie Wonder, Smokey Robinson, Marvin Gaye, Diana Ross, and others just slugged on and on, playing to ever-increasing concert audiences, performing in motion pictures, and producing nostalgic soundtrack music for an array of '80s films. With Motown on the field, popular music (especially for young black artists) became a whole new ball game.

REFERENCES

Bartlette, Reginald J. *Off the Record–Motown by Master Number, 1959-1989: Volume One–Singles.* Ann Arbor, Michigan: Popular Culture, Ink., 1991.

Benjaminson, Peter. *The Story of Motown.* New York: Grove Press, 1979.

Bianco, David. *Heat Wave: The Motown Fact Book.* Ann Arbor, Michigan: Pierian Press, 1988.

Blansky, Bob (comp.). *The Motown Era.* Detroit, Michigan: Jobete Music Company, Inc., 1971.

Brown, Ashley and Michael Heatley (eds.). *The Motown Story.* London: Bedford Press, 1985.

Brown, Stanley H. "The Motown Sound of Money." *Fortune.* LXXVI (September 1, 1967): 103-105ff.

Curtis, Jim. "Detroit Rises for the First Time," in *Rock Eras: Interpretations of Music and Society, 1954-1984* (Bowling Green, Ohio: Bowling Green State University Popular Press, 1987): pp. 90-100.

Davis, Sharon. *Motown: The History.* New York: Sterling Books, 1989.

Dr. Licks. *Standing in the Shadows of Motown: The Life and Music of Legendary Bassist James Jamerson.* Milwaukee, Wisconsin: Hal Leonard Publishing Corporation, 1989.

Frith, Simon. "You Can Make it if You Try: The Motown Story," in *The Soul Book*, by Ian Hoare, Tony Cummings, Clive Anderson, and Simon Frith (New York: Dell Publishing Company, Inc., 1976): pp. 39-73.

George, Nelson. *Where Did Our Love Go? The Rise and Fall of the Motown Sound*. New York: St. Martin's Press, 1985.

Grein, Paul. "Where Did Our Love Go?" *Detroit [Michigan] News*, (July 13, 1988): pp. 1D, 6D.

Hirshey, Gerri. *Nowhere to Run: The Story of Soul Music*. New York: Times Books, 1984.

Holden, Stephen. "The Grooves of Motown." *Atlantic*. CCLIII (May 1984): pp. 104-107.

Landau, Jon. "Motown: The First Ten Years," in *It's Too Late to Stop Now: A Rock and Roll Journal* (San Francisco, California: Straight Arrow Books, 1972): pp. 143-150.

Larkin, Rochelle. "Tales of Two Cities: Memphis and Motown," in *Soul Music!* (New York: Lancer Books, 1970): pp. 77-97.

Lingeman, Richard R. "The Big, Happy Beating Heart of the Detroit Sound." *New York Times Magazine* (November 27, 1966): pp. 48-49, 162-184.

McEwen, Joe and Jim Miller. "Motown," in *The Rolling Stone Illustrated History of Rock and Roll*, edited by Anthony DeCurtis and James Henke, with Holly George Warren (New York: Random House, 1992): pp. 277-292.

Millar, Bill. "Motown Magician." *The History of Rock*. No. 24 (1982): pp. 470-473.

Morse, David. *Motown and the Arrival of Black Music*. New York: Collier Books, 1971.

Partridge, Marianne (ed.). *The Motown Album: The Sound of Young America*. New York: St. Martin's Press, 1990.

Ryan, Jack. *Recollections–The Detroit Years: The Motown Sound by the People Who Made It*. Detroit, Michigan: J. Ryan/Data Graphics and Whitlaker Marketing, 1982.

Shaw, Arnold. *The World of Soul*. New York: Paperback Library, 1971.

Singleton, Raynoma Gordy. *Berry, Me, and Motown: The Untold Story*. Chicago: Contemporary Books, 1990.

Stuessy, Joe. "Soul and Motown," in *Rock and Roll: Its History and Stylistic Development* (Englewood Cliffs, New Jersey: Prentice-Hall, Inc., 1990): pp. 207-235.

Szatmary, David P. "Motown: The Sound of Integration," in *Rockin' in Time: A Social History of Rock-and-Roll*, Second Edition (Englewood Cliffs, New Jersey: Prentice-Hall, Inc., 1991): pp. 134-144.

Taraborrelli, J. Randy. *Motown: Hot Wax, City Cool, and Solid Gold*. Garden City, New York: Dolphin Books/Doubleday and Company, Inc., 1986.

Waller, Don. *The Motown Story: The Inside Story of America's Most Popular Music*. New York: Charles Scribner's Sons, 1985.

Chapter 8

Dance Crazes

Legends and myths are valuable for explaining self and society. The late Joseph Campbell said so in book after book. Improper metaphors, according to Susan Sontag, can hamper perception, cloud logic, and dull sensitivity. Clearly, images that educators employ to describe the contemporary college scene have serious implications.

For the past 15 years, I've listened to faculty members and fellow administrators depict higher education to parents, alumni, trustees, business people, and community leaders. None of the traditional metaphors that are so commonly utilized seem entirely appropriate. Some are downright annoying. For example, the "We are a big, happy family at this college" assertion to incoming students is designed to connote caring, concern, and individual attention. However, real family ties are irrevocable; school ties are not. Poor grades lead to dismissal; flagrant abuse of residence hall policies prompts expulsion. Thus the family metaphor collapses. Another disconcerting analogy is the Commencement dichotomy between "The Halls of Ivy" and "The Real World." This makes a college experience sound more like four years of fiction and fantasy rather than an intense period of intellectual rigor and responsibility.

After much reflection, I've concluded that higher education needs a new analog. The solution hit me recently while I was watching "American Bandstand." Dancing is the perfect metaphor for teaching. It links two human beings in a voluntary association

---

This commentary was developed by B. Lee Cooper under the title "Dancing: The Perfect Educational Metaphor" for presentation at the induction ceremony for Omicron Delta Kappa/Alpha Chi honor students at Olivet College on November 18, 1989. Reprint permission has been granted by the author.

where cooperative achievement is the initial expectation. The activity is intensely personal, yet usually conducted in a group setting. Changing partners is acceptable, just as changing classes or majors or faculty advisors is acceptable. The essential character of instruction–a learning partnership between teacher and student–can readily be envisioned in the dance metaphor. Musical rhythms and dance styles vary throughout an evening. So, too, classes and assignments occur in a variety of formats over a four-year undergraduate career. Dancing, like learning, is a performance-based activity. It requires concentration and creativity, energy and discipline, and concern for others as well as attention to self. There is always room for individual showmanship (independent pursuit of the special project), plus chances to participate in a chorus line (presentation of a group report).

The college setting is similar to a grand ballroom. Here student guests meet genuinely stellar dancers (campus speakers and scholarly honorees), view varying modes of performance apparel (academic regalia, dark suits and ties, and athletic gear), and encounter collegiate tradition in both form and function (Presidential stroll, Dean's shuffle, and Faculty ramble).

Surely, Kenneth P. Mortimer, Howard R. Bowen, Zelda F. Gamson, Alexander W. Astin, Harold L. Hodgkinson, and the other authors of *Involvement in Learning* (N.I.E. Report, 1984) had the dancing metaphor subconsciously in mind when they crafted their exceptional study. What other analogy fits their conclusions? Dancing demands a high level of students' involvement; it requires that performance expectations be mutually understood and skillfully carried out; and it provides immediate feedback. One can readily envision Sandy and Zelda waltzing these key learning ideas by Ken and Bud.

Some may wish to challenge the dancing metaphor as too narrow–or too unacademic. Must learning couples always be male and female? Obviously not. Numerous ballet and chorus line performance models negate this concern. But isn't dance too frivolous a metaphor for the serious business of higher education? Decidedly not. The good feelings, fun, enjoyment, and collegiality of campus life ought to be celebrated and cherished. A dull lecturer or an unprepared student is just as joyless as a clumsy, inept dancing partner.

If the dancing metaphor survives its initial critics, then what kinds of music should accompany this new campus analogy? For contemporary students, something more lively than the minuette or the waltz will be required. Variety in syncopation, singers, and instrumentation will also be needed in the liberal arts ballroom. My specific suggestions for the undergraduate dance card might include: Martha and The Vandellas' "Dancing in the Street" (urban studies), Sheena Easton's "Strut" (women's studies), Lou Monte's "At the Darktown Strutter's Ball" (black culture), Eydie Gorme's "Blame It on the Bossa Nova" (Latin American history), Bobby Freeman's "C'mon and Swim" (aquatics), Klique's "Dance Like Crazy" (psychiatry), Tony Martin's "Dance of Destiny" (futuristic studies), Chubby Checker's "Dance the Mess Around" (leisure studies), Georgia Gibbs' "Dance with Me Henry" (biographical studies on James, Clay, Kissinger, and Aaron), Cozy Powell's "Dance with the Devil" (religious studies and theology), Claudja Barry's "Dancin' Fever" (pre-med studies), The Jackson Five's "Dancing Machine" (technology and automation), The Wilton Place Street Band's "Disco Lucy (I Love Lucy Theme)" (broadcast journalism and telecommunication), Johnny Taylor's "Disco 9000" (algebra, geometry, trigonometry, and calculus), The Commodores' "Fancy Dancer" (merchandising and retailing), Kenny Loggins' "Footloose" (geography), Bob and Earl's "Harlem Shuffle" (black history), Van Halen's "Jump" (physical education and recreation), Cannibal and The Headhunters' "Land of 1,000 Dances" (distribution requirements for general education), Little Eva's "Loco-Motion" (advanced physics), The Ray Bryant Combo's "Madison Time" (constitutional history), Michael Sembello's "Maniac" (deviant behavior), Chubby Checker's "Pony Time" (equestrian activities), Huey Smith's "Rockin' Pneumonia and the Boogie Woogie Flu" (immunology), Dolly Parton's "Save the Last Dance for Me" (final exams), The Olympics' "Shimmy Like Kate" (biographical studies of Hepburn and The Great Russian ruler), The Stray Cats' "Stray Cat Strut" (examinations of Marco Polo, Richard Byrd, and Jack Kerouac), Dire Straits' "Sultans of Swing" (ethnomusicology), The Trashmen's "Surfin' Bird" (ornithology),

The Beatles' "Twist and Shout" (aerobics), The Marvelettes' "Twistin' Postman" (government service), Lee Allen's "Walkin' with Mr. Lee" (civil war studies), The Turbans' "When You Dance" (teacher education), and Loggins and Messina's "Your Mama Don't Dance" (generational conflict analysis).

The dancing metaphor, if adopted and internalized by students and faculty alike, could revitalize the perception of higher education. Teachers desperately need a new bounce in their steps; freshmen and sophomores should view their performance roles more actively; juniors and seniors ought to become high stepping models; and administrators need to strike up the band to support all facets of undergraduate study. Boogie down, college presidents!

Chapter 9

Food Images

Food and drink are central factors in modern life.[1] In many cases, though, it is difficult to perceive any rationale for references to saltwater taffy, shortnin' bread, pumpkin pie, coconuts, mashed potatoes, and cherry wine in popular songs. The necessity of eating, combined with the plethora of available foods and liquid refreshments, seems to make musical commentaries about culinary activities random and undirected. Yet after careful examination, several distinct patterns of food-related observations become apparent. Undeniably, some identifications are strictly serendipitous in regard to individual food items; others are quite specific for either logical or symbolic reasons; and still others utilize the social setting of dining as a means of communicating varying personal feelings.

This chapter identifies 200 food-related recordings and places them in five separate categories. Although some of the songs feature overlapping ideas and a few of the titles are used in two or more categories, the general system seems reasonable, functional, and inclusive. The specific categories represented are: (1) focal point, (2) personal desire, (3) social setting, (4) symbol or image, and (5) nonsense use. The definition for each of these areas is provided below, along with a table of songs to illustrate the category.

This essay by B. Lee Cooper and William L. Schurk was originally published as "Food for Thought: Investigating Culinary Images in Contemporary American Recordings," *International Journal of Instructional Media* XIV, No. 3 (1987), pp. 251-262. Reprint permission has been granted by the co-authors, editor Phillip J. Sleeman, and The Baywood Publishing Company.

FOCAL POINT

Every song has a title, word, or phrase that becomes the formal identification tag for a distinct melody. For most musical compositions, the title is drawn directly from the lyrical content of the song. However, many tunes are strictly instrumental pieces. In these cases, the composer, arranger, performer, or someone else involved in the recording session arbitrarily assigns a title to the composition. Not infrequently, food or drink names are selected. Without rational explanation, Booker T. and the MGs cooked up "Green Onions," Al Hirt served "Java," Ray Charles belted down "One Mint Julep," and Herb Alpert and The Tijuana Brass sweetened the music scene with "Whipped Cream."

The following recordings illustrate the Focal Point theme:

- "Apples and Bananas"
  (Dot 16697)
  Lawrence Welk (1965)

- "Apricot Brandy"
  (Elektra 45647)
  Rhinoceros (1969)

- "Cotton Candy"
  (REG 8346)
  Al Hirt (1964)

- "Fried Onions"
  (London 1810)
  Lord Rockingham's XI (1958)

- "Gravy Waltz"
  (Dot 16457)
  Steve Allen (1963)

- "Green Onions"
  (Stax 127)
  Booker T. and The MGs (1962)

- "Hot Cakes! 1st Serving"
  (Chess 1850)
  Dave "Baby" Cortez (1963)

- "Hot Pepper"
  (RCA 8051)
  Floyd Cramer (1962)

- "Java"
  (RCA 8280)
  Al Hirt (1964)

- "Jellybread"
  (Stax 131)
  Booker T. and The MGs (1963)

- "Mo-Onions"
  (Stax 142)
  Booker T. and The MGs (1964)

- "My Sweet Potato"
  (Stax 196)
  Booker T. and The MGs (1966)

- "One Mint Julep"
  (Impulse 200)
  Ray Charles (1961)

- "Pass the Peas"
  (People 607)
  JB's (1972)

- "Peas 'n' Rice"
  (Prestige 450)
  Freddie McCoy (1967)

- "Saltwater Taffy"
  (Legend 124)
  Morty Jay and The Surferin' Cats (1963)

- "Whipped Cream"
  (A&M 760)
  Herb Alpert and The Tijuana Brass (1965)

PERSONAL DESIRE

Food themes often appear in song lyrics as expressions of personal desire. These feelings range from a child's hunger for "Shortnin' Bread" and "Peanut Butter" to adult cravings for "Another Cup of Coffee," "Java Jive," "Cigarettes and Coffee Blues," "Bottle Of Wine," "Drinking Wine Spo-Dee-O-Dee," and "Scotch and Soda." In times of extreme physical stress, even nonalcoholic liquids seem desirable. Such situations are presented in the desert format of "Cool Water" and in the prison scene of "Jailer, Bring Me Water." Personal slavery to excesses in food and drink is also lyrically documented, though usually from a tongue-in-cheek perspective. Jimmy Buffett describes the listless, unobligated life of an alcoholic in "Margaritaville," and Larry Groce condemns his own weakness for taco chips, Ho-Ho's, Ding-Dong's, and moon pies in "Junk Food Junkie." The following recordings illustrate the Personal Desire theme:

- "Animal Crackers in My Soup"
  (Musicor 1235)
  Gene Pitney (1967)

- "Another Cup of Coffee"
  (Mercury 72266)
  Brook Benton (1964)

- "Bottle of Wine"
  (Atco 6491)
  The Fireballs (1967)

- "Cigarettes and Coffee Blues"
  (Columbia 42701)
  Marty Robbins (1963)

- "Cool Water"
  (Top Rank 2055)
  Jack Scott (1960)

- "Drinking Wine Spo-Dee-O-Dee"
  (Mercury 73374)
  Jerry Lee Lewis (1973)

- "I'll Just Have a Cup of Coffee (Then I'll Go)"
  (Mercury 71732)
  Claude Gray (1961)

- "Jailer, Bring Me Water"
  (Reprise 0260)
  Trini Lopez (1964)

- "Java Jive"
  (Decca 3432)
  The Ink Spots (1941)

- "Junk Food Junkie"
  (Warner Brothers 8165)
  Larry Groce (1976)

- "Little Ole Wine Drinker, Me"
  (Reprise 0608)
  Dean Martin (1967)

- "Margaritaville"
  (ABC 12254)
  Jimmy Buffett (1977)

- "Peanut Butter"
  (Arvee 5027)
  The Marathons (1961)

- "Scotch and Soda"
  (Capitol 4740)
  The Kingston Trio (1962)

- "Shortnin' Bread"
  (Madison 136)
  The Bell Notes (1960)

- "Spill the Wine"
  (MGM 14118)
  Eric Burdon and War (1970)

SOCIAL SETTING

It is impossible to assess food references in popular recordings without acknowledging the influence of social settings in food-related songs. "Tea for Two" is not simply a commercial for non-alcoholic beverages, but an intimate statement describing a quiet interlude: "Champagne Jam" is less a description of a bubbly wine than a commentary about a wild party; and "Scotch and Soda" is not simply an invitation for a friendly drink, but a lightheaded (and similarly lighthearted) commentary about being overwhelmed by the presence of an infatuating woman. Even The Clovers' comic tale of marital entrapment (which was the result of imbibing at least "One Mint Julep") relies on the physical setting and the social environment, rather than just the liquid refreshment mentioned, to produce meaning.

Public dining arenas of diverse reputations, peopled by an array of pickled patrons and spicy waitresses, are grandly depicted in contemporary lyrics. Food is always present, but usually as a means of defining the social context of the dining experience. According to Arlo Guthrie, a customer can secure absolutely anything desired at "Alice's Restaurant." Obviously, there is a menu beyond the actual menu. Although the "Copacabana (At The Copa)" features high-class cuisine, fancy drinks, passionate dancing, and homicidal intrigue, most songs illustrate more plebian settings and more humble entrees. Listeners are invited to go "(Down at) Papa Joe's," to "The House of Blue Lights," to "The Sugar Shack," to the "Rib Joint," to the "Hotel California," and even to "Smokey Joe's Cafe." The latter establishment features a plate of chili beans and a jealous chef who carries a lengthy butcher knife and objects to customers flirting with his waitress girlfriend.

Songs depicting private parties also highlight special foods, beverages appropriate to the festivities, and ample physical surroundings for both culinary and sexual indulgence. Whether romping in the grass on "Blueberry Hill," accepting an invitation to consume a seemingly endless array of gourmet delights from an over-anxious matron in "Come on-a My House," eating a simple "Cheeseburger in Paradise," returning from overseas to the joy of grilled burgers "Back in the U.S.A.," "Having a Party" with coke, pretzels, and chips, feasting on Cajun cooking at a "Jambalaya (On The Bayou)," devouring a ghoulish "Dinner with Drac," enjoying a wild southern community picnic in "Jackson," or attempting to fry up an evening meal in a "Haunted House," the foodstuffs mentioned in the lyrics both give and gain meaning via the social context.

Highly emotional eating environments are common in contemporary recordings. Joyous occasions of youth, punctuated with popcorn and cotton candy, are illustrated in "Saturday Night at the Movies" and "Palisades Park." More chilling, emotion-draining dining occurs in the "Ode to Billie Joe," when a recently discovered suicide is discussed during a family dinner. Worse yet, cannibalism is suggested in "Timothy," the haunting tale of a mining disaster in which the survivors express guilt over the "disappearance" of their friend. And Three Dog Night cannot bear to watch, let alone recount, what is being eaten, drunk, or smoked in the pad where "Mama Told Me (Not to Come)." Finally, a southern plant of questionable nutritional value is the object of Tony Joe White's song ("Polk Salad Annie") about a family of thieves and murderers.

The following recordings illustrate the Social Setting theme:

- "Alice's Restaurant"
  (Reprise 0877)
  Arlo Guthrie (1969)

- "Back in the U.S.A."
  (Chess 1729)
  Chuck Berry (1959)

- "Back in the U.S.A."
  (Asylum 45519)
  Linda Ronstadt (1978)

- "Banana Boat (Day-O)"
  (RCA 6771)
  Harry Belafonte (1957)

- "Banana Boat Song"
  (Glory 249)
  The Tarriers (1957)

- "Blueberry Hill"
  (Imperial 5407)
  Fats Domino (1956)

- "Breakfast for Two"
  (Fantasy 758)
  Country Joe McDonald (1975)

- "Breakfast in Bed"
  (Atlantic 2606)
  Dusty Springfield (1969)

- "Champagne Jam"
  (Polydor 14504)
  The Atlantic Rhythm Section (1978)

- "Cheeseburger in Paradise"
  (ABC 12358)
  Jimmy Buffett (1978)

- "Chug-a-Lug"
  (Smash 1926)
  Roger Miller (1964)

- "Come on-a My House"
  (Columbia 39467)
  Rosemary Clooney (1951)

- "Copacabana (At The Copa)"
  (Arista 0339)
  Barry Manilow (1978)

- "Dinner with Drac"
  (Cameo 130)
  John "The Cool Ghoul" Zacherie (1958)

- "(Down At) Papa Joe's"
  (Sound Stage 2507)
  The Dixiebelles, with Cornbread and Jerry (1963)

- "Greasy Spoon"
  (Federal 12508)
  Hank Marr (1964)

- "Haunted House"
  (Hi 2076)
  Jumpin' Gene Simmons (1964)

- "Having a Party"
  (RCA 8036)
  Sam Cooke (1962)

- "Hotel California"
  (Asylum 45386)
  The Eagles (1977)

- "The House of Blue Lights"
  (Mercury 70627)
  Chuck Miller (1955)

- "Jackson"
  (Reprise 0595)
  Nancy Sinatra and Lee Hazlewood (1967)

- "Jambalaya (On The Bayou)"
  (Fantasy 689)
  The Blue Ridge Rangers (1973)

- "Long Tall Glasses (I Can Dance)"
  (Warner Brothers 8043)
  Leo Sayer (1975)

- "Mama Told Me (Not to Come)"
  (Dunhill 4239)
  Three Dog Night (1970)

- "Mama Told Me (Not to Come)"
  (Atlantic 2909)
  Wilson Pickett (1972)

- "Meet Me at Grandma's Joint"
  (Savoy 1123)
  Georgie Stevenson (1954)

- "Ode To Billie Joe"
  (Capitol 5950)
  Bobbie Gentry (1967)

- "One Mint Julep"
  (Atlantic 963)
  The Clovers (1952)

- "Palisades Park"
  (Swan 4106)
  Freddy Cannon (1962)

- "Polk Salad Annie"
  (Monument 1104)
  Tony Joe White (1969)

- "Rib Joint"
  (Savoy 1505)
  Sam Price (1957)

- "A Rose and a Baby Ruth"
  (ABC-Paramount 9765)
  George Hamilton IV (1956)

- "Saturday Night at the Movies"
  (Atlantic 2260)
  The Drifters (1964)

- "Scotch and Soda"
  (Capitol 4740)
  The Kingston Trio (1962)

- "Scotch and Soda"
  (Viva 29543)
  Ray Price (1983)

- "Smokey Joe's Cafe"
  (Atco 6059)
  The Robins (1955)

- "Stella's Candy Store"
  (Yardbird 1326)
  Sweet Marie (1973)

- "Sugar Shack"
  (Dot 16487)
  Jimmy Gilmer and The Fireballs (1963)

- "Sunday Barbecue"
  (Capitol 3997)
  Tennessee Ernie Ford (1958)

- "Tea for Two"
  (Atco 6286)
  Nino Tempo and April Stevens (1964)

- "Timothy"
  (Scepter 12275)
  The Buoys (1971)

- "Tip On In"
  (Excello 2285)
  Slim Harpo (1967)

- "Wedding Cake"
  (MGM 14034)
  Connie Francis (1969)

- "Whatcha' Got Cookin' in Your Oven Tonight"
  (MCA 52297)
  The Thrasher Brothers (1983)

- "Whiskey, Women, and Loaded Dice"
  (King 4628)
  Stick McGhee (1954)

SYMBOL OR IMAGE

Recordings that use food and drink in a symbolic way tend to emphasize sight and taste to communicate certain attitudes and feelings. For example, the desire for affection is often expressed in terms of hunger, as in Paul Revere's "Hungry" and Bruce Springsteen's "Hungry Heart." The Coasters present even more colorful hunger metaphors in "I'm a Hog for You."

Images of the good life–wealth, security, health, and overall well-being–are often communicated through verbal pictures of feasts of unimaginable proportion. Such extremes of culinary luxury are portrayed in "Big Rock Candy Mountain" and "Long Tall Glasses (I Can Dance)." Matchless liquid satisfaction is displayed in "Drinkin' Wine Spo-Dee-O-Dee." Food is also employed to illustrate the natural order of a continuing personal relationship and the mutual affection felt by a loving couple. Little Milton declares that if his passion isn't genuine, then "Grits Ain't Groceries" and eggs ain't poultry. In similar fashion, O. C. Smith uses the images of "Little Green Apples" to symbolize divine support for his loving feelings.

Sweetness, communicated symbolically in the form of candy, honey, and sugar, is a common referent to many passionate men and women depicted in popular songs. Whether a "Candy Girl" or a "Candy Man," the object of audio affection is always instructed to "Save Your Sugar for Me." Not surprisingly, even interracial dating is couched in sweet symbolism by Neil Young in "Cinnamon Girl" and by The Rolling Stones in "Brown Sugar." More common references to loved ones include "Sugar Dumplin," "Sugar Plum," "Sugar, Sugar," "Sweets for My Sweet," and "What a Sweet Thing that Was." Of course, not all loving relationships last forever. To ensure continued affection, Dusk suggests "Treat Me Like a Good Piece of Candy"; The Guess Who are even more emphatic in declaring that there will be "No Sugar Tonight" if proper standards of behavior aren't followed.

Unsuccessful relationships are also exhibited in food-related imagery. The Osmonds argue that a poor dating experience with "One Bad Apple" shouldn't permanently spoil a young girl's perception of other men. William Bell, chiming the sour grapes of the jilted lover, warns that "You Don't Miss Your Water" until the well of new suitors has gone dry. Yet another recording emphasizes the ability of one person to see value in another even though that individual has been ignored and rejected by a previous lover. This attitude appears in "One Man's Leftovers (Is Another Man's Feast)." Finally, The Newbeats (and, later, Robert John) described in kitchen-centered terms the breakup of a relationship because the girl preferred eating chicken and dumplings with a new boyfriend over preparing "Bread and Butter" and toast and jam for her former beau.

The following recordings illustrate the Symbol or Image theme:

- "Apples, Peaches, Pumpkin Pie"
  (Smash 2086)
  Jay and The Techniques (1967)

- "Big Rock Candy Mountain"
  (Era 3019)
  Dorsey Burnette (1960)

- "Bread and Butter"
  (Hickory 1269)
  The Newbeats (1964)

- "Bread and Butter"
  (Motown 1664)
  Robert John (1983)

- "Brown Sugar"
  (Rolling Stones 19100)
  The Rolling Stones (1971)

- "Candy Girl"
  (Vee-Jay 539)
  The Four Seasons (1963)

- "Candy Man"
  (Monument 447)
  Roy Orbison (1961)

- "Cinnamon Girl"
  (Reprise 0911)
  Neil Young (1970)

- "Coconut Woman"
  (RCA 6885)
  Harry Belafonte (1957)

- "Don't Mess with My Man"
  (Ron 328)
  Irma Thomas (1960)

- "Drinkin' Wine Spo-Dee-O-Dee"
  (Atlantic 873)
  Stick McGhee (1949)

- "Girl with the Hungry Eyes"
  (Grunt 11921)
  Jefferson Starship (1980)

- "Grits Ain't Groceries (All Around the World)"
  (Checker 1212)
  Little Milton (1969)

- "How Blue Can You Get"
  (Decca 27648)
  Louis Jordan (1951)

- "Hungry"
  (Columbia 43678)
  Paul Revere and The Raiders (1966)

- "Hungry Heart"
  (Columbia 11391)
  Bruce Springsteen (1980)

- "I Can't Help Myself"
  (Motown 1076)
  Four Tops (1965)

- "I'm a Hog for You"
  (Atco 6146)
  The Coasters (1959)

- "Let Me Go Home, Whiskey"
  (Aladdin 3164)
  Amos Milburn (1953)

- "Little Green Apples"
  (Columbia 44616)
  O. C. Smith (1968)

- "Long Tall Glasses (I Can Dance)"
  (Warner Brothers 8043)
  Leo Sayer (1975)

- "Maneater"
  (RCA 13354)
  Daryl Hall and John Oates (1982)

- "No Sugar Tonight"
  (RCA 0325)
  The Guess Who (1970)

- "One Bad Apple"
  (MGM 14193)
  The Osmonds (1971)

- "One Man's Leftovers (Is Another Man's Feast)"
  (Hot Wax 7009)
  100 Proof Aged in Soul (1971)

- "One Mint Julep"
  (Atlantic 963)
  The Clovers (1952)

- "Save Your Sugar for Me"
  (Monument 1206)
  Tony Joe White (1970)

- "Sugar Dumpling"
  (RCA 8631)
  Sam Cooke (1965)

- "Sugar Plum"
  (Mercury 71975)
  Ike Clanton (1962)

- "Sugar, Sugar"
  (Calendar 1008)
  The Archies (1969)

- "Sugar, Sugar"
  (Atlantic 2722)
  Wilson Pickett (1970)

- "Sweets for My Sweet"
  (Atlantic 2117)
  The Drifters (1961)

- "Treat Me Like a Good Piece of Candy"
  (Bell 45148)
  Dusk (1971)

- "You Don't Miss Your Water"
  (Stax 116)
  William Bell (1962)

NONSENSE USE

Similar to the Focal Point theme, this section includes food-related songs where the titles appear to be arbitrary. Various dance crazes, and tunes that provide the rhythms for the dancing, have been assigned seemingly random food titles with no apparent rationale. This trend is readily noted in "Mashed Potatoes," "Mashed Potato Time," "Gravy (for My Mashed Potatoes)," "Hot Pastrami," and "Hot Pastrami and Mashed Potatoes." A particularly bouncy, lyrically benign set of songs produced during the late 1960s became known as Bubblegum Music. Their titles reflect hunger for affection in such food-related images as "Chewy Chewy," "Goody Goody Gumdrops," "Jam Up Jelly Tight," and "Yummy Yummy Yummy."

There is also an off-the-wall group of recordings that utilize the names of specific foods as background elements to achieve a sense of comic absurdity. The Kingsmen's vocal interjections of artichokes, green beans, broccoli, cabbage, corn, and so on, in the tale of the "Jolly Green Giant" illustrates this approach. Other bizarre formats for food commentaries appear in "Eat It," "Does Your Chewing Gum Lose Its Flavor (on the Bedpost Overnight)," "I Love Rocky Road," "On Top of Spaghetti," and "Rubber Biscuit." Humorous tales are also concocted about potent elixirs, special medications, and missing meat delicacies. These recordings include "Love Potion No. 9," "Jeremiah Peabody's Poly Unsaturated Quick Dissolving Fast Acting Pleasant Tasting Green and Purple Pills," and "Who Stole the Keeshka?"

The following recordings illustrate the Nonsense Use theme:

- "Bacon Fat"
  (Epic 9196)
  Andre Williams (1957)

- "Beans in My Ears"
  (Philips 40198)
  The Serendipity Singers (1964)

- "Bubble Gum Music"
  (Buddah 78)
  Rock and Roll Dubble Bubble Trading Card Co.
  of Philadelphia–19141 (1969)

- "Chewy Chewy"
  (Buddah 70)
  The Ohio Express (1968)

- "Coconut"
  (RCA 0718)
  Nilsson (1972)

- "(Do the) Mashed Potatoes"
  (Dade 1804)
  Nat Kendrick and The Swans (1960)

- "Does Your Chewing Gum Lose Its Flavor
  (on the Bedpost Overnight)"
  (Dot 15911)
  Lonnie Donegan and His Skiffle Group (1961)

- "The Eggplant that Ate Chicago"
  (Go Go 100)
  Dr. West's Medicine Show and Junk Band (1966)

- "The Fish"
  (Cameo 192)
  Bobby Rydell (1961)

- "Goody Goody Gumdrops"
  (Buddah 71)
  The 1910 Fruitgum Co. (1968)

- "Gravy (for My Mashed Potatoes)"
  (Cameo 219)
  Dee Dee Sharp (1962)

- "Hot Pastrami"
  (Dot 16453)
  The Dartells (1963)

- "Hot Pastrami and Mashed Potatoes"
  (Roulette 4488)
  Joey Dee and The Starliters (1963)

- "I Love Rocky Road"
  (Rock 'n' Roll 03998)
  Weird Al Yankovic (1983)

- "Jam Up Jelly Tight"
  (ABC 11247)
  Tommy Roe (1970)

- "Jelly Jungle (of Orange Marmalade)"
  (Buddah 41)
  The Lemon Pipers (1968)

- "Jeremiah Peabody's Poly Unsaturated Quick Dissolving Fast Acting Pleasant Tasting Green and Purple Pills"
  (Mercury 71843)
  Ray Stevens (1961)

- "Jolly Green Giant"
  (Wand 172)
  The Kingsmen (1965)

- "Love Potion No. 9"
  (United Artists 180)
  The Covers (1959)

- "Mashed Potato Time"
  (Cameo 212)
  Dee Dee Sharp (1962)

- "Mashed Potatoes"
  (Checker 1006)
  Steve Alaimo (1962)

- "Mashed Potatoes U.S.A."
  (King 5672)
  James Brown (1962)

- "On Top of Spaghetti"
  (Kapp 526)
  Tom Glazer and The Do-Re-Mi Children's Chorus (1963)

- "Peppermint Twist"
  (Roulette 4401)
  Joey Dee and The Starliters (1962)

- "The Popcorn"
  (King 6240)
  James Brown (1969)

- "Rubber Biscuit"
  (Josie 803)
  The Chips (1956)

- "Rubber Biscuit"
  (Atlantic 364)
  The Blues Brothers (1979)

- "Strawberry Shortcake"
  (Smash 2142)
  Jay and The Techniques (1968)

- "Who Stole the Keeshka?"
  (Select 719)
  The Matys Brothers (1963)

- "Yummy Yummy Yummy"
  (Buddah 38)
  The Ohio Express (1968)

CONCLUSION

There are few broad conclusions that can be drawn from this preliminary investigation of food-related recordings, although the frequency, variety, and breadth of meaning attributed to various foods in contemporary songs is amazing. The fact that pizza is seldom mentioned, despite its high profile in the American diet, is of singular interest. The distinctions that can be drawn between food as nutritional substance and food as a symbolic reference or a social environment definer are also genuinely significant. Finally, given their apparent mundaneness, it is relatively easy to understand why the most common elements of social life are often overlooked and downplayed in social research. This is why popular-culture studies can be helpful in attempting to understand human behavior. Hopefully, contemporary recordings about the emotional conflicts of a "Junk Food Junkie" and the superstitious beliefs in "Love Potion No. 9" can provide ample food for scholarly thought.

NOTE

1. For general discussions of the social and psychological meanings of dining, consult the following sources: Roland Barthes, "Toward a Psychosociology of Contemporary Food Consumption," in *European Diet from Pre-Industrial to Modern Times*, ed. Elborg Forster and Robert Forster (New York: Harper & Row, 1975), pp. 47-59; Charles Camp, "Foodways in Everyday Life," American Quarterly XXXIV (1982), pp. 278-289; Waverly Root and Richard de Rochemont, *Eating in America: A History* (New York: William Morrow, 1976); and Roger Welsch, "We Are What We Eat: Omaha Food as Symbol," *Keystone Folklore Quarterly* XVI (1971), pp. 165-170. For an investigation of food-related commentaries in early twentieth-century recordings, see William L. Schurk, "'Yes, We Have No Bananas': The Image of Food and Eating in Popular Song" (Mimeographed paper and audio presentation delivered at the Annual Convention of the Midwest Popular Culture Association in Bloomington, Indiana in October 1984), pp. 1-6.

Chapter 10

Games and Music Trivia

Musical Attractions, by Gretchen L. Hovis and Faith A. MacLennan. Dearborn, Michigan: Hovis and MacLennan Games, Inc., 1988. A Board Game.

The appearance of a new musical board game hardly seems noteworthy. From the specialty set of music cards in *Trivial Pursuit* to the telephone quizzes conducted each day by morning zoo disc jockeys, young people have already answered thousands of questions on rock-era songs and performers. But *Musical Attractions* is a game that marches to a different drummer. For once, Ringo Starr and Phil Collins share the popular-music platform with Buddy Rich and Gene Krupa. The music of the 1930s and 1940s is linked to tunes of the 1960s, 1970s, and 1980s in this unique, nostalgia-provoking game.

Sixty-eight-year-old Gretchen Hovis and seventy-three-year-old Faith MacLennan devoted more than three years to creating the game cards for *Musical Attractions.* Their competitive game challenges players to link specific song titles with selected subjects, and to answer trivia-type questions about recordings and artists that have been popular over the last 80 years. The game is played by two to eight people divided into two teams. This game's playing board consists of 56 subject categories (28 topics per team) that must be matched correctly with song titles from a preselected decade. The categories include such items as transportation, beverages, and jewelry–with the appropriate matching songs being "Cruisin'," "Days

---

This essay by B. Lee Cooper was originally published in *Popular Music and Society* XIII (Summer 1989): pp. 115-116. Reprint permission has been granted by the author and The Popular Press.

of Wine and Roses," and "String of Pearls." A team may earn bonus points for accurately remembering facts about other recordings. These trivia questions include such memory testers as: "Who was England's most popular female singer during World War II?" (Vera Lynn); "What song was the trademark of Woody Herman's orchestra?" ("Woodchopper's Ball"); "Who gave Elvis Presley his first guitar?" (his mother, Gladys);" What was Chubby Checker's real name?" (Ernest Evans); and "How did Bobby Darin die?" (during heart surgery in 1973).

Unlike other trivia games, *Musical Attractions* is designed to be a genuinely family-oriented experience. It is also a unique vehicle for popular-culture exploration. The notion that 80 years of American music can be designated decade by decade into 56 identifiable themes acknowledges the oral tradition of recorded lyrics. Hovis and MacLennan, though dynamic personalities and competent physical-therapy workers, are (like most of us) amateurs in the field of contemporary music. Their herculean efforts at creating this audio kaleidoscope of themes and facts is a tribute to their energy, enthusiasm, and ingenuity. But those who will most appreciate their efforts will be the young and old players who discover how ubiquitous music has been in American society. Nostalgia aside, potential history lessons offered in *Musical Attractions* are legion. But the fact that they can be learned in an interacting and intergenerational setting is a highly attractive component to the game.

Musical Attractions, though not yet being produced and marketed by a giant board-game corporation, is the best music theme, information, and trivia project currently available for total family recreation. Hopefully, teachers and media specialists will join the general buying public in identifying this game as a source of education and enjoyment.

Chapter 11

Hit Tunes

THE PERSUASIONS

The practice of reviving songs that have become popular is anything but new. The 1942 Bing Crosby tune "White Christmas" had been successfully covered or revived by nine other performers by 1955. Similarly, Ben E. King's 1961 hit "Stand By Me" was re-recorded by six other artists over the next 24 years. Each of these versions reached *Billboard's* Hot 100. Most covers differ little in lyric, rhythm, and instrumentation from the original recordings. However, there are a few vocal groups that rely almost solely on previous hits to create their repertoires. These a cappella stylists creatively transform golden oldies into fresh, non-instrumented, vibrant sounds. The major names among contemporary a cappella groups are The Darts, The Nylons, and especially The Persuasions.

Songs without instrumental accompaniment may be an effective approach for church choirs or folk artists, but it is rarely utilized by popular-music performers. That's why The Persuasions are a unique recording phenomenon. This five-member group has carved a distinctive niche in the modern musical scene by singing a cappella. Their performing response to each new stylistic fad that has emerged during the past four decades is vocal co-option. They have assimilated songs from soul, rock 'n' roll, gospel, rhythm 'n' blues, pop, and other musical genres into their own recording format, and they have devoted their professional careers to popularizing unaccompanied singing.

This essay by B. Lee Cooper was originally published as "Repeating Hit Tunes, A Cappella Style: The Persuasions as Song Revivalists, 1967-1982," *Popular Music and Society*, XIII (Fall 1989), pp. 17-27. Reprint permission has been granted by the author, editor R. Serge Denisoff, and The Popular Press.

The Persuasions, in their normal five-man format, consist of lead baritone Jerry Lawson, baritone Herbert "Tubo" Rhoad, bass Jimmy "Bro" Hayes, first tenor Jayotis Washington, and second tenor Joe "Jesse" Russell. Two albums produced for A&M records during 1974 featured two significant changes in the group's composition and musical approach: first tenor Jayotis Washington was absent on both discs, replaced by Willie C. Daniels, and the group's thematic signature–"This album contains no instruments other than the human voice"–was also absent. *More Than Before* [SP 3635] features guitar, bass, keyboard, and percussion accompaniment and *I Just Want to Sing with My Friends* [SP 3656] introduces strings and horns in background arrangements. But The Persuasions are at their best with the standard group (Jerry, Tubo, Jimmy, Jayotis, and Jesse) singing in unaccompanied harmony.

According to publicity releases, the group was formed in the mid-1960s in New York City through the assembly of five diversely experienced singers. Jerry Lawson, born January 28, 1944, in Fort Lauderdale, Florida, began perfecting his baritone voice by listening to the records of David Ruffin, Sam Cooke, and Otis Redding. After a youthful period of church-choir singing and drum and trumpet playing in Apopka, Florida, he moved to New York and joined a vocal group called The Shufflers. Jimmy Hayes was already a member of this group. He had sung gospel hymns and rock 'n' roll tunes in Hopewell, Virginia, where he was born November 12, 1943. Street-corner singing united Jimmy and Jerry in Bedford-Stuyvesant, and they made up the core of the group.

Joe Russell, who was born on September 25, 1939, in Henderson, North Carolina, sang with The Southern Echoes in 1957. He visited Madison Square Garden in 1959 as a student member of The New Bethel Gospel Singers. After graduation, he moved to New York City, where he met Tubo Rhoad of Bamberg, South Carolina. Tubo, who was born October 1, 1944, was living in Brooklyn and singing with The Parisians. The fifth member of The Persuasions was born on May 12, 1945, in Detroit, Michigan, but had moved to New York at age ten, growing up on 134th street in Harlem. Jayotis Washington joined the two Shufflers and the two Parisians to form the premier a cappella group of the seventies, The Persuasions. With the exception of a period between 1974 and 1977, when Jay retired from singing to work in a Long Island mental-health center, The Persuasions have been a consistent vocal team since 1967, when they won their first singing contest in Jersey City, New Jersey.

The Persuasions, under the guidance of manager and producer David Dashev, have been the most popular practitioners of unaccompanied singing in the United States during the past 30 years. This assertion is accurate, yet ironic. The art of a cappella performing was a common pursuit in American popular music during the 1940s and 1950s. Geographically, this style reached its zenith in the New York-Philadelphia-New Haven areas, although Detroit, Los Angeles, and several other major cities generated notable vocal groups. The tales of rhythm 'n' blues giants standing on Harlem street corners serenading passers-by bear substantial truth, and mark the initial step on the road to record-producing success for many black groups. Gospel harmony, blues wailing, and the finger-snapping rhythm of The Moonglows, The Flamingos, The Orioles, The Clovers, The Harptones, The Spaniels, The Five Royales, and others still echo in the "Golden Oldie" bins of contemporary music shops. They represent the vocal heritage of The Persuasions.

The problem with a cappella singing during the 1970s and 1980s was that public demand for such albums was remarkably weak. However, the distinctive claim that "This album contains no instruments other than the human voice" has become anachronistically fascinating in an age of multitrack recording, overdubbing, and studio musician dominance. Despite the lack of sales success and *Billboard* Hot 100 recognition, no music historian should fail to note the revivalist heart of The Persuasions' repertoire. This factor is especially significant during an age where the black cultural heritage in music is a major concern.

In order to highlight the song-revivalist tendencies of The Persuasions, this chapter focuses on their album production during a designated 15-year period. Between 1967 and 1982, The Persuasions released 11 albums. Most of these discs were issued by major companies, such as Reprise, Capitol, MCA, A&M, and Elektra. In addition, several minor recording labels–Catamount, Flying Fish, Rounder, and Straight–either reissued previously released tracks or offered new albums for the limited a cappella market. These Persuasions' albums are:

- *Acappella* (Straight RS 6394)–1968
- *Stardust* (Catamount CATA 905)–1969
- *We Came to Play* (Capitol SM 791)–1971
- *Street Corner Symphony* (Capitol ST 872)–1972
- *Spread the Word* (Capitol ST 11101)–1972
- *We Still Ain't Got No Band* (MCA 326)–1973
- *More Than Before* (A & M SP 3635)–1974
- *I Just Want to Sing with My Friends* (A & M SP 3656)–1974
- *Chirpin'* (Elektra 7E–1099)–1977
- *Comin' at Ya* (Flying Fish FF 093)–1979
- *Good News* (Rounder RR 3053)–1982

The following chart lists 80 songs from The Persuasions' first 11 albums. The tunes included below are all revived versions of hit songs. The hit status accorded each song on this chart is defined as achieving at least one week of listing on *Billboard*'s Best Selling Singles pop chart (1950-1955), the Hot 100 chart (1955-1980), the Rhythm and Blues chart (1950-1969), or the Soul chart (1969-1980).

Alphabetical List of Hit Songs Revived by The Persuasions in Their First 11 Albums, 1967-1982[1]

Title (Record Number) Original Artist (Original Release Date)	Persuasions' Release
"A.B.C.'s of Love" (Gee 1022) Frankie Lymon and The Teenagers (1956)	1974
"Ain't That Good News" (RCA 8299) Sam Cooke (1964)	1982
"All I Have To Do Is Dream" (Cadence 1348) The Everly Brothers (1958)	1982
"Any More" (Duke 144) Johnny Ace (1955)	1973
"Baby, Don't Do It" (Apollo 443) The Five Royales (1953)	1969
"Baby, What You Want Me To Do (You Got Me Running)" (Vee-Jay 333) Jimmy Reed (1960)	1973

Title (Record Number) Original Artist (Original Release Date)	Persuasions' Release
"Be Good to My Baby" (Ko Ko 2107) Luther Ingram (1971)	1972
"Beauty's Only Skin Deep" (Gordy 7055) The Temptations (1966)	1974
"Besame Mucho" (Decca 18574) Jimmy Dorsey (1944)	1979
"The Bounce" (Tri Disc 106) The Olympics (1963)	1968
"Bright Lights, Big City" (Vee-Jay 398) Jimmy Reed (1961)	1973
"Buffalo Soldier" (Polydor 14019) The Flamingos (1970)	1972
"Chain Gang" (RCA 7783) Sam Cooke (1960)	1971

Title (Record Number) Original Artist (Original Release Date)	Persuasions' Release
"Chapel of Love" (Red Bird 001) The Dixie Cups (1964)	1973
"Cloud Nine" (Gordy 7081) The Temptations (1968)	1972
"Crying in the Chapel" (Valley 105) Darrell Glenn (1953)	1979
"Cupid" (RCA 7883) Sam Cooke (1961)	1982
"Dance with Me" (Atlantic 2040) The Drifters (1959)	1973
"Don't It Make You Want To Go Home" (Capitol 2592) Joe Smith (1969)	1971
"Don't Let Him Take Your Love from Me" (Motown 1159) The Four Tops (1969)	1979

Title (Record Number) Original Artist (Original Release Date)	Persuasions' Release
"Don't Look Back" (Gordy 7047) The Temptations (1965)	1972
"Drip Drop" (Atlantic 1187) The Drifters (1958)	1979
"Ebb Tide" (London 1358) Frank Chacksfield (1953)	1969
"Good Times" (RCA 8368) Sam Cooke (1964)	1972
"Goodnight, Sweetheart, Goodnight" (Vee-Jay 107) The Spaniels (1954)	1969
"The Great Pretender" (Mercury 70753) The Platters (1956)	1969
"Gypsy Woman" (ABC-Paramount 10241) The Impressions (1961)	1971

Title (Record Number) Original Artist (Original Release Date)	Persuasions' Release
"He Ain't Heavy, He's My Brother" (Epic 10532) The Hollies (1970)	1972
"Heaven Help Us All" (Tamla 54200) Stevie Wonder (1970)	1972
"I Could Never Love Another (After Loving You)" (Gordy 7072) The Temptations (1968)	1972
"I Lost Everything I Ever Had" (Motown 1149) David Ruffin (1969)	1982
"I Won't Be the Fool Anymore" (Rama 222) The Heartbeats (1957)	1982
"I'll Come Running Back to You" (Specialty 619) Sam Cooke (1957)	1982
"I'm a Hog for You" (Atco 6146) The Coasters (1959)	1974

Title (Record Number) Original Artist (Original Release Date)	Persuasions' Release
"I've Got To Use My Imagination" (Buddah 393) Gladys Knight and The Pips (1974)	1974
"Idol with the Golden Head" (Atco 6098) The Coasters (1957)	1973
"It's All in the Game" (MGM 12688) Tommy Edwards (1958)	1974
"Just Because" (ABC-Paramount 9792) Lloyd Price (1957)	1979
"Lean on Me" (Sussex 235) Bill Withers (1972)	1972
"Let It Be" (Apple 2764) The Beatles (1970)	1971
"Let the Good Times Roll" (Aladdin 3325) Shirley and Lee (1956)	1982

Title (Record Number) Original Artist (Original Release Date)	Persuasions' Release
"Let Them Talk" (King 5274) Little Willie John (1959)	1979
"(Loneliness Made Me Realize) It's You That I Need" (Gordy 7065) The Temptations (1967)	1971
"Lookin' for a Love" (Sar 132) The Valentinos (1962)	1974
"Love You Most of All" (Keen 2008) Sam Cooke (1959)	1973
"Loves Me Like a Rock" (Columbia 45907) Paul Simon (1973)	1979
"Message from Maria" (Sound Stage 2617) Joe Simon (1968)	1982
"One Mint Julep" (Atlantic 963) The Clovers (1952)	1979

Title (Record Number) Original Artist (Original Release Date)	Persuasions' Release
"Oh What a Night" (Vee-Jay 204) The Dells (1956)	1974
"Old Man River" (Verve 10262) Jimmy Smith (1962)	1982
"Pappa Oom Mow Mow" (Liberty 55427) The Rivingtons (1962)	1977
"People Get Ready" (ABC-Paramount 10622) The Impressions (1965)	1972
"Return to Sender" (RCA 8100) Elvis Presley (1962)	1979
"Runaway Child, Running Wild" (Gordy 7084) The Temptations (1969)	1972
"Searchin' for My Baby" (Carnival 509) The Manhattans (1965)	1968

Title (Record Number) Original Artist (Original Release Date)	Persuasions' Release
"Send Me Some Lovin'" (Specialty 598) Little Richard (1957)	1963
"Since I Fell for You" (Cadence 1439) Lenny Welch (1963)	1968
"Sincerely" (Chess 1581) The Moonglows (1955)	1969
"Sixty Minute Man" (Federal 12022) The Dominoes (1951)	1977
"So Much in Love" (Parkway 871) The Tymes (1963)	1972
"Speedo" (Josie 785) The Cadillacs (1956)	1969
"Stardust" (Victory 27233) Tommy Dorsey (1940)	1969

Title (Record Number) Original Artist (Original Release Date)	Persuasions' Release
"Steal Away" (Fame 6401) Jimmy Hughes (1964)	1973
"Sunday Kind of Love" (Bruce 101) The Harptones (1953)	1969
"Swanee" (RCA 6182) Jaye P. Morgan (1955)	1969
"The Ten Commandments" (Chess 1705) Harvey and The Moonglows (1958)	1972
"A Thousand Miles Away" (Rama 216) The Heartbeats (1957)	1969
"To Be Loved" (Brunswick 55052) Jackie Wilson (1958)	1977
"Too Late" (RCA 6880) Gene Austin (1957)	1968

Title (Record Number) Original Artist (Original Release Date)	Persuasion's Release
"Up on the Roof" (Atlantic 2162) The Drifters (1963)	1968
"Walk on the Wild Side" (Verve 10255) Jimmy Smith (1962)	1971
"We're All Goin' Home" (MGM 14246) Bobby Bloom (1971)	1974
"The Whole World Is a Stage" (Ric Tic 122) The Fantastic Four (1967)	1968
"Why Don't You Write Me?" (RPM 428) The Jacks (1955)	1969
"Willie and Laura" (Atlantic 2647) Dusty Springfield (1969)	1977
"Win Your Love" (Keen 2006) Sam Cooke (1958)	1977

Title (Record Number) Original Artist (Original Release Date)	Persuasions' Release
"With This Ring" (Musicor 1229) The Platters (1967)	1974
"Without a Song" (Epic 9125) Roy Hamilton (1955)	1972
"You Must Believe Me" (ABC-Paramount 10581) The Impressions (1964)	1973
"You've Got a Friend" (Warner Brothers 7498) James Taylor (1971)	1972

CONCLUSION

The Persuasions are obviously song revivalists, but not in the most traditional sense. They have rarely recorded and released songs written by America's classic tunesmiths of the 1930s and 1940s. The 11 albums surveyed show no tunes attributed to Richard Rodgers, Cole Porter, Noel Coward, Duke Ellington, Johnny Mercer, Sammy Cahn, Jule Styne, Irving Berlin, or Ira Gershwin. Songs by Oscar Hammerstein II, Jerome Kern, Hoagy Carmichael, and George Gershwin are present, but are few in number. The Persuasions have also ignored the realm of country music. They include no songs by Hank Williams, Jimmie Rodgers, Mel Tillis, Bob Gibson, Fred Rose, Tex Ritter, Merle Travis, Gene Autry, Jimmy

Wakely, Ernest Tubbs, Eddy Arnold, Webb Pierce, or Buck Owens in their albums. The lone country-oriented song produced between 1967 and 1982 was the Everly Brothers' classic "All I Have To Do Is Dream" written by Bodeleaux Bryant. The songwriters who have provided the majority of material for The Persuasions are urban tunesmiths from Chicago, Detroit, and New York. This group of composers and lyricists includes the cream of 1950-1970 popular music writers: Jerry Leiber and Mike Stoller, Gerry Goffin and Carole King, William "Smokey" Robinson and Ronald White, Berry Gordy, Jr., Eddie Holland, Barrett Strong and Norman Whitfield, Sam Cooke, and Curtis Mayfield. It is somewhat strange, though, that the rhythm and blues repertoire of The Persuasions doesn't feature many more songs by Otis Blackwell, Buck Ram, James Sheppard, Jimmy Reed, or Don Robey, and contains no numbers by Doc Pomus and Mort Shuman, Otis Redding, Ray Charles, Bo Diddley, Chuck Berry, Hank Ballard, Willie Dixon, Fats Domino, Chuck Willis, or Marvin Gaye.

Beyond the songs and composers, it is also interesting to note the stylistic influences on The Persuasions' revival activities. Their chief singing style/musical arrangement models are Curtis Mayfield and The Impressions, Sam Cooke, Billy Ward and The Dominoes, The Temptations, Harvey Fuqua and The Moonglows, The Flamingos, Jackie Wilson, The Coasters, Clyde McPhatter and The Drifters, James Sheppard and The Heartbeats, and The Four Tops. Finally, although The Persuasions have recorded a vast array of classic tunes, it is fascinating to note the large number of traditionally popular a cappella songs that they have not released. Among these tunes are: "In the Still of the Night," "To the Aisle," "Why Do Fools Fall in Love," "Unchained Melody," "I Only Have Eyes for You," "You Send Me," and "Fever."

NOTE

1. Sources used to compile this listing include: Nat Shapiro and Bruce Pollock, eds., *Popular Music, 1920-1979: A Revised Cumulation*, 3 Volumes (Detroit, Michigan: Gale Research Company, 1985); Joel Whitburn, comp., *Pop Memories, 1890-1954: The History of American Popular Music* (Menomonee Falls, Wisconsin: Record Research, Inc., 1986); Joel Whitburn, comp., *Top Pop Singles, 1955-1986* (Menomonee Falls, Wisconsin: Record Research, Inc., 1987); and Joel

Whitburn, comp., *Top R&B Singles, 1942-1988* (Menomonee Falls, Wisconsin: Record Research, Inc., 1988).

REFERENCES

Brown, Ashley. "The Alchemists." *The History of Rock* No. 15 (1982): pp. 281-283.

Brown, Geoff. "Doo-Wop." *The History of Rock* No. 4 (1982): pp. 69-73.

Cummings, Tony. "Doo-Wop: The Streetcorner Harmonizers." In *The Sound of Philadelphia*. London: Methuen Press, 1975.

Geberer, Raanan. "A Cappella–In the Mid-1960s." *Goldmine* 90 (November 1983): p. 174ff.

George, Nelson. *The Death of Rhythm and Blues*. New York: Pantheon Books, 1988.

Gribin, Anthony J., and Matthew M. Schiff. *Doo-Wop: The Forgotten Third of Rock 'n' Roll*. Iola, WI: Krause Publications, 1992.

Groia, Philip. *They All Sang on the Corner: A Second Look at New York City's Rhythm and Blues Vocal Groups* (revised edition). West Hempstead: Phillie Dee Enterprises, 1984.

Hansen, Barry. "Doo-Wop." In *The Rolling Stone Illustrated History of Rock and Roll*. Edited by Jim Miller. New York: Random House/Rolling Stone Press, 1976.

King, Woodie, Jr. "Searching for Brothers Kindred: Rhythm and Blues of the 1950s." *The Black Scholar* VI (November 1974): pp. 19-30.

Marion, Jean-Charles. "The Aesthetics of Lead Vocals: Upfront Variations in Style of the R&B Groups of the 50s." *Record Exchanger* 8 (1971): pp. 16-17.

Nickols, Pete. "Doo-Wop." *Record Collector* 88 (December 1986): pp. 45-49.

Redmond, Mike, and Mary Goldberg. "The Doo-Wah Sound: Black Pop Groups of the 1950s." *Yesterday's Memories* 1 (1975): pp. 22-24, 26.

Shaw, Arnold. *Honkers and Shouters: The Golden Years of Rhythm and Blues*. New York: Collier Books, 1978.

Tamarkin, Jeff. "Ambient Sound Records: Group Harmony in the '80s." *Goldmine* 70 (March 1982): p. 20ff.

Tamarkin, Jeff. "New Jersey: The Home of Doo-Wop." *Goldmine* 75 (August 1982): pp. 27-28.

Chapter 12

Imported Recordings

TEACHING ABOUT IMPERIALISM THROUGH IMPORTED RECORDINGS

Imperialism is a distant, obscure concept to most social studies students. Whether related to the Balkan origins of World War I, the British experience with Ghandi in India, or the rise of nationalism throughout colonial Africa, the intellectual interest of young Americans is rarely piqued by tales about European subjugations of distant, underdeveloped countries. However, history teachers can utilize the American experience of cultural and economic dominance in postwar Great Britain to define and illustrate the process of non-political hegemony. During the middle of this century, American music was overwhelmingly accepted in the United Kingdom as *the* standard of contemporary popular art. Commercial recordings from the States dotted British music charts from 1953 until the mid-1960s. Then things changed. The Beatles, The Rolling Stones, and hundreds of other British beat groups found their own distinctive voices. The post-1964 era of the British Invasion saw the U.K. record charts listing Liverpool musicians in the Top Ten, while *Billboard* and *Cash Box* Hot 100 listings also featured more and more hits by British groups. How did the American cultural imperialism of the fifties get turned around? What factors enabled British

---

This study by Laura E. Cooper and B. Lee Cooper was originally published as "Exploring Cultural Imperialism: Bibliographic Resources for Teaching About American Domination, British Adaptation, and the Rock Music Interchange, 1950-1967." *International Journal of Instructional Media* XVII (1990): pp. 167-177. Reprint permission has been granted by the authors, editor Phillip J. Sleeman, and The Westwood Press.

artists to emerge as celebrities of international rank? The following bibliographic outline suggests a teaching format for examining this brief incident of cultural imperialism.

1950-1959: AMERICAN SOCIETY EMBRACES RHYTHM 'N' BLUES AND ROCK 'N' ROLL AS ITS POPULAR-MUSIC CULTURE

Teachers should begin this historical investigation by noting that during the fifties American society initiated a variety of major changes. Integration of blacks, challenges to several sources of traditional authority, the rise of sexual openness, increasing economic affluence, youthful rebellion, and other significant cultural themes had vast political and social implications in the sixties. Music functioned as both a catalyst and a reflector for many of these events. The following books are good sources of information on this era:

- Busnar, Gene. *It's Rock 'n' Roll: A Musical History of the Fabulous Fifties*. New York: Wandered, 1979.
- Gillett, Charlie. *The Sound of the City: The Rise of Rock and Roll*. New York: Outerbridge and Dienstfrey, 1970.
- Shapiro, Nat (ed.). *Popular Music: An Annotated Index of American Popular Songs: Volume One, 1950-1959*. New York: Adrian, 1964.
- Shaw, Arnold. *Honkers and Shouters: The Golden Years of Rhythm and Blues*. New York: Collier, 1978.
- Shaw, Arnold. *The Rockin' 50s: The Decade that Transformed the Pop Music Scene*. New York: Hawthorn, 1974.

1950-1963: BRITISH SOCIETY BECOMES A RECEPTIVE SITE FOR AMERICAN CULTURAL IMPERIALISM

There are many reasons why the United States was able to impose its popular-music culture on the United Kingdom. Anglo-American history, language similarity, British topography, established communication links from the trans-Atlantic telephone cable in 1956 to Telstar in 1962, international trade ties, newspapers, tourism, and the presence of U.S. soldiers from NATO contributed to the initiation and triumph of rock music in the British Isles. The following sources provide a wealth of information on this era:

- Leigh, Spencer. "Larry Parnes." *Record Collector* 122 (October 1989): pp. 86-88.
- Marwick, Arthur. *British Society Since 1945*. New York: Penguin, 1982.
- Reines, Bernard. "United Kingdom." In *Europe–Worldmark Encyclopedia of the Nations*. Edited by Louis Barron. New York: Harper & Row, 1963.
- Steele-Perkins, Crispan, and Richard Smith (comps.). *The Teds*. London: Traveling Light Photography, 1979.
- Watson, Ian. *Song and the Democratic Culture in Britain*. New York: St. Martin's, 1983.
- Watts, Michael. "The Call and Response of Popular Music: The Impact of American Pop Music in Europe." In *Superculture: American Popular Culture and Europe*. Edited by C. W. E. Bigsby. Bowling Green: Bowling Green University, 1975.

1960-1964: MAXIMUM AMERICAN DOMINATION OVER THE BRITISH POPULAR-MUSIC SYSTEM

The first five years of the 1960s demonstrated how American recording artists and popular songs totally dominated British popular-music charts. The irony, of course, is that Paul McCartney, Eric Burdon, Mick Jagger, John Lennon, Eric Clapton, Keith Richards, and other young British singers and bands learned their craft and developed their performing repertoires from the vinyl artifacts of an overseas culture. The following sources trace these developments:

- Barnes, Richard (comp.). *Mods!* London: Eel Pie, 1980.
- Chambers, Iain. *Urban Rhythms: Pop Music and Popular Culture*. New York: St. Martin's, 1985.
- Chapple, Steve, and Reebe Garofalo. *Rock 'n' Roll Is Here to Pay: The History and Politics of the Music Industry.* Chicago: Nelson-Hall, 1977.
- London, Herbert I. *Closing the Circle: A Cultural History of the Rock Revolution*. Chicago: Nelson-Hall, 1984.
- Pielke, Robert G. *You Say You Want a Revolution: Rock Music in American Culture*. Chicago: Nelson-Hall, 1986.
- Rice, Jo and Tim, Paul Gambaccini, and Mike Read (comps.). *The Guinness Book of British Hit Albums*. London: Guinness Superlatives, Ltd., 1983.

1962-1967: THE RISE OF THE BEATLES AND THE ROLLING STONES

The British Invasion in 1964, led by The Beatles and The Rolling Stones, demonstrated how effectively American cultural imperialism had transformed U.K. music into a reasonable, exportable facsimile of U.S. popular music. The following books and articles provide a good overview of the British Invasion years:

- Bacon, David and Norman Maslov. *The Beatles' England: There Are Places I'll Remember.* San Francisco: 910, 1982.
- Brown, Ashley. "The U.K. Rocks–Rock 'n' Roll Hit the Shores of Great Britain Like a Tidal Wave: Music Was Never the Same Again." *History of Rock* No. 7 (1982): pp. 121-123.
- Castleman, Harry, and Wally Podrazik. "The Case of the Belittled Beatles Tapes." *Stereo Review* XXXIX (November 1977): pp. 66-68.

- Colman, Stuart. *They Kept on Rockin': The Giants of Rock 'n' Roll.* Poole, Dorset, England: Blandford, 1982.

- DeWitt, Howard A. *The Beatles: Untold Tales.* Fremont: Horizon, 1985.

- Escott, Colin. "The Beatles on Stage–August 12, 1963." *Goldmine* No. 132 (August 16, 1985): pp. 16-18.

- Freeman, Robert. *Yesterday: The Beatles, 1963-1965.* New York: Holt, Rinehart, and Winston, 1983.

- Griffin, Alistair. *On the Scene at the Cavern.* London: Hamish Hamilton, 1964.

- Howlett, Kevin. *The Beatles at the BeeB, 1962-65: The Story.* London: British Broadcasting Corporation, 1982.

- Norman, Philip. *Symphony for the Devil: The Rolling Stones Story.* New York: Linden/Simon and Schuster, 1984.

- O'Grady, Terence J. *The Beatles: A Musical Evolution.* Boston: Twayne Publishers, 1983.

- Okun, Milton, Ed Caraeff et al. (comps.). *The Compleat Beatles: Volume One, 1962-1966.* New York: Delilah/ATV/Bantam, 1981.

- Paytress, Mark. "The Rolling Stones at the BBC." *Record Collector* No. 117 (May 1989): pp. 3-8.

- Pidgeon, John. "Blues in the Basement." *History of Rock* No. 30 (1982): pp. 598-600.

- Schultheiss, Tom (comp.). *The Beatles–A Day in the Life: The Day-by-Day Diary, 1960-1970.* New York: Quick Fox, 1981.

- Tamarkin, Jeff. "Roots of The Beatles: What Did They Listen To?" *Goldmine* No. 219 (December 16, 1988): pp. 95-96.

• Vollmer, Jurgen. *Rock 'n' Roll Times: The Style and Spirit of the Early Beatles and Their First Fans*. Woodstock: Overlook, 1983.

• Wells, John D. "Me and the Devil Blues: A Study of Robert Johnson and the Music of the Rolling Stones." *Popular Music and Society* IX (1983): pp. 17-24.

1964-1967: THE WHITE U.S. POT CALLING THE WHITE BRITISH KETTLE BLACK

The triumph of numerous British groups in the States was greeted by many American journalists, record-company executives, black artists, and elite snobs with anger, derision, and charges of blatant cultural copying. The public exposure, financial success, and creative opportunity to search for their own artistic voices launched The Beatles and The Rolling Stones on their own distinctive performing, songwriting, and culture defining careers. The following sources trace these developments:

• Almost Slim. "The Beatles Visit New Orleans." *Wavelength* No. 34 (August 1983): pp. 11-13.

• Aronowitz, Alfred G. "Yeah! Yeah! Yeah! Music's Gold Bugs: The Beatles." *Saturday Evening Post* CCXXXVII (March 21, 1964): pp. 30-35.

• Beckett, Alan. "The Stones." *New Left Review* XLVII (January/February 1968): pp. 24-29.

• "Beatles Success in U.S.: A Trend for the British?" *Variety* CCXXXIII (February 5, 1964): p. 46.

• Castleman, Harry, and Walter Podrazik. "The Beatles from Others." In *All Together Now: The First Complete Beatles Discography, 1961-1975*. New York: Ballantine, 1975.

• Clayson, Alan. *Call Up the Groups! The Golden Age of British Beat, 1962-1967*. Poole, Dorset, England: Blandford, 1985.

- Coleman, Ray. "1964: The Year of the Beatles." *Melody Maker* XXXIX (December 19, 1964); pp. 2-3ff.
- Cross, Colin, with Paul Kendall and Mick Farren (comps.). *Encyclopedia of British Beat Groups and Solo Artists of the Sixties*. London: Omnibus, 1980.
- Dove, Ian. "January 1-March 31, 1964: 90 Days that Shook the Industry." *Billboard* LXXXI (December 27, 1969): p. 126.
- Gabree, John. "The Beatles in Perspective." *Down Beat* XXXIV (November 16, 1967): pp. 20-22ff.
- Hellmann, John J., Jr. " 'I'm a Monkey': The Influence of the Black American Blues Argot on The Rolling Stones." *Journal of American Folklore* LXXXVI (October-December 1973): pp. 367-373.
- May, Chris. *British Beat*. London: Socion, 1974.
- Poirier, Richard. "Learning from The Beatles." *Partisan Review* XXXIV (Fall 1967): pp. 526-546.
- Price, June. "The Beatles' Arrival: Mania in the Media." *Goldmine* No. 224 (February 24, 1989): pp. 8, 93.
- Schaffner, Nicholas. *The British Invasion: From the First Wave to the New Wave*. New York: McGraw-Hill, 1983.
- "U.K. Rock 'n' Rollers Are Called Copycats." *Billboard* LXXVIII (June 19, 1965): p. 12.
- "U.S. Rocks and Reels from Beatles Invasion." *Billboard* LXXVI (February 15, 1964): p. 1ff.
- Watkins, R. "Rocking Redcoats Are Coming: Beatles Lead Massive Drive." *Variety* CCXXXIII (February 19, 1964): p. 1ff.

1967: THE WORLDWIDE INFLUENCE OF THE BEATLES

The release of *Sergeant Pepper's Lonely Hearts Club Band* by The Beatles in 1967 marked the high point in U.K. popular-music artistic creativity. It was, in many respects, the musical equivalent of a declaration of independence by a colonized nation (Great Britain) from its imperialist neighbor (The United States). Obviously, The Rolling Stones also continued to carve their own unique niche in international music as well. The following sources document The Beatles' and The Rolling Stones' artistic directions:

- Christgau, Robert. "The Rolling Stones." In *The Rolling Stone Illustrated History of Rock and Roll* (revised edition). Edited by Jim Miller. New York: Random House/Rolling Stone, 1980.

- Dalton, David. *The Rolling Stones: The First Twenty Years.* New York: Alfred A. Knopf, 1981.

- Doggett, Peter. "*Sgt. Pepper*–The Album." *Record Collector* 94 (June 1987): pp. 3-6.

- Friede, Goldie, Robin Titone, and Sue Weiner (comps.). *The Beatles: A to* Z. New York: Methuen, 1980.

- Frith, Simon. *Sound Effects: Youth, Leisure, and the Politics of Rock 'n' Roll.* New York: Pantheon, 1981.

- Greenfield, Jeff. "They Changed Rock, Which Changed the Culture, Which Changed Us." *New York Times Magazine* (February 16, 1975): pp. 12-13, 37ff.

- Harker, Dave. *One for the Money: Politics and Popular Song.* London: Hutchinson and Company, 1980.

- Mellers, Wilfrid. *The Music of The Beatles: Twilight of the Gods.* New York: Schirmer, 1973.

- Norman, Philip. *Shout! The Beatles in Their Generation.* New York: Fireside/Simon and Schuster, 1981.

- Okun, Milton, Ed. Caraeff et al. (comps.). *The Compleat Beatles: Volume Two, 1966-1970.* New York: Delilah/ATV/Bantam, 1981.

- Pichaske, David R. "Sustained Performances: *Sgt. Pepper's Lonely Hearts Club Band.*" In *The Beatles Reader: A Selection of Contemporary Views, News, and Reviews of The Beatles in Their Heyday.* Edited by Charles P. Nelses. Ann Arbor: Pierian, 1984.

- Reinhart, Charles. "*Sgt. Pepper's Lonely Hearts Club Band:* It's 20 Years Later Now . . . And Still a Landmark." *Goldmine* No. 182 (July 17, 1987): pp. 18-20.

- Schaffner, Nicholas. *The Boys from Liverpool: John, Paul, George, and Ringo.* New York: Methuen, 1980.

1950-1967: DISCOGRAPHIC RESOURCES ON AMERICAN AND BRITISH RECORDINGS

In order to trace the magnitude of American popular-music hegemony in Great Britain from 1950 to 1963 and the subsequent rise of United Kingdom performers to dominant roles on U.S. music charts from 1964 to 1967, the following reference guides are required:

- Aeppli, Felix (comp.). *Heart of Stone: The Definitive Rolling Stones Discography, 1962-1983.* Ann Arbor: Pierian, 1985.

- Carr, Roy. *The Rolling Stones: An Illustrated Record.* New York: Harmony, 1976.

- Carr, Roy, and Tony Tyler. *The Beatles: An Illustrated Record* (revised edition). New York: Harmony, 1978.

- Castleman, Harry, and Walter J. Podrazik (comps.). *All Together Now: The First Complete Beatles Discography, 1961-1975.* New York: Ballantine, 1975.

- Doggett, Peter. "Rolling Stones' U.K. Singles." *Record Collector* No. 30 (February 1983): pp. 4-13.

- Doggett, Peter. "The Rolling Stones' U.S. Singles." *Record Collector* No. 49 (September 1983): pp. 8-10.

- Rice, Jo and Tim, Paul Gambaccini, and Mike Read (comps.). *The Guinness Book of British Hit Singles* (second edition). London: Guinness Superlatives, 1979.

THE CHUM CHART BOOK

The CHUM Chart Book, 1957-1983: A Complete Listing of Every Charted Record. By Ron Hall. Rexdale, Ontario, Canada: Stardust, 1984. Illustrated. 345 pp.

The CHUM Chart Book presents 2,200 recording artists and 6,700 titles that have appeared on Toronto radio station CHUM's Top Fifty Records of the Week between May 27, 1957, and December 31, 1983. The text is divided into two sections. The "Artist" section (pp. 1-204) contains an alphabetical list of performers, with their hit tunes arranged chronologically. This section also displays the month, year, and total number of weeks the record spent on the CHUM chart, the peak charted position, and the record label and number of each charted disc. The "Index of Song Titles" section (p. 205-317) features an alphabetical listing of all CHUM-charted recordings. The remainder of the book offers specialty information–including a chronological listing of all number one records from 1957 ("All Shook Up" by Elvis Presley) through 1983 ("Say Say Say" by Paul McCartney and Michael Jackson), a list of charted LP and EP cuts (songs that were not released commercially as singles), and the most frequently charted performers who placed at least ten tunes on the CHUM charts. This resource guide is handsomely bound, clearly printed, and easy to understand.

What interesting facts or trends are revealed by the statistics in *The CHUM Chart Book*? James Brown–Macon, Georgia's powerhouse hitmaker and the undisputed godfather of soul–had 90 *Billboard*-charted Hot 100 songs between 1958 and 1977, but placed only nine tunes on the CHUM chart. Other popular U.S. artists who also fell short on the Canadian charts include Ray Charles, Wilson Pickett, Jerry Lee Lewis, Smokey Robinson and The Miracles, Kenny Rogers, Jimmy Reed, Sam Cooke, Aretha Franklin, and Charlie Rich. In contrast, Ronnie Hawkins, who compiled only three *Billboard* Hot 100 hits, placed 11 songs on the CHUM chart.

There also appears to be considerably fewer novelty tunes charted in Toronto, with such comic forces as Buchanan and Goodman, Allan Sherman, and Stan Freberg barely represented. However, several CHUM disc jockeys did achieve Canadian chart recognition while never gaining American *Billboard* listings.

Does Ron Hall's compilation of chart data have any significance beyond the offices of radio station CHUM (1050 AM)? Do the CHUM charts actually reflect the musical tastes of listeners and record buyers throughout southern Ontario? Will collectors who utilize chart and survey information perceive any major variations between popular music in Canada and the U.S.? Could any major U.S. city validly offer the popularity charts (or even the playlists) of its top radio station as the barometer of the nation's musical interest? These questions cannot be answered here. Yet, they remain part of a needed investigation into a larger issue: What *is* popular music?

The documentation of record-chart listings is an interesting phenomenon. Wisconsin analyst Joel Whitburn is the dean of survey surveyors. His Record Research, Inc. data factory churns out *Billboard*-based information from 1940 to the present on numerous styles (pop, country, easy listening, disco, and black contemporary) and speeds (33 1/3, 45, and 78 rpm's) of recordings. Recently, Texas historian/librarian Frank Hoffmann produced chart-list compilations for pop, country, and rhythm-and-blues singles from previously untapped *Cash Box* files. Across the Atlantic, British hit charts from *Record World*, *Melody Maker*, *Record Retailer*, *Record and Tape Retailer*, *Music Week*, and *Record Mirror* have provided statistical data for books by Clive Solomon, Charles Miron, Jo and Tim Rice, Paul Gambaccini, and Mike Read. Yet all national song charting remains suspect because (1) it is subject to the pressure and influence of major recording company propaganda; (2) it relies on urban-oriented reporting of commercial sales; and (3) it lacks the ability to reflect on the meaning of the long-term impact of particular artists or songs.

What alternatives exist to the national surveys of weekly record popularity? A particularly hardnosed materialistic viewpoint about identifying top recordings was expounded by Peter E. Berry in his 1977 study "*. . . And the Hits Just Keep on Comin'*." He contended that the only accurate barometer of a song's value is commercial merit. Berry eschewed survey charts from trade journals and radio stations in favor of "audited" gold records certified by the Recording Industry Association of America (RIAA). Regrettably, Berry overlooked the fact that RIAA statistics are either unavailable for some labels or simply unreliable for much of the 1950-1970 period. Such broad-scale assessments seem less than objective, consistent, or wholly valid.

The other end of the vinyl ranking spectrum–the subjective, personal analysis of individual recordings–is even less satisfying as a means of assessing the impact and value of particular releases. Most record collectors, for instance, tend to respond more favorably to scarcity and rarity rather than popularity. So do many music critics, who prefer to laud particular vocal or instrumental innovations, trend-setting or trend-defying performances, and other imaginative artistic strides. Obviously, there is no way to assess the song popularity system through the behaviors or interests of either esoteric collectors or technically oriented music buffs.

If objectivity is impossible and subjectivity is of little value, how should the popularity of contemporary recordings be defined? Realism demands the use of multiple perspectives. Whitburn and Hoffmann offer consistent, longitudinal national trade-journal data; the RIAA compiles statistics of the sales of vinyl commodities; and radio station chart lists reflect regional involvement in or reaction to or rebellion against mass-market trends. *The CHUM Chart Book* provides American and British music researchers with a new and potentially valuable Canadian perspective on contemporary songs. If nothing else, it is an intriguing tool for examining the Toronto reaction to such diverse Canadian-born international singing stars as Bryan Adams, Gordon Lightfoot, The Guess Who (and Burton Cummings), Joni Mitchell, The Diamonds, Paul Anka, Helen Reddy, Leonard Cohen, and Anne Murray.

One would hope that the appearance of the CHUM chart compilation and the availability of data-entry technology might stimulate several major U.S. radio stations to examine their own historical definitions (and survey charts) of popular music. This desire is academically self-serving, of course. It is far more beneficial to scholars, archivists, collectors, and teachers than to record-industry moguls or commercial radio-station managers. For this reason alone, *The CHUM Chart Book* must be acknowledged as a delightful, surprising, and helpful survey discography.

Beyond Ron Hall's new publication, readers interested in chartlist discographies may wish to contact Guinness Superlatives (London), Record Research (Wisconsin), and The Scarecrow Press (Metuchen) for further resources.

Chapter 13

Journalists and Critics

DAVE MARSH

Fortunate Son, by Dave Marsh. New York: Random House, 1985. 337 pp.

Dave Marsh is a rock 'n' roll evangelist. Readers of his *Fortunate Son* anthology will marvel at his religious intensity in depicting those who speak in sacred tongues (Bob Marley and Bruce Springsteen); those who have betrayed or abandoned the truth faith (Peter Frampton, Mike Love, Robbie Robertson, Mick Jagger, Doug Fleger, and the MTV production staff); early prophets (MC5, Bob Seger, Pete Townshend, and Sylvester Stewart); revivals and second comings (John Fogerty, Rudy Martinez, and James Brown); anointed preachers and other soul savers (Stevie Wonder, Smokey Robinson, Sam Phillips, and The Electrifying Mojo); and eternal lights (Marvin Gaye, James Jamerson, Elvis Presley, and Muddy Waters). Marsh's sacred text can spark born-again feelings: Rock Lives! (We're all fortunate sons for this fact.)

Religious metaphors aside, this is a spectacular journalistic review of contemporary American music, and the author readily acknowledges his personal and political biases throughout the book. *Fortunate Son* is structured in ten chapters, with previously published essays of 1970-1985 vintage presented in each of these chapters. Marsh has carefully edited these pieces and provides thought-provoking introductions to each essay. His transitional observations are genuinely helpful, and his insights are stimulating.

This review by B. Lee Cooper was originally published as "The Heart of Rock and Soul," *Michigan Academician* XXIII (Spring 1991): pp. 203-205. Reprint permission has been granted by the author.

Dave Marsh's writing style evokes intensely personal feelings. His Pontiac, Michigan, childhood and Detroit musical roots thunder across the pages. The heroes and events he fondly mentions–from the 1963 Smokey Robinson recording "You've Really Got a Hold on Me" and numerous MC5 concerts to private chats with Bob Seger and reveries about the talent of Marvin Gaye–clearly delineate the Motor City focus of his personal rock perspective. Yet Marsh is anything but provincial about his music. To him, rock 'n' roll is a national vehicle for fighting racism, sexism, profit-mongering conglomerates, stupid/inhumane/lethal politicos, and all forms of social and economic injustice. Marsh's idealism–born out of intellectual toughness rather than ideological rigidity or pantheistic mush–attacks bigotry, slavery (to wages, to political systems, and to outdated modes of thought), inconsistency, and hypocrisy. This man is difficult to please, and that's what makes his writing so special.

Marsh's credentials for presenting a text headlined by the bodacious subtitle "Criticism and Journalism by America's Best-Known Rock Writer" are reasonable. He has penned biographies on Bruce Springsteen, Elvis Presley, and The Who; he was founding editor of *Creem*, a former editor for *Rolling Stone*, and co-editor of *The Rolling Stone Record Guide*. The essays in *Fortunate Son* have been culled from such diverse literary sources as *Creem*, *Musician*, *The Record*, *Boston Phoenix*, *Rolling Stone*, *Film Comment*, and the author's own books. Duplication is minimal (although a Buddy Holly segment is repeated twice); the selection of topics is remarkably diverse; and the commentaries are lively, pointed, and logical. It is too bad that the Random House editorial staff failed to provide two helpful items: an alphabetized subject index to the entire book and a full bibliography of the published works of Dave Marsh. These additions would have completed an otherwise extremely well-constructed study.

Rock journalism is a terribly mixed bag, or (with apologies to Earl King) a trick bag. A critic often appears to be either a puppet or a cheerleader rather than an analyst or a commentator. However, among the thousands of concert attenders, record and book reviewers, and writers of biographies, there are only a handful of authors who really deserve to be anthologized. Dave Marsh is one. Others, including Peter Guralnick, Paul Williams, Michael Lydon, Jon Landau, and Greil Marcus, have already had portions of their journalistic works compiled and printed. But as the rock era's shadow lengthens (Marsh is somewhat sketchy about the lives of many key '50s rock 'n' rollers) and as copies of many fine rock magazines become less and less available to fans, scholars, teachers, musicians, critics, collectors, and popular-culture buffs, the words of the best rock writers deserve to be preserved. Marsh's self-designed text is a model for living authors, but posthumous commentaries should also be assembled.

Fortunate Son is the literary equivalent of a "Greatest Hits" LP album containing "Lucille" by Little Richard, "Whole Lotta Shakin' Goin' on" by Jerry Lee Lewis, "Mystery Train" by Elvis Presley, "In the Midnight Hour" by Wilson Pickett, "Mind Over Matter" by Nolan Strong and The Diablos, and "I Heard It Through the Grapevine" by Marvin Gaye. If you still believe in magic, then *Fortunate Son* is required reading.

The Heart of Rock and Soul: The 1001 Greatest Singles Ever Made, by Dave Marsh. New York: New American Library, 1989. 717 pp.

Although Marsh's credentials are awesome, one must be immediately skeptical about any author who subtitles a work "The 1001 Greatest Singles Ever Made." Dave Marsh deserves applause for just attempting to distill 40 years of recorded music into a precise set of rhythms, lyrics, and performers. Where he succeeds, he does so with insight, enthusiasm, and sound judgment; where he fails, he falls victim to his own enormous ego and to glaring omissions. *The Heart of Rock and Soul* is a study that should be read, debated, freely revised, and cherished as a kaleidoscopic vision of contemporary audio artistry.

In stating the obvious, Marsh brands himself as a revolutionary. He acknowledges the primacy of individual songs over either albums or compact discs. "Singles are the essence of rock and roll," he declares. "They occupy the center of all pop music that came after it. They're the stuff of our everyday conversations and debates about music, the totems that trigger our memories. Everyone who listens with half an ear must know this. But nobody writes as if it were true" (p. ix). Actually, several folk do write with this generally unacknowledged truth in mind. Charlie Gillett's *The Sound of the City: The Rise of Rock and Roll* (Outerbridge and Dienstfrey, 1970) is still the best singles-driven study available. Joel Whitburn's magnificent Record Research fact books also focus solely on singles. So do George Albert and Frank Hoffmann's book-length *Cashbox* surveys.

Other researchers have produced works that rely on single songs as key popular-music reflectors. B. Lee Cooper traces 15 socially significant topics found in 45-rpm recordings in *A Resource Guide to Themes in Contemporary American Song Lyrics, 1950-1985* (Greenwood, 1986); Bob Shannon and John Javna serve up tasty trivia about singles in *Behind the Hits: Inside Stories of Classic Pop and Rock and Roll* (Warner, 1986); and Fred Bronson tells delightful stories about the origins of each top-charted tune between 1955 and 1988 in the second edition of *The Billboard Book of Number One Hits* (Billboard, 1988). Other compilations also make singles the chief coin of rock's realm.

What Marsh is arguing against, of course, is the post-1967 tendency of journalists, reviewers, critics, scholars, deejays, and collectors to contend that 33 1/3-rpm recordings, especially so-called concept albums, are the true bearers of rock's heritage. Tom Hibbert's audacious *The Perfect Collection* (Proteus, 1982), which lists the 200 rock albums that everyone should own, is the kind of publication that Marsh despises. For Marsh, even The Beatles' remarkable *Sgt. Pepper* album is a collection of magnificent singles–"Lucy in the Sky with Diamonds," "A Little Help from My Friends," "When I'm Sixty-Four," and "Lovely Rita."

Once the primacy of the singles concept has been established, how well does Marsh do in selecting and describing the 1,001 "greatest" records over the past four decades? It's a mixed bag. Many of the songs he presents are incontestably trademarks of the rock era: "Satisfaction," "What'd I Say," "Respect," "Great Balls of Fire," "Johnny B. Goode," and "Billie Jean." But, regrettably, Marsh then glides off into the thin air of his own decision making, unfettered by record charts or the critical judgments of others. For example, he lists "Purple Haze" but not "Purple Rain"; "Bad Girls" but not "Bad to the Bone"; "Little Sister" but not "Little Queenie"; and "Walk This Way" but not "The Walk."

Other omissions are even more mind-boggling. It is hard to conceive the absence of the twice-charted garage-band tune "Tall Cool One" by The Wailers. Similarly inexplicable omissions include: "At

My Front Door (Crazy Little Mama)" by The El Dorados; "Irresistible You" by The Bobby Peterson Quintet; "Cry Baby" by Garnet Mimms and The Enchanters; "Slow Walk" by Sil Austin; "There's Something on Your Mind (Part Two)" by Bobby Marchan; and "I Like It Like That" by Chris Kenner. In the novelty-tune genre, neither "Ape Call" nor "Transfusion" by Nervous Norvus (Jimmy Drake) are mentioned. Neither are "The Flying Saucer" by Buchanan and Goodman or "The Streak" by Ray Stevens. If rock-era humor is sold short by Marsh, one fears that many rock-and-soul classics are doomed to his historical dungeon. Thus, if Marsh elects to leave out "Wild Thing" by The Troggs, one suspects that Tone Lōc's "Wild Thing" or the even more hilarious "Funky Cold Medina" don't have a prayer of scoring in this strangely skewed charting system. Will future slots be reserved for "When Love Comes to Town" by U2 (with B. B. King), "Simply Irresistible" by Robert Palmer, and "Roll With It" by Steve Winwood?

Finally, one must question not just omissions but a series of unexplainable inclusions in *The Heart of Rock and Soul.* The following songs are simply not part of any reasonable greatest-singles compendium: "Across the Street" by Lenny O'Henry; "Free Nelson Mandela" by Special AKA; "The Adventures of Grandmaster Flash on the Wheels of Steel" by Grandmaster Flash and The Furious Five; "Devil with a Blue Dress" by Shorty Long; "Hurt" by Elvis Presley; "Gina is a Coward" by Gino Washington; "I Don't Want To Go Home" by Southside Johnny and The Asbury Jukes; and "You Left the Water Running" by Otis Redding.

While one might be shocked by a few specific omissions, befuddled by certain inclusions, and confused by a couple of inappropriate attributions (such as listing "Twist and Shout" as a Beatles' tune rather than as an Isley Brothers' triumph), most of Marsh's study is absolutely ingenious. This is the saving grace of all of Marsh's literary work. His intellectual power, understanding of the sweep of rock history, insight into the machinations of the record industry, and personal access to performers, journalists, disc jockeys, and production personnel makes the majority of his comments pithy, perceptive, and powerful. Marsh is a driven man. Riding along with him requires insurance and a seat belt. But if one wishes to tour Rock City, then there is no better chauffeur than "Wild Dave."

Chapter 14

Mass Media

Throughout history, humankind has utilized both oral and written communications to transmit feelings of love and hate, to preserve documents of public significance and ideas of personal value, and to provide individuals and groups with resources for examining themselves and their predecessors. Both songs and books are central to historical investigation. We live at a time when different mediums of communication (radio, television, and motion pictures) dramatically affect, and in some cases even become, intellectual messages. Writers like Marshall McLuhan have speculated that the human senses, of which all media are merely extensions, function to configure the awareness and the experiences of each of us. Thus, the products of modern electronic technology frequently become the content of learning and understanding during late-twentieth-century America. When one medium of communication either comments on or draws its imagery from another medium, the perception of individuals is broadened by both the technology and the mediated thought. The ability of human beings to conceive and interpret ideas, issues, and problems through films, newspapers, magazines, radio programs, and television shows is often illustrated in popular-song lyrics.

MOTION PICTURES

In 1919, Billy Murray urged frustrated suitors to "Take Your Girlie to the Movies" if she can't be induced to cooperate at home. A

This essay by B. Lee Cooper originally appeared as "Communications Media" in *A Resource Guide to Themes in Contemporary American Song Lyrics, 1950-1985*. (Westport: Greenwood, 1986). Reprint permission has been granted by the author and The Greenwood Press Publishing Group, Inc.

decade later, a more amorous Belle Baker crooned, "If I Had a Talking Picture of You." By 1934, The Ziegfeld Follies introduced the universal idea "You Oughta Be in Pictures." Tony Alamo and Judy Johnson, singing with The Sammy Kay Orchestra in 1950, repeated the same sentiments. But it was Johnny "Scat" Davis, backed by Benny Goodman and his band in 1937, who trumpeted the most famous paean to the motion-picture capital–"Hooray for Hollywood." The silver screen was so deeply ingrained in American popular culture by the mid-twentieth century that many film celebrities' names were more readily recognized by the general public than those of wealthy businesspeople or successful politicians.

Between 1950 and 1985, motion pictures continued to hold a dominant position in American thought and life. Attendance at films is chronicled in a variety of recordings. Eddie Cochran urged his girl to join him at a "Drive-In Show"; he also suggested that they could enjoy undescribed adolescent delights while "Sittin' in the Balcony" in the very last row. Carl Perkins attempted to hide from the overly watchful eyes of a suspicious, gun-toting father by taking his girlfriend to a show in "Movie Magg." The Drifters echoed Cochran's suggestive sentiments in "Saturday Night at the Movies," while The Steve Miller Band reminisced about a first romance that began in the back seat of a car at the drive-in movie in "Circle of Love." The most humorous tale of movie-related teenage problems is recounted in "Wake Up Little Susie," where a couple falls asleep during a film and finally awakes to discover the movie's over, it's 4 a.m., and they're in deep trouble.

Motion pictures–aside from providing excuses for meeting friends and loved ones or for escaping from suspicious parents–offer a world of personal fantasy to each viewer. Individual satisfaction with film images varies greatly. In "Sad Movies (Make Me Cry)," Sue Thompson reflects on personal affairs that have failed, while in "Are You Getting Enough Happiness," Hot Chocolate notes that every time they go to the movies, all they see is happy love on the silver screen. Obviously, fantasy expectations often dictate interest in particular films. The most traditional hero-wins-out-over-villain scenes are laughingly recalled by The Coasters (and again by Ray Stevens) in the novelty tune "Along Came Jones." Bertie Higgins depicts his own love life in "Key Largo," when he contends that he and his girl had it all, just like Bogey and Bacall (who are only two of an innumerable list of movie stars who are mentioned in popular recordings). Marilyn Monroe was idealized by Teddy and The Twilights in "Woman Is a Man's Best Friend," while Kim Carnes used a distinctive facial feature to conjure up a mysterious female persona in "Bette Davis Eyes." And if Michael Jackson viewed "Billie Jean" as a beauty queen from the movie screen, he only echoed the thoughts of The Bellamy Brothers who, after admitting that they go to the movies to see Sophia Loren and Brigitte Bardot, still assert loyalty to their hometown girl in "You're My Favorite Star."

Hollywood offers a get-rich-quick, become-a-celebrity-overnight myth to many Americans. This idea is reinforced in films, through media hype on both radio and television, and by authentic (although statistically rare) instances of a pretty girl or handsome boy from Peoria achieving fame and fortune in Los Angeles. Chuck Berry and Elvis Presley described Southern California's movie sets as "The Promised Land" for aspiring performers. The Beatles and Buck Owens noted that all you've got to do to be successful in films is just "Act Naturally." The exciting West Coast lifestyle is lauded by Carl Perkins in "Hollywood City" and by Kool and The Gang in "Hollywood Swinging." But in the pursuit of John Stewart's "Gold" and in the excitement of chasing "Star Baby" with The Guess Who, the movie capital of America also harbors rejection, failure, and lost hope. These sentiments are contained in Gladys Knight and The Pips' "Midnight Train to Georgia," Eric Clapton's "Tulsa Time," and Don Williams' "If Hollywood Don't Need You (Honey, I Still Do)."

TELEVISION SHOWS

In terms of hourly viewing, Americans watch television to a far greater extent than they attend movie theaters. However, with the advent of cable movie networks, there has been considerable blurring of the notions of feature films versus TV programs as distinct media sources. Clearly, the ideas, images, personalities, and techniques of communication between motion pictures and television shows have dramatically overlapped since 1980. The Statler Brothers, in "A Child of the Fifties," nostalgically recall the early days of black-and-white broadcasting, when TV was their friend, particularly in the form of *I Love Lucy* and *Rin Tin Tin*. It is interesting to note that Lucille Ball reruns were united with a late-1970s dance fad in The Wilton Place Street Band's hit recording of "Disco Lucy (*I Love Lucy* Theme)."

The lyrical depiction of television as a social force varies significantly from 1950 to the present. The humor of The Coasters employing the arcane tricks of TV detectives while "Searchin'" for their missing sweetheart was echoed by The Olympics, who were frustrated by girls who prefer sitting at home watching lawmen and desperadoes in "Western Movies" to dating, dancing, and romancing. With considerable remorse, Mac Davis declared that you can't even look at TV these days without getting scared to death. Regrettably, the images presented in his "The Beer Drinkin' Song" are the product of contemporary visual horrors ranging from napalm atrocities in Vietnam to kidnapping and mass hysteria in Iran to saturation bombing in Lebanon to any number of war zones within American cities. Mac Davis concluded this early-1980s analysis by admitting that eyewitness news programs leave him abused and gasping for breath.

Only Don Henley's "Dirty Laundry" presents a more caustic indictment of broadcast journalism run amuck. Henley notes that TV news is presented by an attractive female reporter who can describe a grisly plane crash with a gleam in her eye. He notes that morbidity, scandal, sensationalism, death, and other subhuman values seem to motivate the ratings chase within the television news industry. Other recent recordings offer only two solutions to the constant flow of bad news. Junior rejoices that the TV's out of order so he won't see the news at ten in "Communication Breakdown," and Joe Jackson pleads with his girlfriend to leave the television and radio behind and go "Steppin' Out" for an evening unencumbered by reports of international warfare or domestic tragedy. The rock group Styx adopts George Orwell's 1984 vision of TV as a mind control device. In "High Times," they note with sinister fear that the "mind police" are coming.

RADIO BROADCASTS

In terms of public exposure, both motion pictures and television programs are overshadowed by ubiquitous radio broadcasts. From the morning bedside chatter of a wake-up disc jockey, to a day-long experience of transistorized portable tunes, news, and weather reports, to heading home in a car humming with AM-FM stereo, to unwinding in the early evening with AOR/Country Rock/MOR/Rock sounds, and, finally, to retiring to quiet sounds by The Beatles, Bread, and Three Dog Night, radio is omnipresent. It is undeniable, though, that there is an element of public unrest about the "dirty laundry" being pushed by the radio as well as by the video media. Songs such as "Silent Night/Seven O'Clock News" by Simon and Garfunkel and "In Times Like These" by Barbara Mandrell convey this feeling.

Somehow, there is a more controllable sense and a more personalized connection between listeners and broadcast celebrities in lyrics that assess radio as a communication medium. Mark Dinning notes that the essentials of pop radio programming are "Top Forty, News, Weather, and Sports." Throughout the 1950-1985 period, various personalities have ruled the airwaves. From Alan Freed and Wolfman Jack to Norm N. Nite and Casey Kasem, the identifiable "platter chatter" of a friendly disc jockey has set the tempo for modern musical messages. Rene and Angela comment fondly about the comforting voice on the radio, your favorite D.J., just going with the flow in "Banging the Boogie." Other salutes to disc jockeys include "Kansas City Star" by Roger Miller, "Clap for the Wolfman" by The Guess Who, and "#1 Dee Jay" by Goody Goody. The 1959-1960 scandal involving bribes being paid to radio-station managers and disc jockeys to promote specific records is humorously chronicled by Stan Freberg in "The Old Payola Roll Blues." But for the most part, radio personalities (even the zany fictional jocks at *WKRP in Cincinnati*) deliver satisfying musical interludes to individuals who are "Wired for sound" and to those listening to "FM (No Static at All)."

There is an overtly sexist, or at least somewhat sexy, tone to other images of broadcast music. Freddy Cannon describes a radio-listening fanatic as "Transistor Sister." And Dexy's Midnight Runners remind their date in "Come on Eileen" that Johnny Ray sounded sad on the radio as he moved a million hearts. This kind of airplay foreplay is addressed by Don Williams in "Listen to the Radio" and by The Younger Brothers, who reminisce about how good their date looked with "Nothing But the Radio on."

PRINT MEDIA

Beyond the realm of the electronic media, lyrical attention has also focused on newspapers, books, and magazines. However, recordings illustrating print-media activities are far less numerous than those examining or alluding to motion pictures, television shows, or radio programs. This is perhaps indicative of the nonprint style of the post-1960 period, particularly in regard to the more youthful generation. Neil Diamond observes that heartbreak isn't a "Front Page Story" and probably won't even make the papers, while Christopher Cross says just the opposite in "No Time for Talk." Although The Silhouettes seemed content to search the want ads just to "Get a Job," Rupert Holmes felt compelled to seek a new relationship through a classified newspaper ad in "Escape (The Piña Colada Song)." Beauty is assessed by The J. Geils Band in terms of making a magazine "Centerfold." For George Jones in "Shine on (Shine All Your Sweet Love on Me)," the judgment that his girl will never grace the centerfold of *Playboy* magazine is followed by his criterion for physical excellence: in her jeans, she's as sexy as a dream. The ultimate print-market achievement for a rock band is not just to be lauded in *Playboy*, *Variety*, *Billboard*, *Cash Box*, or *The New Musical Express*. If Dr. Hook and his band speak for most, the ultimate goal is to have their picture on "The Cover of 'Rolling Stone'."

Below is a selected discography of tunes from 1950 to 1985 that have drawn on media images for their lyrics.

Motion Pictures

- "Act Naturally"
  (Capitol 5498)
  The Beatles (1965)

- "Along Came Jones"
  (Atco 6141)
  The Coasters (1959)

- "Along Came Jones"
  (Monument 1150)
  Ray Stevens (1969)

- "Are You Getting Enough Happiness"
  (EMI America 8143)
  Hot Chocolate (1982)

- "'B' Movie"
  (Arista 0647)
  Gil Scott-Heron (1981)

- "Bette Davis Eyes"
  (EMI American 8077)
  Kim Carnes (1981)

- "Billie Jean"
  (Epic 03509)
  Michael Jackson (1983)

- "Circle of Love"
  (Capitol 5086)
  The Steve Miller Band (1982)

- "Drive-In Show"
  (Liberty 55087)
  Eddie Cochran (1957)

- "Gold"
  (RSO 931)
  John Stewart (1979)

- "Good Guys Only Win in the Movies"
  (Bamboo 109)
  Mel and Tim (1970)

- "Hollywood"
  (MGM 13039)
  Connie Francis (1961)

- "Hollywood"
  (ABC 12269)
  Rufus, featuring Chaka Khan (1977)

- "Hollywood"
  (Columbia 10679)
  Boz Scaggs (1978)

- "Hollywood"
  (Epic 02755)
  Shooting Star (1982)

- "Hollywood City"
  (Columbia 42045)
  Carl Perkins (1961)

- "Hollywood Hot"
  (20th Century 2215)
  Eleventh Hour (1975)

- "Hollywood Nights"
  (Capitol 4618)
  Bob Seger and The Silver Bullet Band (1978)

- "Hollywood Swinging"
  (DeLite 561)
  Kool and The Gang (1974)

- "If Hollywood Don't Need You (Honey, I Still Do)"
  (MCA 52152)
  Don Williams (1982)

- "If You Could Read My Mind"
  (Reprise 0974)
  Gordon Lightfoot (1970)

- "Just Like in the Movies"
  (Swan 4010)
  The Upbeats (1958)

- "Key Largo"
  (Kat Family 02524)
  Bertie Higgins (1981)

- "Last of the Silver Screen Cowboys"
  (Warner Brothers 50035)
  Rex Allen, Jr. (1982)

- "Like an Old Time Movie"
  (Ode 105)
  Scott McKenzie (1967)

- "Midnight Train to Georgia"
  (Buddah 383)
  Gladys Knight and The Pips (1973)

- "Movie Day"
  (Kapp 936)
  Don Scardino (1968)

- "Movie Magg"
  (Flip 501)
  Carl Perkins (1955)

- "Movie Star Song"
  (Epic 10640)
  Georgie Fame (1970)

- "The Movies"
  (Mercury 73877)
  The Statler Brothers (1977)

- "Norma Jean Wants To Be a Movie Star"
  (Polydor 14312)
  Sundown Company (1976)

- "Pop Goes the Movies"
  (Arista 0660)
  Meco (1982)

- "Promised Land"
  (Chess 1916)
  Chuck Berry (1965)

- "Promised Land"
  (RCA PB-10074)
  Elvis Presley (1974)

- "Sad Movies (Make Me Cry)"
  (Hickory 1153)
  Sue Thompson (1961)

- "Saturday Night at the Movies"
  (Atlantic 2260)
  The Drifters (1964)

- "Say Goodbye to Hollywood"
  (Columbia 02518)
  Billy Joel (1981)

- "Sittin' in the Balcony"
  (Liberty 55056)
  Eddie Cochran (1957)

- "Star Baby"
  (RCA 0217)
  The Guess Who (1974)

- "Tulsa Time"
  (RSO 1039)
  Eric Clapton (1980)

- "Wake Up Little Susie"
  (Cadence 1337)
  The Everly Brothers (1957)

- "Wake Up Little Susie"
  (Warner Brothers 50053)
  Simon and Garfunkel (1982)

- "Woman Is a Man's Best Friend"
  (Swan 4102)
  Teddy and The Twilights (1962)

- "You're My Favorite Star"
  (Warner/Curb 49815)
  The Bellamy Brothers (1981)

Newspapers, Books, and Magazines

- "Centerfold"
  (EMI America 8102)
  The J. Geils Band (1981)

- "The Cover of 'Rolling Stone'"
  (Columbia 45732)
  Dr. Hook (1972)

- "Escape (The Piña Colada Song)"
  (Infinity 50035)
  Rupert Holmes (1979)

- "Front Page Story"
  (Columbia 03801)
  Neil Diamond (1983)

- "Get a Job"
  (Ember 1029)
  The Silhouettes (1958)

- "The Girl on Page 44"
  (Columbia 41310)
  The Four Lads (1959)

- "Headline News"
  (Ric-Tic 114)
  Edwin Starr (1966)

- "A Little Good News"
  (Capitol 5263)
  Anne Murray (1983)

- "Movie Magazine, Stars in Her Eyes"
  (Playboy 6043)
  Barbi Benton (1975)

- "No Time for Talk"
  (Warner Brothers 29662)
  Christopher Cross (1983)

- "Put It in a Magazine"
  (Highrise 2001)
  Sonny Charles (1982)

- "Shine on (Shine All Your Sweet Love on Me)"
  (Epic 03489)
  George Jones (1983)

- "Want Ads"
  (Hot Wax 7011)
  Honey Cone (1971)

Radio

- "Banging the Boogie"
  (Capitol 5220)
  Rene and Angela (1974)

- "Clap for the Wolfman"
  (RCA 0324)
  The Guess Who (1974)

- "Come on Eileen"
  (Mercury 76189)
  Dexy's Midnight Runners (1983)

- "Dear Mr. D.J. Play It Again"
  (Mercury 71852)
  Tina Tobin (1961)

- "'DJ' Man"
  (Prelude 8066)
  Secret Weapon (1983)

- "FM (No Static at All)"
  (MCA 40894)
  Steely Dan (1978)

- "H.A.P.P.Y. Radio"
  (20th Century 2408)
  Edwin Starr (1979)

- "In Times Like These"
  (MCA 52206)
  Barbara Mandrell (1983)

- "Juke Box Baby"
  (RCA 6427)
  Perry Como (1956)

- "Juke Box Hero"
  (Atlantic 4017)
  Foreigner (1982)

- "Kansas City Star"
  (Smash 1998)
  Roger Miller (1965)

- "Last Night a D.J. Saved My Life"
  (Sound New York 602)
  Indeep (1983)

- "Listen to the Radio"
  (MCA 52037)
  Don Williams (1982)

- "Love on the Airwaves"
  (Planet 47921)
  Night (1981)

- "Mexican Radio"
  (I.R.S. 9912)
  Wall of Voodoo (1983)

- "Mr. D.J. (5 for the D.J.)"
  (Atlantic 3289)
  Aretha Franklin (1975)

- "Nothing But the Radio On"
  (MCA 52076)
  The Younger Brothers (1982)

- "#1 Dee Jay"
  (Atlantic 3504)
  Goody Goody (1978)

- "The Old Payola Roll Blues"
  (Capitol 4329)
  Stan Freberg (1960)

- "Old Songs"
  (Juana 3700)
  Frederick Knight (1981)

- "Old Time Rock and Roll"
  (Capitol 5276)
  Bob Seger and The Silver Bullet Band (1983)

- "On the Radio"
  (Casablanca 2236)
  Donna Summer (1980)

- "Play That Beat Mr. D.J."
  (Tommy Boy 836)
  G.L.O.B.E. and Whiz Kid (1983)

- "A Prayer and a Juke Box"
  (End 1047)
  Little Anthony and The Imperials (1959)

- "Radio Activity (Part I)"
  (Sutra 126)
  Royalcash (1983)

- "Radio Free Europe"
  (I.R.S. 9916)
  R.E.M. (1983)

- "Radio Ga Ga"
  (Capitol 5317)
  Queen (1984)

- "Radio Man"
  (Island 791)
  World's Famous Supreme Team (1984)

- "Rock Radio"
  (Capitol 4996)
  Gene Dunlap (1981)

- "Rockin' Radio"
  (Arista 9088)
  Tom Browne (1983)

- "Silent Night/Seven O'Clock News"
  (Columbia Album)
  Simon and Garfunkel (1966)

- "Sleepin' with the Radio On"
  (Epic 02421)
  Charly McClain (1981)

- "Song on the Radio"
  (Arista 0389)
  Al Stewart (1979)

- "The Spirit of Radio"
  (Mercury 76044)
  Rush (1981)

- "That Old Song"
  (Arista 0616)
  Ray Parker, Jr. and Raydio (1981)

- "Pop Forty, News, Weather and Sports"
  (MGM 12980)
  Mark Dinning (1961)

- "Transistor Sister"
  (Swan 4078)
  Freddy Cannon (1961)

- "Union of the Snake"
  (Capitol 5290)
  Duran Duran (1983)

- "Video Killed the Radio Star"
  (Island 49114)
  The Buggles (1979)

- "Voice on the Radio"
  (Montage 1210)
  Conductor (1982)

- "Who Listens to the Radio"
  (Arista 0468)
  The Sports (1979)

- "Wired for Sound"
  (EMI American 8095)
  Cliff Richard (1981)

- "WKRP in Cincinnati"
  (MCA 51205)
  Steve Carlisle (1981)

- "You Can't Judge a Book by the Cover"
  (Checker 1019)
  Bo Diddley (1962)

- "You Turn Me on, I'm a Radio"
  (Asylum 11010)
  Joni Mitchell (1972)

Television

- "The Beer Drinkin' Song"
  (Mercury 2355)
  Mac Davis (1982)
- "A Child of the Fifties"
  (Mercury 76184)
  The Statler Brothers (1982)
- "Communication Breakdown"
  (Mercury 812397)
  Junior (1983)
- "Dirty Laundry"
  (Asylum 69894)
  Don Henley (1982)
- "Disco Lucy (*I Love Lucy* Theme)"
  (Island 078)
  The Wilton Place Street Band (1977)
- "High Time"
  (A&M 2568)
  Styx (1983)
- "Love Busted"
  (Capricorn 5139)
  Billy "Crash" Craddock (1982)
- "Searchin'"
  (Atco 6087)
  The Coasters (1957)
- "Star on a TV Show"
  (AVCO 4549)
  The Stylistics (1975)

- "Steppin' Out"
  (A&M 2428)
  Joe Jackson (1982)

- "T.V. Mama"
  (Casablanca 814217)
  Leon Haywood (1983)

- "TV Mama"
  (Atlantic 1016)
  Joe Turner (1953)

- "Video Baby"
  (Boardwalk 179)
  Earons (1983)

- "Western Movies"
  (Demon 1508)
  The Olympics (1958)

Chapter 15

Memorabilia and Collectibles

ELVIS PRESLEY

The Elvis Catalog: Memorabilia, Icons, and Collectibles Celebrating the King of Rock 'n' Roll, by Lee Cotten. Garden City: Doubleday, 1987. Illustrated. 255 pp.

Rock memorabilia auctions conducted in London, New York, and Los Angeles have featured all imaginable items from the personal lives and professional careers of John Lennon, Paul McCartney, and other contemporary-music luminaries. Sacramento-based scholar Lee Cotten has assembled a well-illustrated, chronologically organized guide to Elvis icons and collectibles. This study was authorized by "Elvis Presley Enterprises," whose commercial authorization probably opened the door for Cotten to examine, analyze, photograph, and secure prices on the broadest scope of Elvis memorabilia.

The Elvis Catalog is divided into six chapters. These segments represent and illustrate unequal portions of Elvis' early life, his singing and motion picture career, and his post-burial celebrity. "The Early Years" (pp. 12-45) cover everything from Tupelo, Mississippi, bumper stickers to the December 1956 issue of *16 Magazine*. "The Phenomenon Explodes" (pp. 46-94) features Elvis drinking glasses, *Love Me Tender* movie posters, and a 1958 "Elvis and the Colonel [Parker]" Christmas postcard. "Follow That

---

These reviews by B. Lee Cooper were originally published as "The Elvis Catalog," *Popular Music and Society* XIII (Fall 1989): pp. 97-98 and "Directory of Popular Culture Collections," *Journal of Popular Culture* XXIII (Fall 1989): pp. 163-164. Reprint permission has been granted by the author and The Popular Press.

Dream" (pp. 94-140) presents Elvis bubble-gum card wrappers, 1959 Gold Standard picture sleeves, and a burnished-steel Elvis medallion. "Viva Las Vegas" (pp. 141-182) reviews Las Vegas Hilton postcards, 1969 *Rolling Stone* magazines, and stuffed Elvis Presley hound dogs. "The Final Curtain" (pp. 183-217) offers Elvis concert pennants, numerous bootleg albums, and a gold beretta. Finally, "The King Lives On" (pp. 218-252) features such post-1977 items as the front-page obituary of Elvis from *The Memphis Press-Scimitar*; pewter, porcelain, and plaster busts of Elvis; and 1978 Elvis bubble-gum cards. Cotten provides both color and black-and-white illustrations for nearly every item he depicts.

Although any hack memorabilia merchandiser could have assembled a colorful picture catalog of Presleyanna, the historical expertise of Lee Cotten makes *The Elvis Catalog* a very special guide. This resource compilation is a model for detailing and portraying rock collectibles.

POPULAR CULTURE COLLECTIONS

Directory of Popular Culture Collections, compiled by Christopher D. Geist, Ray B. Browne, Michael T. Marsden, and Carole Palmer. Phoenix, Arizona: Oryx, 1989. 234 pp.

This resource-identification guide contains information about 667 popular-culture collections located in the United States and Canada. Presented alphabetically by state and province, the authors explore special materials from the (Birmingham) Alabama Sports Hall of Fame and Museum (p. 1) and the (Sioux Falls, South Dakota) Center for Western Studies (p. 143) to the (Whitehorse) Yukon Territory Archives (p. 178). Each citation features the full local address of the collection, the main contact person, the hours of operation, the degree of public or scholarly accessibility, and any special considerations concerning resource availability. A brief description of all special materials featured in each archive is also provided.

For music enthusiasts, the *Directory* is a goldmine. The compilers list multiple resource locations for music collections featuring blues (9), Cajun (2), country and western (7), folk (35), gospel (8), jazz

(19), popular (52), and rock 'n' roll (17). Single archival holdings are reported for new wave, punk, reggae, and soul. Beyond genre identification, ethnic and national music resources are also cited: Africa (2), American Indians (2), Blacks (6), British (3), Canada (5), Hawaii (1), and West Indies (1). The magnificent holdings of the Bowling Green State University Music Library and Sound Recordings Archive, the University of Mississippi Blues Archive, Tulane University's William Ransom Hogan Jazz Archives, and the County Music Foundation Library and Media Center are amply depicted too. What was once a very restricted audio-resource preserve of private record collectors is now becoming an area for intercollegiate scholarly research on an international scale.

This volume is similarly valuable to students of advertising, art, cartoons, comic books, film, magazines, oral history, postcards, posters, science fiction, and hundreds of other popular-culture fields. Over the next ten years, the number of archival sites will likely increase dramatically as private collectors recognize both the economic advantages and the preservation stability of donating items to scholarly collections. Hopefully, Christopher Geist and his colleagues will be ready with a second edition of this *Directory* by 1999.

Chapter 16

Nursery Rhymes

Music educators often feel trapped. Each day, they encourage students to investigate Bach, Beethoven, or Mozart; yet they cannot escape classroom references to the latest radio or MTV renderings by Eric Clapton, Madonna, or Bruce Springsteen. Too often, this musical dichotomy is characterized as a conflict between good and evil, a battle over quality and squalor, or a war of high art against commercialism. A more constructive instructional perspective should emphasize the learning potential inherent in *all* musical expression, including popular music and folk songs. Since the potential of classical music is already reinforced in all graduate programs, this chapter suggests teaching methods, audio resources, and bibliographical materials designed to help harried music teachers deal with and utilize oral traditions found in rock-era songs. Hopefully, recognition of the potential value of examining popular songs that borrow from nursery rhymes or folk conventions may lead students to be less surly and thus allow teachers to be more effective.

Lyricists of popular songs derive their ideas from every imaginable source.[1] They often adapt and reinterpret traditional characters and themes from established cultural artifacts. During the past four decades, scores of *Billboard*-charted songs have utilized characters and images from children's literature to define lyrical passages.

A portion of this essay by B. Lee Cooper was originally entitled "Them Three Little Pigs Done Got Hip! Adaptations of Children's Literature to Commercial Song Lyrics." It was presented at the 40th Annual Convention of the Michigan College English Association on October 5, 1991. Reprint permission has been granted by the author. For a more detailed examination of this topic, see B. Lee Cooper, "Nursery Rhymes and Fairy Tales," in *Popular Music Perspectives: Ideas, Themes, and Patterns in Contemporary Lyrics* (Bowling Green: Bowling Green State University Popular Press, 1991), pp. 155-171.

Most scholars who examine the lyrical content of modern music tend to concentrate on predetermined social issues such as courtship, death, education, and women's roles.[2] Other analysts investigate specific historical periods or significant individual events cited in particular recordings.[3] It is rare to encounter studies searching lyrics for the sources of images, ideas, allegories, and metaphors from classic literary sources or from longstanding oral traditions.[4] The information assembled in Table A illustrates literature-to-lyric transition. It is important to note that sources such as The Holy Bible, Shakespeare's plays, and books by Lewis Carroll and Charles Dickens are freely intermingled with popular culture references to television programs, motion pictures, and comic strips in the eclectic scheme of song lyrics.

TABLE A

SELECTED ILLUSTRATIONS OF LITERARY RESOURCES ADAPTED FOR THE LYRICS OF POPULAR SONGS, 1950-1990

Title of Popular Recording (Record Company and Number)	Year of Release	Resource for Images or Illustrations in Song Title or Lyric
1. "Adam and Eve" (ABC-Paramount 10082)	1960	Old Testament
2. "Alice in Wonderland" (RCA 8137)	1963	Lewis Carroll's *Alice's Adventures in Wonderland*
3. "Alley-Oop" (Lute 5905)	1960	Newspaper Comic Strip
4. "The Bible Tells Me So" (Coral 61467)	1955	New Testament
5. "Garden of Eden" (Vik 0226)	1956	Old Testament
6. "Guitarzan" (Monument 1131)	1969	Edgar Rice Burroughs' *Tarzan of the Apes*

7. "House at Pooh Corner" (United Artists 50769)	1971	A.A. Milne's *The House at Pooh Corner*
8. "(Just Like) Romeo and Juliet" (Golden World 9)	1964	William Shakespeare's *Romeo and Juliet*
9. "Magic Carpet Ride" (Dunhill 4161)	1968	"Aladdin and the Wonder Lamp" from *The 1,001 Arabian Nights*
10. "Oliver Twist" (Spiral 1407)	1962	Charles Dickens' *Oliver Twist*
11. "The Return of The Red Baron" (Laurie 3379)	1967	Newspaper Comic Strip by Charles Schulz
12. "Rip Van Winkle" (Roulette 4541)	1964	Washington Irving's *Rip Van Winkle*
13. "Tom Sawyer" (Mercury 76109)	1981	Mark Twain's *The Adventures of Tom Sawyer*
14. "Turn! Turn! Turn!" (Columbia 43424)	1965	Old Testament
15. "White Rabbit" (RCA 9248)	1967	Lewis Carroll's *Alice's Adventures in Wonderland*

Beyond the realm of traditional literature, contemporary lyricists are also influenced by the broad variety of children's stories, games, toys, chants, fads, mythical heroes, and nonsense word play. That such ephemeral popular culture material informs lyrical content is hardly surprising. Nostalgia is not limited to middle-aged men and women. Familiar lines from childhood experiences, linked to powerful rhythm bases, are immensely attractive to teenage record buyers. This observation is not meant to imply that *every* childhood game or *every* personal experience can be translated into a pop hit. Still, the tendency to utilize youthful ideas and verbal play to create lyrical images is evident in songs listed in Table B.

TABLE B

SELECTED ILLUSTRATIONS OF CHILDHOOD GAMES AND VERBAL TERMS ADAPTED TO THE TITLES AND LYRICS OF POPULAR SONGS, 1950-1990

Title of Popular Recording (Record Company and Number)	Year of Release	Resource for Images or Illustrations in Song Title or Lyric
1. "ABC" (Motown 1163)	1970	Alphabet Game
2. "Double Dutch Bus" (WMOT 5356)	1981	Jump Rope Chant
3. "Finders Keepers, Losers Weepers" (Wand 171)	1965	Children's Chant
4. "Hide and Go Seek" (Mala 451)	1962	Children's Game
5. "Hop Scotch" (Canadian American 124)	1961	Children's Game
6. "The Hula Hoop Song" (Roulette 4106)	1958	Child's Toy
7. "Liar, Liar" (Soma 1433)	1965	Children's Chant
8. "Pin the Tail on the Donkey" (Columbia 43527)	1966	Children's Game
9. "Pop Goes the Weasel" (London 9501)	1961	Children's Game
10. "Rubber Ball" (Liberty 55287)	1960	Child's Toy
11. "Simon Says" (Buddah 24)	1968	Children's Game
12. "Skip a Rope" (Monument 1041)	1967	Children's Game
13. "Sticks and Stones" (ABC-Paramount 10118)	1960	Children's Tease

Tables A and B constitute a lengthy preamble for the remainder of this chapter. Although it is obvious that many song titles and lyric lines are directly linked to childhood experiences, few sources are as significant as nursery rhymes and fairy tales.[5] Simple poetry from distant times continues to fuel our imaginations; humorous tales of rabbits and wolves, farmers and puppets, and Jacks, Jills, and Kings are part of the longstanding oral tradition of American society. The adaptation of these stories to popular recordings occurs in varying ways. First, a catchy melody and rhythm pattern are added. Second, characters from the rhymes are translated into a story setting suitable for a two-and-a-half minute vocal recitation. Finally, the story is told not by a loving grandparent, a mother, a father, or a babysitter, but by a commercial recording artist.

Popular music's use of nursery rhymes and other childhood tales is quite distinctive. The mere recitation of a particular character's name–Little Jack Horner, The Pied Piper, or Old MacDonald–often symbolizes a distinctive attitude or specific set of behaviors. The assumption is that everyone listening to the recorded lyric understands the implied meaning undergirding the fictional character's personality. Great latitude is also permitted in retelling a fairy tale or nursery rhyme. Double entendre humor is often built into the updated lyrical children's stories. Wolves are two-legged women chasers; Red Riding Hood is a sleek, sexy, fleeting object of libidinal desire. The delivery styles of artists such as The Big Bopper, Sam the Sham and The Pharoahs, and The Coasters are fashioned in accord with the vocal extremes and oral pyrotechnics that typify the very best children's storytellers. No hoots, howls, huffs, puffs, snarls, wails, or giggles are spared.

The remainder of this chapter outlines the adaptations of four children's tales to the lyrics of several popular recordings. A selected discography containing more than 50 records arranged alphabetically according to nursery rhyme or fairy tale title is also presented in Table C.

JACK THE GIANT KILLER

When good King Arthur reigned, there lived near the land's end of England, in the county of Cornwall, a farmer

> who had only one son called Jack . . . One day Jack happened to be at the town hall when the magistrates were sitting in council about the giant. He asked, "What reward will be given to the man who kills the Cormoran?" "The giant's treasure," they said, "will be the reward."

Except for the opening "Fe, Fi, Fo, Fum" chant, drawn directly from the mythic giant who claimed that he could smell the blood of an Englishman, The Coasters offer no other direct reference to this fairy tale. Nevertheless, the iconoclastic "Charlie Brown" is undeniably a contemporary anti-establishment hero. Charlie Brown confronts the giant dimensions of public school bureaucracy, and lives to tell the tale. He breaks rules by smoking in the auditorium, by gambling in the gymnasium, by throwing spitballs in the classroom, by writing on the wall, and by goofing in the hallways. Charlie Brown even has the audacity to call his English teacher "Daddy-O." This defiance of authority is reflected by the main character's mocking refrain: "Why is everybody always picking on me?" The Cormoran-like authoritarianism of the public school environment is thus short-circuited by a wily, daffy, Jack-of-all-mischief.

LITTLE RED RIDING HOOD

> There was once upon a time a little village girl, the prettiest ever seen or known, of whom her mother was dotingly fond. Her Grandmother was even fonder of her still, and had a little red hood made for the child, which suited her so well that wherever she went she was known by the name of Little Red Riding Hood. . . .

With introductory wolf-like howls, Sam the Sham greets a big-eyed, full-lipped "Li'l Red Riding Hood" and escorts her through the spooky old woods, carefully camouflaged in his best sheep-suit. What a big heart he has! The initial physical attraction continues throughout the recording, which ends prior to the couple's arrival at Grandma's house. In contrast to that woodsy setting, The Big Bopper comes calling directly at Red's home, claiming that he has heard about her good looks from the Three Little Pigs. Using a catchy bing-bang-biddley-bang knock punctuated by threats to huff and puff and blow her house down, The Bopper (admitting that he's actually the notorious Big Bad Wolf of the neighborhood) pleads with the young lady for some personal attention. His stated desire is to shake the shack with rock 'n' rollin' Red until her grandma returns. But "Little Red Riding Hood" refuses his insistent pleas to go tick-a-locka, tick-a-locka and let him in.

Dee Clark also describes a wolf who wants to rock 'n' roll. But this crooning lobo follows the traditional fairy tale more closely by putting Grandma out of her house and then surprising Red with his big eyes and big arms. Although "Little Red Riding Hood" remains an undescribed delicacy in Clark's lyrical version, the conclusion of his story is left to the listener's imagination.

Meanwhile, The Coasters deliver an upbeat, hepcat story about a red-caped chick that *every* wolf desires. In "Ridin' Hood" the heroine is spied on her way to Grandma's house with a sack full of goodies. Her groovy motivation attracts an ugly wolf who seeks to become her chaperon. "Later dad," she responds. Although the cunning wolf dashes ahead to Grandma's house, Granny is prepared for the intruder and whomps him on the head ten times with her cane. The wounded wolf flees the unfriendly scene howling into the nearby woods.

Finally, in a parody of Jack Webb's popular "Dragnet" series, Stan Freberg investigates a gun-toting "Little Blue Riding Hood," ties Grandma up in order to get the facts on the sweet-talking, goodies ring participant, and then arrests the little female thief and her elderly relative.

With the exception of Freberg's bizarre detective yarn, all lyrical references to Little Red Riding Hood are oriented toward potential sexual involvement. The carnivore in each story is attracted by the prey's shapely frame; he desires a dance, a walk, or some other form of companionship as a prelude to further physical involvement. No notion of eating Grandma or stealing baked goodies is considered or communicated. Thus the traditional guidelines of "don't talk to strangers" evolves into a more updated, anti-chauvinist theme concerning male lasciviousness toward lonely, innocent young women.

MARY'S LITTLE LAMB

Mary had a little lamb,
Its fleece was white as snow;
And everywhere that Mary went,
The lamb was sure to go. . . .

The Coasters recite the first four lines of the original nursery rhyme, and then personalize their own situation by observing that the little lamb's behavior parallels a lover's subservient tendencies toward his loved one. Stevie Ray Vaughan is slightly more adaptive. His lyrical commentary reproduces the first four lines intact, but then he deviates into a jive talkin' version of the little lamb sparkin' a wild time in the old schoolyard. No specifics of dancin', prancin', or romancin' are detailed. However, the playful guitar solo by Vaughan hints at a casual, joy-filled romp that–in Vaughan's own terms–broke *all* the teacher's rules.

THERE WAS AN OLD WOMAN WHO LIVED IN A SHOE

There was an old woman who lived
in a shoe,
She had so many children she didn't
know what to do.
She gave them some broth
without any bread,
Then whipped them all soundly
and sent them to bed.

After identifying the traditional nursery rhyme situation in the initial stanzas of "All Mama's Children," Carl Perkins shifts toward a contemporary social mobility theme. Once the footwear-dwelling youngsters see urban life and the accompanying downtown party styles, they *all* want to bop. Dancing symbolizes personal freedom; remodeling the old, battered shoe into a new blue suede model (a not very subtle salute to Perkin's classic rockabilly tune) illustrates the family's materialistic success. The singer qualifies the movement from lower class life to more wealthy existence by claiming that the kids don't want to live too fast, they just want to live in class. The tune concludes with music echoing through the night from the blue suede mansion on the hill.

TABLE C

SELECTED ILLUSTRATIONS OF CONTEMPORARY RECORDINGS CONTAINING REFERENCES TO NURSERY RHYMES, FAIRY TALES, AND OTHER CHILDREN'S STORIES[6]

1. Baa-Baa Black Sheep, Have You Any Wool?

   "Black Sheep" (MGM 13747)
   by Sam the Sham and The Pharoahs (1967)

2. Cinderella and the Glass Slipper

   "Cinderella" (ABC-Paramount 10239)
   by Paul Anka (1961)

   "Cinderella" (Atlantic 3392)
   by Firefall (1977)

   "Cinderella" (Capitol 4078)
   by The Four Preps (1958)

   "Cinderella" (Dot 16333)
   by Jack Ross (1962)

   "Cinderella Rockefella" (Philips 40526)
   by Ester and Abi Ofarim (1968)

   "Cinderella Sunshine" (Columbia 44655)
   by Paul Revere and The Raiders (1968)

3. Hey Diddle Diddle, the Cat and the Fiddle

   "(Ain't That) Just Like Me" (ATCO 6210)
   by The Coasters (1961)

   "Cat's in the Cradle" (Elektra 45203)
   by Harry Chapin (1974)

   "Hi Diddle Diddle" (Symbol 924)
   by Inez Foxx (1963)

   "Triangle of Love (Hey Diddle Diddle)"
   (Sussex 212)
   by The Presidents (1971)

4. Hickory, Dickory, Dock, The Mouse Ran up the Clock

"Hickory, Dick, and Dock" (Liberty 55700)
by Bobby Vee (1964)

5. Humpty Dumpty Sat on a Wall

"(Ain't That) Just Like Me" (ATCO 6210)
by The Coasters (1961)

"All the King's Horses" (Atlantic 2883)
by Aretha Franklin (1972)

"Humpty Dumpty" (Co+Ce 234)
by The Vogues (1964)

"Humpty Dumpty Heart" (Atlantic 1150)
by LaVern Baker (1957)

6. The Inky Dinky Spider

"Inky Dinky Spider (The Spider Song)"
(4 Corners 129)
by The Kids Next Door (1956)

7. Jack and Jill Went up the Hill

"Jack and Jill" (Arista 0283)
by Raydio (1978)

"Jack and Jill" (ABC 11229)
by Tommy Roe (1969)

"Jack and Jill Boogie"
by Sleepy LaBeef

8. Jack Be Nimble, Jack Be Quick

"American Pie" (United Artists 50856)
by Don McLean (1971)

9. Jack The Giant Killer

"Charlie Brown" (ATCO 6132)
by The Coasters (1959)

10. Little Boy Blue, Come Blow Your Horn

"Little Boy Blue" (Challenge 59014)
by Huelyn Duvall (1959)

"Little Boy Blue" (Dot 15444)
by Billy Vaughn (1956)

11. Little Jack Horner Sat in the Corner

"Ain't Misbehavin'" (Warner Brothers 28794)
by Hank Williams, Jr. (1986)

"Cherry Pie" (Brent 7010)
by Skip and Flip (1960)

"Nursery Rhyme" (Checker)
by Bo Diddley (1961)

12. Little Red Riding Hood

"Little Blue Riding Hood" (Capitol 1697)
by Stan Freberg (1951)

"Li'l Red Riding Hood" (MGM 13506)
by Sam the Sham and The Pharoahs (1966)

"Little Red Riding Hood" (Mercury 713775)
by The Big Bopper (1958)

"Little Red Riding Hood" (Vee-Jay n.n.)
by Dee Clark (1960)

"Ridin' Hood" (ARCO 6219)
by The Coasters (1961)

13. Mary Had a Little Lamb, Its Fleece Was White as Snow

"(Ain't That) Just Like Me" (ATCO 6210)
by The Coasters (1961)

"Mary Had a Little Lamb" (Apple 1851)
by Paul McCartney (1972)

"Mary Had a Little Lamb" (Epic n.n.)
by Stevie Ray Vaughan (1983)

"Mary's Little Lamb" (Colpix 644)
by James Darren (1962)

14. There Was a Crooked Man, and He Walked a Crooked Mile

"Don't Let the Rain Come Down
(Crooked Little Man)" (Philips 40175)
by The Serendipity Singers (1964)

15. There Was an Old Woman Who Lived in a Shoe

"All Mama's Children" (Sun 243)
by Carl Perkins (1956)

16. Three Little Pigs

"The Hair on My Chinny Chin Chin" (MGM 13581)
by Sam the Sham and The Pharoahs (1966)

"Three Little Pigs" (King 5966)
by James Duncan (1964)

What generalizations can be drawn from surveying hundreds of commercial recordings containing lyrical references to nursery rhymes and fairy tales? There are several. First, anthropomorphic imagery is alive and well in American popular songs. Appearances of talking animals, long a staple within novelty tune categories, are often used for comic effect in standard pop lyrics as well. Second, particular artists have adapted their broad vocal ranges to depict nursery rhyme characters with great gusto. Dee Clark, Sam the Sham, and The Big Bopper have been particularly creative in vocalizing either initial hooks or other attention-getting sounds. The comedy routines and harmonic vocal interplay of The Coasters creates priceless dialogues among wolves, sheep, and pigs, as well as between distressed parents, hassled students, and frustrated school teachers. Third, many fairly tale characters are lifted from their traditional rural settings and inserted into contemporary social problems (divorce, lost love, infidelity, drunkenness, greed, and poverty) and into modern physical arenas (hotel or motel rooms, living rooms, bars, and schools.) Simple wooded environs are apparently inappropriate for 32-bar urban tales of intrigue, conflict, and romance. Fourth, it is difficult to imagine a more diverse group of artists–white blues guitarist Stevie Ray Vaughan, black doo-wop singer Nolan Strong, classic pop crooner Frank Sinatra, sassy-brassy R&B vocalist LaVern Baker, and groups like The Searchers, The Five Keys, and The Serendipity Singers–utilizing nursery rhyme formats to produce pop hits. Finally, as a research afterthought, it should be noted how difficult it is to locate 1950s and 1960s recordings of nursery rhymes and fairy tales.

CONCLUSION

Popular music contains a goldmine of teaching topics. Music educators should not view sounds favored by their students as unworthy of investigation. The mark of a learned person is the ability to perceive universal questions in all forms of human experience. Aesthetic quality, redeeming social value, political perception, and moral standards cannot be honed in students without discussion and debate. The realization that all music has some traditional or historical meaning is a lesson in itself.

NOTES

1. A broad examination of personal concerns, social issues, and historical events which have informed modern lyrics over the past forty years is found in B. Lee Cooper, *A Resource Guide to Themes in Contemporary American Song Lyrics, 1950-1985* (Westport, Connecticut: Greenwood Press, 1986.)

2. B. Lee Cooper, "It's a Wonder I Can Think at All: Vinyl Images of American Public Education, 1950-1980," *Popular Music and Society,* IX (1984), pp. 47-65; B. Lee Cooper, "Women's Studies and Popular Music: Using Audio Resources in Social Studies Instruction," *The History and Social Science Teacher,* XIV (Fall 1978), pp. 29-40; R. Serge Denisoff, "Death Songs and Teenage Roles," in *Sing a Song of Social Significance* (Bowling Green, Ohio: Bowling Green University Popular Press, 1972), pp. 171-176; John C. Thrush and George S. Paulus, "The Concept of Death in Popular Music: A Social Psychological Perspective," *Popular Music and Society,* VI (1979), pp. 219-228; R. Serge Denisoff, " 'Teen Angel' Resistance, Rebellion, and Death–Revisited," *Journal of Popular Culture,* XVI (Spring 1983), p. 121; and James T. Carey, "Changing Courtship Patterns in the Popular Song," *American Journal of Sociology,* LXXIV (May 1969), pp. 720-731. For a broad survey of this topical approach, see George H. Lewis, "The Sociology of Popular Music: A Selected and Annotated Bibliography," *Popular Music and Society,* VII (1979), pp. 57-68.

3. David Pichaske, *A Generation in Motion: Popular Music and Culture in the Sixties* (New York: Schirmer Press, 1979); John P. Morgan and Thomas C. Tulloss, " The Jake Walk Blues: A Toxicologic Tragedy Mirrored in American Popular Music," *Annals of Internal Medicine,* LXXXV (December 1976), pp. 804-808; William Graebner, "Teaching 'The History of Rock 'n' Roll," *Teaching History: A Journal of Methods,* IX (Spring 1984), pp. 2-20; B. Lee Cooper "Oral History, Popular Music, and American Railroads, 1920-1980," *Social Studies,* LXXIV (November-December 1983), pp. 223-231; B. Lee Cooper, "Controversial Issues in Popular Lyrics, 1960-1985: Teaching Resources for the English Classroom" *Arizona English Bulletin,* XXIX (Fall 1986), pp. 174-187; and Jerome L. Rodnitzky, *Minstrels of the Dawn: The Folk-Protest Singer as a Cultural Hero* (Chicago: Nelson-Hall Publishers, Inc., 1976.)

4. David Pichaske, *Beowulf to Beatles and Beyond: The Varieties of Poetry* (New York: Macmillan Company, 1981.)

5. Sources consulted for this study include: Edna Johnson, Evelyn R. Sickels, and Frances Clarks Sayers (comps.), *Anthology of Children's Literature,* third edition (Boston: Houghton Mifflin Company, 1959); Iona and Peter Opie (eds.), *The Oxford Dictionary of Nursery Rhymes* (London: Oxford University Press, 1951); Betty O'Conner (ed.), *Better Homes and Gardens Story Book* (New York: Better Homes and Gardens Books, 1972); *Dean's Mother Goose Book of Rhymes* (New

York: Playmore Publishers, Inc., 1977); and Humphrey Carpenter and Mari Prichard (comps.), *The Oxford Companion to Children's Literature* (New York: Oxford University Press, 1984.)

6. An expanded version of this list appears in B. Lee Cooper, *Popular Music Perspectives: Ideas, Themes, and Patterns in Contemporary Lyrics* (Bowling Green, Ohio: Bowling Green State University Popular Press, 1991), pp. 155-171. Also see B. Lee Cooper, "Rhythm 'n' Rhymes: Character and Theme Images from Children's Literature in Contemporary Recordings, 1950-1985," *Popular Music and Society*, XIII (Spring 1989), pp. 53-71 and B. Lee Cooper, "Lyrical Commentaries: Learning from Popular Music," *Music Educators Journal*, LXXVII (April 1991), pp. 56-59.

Chapter 17

Radio Broadcasters

DISC JOCKEYS

The Pied Pipers of Rock 'n' Roll: Radio Deejays of the 50s and 60s, by Wes Smith. Marietta: Longstreet, 1989. Illustrated. 300 pp.

Chicago Tribune writer Wes Smith has assembled an anecdotal menagerie featuring the wild, woolly predecessors of "Morning Zoo" radio. The announcers, pitchmen, and alcoholics who became disc jockeys during the heyday of rock 'n' roll are portrayed as working stiffs, egomaniacs, voyeurs, and materialistic audio-nomads in Smith's study. Rather than being either musical visionaries or prophetic luminaries, most 1950s deejays are portrayed as victims of their own short-sighted greed (payola-plus-sexola during a 1959 Miami Beach Convention) and as pawns in the great recording industry/radio merchandising game of chance. Few were kingmakers; few were even music lovers. The story told in *The Pied Pipers of Rock and Roll* isn't an authentic tragedy, since neither the heroes (Alan Freed, Gene Nobles, or John R. Richbourg) nor the villains (Congressman Oren Hatch, Dick "Clarkola" Clark, or Mitch Miller) are truly larger than life. The purported demise of radio's personality jocks after 1969 is also difficult to discern, especially in a book that concludes with a lengthy chapter on the howling greybeard of current rock broadcasting, Wolfman Jack.

This essay by B. Lee Cooper was originally published as "From Anonymous Announcer to Radio Personality, from Pied Piper to Payola: The American Disc Jockey, 1950-1970," *Popular Music and Society* XIV (1990): pp. 89-95. Reprint permission has been granted by the author and The Popular Press.

There are undeniable strengths in Wes Smith's slim volume. First, he has personally interviewed numerous rock performers and broadcasting co-workers who knew the '50s disc jockeys well–and many humorous tales are resurrected. Second, the author presents a variety of interesting black-and-white photos reportedly culled from Cleveland *Plain Dealer* and *Chicago Tribune* archives. Third, an amazingly detailed index has been compiled to assist readers in locating individual artists, record-company executives, and deejays mentioned throughout the text. Fourth, Smith provides a brief but entertaining section on women disk jockeys by featuring vignettes on Martha Jean "The Queen" Steinberg, Gladys "Dizzy Lizzy" Hill, and Novella Smith. Finally, he offers lengthy glimpses at the big names of '50s rhythm 'n' blues radio: Hugh Baby Jarrett, Zena Sears, Hunter Hancock, Jocko Henderson, Hoss Allen, Dick Biondi, Al Benson, Vernon "Poppa Stoppa" Winslow, Ken "Jack the Cat" Elliott, Riley "Blues Boy" King, Rufus Thomas, and Lavada "Dr. Hepcat" Durst.

Despite the many attributes of Smith's biographical history, one is puzzled by a series of omissions. Some of these are remarkable in a research work; others are merely disappointing as either historical gaffs or editorial oversights. The scholarly shortcomings begin with the total absence of citations to sources quoted within the text. Facts, opinions, tall tales, myths, and memories blur throughout the report. Books and authors, relatives, and broadcasting colleagues are frequently mentioned, but nowhere does the line between fact and fantasy emerge. This is a disservice to the characters being analyzed and to readers seeking to interpret Smith's commentary. The brevity of his bibliography casts additional doubt on the validity of the images crafted by Smith. Finally, there is a lingering sense that neither the disc jockeys mentioned nor Smith himself either knew, liked, or cared much about the 1950s R&B music they hyped so fervently. If this is true, it's particularly sad. If it's false, then Smith has misrepresented his subjects as charlatans rather than Pied Pipers.

The distinct feeling that is communicated, though, is that music and teenage discretionary wealth were convenient pathways to booze, broads, and bribes for some; to the merchandising of beer, baby chicks, and records to many; and to personal power and corporate wealth for a select, cunning few. Nowhere does the sheer love of music seem to motivate any 1950s announcer to simply bust loose with uninhibited joy. The audience and the performers (the *real* music lovers of the day) were apparently united by sanctimonious, but unsanctified, audio gatekeepers.

The Pied Pipers of Rock 'n' Roll is a volume that should be examined with a critical eye. Nevertheless, it deserves study because of its broad disc jockey coverage, its careful acknowledgment of black and white deejays who promoted R&B to increasingly integrated teen groups, and its attempt to explore the broadcasting roots of America's most controversial musical contribution to the twentieth-century culture.

After reading Smith and perusing his brief booklist, those interested in examining disc jockeys in greater detail should track down the studies listed below:

GENERAL RADIO/DISC JOCKEY STUDIES

- Barnes, Ken. "Top 40 Radio: A Fragment of the Imagination." In *Facing the Music.* Edited by Simon Frith. New York: Pantheon, 1988.
- Blackburn, Richard. "Alan Freed May Have Invented Rock 'n' Roll Radio–But He Had Help: The Amazing Stories of Dr. Hepcat, Professor Bop, Groover Boy, and Jack the Cat." *Waxpaper* IV (May 4, 1979): pp. 20-23ff.
- Blackburn, Richard. "Rock 'n' Roll Disc Jockeys." *Contemporary Music Almanac 1980/81.* Compiled by Ronald Zalkind. New York: Schirmer, 1980.
- Chapple, Steve, and Reebee Garofalo. "Rock 'n' Roll Radio." In *Rock 'n' Roll Is Here to Pay: The History and Politics of the Music Industry.* Chicago: Nelson-Hall, 1977.
- Courtney, Ron. "Blues in the Night: The Story of WLAC Radio." *Goldmine* No. 93 (February 1984): pp. 183-184.
- Denisoff, R. Serge. "The Evolution of Pop Music Broadcasting, 1920-1972." *Popular Music and Society* II (Spring 1973): pp. 202-226.

- Denisoff, R. Serge. "The Gatekeepers of Radio." *Solid Gold: The Popular Record Industry.* New Brunswick, New Jersey: Transaction, 1975.

- Dexter, Dave. "Disk Jockey: Origin of the Species, 1930-1945." *Billboard* LXXXI (December 27, 1969): pp. 56-58.

- Farren, Mick. "Voices: Dr. Johnny Fever, Where Are You Now?" *M & SO* III (May-June 1983): pp. 10, 18.

- Garofalo, Reebe, and Steve Chapple. "From ASCAP to Alan Greed: The Pre-History of Rock 'n' Roll." *Popular Music and Society* VI (1978): pp. 72-80.

- Grendysa, Peter A. "DJ Copy." *Record Exchanger* No. 29 (1981): pp. 24-25.

- Hall, Claude, and Barbara Hall, *The Business of Radio Programming: A Comprehensive Look at Modern Programming Techniques Used Throughout the Radio World.* New York: Billboard, 1977.

- Hesbacher, Peter, Nancy Clasby, Bruce Anderson, and David G. Berger. "Radio Format Strategies." *Journal of Communication* XXVI (Winter 1976): pp. 109-117.

- Kinder, Bob. "Rock Radio." *The Best of the First: The Early Days of Rock and Roll.* Chicago: Adams, 1986.

- MacFarland, David T. *The Development of the Top 40 Radio Format.* Salem: Ayer, 1979.

- Marion, Jean-Charles. "The New York Disc Jockeys." *Record Exchanger* No. 31 (1983): pp. 16-17, 24.

- Marsh, Dave. "American Grandstand: Alan Freed Wept." *The Record* II (October 1983): p. 15.

- Moffitt, Phillip. "The Sound of Soul." *Esquire* CLLL (May 1985): pp. 21-22.

- Morthland, John. "The Rise of Top 40 AM." *The Rolling Stone Illustrated History of Rock and Roll* (revised edition). Edited by Jim Miller. New York: Random House/Rolling Stone, 1980.

- Osgood, Dick. *WYXIE Wonderland: Diary of a Radio Station.* Bowling Green, Ohio: Bowling Green State University Popular Press, 1981.

- Paglin, Jules. "Louisiana Disc Jockeys." *Blues World* No. 31 (June 1970): pp. 7-10.

- Peterson, Richard A., and David G. Berger. "Cycles in Symbol Production: The Case of Popular Music." *American Sociological Review* XL (April 1975): pp. 158-173.

- Rea, Steven X. "They Only Come Out at Night." *Waxpaper* IV (April 6, 1979): pp. 4-7.

- Reid, J. R. "Buffalo Rock Radio–The Early Years." *Goldmine* No. 37 (June 1979): p. 34.

- Russell, Tony. "Music in the Air." *The History of Rock* No. 3 (1982): pp. 55-58.

- Williams, Gilbert A. "The Black Disc Jockey as a Cultural History." *Popular Music and Society* X (1986): pp. 79-90.

INDIVIDUAL DISC JOCKEYS

Jerry Blavat

- Friedman, Bruce Jay. "Number One Cat: Geator with the Heater of Philadelphia." *Saturday Evening Post* CCXXXIX (September 24, 1966): pp. 36-42.

- Furek, Maxim W. "East Coast Radio Days." *DISCoveries* I (December 1988): pp. 38-39.

Porky Chedwick

- Amber, Arnie. "Porky Chedwick: Pittsburgh's Platter Pushin' Papa." *Goldmine* No. 45 (February 1980): p. 120.

Lee Diamond

- Pruter, Robert. "Lee Diamond Recalls Early Chicago R&B." *Goldmine* No. 83 (April 1983): p. 186.

Chuck Dunaway

- Hall, Claude. "Dunaway's Stormy Career." *Billboard* LXXXIX (December 24, 1977): pp. 34, 38.

- Hall, Claude. "Dunaway's 'Insanity' in Early 1950s." *Billboard* XC (January 7, 1978): pp. 22, 27, 45.

- Hall, Claude. "Only Memories for Dunaway." *Billboard* XC (January 14, 1978): pp. 21, 31.

Alan Freed

- Belz, Carl. "The Role of the Disk Jockey: Alan Freed." In *The Story of Rock* (second edition). New York: Harper & Row, 1972.

- Bundy, June. "Freed Replies to R&B Slurs." *Billboard* LXVIII (April 28, 1956): p. 19.

- Cotten, Lee. "Alan Freed." In *Shake, Rattle, and Roll–The Golden Age of American Rock 'n' Roll: Volume One, 1952-1955*. Ann Arbor: Pierian, 1989.

- Fanselow, Julie. "Alan Freed–Mr. Rock 'n' Roll Remembered." *The* [Cleveland] *Plain Dealer* (September 6, 1985): pp. 3, 14.

- Jackson, John. "Spotlight on Alan Freed." *Rockin' 50s* No. 1 (August 1986): pp. 8-15.

- John, Mike. "In the Beginning Was Alan Freed." In *Rock: From Elvis Presley to The Rolling Stones*. New York: Quadrangle, 1973.

- Kozak, Roman. "When It Got Its Chance, Rock 'n' Roll Was a Riot." *Billboard* XCIV (March 20, 1982): p. 12.

- Millar, Bill. "Mr. Rock 'n' Roll." *The History of Rock* No. 11 (1982): pp. 215-217.

- Ochs, Ed. "'Rock' of Ages: Born Freed." *Billboard* LXXXI (December 27, 1969): p. 110.

- Rathbun, Keith. "The Moondog Coronation Ball: Happy Birthday, Rock 'n' Roll." *Scene* XVII (March 20-26, 1986): p. 9.

- Richard, Mike. "Banned in Boston!" *Goldmine* No. 41 (October 1979): pp. 125-126.

- Rutledge, Jeffrey L. "Alan Freed: The Fall from Grace of a Forgotten Hero." *Goldmine* No. 118 (February 1, 1985): pp. 22, 54, 57.

- Scott, Jane. "30 Years Ago, 'Moon Dog' Howled." *The* [Cleveland] *Plain Dealer* (March 14, 1982): pp. 1, 12.

- Scott, Jane. "When 'Moon Dog' Howled in Cleveland." *The* [Cleveland] *Plain Dealer* (September 6, 1985): p. 3.

Casey Kasem

- Lissone, Mary. "Casey Kasem: Behind the Voice Behind the Hits." *Goldmine* No. 99 (May 11, 1984): pp. 68-70.

- Sutherland, Sam. "Things Still Looking Up for Kasem's Countdown." *Billboard* XCV (February 19, 1983): p. 16.

Murray Kaufman

- Bashe, Philip. "Do You Remember Rock and Roll Radio?" *Circus* No. 274 (December 31, 1982): p. 32.

- Colmes, A. "Goodphone Commentaries: The End of an Era." *Billboard* XCIV (March 20, 1982): p. 27.

- Kaufman, Murray. *Murray the K: Tell It Like It Is, Baby.* New York: Holt, Rinehart and Winston, 1966.

- Loder, Kurt. "Murray Kaufman: 1922-1982." *Rolling Stone* No. 367 (April 15, 1982): pp. 18, 93.

- "Murray the K Dead at 60: Spread the Rock 'n' Roll Sound." *Billboard* XCIV (March 6, 1982): p. 26.

- Price, Richard. "Going Down with Murray the K." *Rolling Stone* No. 367 (April 15, 1982): pp. 16-18, 92.

- "Rock 'n' Roll Heaven: Murray the K, Alex Harvey." *Trouser Press* IX (May 1982): p. 4.

- Skuce, Larry. "Murray the K." *Goldmine* No. 57 (February 1981): pp. 15-16.

- Sutherland, Sam. "Multiple Acts Books for Kaufman Tribute in New York." *Billboard* XCIII (April 11, 1981): p. 21ff.

- Tiegel, E. "Murray the K: Rock DJ of '60s Returns to the Spotlight with Several Projects." *Billboard* XCI (October 20, 1979): p. 6.

Kid Leo

- Biddle, Daniel R. "Behind the Scenes–Kid Leo: The Voice of Cleveland." *Rolling Stone* No. 284 (February 8, 1979): pp. 23, 27.

- Neff, James. "Leo: A Seasoned Kid on the Radio Block." *The* (Cleveland) *Plain Dealer* (February 14, 1982): pp. 1, 2.

George "Hound Dog" Lorenz

- McSparrin, Charles. "You Ain't Nothing But a (Legendary) Hound Dog." In *Our Best to You–From Record Digest*. Edited by Jerry Osborne. Prescott: Record Digest, 1979.

- Skurzewski, Bob. "Gone Forever: The Grand-Daddy of Rock and Roll." *Record Exchanger* III (1972): pp. 16-17, 20.

Jim Lounsbury

- "Jim Lounsbury." *Rockin' '50s* No. 16 (February 1989): pp. 18-19.

Larry Lujack

- Lujack, Larry. *Super Jock: The Loud, Frantic, Nonstop World of a Rock Radio DJ*. Chicago: Henry Regnery, 1975.

Pete "Mad Daddy" Meyers

- DeLuca, David. "The Mad, Mad Daddy of Cleveland Radio." *Cleveland Magazine* (September 1984): pp. 82-85, 151-153.

Bruce Morrow

- Tamarkin, Jeff. "Bruce 'Cousin Brucie' Morrow: A Top 40 Legend Fights to Save Radio." *Goldmine* No. 80 (January 1983): pp. 7-9.

Johnny Otis

- Cotten, Lee. "Johnny Otis." In *Shake, Rattle, and Roll–The Golden Age of American Rock 'n' Roll: Volume One, 1952-1955*. Ann Arbor, Michigan: Pierian, 1989.

B. Mitchell Reed

- Pond, Steve. "B. Mitchell Reed." *Rolling Stone* No. 395 (May 12, 1983): p. 68.

- "Reed's Career Parallels Rock Radio Evolution." *Billboard* XC (June 17, 1978): pp. 19, 22.

Don K. Reed

- Tamarkin, Jeff. "Don K. Reed: New York's Doo Wop Disc Jockey." *Goldmine* No. 64 (September 1981): pp. 10-11.

Bob Reitman

- Hintz, Martin. "Oldtimer of Underground DJs: Bob Reitman Is Midwest's Original Rock Music Guru." *Billboard* XCI (May 5, 1979): pp. 33-34.

John R. Richbourg

- Courtney, Ron. "John R.: A Man and the Blues." *Goldmine* No. 136 (October 11, 1985): p. 20.

- Hoskyns, Barney. "John Richbourg." *Soul Survivor* No. 7 (Summer 1987): pp. 8-10.

- Pruter, Robert. "John 'John R' Richbourg, Pioneer R&B Deejay, Dead at Age 75." *Goldmine* No. 149 (April 11, 1986): p. 84.

Red Robinson

- Robinson, Red, and Peggy Hodgins. *Rockbound: Rock 'n' Roll Encounters, 1955 to 1969*. Surey, British Columbia, Canada: Hancock House, 1983.

Peter Tripp

- Baer, Jon. "Peter Tripp and 50s New York Radio." *Record Exchanger* V (1977): pp. 22-23.

Vernon Winslow

- Hannusch, Jeff. "Dr. Daddy-O: New Orleans' First Black Radio Personality." In *I Hear You Knockin': Rhythm and Blues.* Ville Platte, Louisiana: Swallow, 1985.

THE PAYOLA SCANDAL, 1959-1960

- Austin, Mary. "Petrillo's War." *Journal of Popular Culture* XII (Summer 1978): pp. 11-18.

- Brown, Ashley. "DJs in Bribes Shock." *The History of Rock* No. 11 (1982): pp. 218-220.

- DeMine, Shields. "Payola." *American Mercury* XC (March 1960): pp. 30-42.

- Grendysa, Pete. "No Pay–No Play: The Story of the Music Licensing Societies (Part One)." *Goldmine* No. 32 (January 1979): pp. 25-26.

- Grendysa, Pete. "The Forty-Year War: The Story of the Music Licensing Societies (Part Two)." *Goldmine* No. 33 (February 1979): pp. 22-23.

- Grendysa, Pete. "Paying for Playing: The Story of the Music Licensing Societies (Part Three)." *Goldmine* No. 34 (March 1979): pp. 30-31.

- Hugunin, Marc. "ASCAP, BMI, and the Democratization of American Popular Music." *Popular Music and Society* VII (1979): pp. 8-17.

- Jackson, John. "Payola: Grease for the Star-Making Machinery (Part One)." *Goldmine* No. 54 (November 1980): pp. 14-15.

- Jackson, John. "Payola: Grease for the Star-Making Machinery (Part Two)." *Goldmine* No. 55 (December 1980): pp. 172-173.

- Morthland, John. "The Payola Scandal." *The Rolling Stone Illustrated History of Rock and Roll* (revised edition). Edited by Jim Miller. New York: Random House/Rolling Stone, 1980.

- Szatmary, David P. "Dick Clark, Philadelphia Schlock, and Payola." *Rockin' in Time: A Social History of Rock and Roll.* Englewood Cliffs, New Jersey: Prentice-Hall, 1987.

Chapter 18

Record Charts

FATS DOMINO

The lilt of his music is unmistakable. His piano-playing technique is pure New Orleans style. His voice–with that quality of munched rather than simply spoken words–is magnificently distinctive. The Fats Domino sound dominated American popular music for two decades. On the "rhythm and blues" side of the ledger, only Ray Charles and James Brown rivaled Fats Domino's hit-record production between 1950 and 1969. In the Hot 100 category, Fats' record-selling popularity was exceeded only by Elvis Presley, The Beatles, Pat Boone, Ricky Nelson, and Connie Francis.

The popular-music ascension of Fats Domino as a 20-year phenomenon marked the ultimate triumph of style over substance. The keys to his success were, in retrospect, quite simple. His arrangements were consistently uncluttered (the handiwork of brilliant New Orleans studio engineer Cosimo Matassa; frequent co-author and arranger Dave Bartholomew also aided significantly). The artist's own persona–affable, yet shy; boyish, yet fatherly; and always smiling–provided a solid base for long-term public exposure. Finally, the songs themselves were unpretentious. As freelance journalist Peter Guralnick observed in *The Rolling Stone Illustrated History of Rock and Roll* (1980), "The tunes of Fats Domino invariably featured clean arrangements, simple melodies, a casual feel, and catchy lyrics" (p. 47). No wonder he produced hit after hit.

Although Fats produced 11 R&B-charted songs between 1950

This study by B. Lee Cooper was originally published as "The Fats Domino Decades, 1950-1969." *Record Profile Monthly* No. 5 (May 1984): pp. 56-58, 71. Reprint permission has been granted by the author.

and 1955, his first major pop tune was "Ain't It a Shame." This marked the beginning of ten consecutive years when at least one Fats song attained a ranking on *Billboard*'s Hot 100 chart. Between 1950, when "The Fat Man" first reached the *Billboard* Rhythm and Blues chart for three weeks, and 1968, when "Lady Madonna" was on the Hot 100 chart for two weeks, the Domino magic spawned the 85 hit records listed below in Table A.

TABLE A.
Two Decades of Musical Dominance: The Charted 45-r.p.m. Releases of Fats Domino, 1950-1969[1]

Song Title (Record Number) Release Date	Weeks on R&B Chart	Weeks in Hot 100
"The Fat Man" (Imperial 5058) 1950	9	0
"Every Night About This Time" (Imperial 5099) 1950	9	0
"Rockin' Chair" (Imperial 5145) 1951	1	0
"Goin' Home" (Imperial 5180) 1952	20	0
"Poor, Poor Me" (Imperial 5197) 1952	1	0

Song Title (Record Number) Release Date	Weeks on R&B Chart	Weeks in Hot 100
"How Long" (Imperial 5209) 1952	1	0
"Goin' to the River" (Imperial 5231) 1953	14	0
"Please Don't Leave Me" (Imperial 5240) 1953	12	0
"Rose Mary" (Imperial 5251) 1953	1	0
"Something's Wrong" (Imperial 5262) 1953	11	0
"You Done Me Wrong" (Imperial 5272) 1954	1	0
"Thinking of You" (Imperial 5323) 1955	1	0
"Don't You Know" (Imperial 5340) 1955	7	0
"Ain't That a Shame" (Imperial 5348) 1955	26	13

Song Title (Record Number) Release Date	Weeks on R&B Chart	Weeks in Hot 100
"All By Myself" (Imperial 5357) 1955	14	0
"Poor Me" (Imperial 5369) 1955	12	0
"I Can't Go On" (Imperial 5369) 1955	4	0
"Bo Weevil" (Imperial 5375) 1956	13	9
"Don't Blame It on Me" (Imperial 5375) 1956	4	0
"I'm in Love Again" (Imperial 5386) 1956	20	23
"My Blue Heaven" (Imperial 5386) 1956	14	20
"When My Dreamboat Comes Home" (Imperial 5396) 1956	13	16
"So-Long" (Imperial 5396) 1956	11	13

Song Title (Record Number) Release Date	Weeks on R&B Chart	Weeks in Hot 100
"Blueberry Hill" (Imperial 5407) 1956	23	27
"Honey Chile" (Imperial 5407) 1956	5	0
"Blue Monday" (Imperial 5417) 1956	16	18
"What's the Reason I'm Not Pleasin' You" (Imperial 5417) 1956	2	10
"I'm Walkin'" (Imperial 5428) 1957	16	25
"The Rooster Song" (Imperial EP 147) 1957	1	0
"Valley of Tears" (Imperial 5442) 1957	11	18
"It's You I Love" (Imperial 5442) 1957	4	12
"When I See You" (Imperial 5454) 1957	3	10

Song Title (Record Number) Release Date	Weeks on R&B Chart	Weeks in Hot 100
"What Will I Tell My Heart" (Imperial 5454) 1957	1	6
"Wait and See" (Imperial 5467) 1957	6	13
"I Still Love You" (Imperial 5467) 1957	0	4
"The Big Beat" (Imperial 5477) 1957	1	9
"I Want You to Know" (Imperial 5477) 1957	0	11
"Yes, My Darling" (Imperial 5492) 1958	4	7
"Sick and Tired" (Imperial 5515) 1958	5	11
"No, No" (Imperial 5515) 1958	2	7
"Little Mary" (Imperial 5526) 1958	3	6

Song Title (Record Number) Release Date	Weeks on R&B Chart	Weeks in Hot 100
"Young School Girl" (Imperial 5537) 1958	2	1
"Whole Lotta Loving" (Imperial 5553) 1958	15	15
"Coquette" (Imperial 5553) 1958	3	1
"When the Saints Go Marchin' In" (Imperial 5569) 1959	0	8
"Telling Lies" (Imperial 5569) 1959	7	9
"I'm Ready" (Imperial 5585) 1959	9	11
"Margie" (Imperial 5585) 1959	0	8
"I Want to Walk You Home" (Imperial 5606) 1959	13	13
"I'm Gonna Be a Wheel Some Day" (Imperial 5606) 1959	4	13

Song Title (Record Number) Release Date	Weeks on R&B Chart	Weeks in Hot 100
"Be My Guest" (Imperial 5629) 1959	14	14
"I've Been Around" (Imperial 5629) 1959	5	9
"Country Boy" (Imperial 5645) 1960	0	10
"If You Need Me" (Imperial 5645) 1960	0	1
"Tell Me That You Love Me" (Imperial 5660) 1960	0	7
"Before I Grow Too Old" (Imperial 5660) 1960	0	2
"Walking to New Orleans" (Imperial 5675) 1960	11	14
"Don't Come Knockin'" (Imperial 5675) 1960	3	11
"Three Nights a Week" (Imperial 5687) 1960	5	11

Song Title (Record Number) Release Date	Weeks on R&B Chart	Weeks in Hot 100
"Put Your Arms Around Me Honey" (Imperial 5687) 1960	0	6
"My Girl Josephine" (Imperial 5704) 1960	12	15
"Natural Born Lover" (Imperial 5704) 1960	1	9
"What a Price" (Imperial 5723) 1961	7	9
"Ain't That Just Like a Woman" (Imperial 5723) 1961	7	8
"Shu Rah" (Imperial 5734) 1961	0	7
"Fell in Love on Monday" (Imperial 5734) 1961	0	6
"It Keeps on Rainin'" (Imperial 5753) 1961	5	11
"Let the Four Winds Blow" (Imperial 5764) 1961	12	11

Song Title (Record Number) Release Date	Weeks on R&B Chart	Weeks in Hot 100
"What a Party" (Imperial 5779) 1961	0	8
"Rockin' Bicycle" (Imperial 5779) 1961	0	1
"I Hear You Knocking" (Imperial 5796) 1961	0	2
"Jambalaya (On the Bayou)" (Imperial 5796) 1961	0	7
"You Win Again" (Imperial 5816) 1962	0	10
"Ida Jane" (Imperial 5816) 1962	0	2
"My Real Name" (Imperial 5833) 1962	2	7
"Nothing New (Same Old Thing)" (Imperial 5863) 1962	0	5
"Dance with Mr. Domino" (Imperial 5863) 1962	0	1

Song Title (Record Number) Release Date	Weeks on R&B Chart	Weeks in Hot 100
"Did You Ever See a Dream Walking" (Imperial 5875) 1962	0	5
"There Goes My Heart Again" (ABC Paramount 10444) 1963	0	7
"Red Sails in the Sunset" (ABC Paramount 10484) 1963	2	8
"Who Cares" (ABC Paramount 10512) 1964	5	5
"Lazy Lady" (ABC Paramount 10531) 1964	2	2
"Sally Was a Good Old Girl" (ABC Paramount 10584) 1964	2	2
"Heartbreak Hill" (ABC Paramount 10596) 1964	2	2
"Lady Madonna" (Reprise 0763) 1968	0	2

[1] Information presented in this table drawn from *Top Rhythm and Blues Singles, 1942-1988* (1988) and *Top Pop Singles, 1955-1986* (1987) compiled by Joel Whitburn (Menomonee Falls, Wisconsin: Record Research, Inc.).

Fats Domino illustrates the classic case of cross-over success from one musical genre to another. For five years, he labored successfully in the rhythm-and-blues market. After 1955, however, the rock 'n' roll revolution opened his talent to a much wider audience, and he responded with an astonishing chain of hit songs. As so often occurred between 1954 and 1959, white performers pounced on several of these Fats-recorded tunes and re-recorded them. The results were twofold. The Domino songs became fine material for Elvis Presley ("Blueberry Hill"), Pat Boone ("Ain't That a Shame"), and Ricky Nelson ("I'm Walkin' "); but the tunes themselves remained the stylistic property of the magical black performer from the Crescent City of Louisiana.

If there is one thing about the brilliant career of Fats Domino that is bewildering, it is his disappearance from the record charts during the '70s. Certainly, he was older than many of his contemporaries, yet he is only two years older than Ray Charles, whose performing career flourished throughout the '70s and into the '80s. Peter Guralnick has speculated about Fats' chart absence. He lamented, "Lately you don't hear so much from Fats. Perhaps he is simply played out, with those hundreds of songs, that vast repertoire of absolutely consistent product, forming a weight which makes it impossible to go forward. And, too, they say that the bands he fronts nowadays–after death, retirement, and disastrous road accidents have taken their toll–are pale imitations of the old days. Maybe so. But it's hard to believe that Fats will not come ambling back someday . . ." (p. 47). Irwin Stambler, editor of *The Encyclopedia of Pop, Rock, and Soul*, offers a more upbeat, diversified explanation for the demise of Fats Domino's 45-r.p.m. hit production. Stambler speculates that increasing age, the desire for more family life, comfortable financial circumstances, and geographic preference combined to alter the hit-after-hit productivity of the 1950-1969 period. Fats turned 40 in 1968. For a popular-music performer, as for a professional athlete, that's a significant milestone. Although Fats cut back sharply on his concert tours during the early '70s in order to spend more time with his wife and their eight children in his beloved New Orleans home, the performances that he did accept at the Flamingo Hotel in Las Vegas and on the Lake Tahoe resort circuit were far more lucrative than the checks that he earned during those old studio recordings days.

Fats Domino fans continue to applaud his performances and to play the reissued anthologies of his numerous hit songs. But in the history of rock 'n' roll, the outstanding elements of a performer's career are public recognition and the longevity of hit production. As the discography presented in Table A attests, the Domino decades marked a lengthy period of popular approval that is as rare as the distinctive talent of the man who etched the achievement in vinyl.

REFERENCES

Anderson, Clive. "The Fat Man." *The History of Rock* No. 8 (1982): pp. 144-147.

Coleman, Rick. "42 Things You Probably Don't Know About Fats Domino." *Wavelength*. No. 79 (May 1987): pp. 22-23.

Coleman, Rick. "The Imperial Fats Domino." *Goldmine*. No. 282 (May 17, 1991): pp. 8-12.

Coleman, Rick. "The New Orleans Sound of Fats Domino and Dave Bartholomew." *Goldmine*. No. 282 (May 17, 1991): pp. 12-13.

Coleman, Rick. "Rare Domino." *Goldmine*. No. 282 (May 17, 1991): pp. 13, 20.

Colman, Stuart. "Fats Domino: 'They Call Me the Fat Man'." In *They Kept on Rockin'*. Poole, Dorset: Blandford, 1982.

Cotten, Lee. "Fats Domino." In *Shake, Rattle and Roll–The Golden Age of American Rock 'n' Roll.* Ann Arbor, Michigan: Pierian Press, 1989.

Dahl, Bill. "Review of Fats Domino: 'They Call Me the Fat Man'." *Goldmine*. No. 297 (December 31, 1991): pp. 28-29.

"Fats Domino." *The Golden Age*. No. 1 (October 1986): pp. 8-19.

"Fats Domino." *The Golden Age*. No. 2 (November 1986): pp. 11-13.

"Fats Domino: The Classic Singles." *Record Collector*. No. 111 (November 1988): pp. 47-50.

Gordon, Mike. "Fats Domino." *Record Collector*. No. 15 (November 1980): pp. 24-27.

Griggs, Bill. "Mike Vice: Saxophone Player for Fats Domino." *Rockin' 50s*. No. 33 (December 1991): pp. 12-14.

Guralnick, Peter. "Fats Domino." In *The Rolling Stone Illustrated History of Rock and Roll* (second edition). Edited by Jim Miller. New York: Random House, 1980.

Harris, Paul. "Hey! Fat Man." *Blues and Rhythm*. No. 66 (January 1992): pp. 4-8.

Hilburn, Robert. "Fats Domino: The Quiet Giant of Rock 'n' Roll." *Los Angeles Times*. (August 21, 1985): pp. 1, 5.

Jones, Wayne. "Fats Domino." *Goldmine*. No. 57 (February 1981): pp. 8-9.

Joyce, Mike, with Fats Domino and Dave Bartholomew. "Intermission with Fats." *Living Blues*. (November-December 1977): pp. 16-22.

Preston, Peter. "Paramount Days of ABC." *The Golden Age*. No. 2 (November 1986): pp. 4-7.

Preston, Peter. "Fats Domino: Mercury Moves." *The Golden Age*. No. 14 (1988): pp. 11-17.

St. Pierre, Roger. "The Blues and Soul Hall of Fame: No. 28/Fats Domino." *Blues and Soul*. No. 596 (October 1-14, 1991): pp. 22-24.

Slevigen, Jan. "At the Fat Man's Hop." *Now Dig This*. No. 56 (November 1987): pp. 8-9.

Stafford, John. "'I Call It Music with a Beat': A Chat with Fats Domino." *Now Dig This*. No. 38 (May 1986): pp. 18-19.

Umphred, Neal. "Fats Domino U.S. Discography and Price Guide." *Goldmine*. No. 282 (May 17, 1991): pp. 14-20.

Chapter 19

Rock 'n' Roll Legends

JERRY LEE LEWIS

Jerry Lee Lewis: The Sun Years. (Sun Box 102). London: Charly Records, 1982.

Rock 'n' roll is aging, if not maturing. Numerous rock journalists, popular-culture scholars, and record-company executives have penned studies describing the evolution of modern music.[1] But even the best of these literary efforts invariably shortchange the audio heritage of rock. Only records, those vinyl orbs of oral history, can capture rock's dynamism. For many years, single-volume anthology albums were sufficient to illustrate the greatest hits of particular artists. In recent years, however, a new collection vehicle has emerged: the boxed set, a multi-disc anthology that offers fans and scholars the opportunity to gain a broad historical perspective on the words of the most influential rock performers. One such set is *Jerry Lee Lewis: The Sun Years.*

The value of Sun Box 102 to record collectors was heralded in a large advertisement in the *Down Home Music, Inc. Newsletter* of

---

The first essay, by B. Lee Cooper and James A. Creeth, was originally published as "Present at the Creation: The Legend of Jerry Lee Lewis on Record, 1956-1963." *JEMF Quarterly* XIX (Summer 1983): pp. 123-129. The second essay, by B. Lee Cooper, was originally published as "In Search of Jerry Lee Lewis," *JEMF Quarterly* XVIII (Fall 1982/Winter 1983): pp. 192-193. The final study, by B. Lee Cooper and William L. Schurk, was originally entitled "The First Tribute to a Rock Legend: Snuff Garrett's Salute to Buddy Holly–February 3, 1959." This paper was presented at the 7th annual meeting of The Midwest Popular Culture Association on October 11, 1979. Reprint permission has been granted by the authors.

March 1983. Store manager Frank Scott lauded it in the following fashion:

> This is it! The definitive collection of vintage recordings by one of the greatest rock 'n' roll artists of all time. Twelve LP box set containing 209 recordings of pounding rock 'n' roll and rhythm 'n' blues, low down blues and boogie, and moving country weepers. The set features 57 cuts that were originally issued by Sam Phillips' Sun Record Company, 77 tracks that were first issued after Sun Records was bought by Shelby Singleton in 1969 (many issued here in original mono for the first time), 60 previously unissued alternative takes of issued songs, 7 tracks that are issued here in their original form (commercial issues featured vocal or instrumental overdubs), and 9 songs that have never been issued before in any form. The set includes false starts and studio chat, including the famous conversation about religion between Sam Phillips and Jerry Lee which is here in a listenable form. Each album has its own photo sleeve with analysis of each performance and the set comes with a 36-page album-sized book which includes an introduction by Sam Phillips, an overview of Jerry Lee's career at Sun Records, a complete Sun session discography, photos, press clippings, and other memorabilia. A must!![2]

One might suspect that Scott's zealous comments were merely excessive commercial hype if they were not echoed and reinforced by more critical Jerry Lee Lewis fans and other more objective journalists. Wim de Boer, Dutch president of the Jerry Lee Lewis International Fan Club and editor of the bi-monthly fan magazine *Fireball Mail*, participated actively in the construction of Sun Box 102. In September 1982, de Boer published an enthusiastic pre-release "Sun Box Report," which was written by Barrie Gamblin. This rave review asserted that the forthcoming 12-LP set was compiled "without thought of financial gain" by several people who believe Jerry Lee to be an authentic "legend in his own time." Gamblin concluded, with no hint of modesty and with full knowledge of the highly critical expectations of Jerry Lee's closest followers, that Sun Box 102 was "put together by fans for the fans."[3]

No sooner had the British Sun Box 102 hit American record stores, than *Time* magazine printed a full-page review entitled "A Few Rounds with The Killer: Twelve New Records Celebrate Jerry Lee Lewis' Glory Days." Music critic Jay Cocks drew heavily on Nick Tosches' sinister biography, *Hellfire*, to place the subject of his extended review in a musical, psychological, and social context. Although Cocks is too brief and too flashy in his viewpoint, the commentary speaks positively to the power of the songs and to the oral history found in the vinyl grooves.[4]

What makes Sun Box 102 such a remarkable documentary product? The breadth and quality of the recordings featured throughout the set are noteworthy. The photographs on the 12 LP sleeves are clear, exciting, and historically accurate. The authenticity of the entire project is linked directly to the high level of cooperation achieved among the diverse groups that constructed the package. Cliff White, project supervisor, enlisted the assistance of a knowledgeable and experienced team of record-producing, research, and writing personnel. Authentication, in terms of detailed song-related information and the designation of specific recording session participants, was skillfully handled by White, Hank Davis, Colin Escott, and Martin Hawkins. Escott and Hawkins are the unparalleled authorities on the history of Sun Records.[5] The photo research and newspaper clippings that adorn the box set were compiled by White, Hawkins, Barrie Gamblin, John Pearce, Adam Komorowski, Bill Millar, and Tony Wilkinson. Other information was drawn from trade journals, fan magazines, and personal interviews with key Sun Records personnel, including Jack Clement, Roy Hall, Roland Janes, Judd Phillips, Sam Phillips, and Jimmy Van Eaton. Finally, the entire project was recorded and marketed by the experienced British vintage rock 'n' roll and rhythm 'n' blues label, Charly Records. There could be no finer tribute, no more thorough presentation of the artistry of Jerry Lee Lewis.

The big question that might linger in the minds of some is, "Why produce such a weighty set of albums on one artist?" Antiquarianism, the mindless reverence for all things from the past, often justifies the preservation of the most obscure 1950s recording figures. However, Jerry Lee Lewis is a legitimate candidate for historical study. Put simply, he was present at the creation of America's rock 'n' roll revolution. The concluding paragraphs of this chapter will hopefully provide a rationale for the loving, diligent labors of those who assembled Sun Box 102.

Since 1956, the professional career of Ferriday, Louisiana, rocker Jerry Lee Lewis has been a roller coaster of audience appreciation and public ridicule. Only one fact cannot be disputed: Jerry Lee is a gifted living legend of rock 'n' roll. His ascension to the status of "the greatest living rock 'n' roller" is based on a dozen distinctive activities, achievements, and events.

First, it must be acknowledged that Jerry Lee was one of many rock 'n' roll giants who emerged during the late 1950s. Although they had been schooled in several established musical genres, these early rockers launched a dynamic, disturbing new sound that provided the creative base for future singers. "Whole Lotta Shakin' Goin' On," Jerry Lee's second Sun Records release, was his farewell address to his hometown, to the Southwestern Bible Institute in Waxahachie, Texas, and to the Wagon Wheel Inn at Natchez. The record reportedly sold six million copies worldwide. As Nick Tosches notes, "By 1958 Jerry Lee Lewis was on top. Of all the rock-and-roll creatures, he projected the most hellish persona."[6] This observation is central to understanding Jerry Lee's legendary stature.

Second, public recognition and performing longevity are two undisputed factors in achieving the status of a legend. Several brilliant singers of the early rock 'n' roll era–Buddy Holly, Eddie Cochran, and Ritchie Valens–died prematurely. Other early rockers, like Carl Perkins and Gene Vincent, sustained unfortunate, career-damaging injuries. Very few stars from the '50s continued to measure their music to a rock 'n' roll beat during the following decades. However, Jerry Lee has accumulated more than 25 years of recording and performing success.

Third, the degree of fame, popularity, and notoriety that a singer achieves is a prime measure of his stylistic leadership and influence. Jerry Lee Lewis dominated *Billboard*'s Top 100, Country, and Rhythm 'n' Blues charts in 1957 with "Whole Lotta Shakin' Goin' On." His next two records, "Great Balls of Fire" and "Breathless," were also blockbusters. However, public opinion hurdled downward on Jerry Lee in 1958 after the British press castigated him for marrying his 13-year-old cousin; as a result, American record distributors and radio broadcasting executives clamped a virtual ban on playing his recordings. This airwave freeze lasted until 1967. Throughout that period, the nightclub circuit continued to be the sustaining public medium for rockin' Jerry Lee. Some of his most dynamic albums, including *The Greatest Live Show on Earth* for Smash Records, were produced during early '60s concert performances. The road back to prominence was paved with winning country tunes: "What Made Milwaukee Famous (Has Made a Loser Out of Me)," "Another Place Another Time," and "Would You Take Another Chance on Me." But his legendary rock 'n' roll soul never cooled. In the early '70s, Jerry Lee's Mercury label released "Chantilly Lace" and "Drinking Wine Spo-Dee O-Dee." By 1978, his new albums featured equal portions of country tunes and joyous, animated rock songs. It is a delight to hear the living legend continue rockin' his life away.

Fourth, the career and image of Elvis Presley overshadowed nearly everything that Jerry Lee Lewis accomplished during the '50s, '60s, and '70s. This frustrated Jerry Lee. No one could challenge the unprecedented record sales or the widespread fan support that surrounded Elvis during his life and after his death. Yet there are several reasons why "The Killer" deserves the title of a rock 'n' roll legend more fully than even "The King" does. Elvis' rock 'n' roll sound and feeling peaked between 1955 and 1958. His Sun years and his early RCA recordings still emanate vintage rock 'n' roll brilliance. However, after Elvis returned from military service, his performing dynamism declined, his public visibility waned, and his grade-B motion-picture work consumed his time and energy. The strict management of Col. Tom Parker emasculated the musical vitality of Elvis. Since the essence of rock music is spontaneity, enthusiasm, unpredictability, and public exposure, Jerry Lee has legitimately outdone Elvis since 1960. Ironically, RCA records, Col. Parker, and the entire Elvis management created "The King of Rock 'n' Roll" mantle during the same period that Jerry Lee Lewis was actually performing as rock royalty in small clubs, at revival concerts, on TV shows, and in recording studios. Jerry Lee identified the essential difference between Elvis and himself in an interview with columnist John Hubner: "There's a difference between a phenomenon and a stylist. I'm a stylist; Elvis was the phenomenon. And don't you ever forget it."[7] Elvis' premature passing left the stage vacant for the rocking stylist.

Fifth, a unique singing style and distinctive piano-playing technique make every tune produced by Jerry Lee Lewis a personalized experience. The numerous alternate takes presented in Sun Box 102 illustrate this fact. Few performers ever achieve this kind of distinctive sound. Among contemporary vocal stylists, only Ray Charles and Frank Sinatra are capable of producing this type of universally identifiable sound. Jerry Lee has characteristically noted that besides himself, there have been only three authentic American song stylists: Al Jolson, Jimmie Rodgers, and Hank Williams. Piano skills are also distinctive signatures of "The Killer" 's work. Writing in *Rolling Stone*, Robert Palmer has noted, "Lewis has often insisted that he always played rock and roll, and since his earliest recordings, there are no serious grounds for doubting him." Still, other writers have speculated that Jerry Lee is actually a dervish-like amalgam of Amos Milburn, Cecil Gant, Merrill Moore, Del Wood, and Moon Millican. Palmer concludes his brief analysis by observing, "My guess is that the Lewis Boogie, as he called it on an early Sun single, was a mixture of local black influences, the hillbilly boogie and rhythm and blues that were popular on Southern jukeboxes when he was growing up, and–the most crucial ingredient–the Killer's individual musical genius."[8]

Sixth, Jerry Lee Lewis' personality and vocal artistry have successfully ventured beyond rock 'n' roll into a variety of musical forms. Although he maintains that "Rockin' My Life Away" is his personal theme song, Jerry Lee's fans variously regard him as an accomplished singer of country, R&B, pop, and gospel numbers. His repertoire is unbelievably varied. Sun Box 102 beautifully illustrates this eclecticism, too. As one journalist wrote in 1979: "There has never been another American pop musician with Lewis' particular mixture of egotistical self-confidence, innate taste and sensitivity, eclecticism (he will play Chuck Berry, Hoagy Carmichael, Jim Reeves, Artie Shaw, spirituals, blues, low-down honky tonk or all-out rock and roll, as the mood strikes him), formidable and entirely idiosyncratic technique (both instrumental and vocal), and sheer bravura."[9] Yet, "The Killer" has his own musical priorities.

To quote Jerry Lee again, "I've had over 30 country hits, but I believe I'd rather do the rockers. I love rock and roll. Country is basically just pretty songs. A lot of guys can sing pretty songs, but there's only one man who can rock his life away. I'm the only one left that's worth a damn. Everyone else is dead or gone. Only 'The Killer' rocks on."[10]

Seventh, the most frequently mentioned characteristic of Jerry Lee Lewis' musical career is his show-stopping, uninhibited stage personality. While avoiding the million-dollar props and supporting orchestration employed by many performers, Jerry Lee and his small band use only the power of personality and piano pyrotechnics to produce musical mayhem and emotional exhaustion wherever they work. This is not meant to underrate the audience excitement associated with the performances of Ted Nugent, Bruce Springsteen, The Who, Bob Seger, Ike and Tina Turner, The Rolling Stones, or even James Brown. Nor does it discount the universal fan hysteria that surrounded The Beatles. But no single artist has ever criss-crossed the U.S. so frequently, played so often and with such continuing gusto for so many years, and created a sustained aura of excitement like Jerry Lee Lewis.[11]

Eighth, even at their wildest, most destructive, most lurid and abusive, or most law-breaking, it is hard to imagine that Jim Morrison, Pete Townshend, Mick Jagger, Keith Richards, or Jimi Hendrix have ever exceeded the drinking, drug-use, fighting, and general antics attributed to Jerry Lee Lewis. Nick Tosches captured this Lewis aspect in a 1978 article in *Creem* magazine: "Jerry Lee Lewis is a creature of mythic essence. . . . He is the heart of redneck rock-and-roll depravados: Jerry Lee makes them all look like Wayne Newton. Jerry Lee can out-drink, out-dope, out-fight, out-cuss, out-shoot, and out-f___ any man in the South. He is the last American wild man, *homo agrestic Americanus ultimus* . . ."[12] Undeniably related to this aberrant behavior are a series of genuinely heart-rending personal tragedies–including several divorces, the death of two sons and both parents, public censure and professional banishment for an unseemly marriage, numerous physical illnesses, and several other personal problems. Still, Lewis continues to blend sexual innuendo, raucous stage gestures, and driving piano rhythm to ignite his cheering audiences. The psychological sources of Jerry Lee's inflammatory character are too complex to unravel. The roots of his personality are as distinctive as his legendary lifestyle.[13]

Ninth, singularity of attention to music is another characteristic that sets Jerry Lee apart from most of his fellow rockers. This trait is both a strength and a weakness. Numerous contemporary musicians have elected to divide their professional lives in order to become actors, producers, managers, record-company owners, or even corporate heads of non-music-related enterprises. Jerry Lee Lewis has not diversified his attention or broadened his sources of income. In fact, he has probably encountered more problems with the Internal Revenue Service precisely because he has been unwilling to accept professional financial management advice about handling his personal wealth. The central concern in Jerry Lee's existence is his music. The rock boogie woogie totally dominates his soul. Ironically, the instability of this live-for-today attitude is part of the force that makes Jerry Lee a legend.

Tenth, songwriting is not one of Lewis' strong points. He has authored only a handful of the hundreds of tunes that he has recorded: "End of the Road," "High School Confidential," "Lewis Boogie," "Lincoln Limousine," and "He Took It Like a Man." This fact denies him membership in the exclusive league of rock singer/songwriters such as Chuck Berry, Paul Simon, Stevie Wonder, Sam Cooke, and Buddy Holly. But rock 'n' roll music is generally less cerebral than emotional, and no one is more emotional than Jerry Lee. Colin Escott and Martin Hawkins, in a chapter from *Sun Records: The Brief History of the Legendary Record Label*, attack the issue of Lewis' reliance on other people's tunes in the following manner: "Some critics have remarked that Jerry is handicapped because he does not write his own material. It is certainly true that he has written very little, although he maintains that he could if he wanted to. . . . He compensates by treating other writer's songs as if they were his own. Jerry has never been cowed by a good song, always believing that he can make a greater version and this self-confidence has usually been well justified."[14]

Eleventh, Jerry Lee Lewis did not fall into a trap like the one that grabbed Bill Haley. The European adoration for Elvis Presley, Fats Domino, Jerry Lee Lewis, Chuck Berry, Gene Vincent, Eddie Cochran, and other American rock 'n' roll originals was amply showered on Haley throughout the heights and depths of his performing career. Particularly in Great Britain, the "Rock Around the Clock" anthem will forever symbolize the dawning of the rock 'n' roll era. Haley emerged from the country-music shadows between 1952 and 1955, leaving The Four Aces of Western Swing and The Saddlemen behind and adopting a new group called The Comets. But after his sensational performances during the '50s, Haley never regained his hit-making stride and simply continued to revive his classic rock tunes for worshipping fans. Regrettably, he succumbed to the kind of time-warp popularity that Rick Nelson described so brilliantly in his 1972 tune "Garden Party." Jerry Lee avoided this trap for several reasons. He was a decade younger than Haley when his career began; he was more stylistically creative and flexible than Haley. He was also more ornery, antagonistic, and egotistical than the gentle Haley. And, finally, he was the kind of devastating showman that commanded public attention far beyond Haley's capabilities.[15]

Of course, any one of the eleven preceding assertions can be challenged. Death has not lessened the musical influence of Buddy Holly. Nor has Elvis' image dimmed since 1977. And the opening lines to Bill Haley's most popular recording remain universally recognized, if not immortal. Among the living giants of rock, Chuck Berry is still an awesome talent. So is the more musically diversified Ray Charles. The same can be said for Bo Diddley, Fats Domino, Little Richard, Carl Perkins, as well as several others. The weight of the eleven points presented above is designed to be cumulative, though. From his emergence as the piano-pumping rocker in Sam Phillip's Sun organization until today, Jerry Lee Lewis remains the living incarnation of rock 'n' roll music. The release of Sun Box 102 simply substantiates what so many music fans have always known.

JERRY LEE LEWIS NOTES

1. Carl Belz, *The Story of Rock*, second edition (New York: Harper & Row, 1972); Gene Busnar, *It's Rock 'n' Roll: A Musical History of the Fabulous Fifties* (New York: Wanderer, 1979); Steve Chapple and Reebee Garofalo, *Rock 'n' Roll Is Here to Pay: The History and Politics of the Music Industry* (Chicago: Nelson-Hall, 1977); Clive Davis, with James Willwerth, *Clive: Inside the Record Business* (New York: William Morrow, 1974); R. Serge Denisoff, *Solid Gold: The*

Popular Record Industry (New Brunswick: Transactions, 1975); Simon Frith, *Sound Effect: Youth, Leisure, and the Politics of Rock 'n' Roll* (New York: Pantheon, 1981): Charlie Gillett, *The Sound of the City: The Rise of Rock and Roll*, revised edition (New York: Outerbridge and Dienstfrey, 1983); Greil Marcus, *Mystery Train: Images of America in Rock 'n' Roll Music* (New York: E. P. Dutton, 1975); Jim Miller (ed.), *The Rolling Stone Illustrated History of Rock and Roll*, revised edition (New York: Random House/Rolling Stone, 1980); David Pichaske, *A Generation in Motion: Popular Music and Culture in the Sixties* (New York: Schirmer Books, 1979); Arnold Shaw, *Honkers and Shouters: The Golden Years of Rhythm and Blues* (New York: Collier, 1978); Arnold Shaw, *The Rockin' 50's: The Decade that Transformed the Pop Music Scene* (New York: Hawthorn, 1974); and Ritchie York, *The History of Rock 'n' Roll* (New York: Methuen, 1976).

2. Frank Scott, "Rockabilly, 50's Rock and Roll, Rhythm and Blues, Rock and Roll Revival," *Down Home Music, Inc. Newsletter* No. 32 (March 1983):p. 6.

3. Barrie Famblin, "Sun Box Report," *Fireball Mail* XX (September-October 1982): p. 4.

4. Jay Cocks, "A Few Rounds with The Killer," *Time* (March 13, 1983): p. 98.

5. Colin Escott and Martin Hawkins (comps.), *The Complete Sun Label Session Files*, revised edition (Bexhill-on-Sea, Sussex: Swift, 1978), and *Sun Records: The Brief History of the Legendary Record Label* (New York: Quick Fox, 1980).

6. Nick Tosches, *Country: The Biggest Music in America* (New York: Dell, 1977), p. 65.

7. John Hubner, "Jerry Lee Lewis: The Killer at 45," *Goldmine* No. 62 (July 1981): pp. 23-25.

8. Robert Palmer, "The Devil and Jerry Lee Lewis," *Rolling Stone* (December 13, 1979): pp. 57-61. Also see: Colin Escott and Martin Hawkins, "Jerry Lee Lewis," in *Sun Records: The Brief History of the Legendary Record Label* (New York: Quick Fox, 1980), pp. 103-115.

9. Palmer, *op cit*, p. 59.

10. Hubner, *op cit*, p. 23.

11. Ren Grevatt, "Jerry Lee Lewis Is the Wildest of Them All!" *Melody Maker* XXXIII (January 25, 1958): pp. 8-9; Mark Humphrey, "Jerry Lee Puts Rumor of His Demise to Rest," *Los Angeles Herald Examiner* (October 20, 1982); Bill Littleton, "Jerry Lee Lewis: There's Still 'A Whole Lotta Shakin' Goin' On,'" *Country Style* No. 69 (August 1981): pp. 28-31; Kristine McKenna, "Jerry Lee Lewis: Rock Incarnate," *Los Angeles Times* (October 20, 1982); Billy Miller, "88 Keys of Fury: The Killer Slays New York!" *Kicks* No. 2 (1979): pp. 43-44; and Bill Williams, "Jerry Lee Lewis: Super Showman/Paradox," *Billboard* LXXXV (March 13, 1973): pp. 39-46.

12. Nick Tosches, "Nashville Babylon–Loud Covenants: Jerry Lee Lewis, God's Garbage Man," *Creem* IX (March 1978): 49.

13. Nick Tosches, *Hellfire: The Jerry Lee Lewis Story* (New York: Dell Publishing Company, Inc., 1982) pp. 175-263; Robert Palmer, *Jerry Lee Lewis Rocks!*

(New York: Delilah, 1981); Peter Guralnick, "Jerry Lee Lewis: Hang up My Rock 'n' Roll Shoes," in *Feel Like Going Home: Portraits in Blues and Rock 'n' Roll* (New York: Outerbridge and Dienstfrey, 1971), pp. 146-162; Park Humphrey, "Jerry Lee Lewis: Where The Lord and The Devil Both Have Their Way," *Esquire* XCVII (June 1982): pp. 60-108; and Jack Hurst, "Child Bride Tells Jerry Lee's Story," *Detroit Free Press* (July 4, 1982): pp. F1, 5.

14. Escott and Hawkins, *Sun Records*, p. 115.

15. For descriptions of the classic rock 'n' roll performers, see Miller (comp.), *The Rolling Stone Illustrated History of Rock and Roll*, pp. 1-142; Stuart Colman, *They Kept on Rockin': The Giants of Rock 'n' Roll* (Dorset: Blandford, 1982), pp. 12-135; and Howard Elson, *Early Rockers* (New York: Proteus, 1982), pp. 1-127.

JERRY LEE LEWIS BIOGRAPHIES

Great Balls of Fire: The Uncensored Story of Jerry Lee Lewis, by Myra Lewis, with Murray Silver. New York: Quill, 1982. 332 pp.

Hellfire: The Jerry Lee Lewis Story, by Nick Tosches. New York: Delacorte, 1981. 263 pp.

Jerry Lee Lewis Rocks! by Robert Palmer. New York: Delilah, 1981. 128 pp.

Whole Lotta Shakin' Goin' On: Jerry Lee Lewis, by Robert Cain. New York: Dial, 1981. 143 pp.

Jerry Lee Lewis has captured newspaper attention from a Tennessee hospital bed, has appeared on several nationally televised talk shows and special music-awards programs, and has produced a series of pop albums for the Elektra and MCA recording companies. It is not surprising that, in addition to Sun Box 102, this recent public visibility also spawned the publication of four book-length biographies on the rocker. The authors of these studies follow a notable line of journalists and music critics–including Colin Escott, John Grissim, Peter Guralnick, Martin Hawkins, Bob Kinder, and Jim Miller–who have attempted to define, characterize, categorize, and accurately pigeonhole the irrepressible Jerry Lee. No study has yet succeeded in achieving this goal. None ever will.

The enigmatic, eccentric nature of Jerry Lee Lewis defies pen-and-paper analysis. His personal drive and stylistic talents are uniformly acknowledged; his egotism, eroticism, and penchant for verbal and physical violence have been amply chronicled; his wizardry with audiences and his onstage persona are legendary; and his premarital and extramarital shenanigans and family-related tragedies are also well-documented. One of his business colleagues attempted to simplify this mystery by noting, "Jerry is one of those persons who exists like fixed points on a compass by which everything else must be judged" (Silver, p. 294). Not unlike a magnetic pole, Jerry Lee has garnered the attention of nearly every American at one time or another during his blustery 25-year musical career. His private being remains encased in ice that appears transparent, but is remarkably hard and cold. Beneath this barrier lurks an unfathomable man.

Robert Cain offers an uncritical, laudatory, and generally apologetic picture of Jerry Lee Lewis in *Whole Lotta Shakin' Goin' On*. The pictures in the book are entertaining and the discography is well organized. However, the text is sadly spotty, and the interviews with Mickey Gilley, Steve Allen, Shelby Singleton, Tom Jones, and Jerry Kennedy are consistently shallow. Robert Palmer's study, *Jerry Lee Lewis Rocks!*, moves up a notch in both writing style and critical insight, but it is flawed by the author's attempt to blend a psycho-historical self-interview with Jerry Lee's biography. The photos, supplied mostly by Ron and Keith Kellerman, are superb. Despite Palmer's efforts to assemble observations by former band members, fan-club president Kay Martin, and Sam Phillips into an upbeat, socio-psychological analysis, his effort falls short of success. Under the title "The Devil and Jerry Lee Lewis," Palmer presented a more concise and cogent study of this performer in a five-page *Rolling Stone* article in 1979.

Nick Tosches originally approached the Jerry Lee Lewis phenomenon in his fascinating and controversial 1977 study *Country: The Biggest Music in America*. *Hellfire* expands his original interpretation with an awesome quality of mystical reporting. This does not mean that facts are ignored or that historical chronology is abandoned. Quite the contrary. Tosches functions as a journalistic James Michener/William Faulkner in presenting the reader with a diabolical tale of inherited evil. The burdens of highlighting Lewis family rifts and tragedies, depicting the polar elements of religious hymns and the devil's music in Jerry Lee's heart and soul, and weaving equal elements of promiscuity, alcoholism, violence, and drug abuse within a single musician's career create a text that sometimes begs for translation. Nevertheless, Tosches is a brilliant writer, even if a trifle excessive in his imagery. The tone of his work is sinister, but he gives Jerry Lee life as few other biographers could hope to do.

Murray Silver's *Great Balls of Fire*, penned through the cooperation, advice, memory, and understandable biases of Jerry Lee's third wife, Myra Lewis, is a remarkably thorough and candid study. Although it covers only two-thirds of the rock singer's career (1950-70), it is elegantly written, thoughtfully organized, and amazingly detailed. Jerry Lee is surrounded by heroes (Judd Phillips and Myra) and villains (Mamie Lewis and Sam Phillips), and he is faced with numerous personal tragedies of dramatic proportions. The portraits of Jerry Lee's family, friends, business associates, and fans are painted with penetrating strokes. The depth of Silver's biographical work surpasses even the stunning rock chronicles produced by Jerry Hopkins in *Elvis: A Biography* (1971) and *Elvis: The Final Years* (1981). The author uses intimate details provided by the subject's former wife to weave a complex fable that depicts a family's struggle with sudden fame and outrageous fortune. The book also details the nature of the American music industry (focusing on recording, retailing, and promoting activities), the impact of mass-media reporting on personal lives and public careers, and the rigors of performing popular music during the period from Elvis Presley's rise to prominence until the breakup of The Beatles. Silver has produced an epic tale indeed.

But with all of the literary hoopla about his dynamic stage presence, his personal predilections for revelry and devilment, his troubled fundamentalist soul, and his never-ending search for Elvis' crown as the "King of Rock 'n' Roll," Jerry Lee Lewis remains a masked man throughout these four biographies. Traditional Jerry Lee vignettes are told and retold, but the actor is never stripped of his grease paint. Is Jerry Lee actually a Pentecostal? Is he a racist Bayou redneck? Does his unmanageability stem from his own internal stubbornness, or is it a logical reaction to confrontations with external greed and duplicity? The real Jerry Lee may be as much of a secret to himself as he is to his biographers simply because he remains so determined to be famous that he has sublimated all that is soft, warm, personal, and humane in his personality. The outer shell–which effectively wards off the death of close relatives, the barbs of nosy reporters, the embarrassments of arrogant fans, the demands of money-hungry supplicants, and even the love of those who genuinely treasure his talents–is all that can be depicted. It would be too bad if that were all that was left of this dynamic, persevering, crowd-pleasing artist.

JERRY LEE LEWIS REFERENCE SOURCES

A. Sun Records: The Memphis Launching Pad

Barnes, Barbara. "Sun Records: An Insider's View," *New Kommotion*, II (Spring 1977), pp. 30-31.

Becker, Robert. "The Sun Sound," *Record Exchanger*, III (February 1973), pp. 12-14.

Cooper, B. Lee and James A. Creeth. "Present at the Creation: The Legend of Jerry Lee Lewis on Record, 1956-1963," *Fireball Mail*, XXII (May/June 1984), pp. 9-12.

Davis, Hank. "The Jerry Lee Lewis Sun Sound," *Goldmine*, No. 234 (July 14, 1989), p. 14.

Doggett, Peter. "Sun Records: The Golden Years," *Record Collector*, No. 92 (April 1987), pp. 24-25.

Doggett, Peter. "Sun Records on CD," *Record Collector* No. 95 (July 1987), pp. 15-18.

Escott, Colin, with Martin Hawkins, *Good Rockin' Tonight: Sun Records and the Birth of Rock 'n' Roll*. New York: St. Martin's Press, 1991.

Escott, Colin and Martin Hawkins, *Sun Records: The Brief History of the Legendary Record Label*. New York: Quick Fox, 1980.

Escott, Colin and Martin Hawkins (comps), *Sun Records: The Discography*. Bremen, West Germany: Bear Family Records, 1987.

Finnis, Robert. "The Rise and Set of Sun," *Rock*, XI (December 14, 1970), pp. 9-10, 31.

Guralnick, Peter. "The Million Dollar Quartet," *New York Times Magazine*, (March 25, 1979), pp. 28-30, 41-45.

Hall, Claude. "Phillips, Presley, Cash, Sun," *Billboard*, LXXXI (December 27, 1969), p. 110.

Koda, Cub. "The Rockin' Sun Year: Sumpin' for Cool-in-the-Know Folks," *Goldmine*, No. 182 (July 17, 1982), pp. 78-79.

Koda, Cub. "The Sun Blues Box: A Killer by Any Standard," *Goldmine*, No. 151 (May 9, 1986), pp. 68, 70.

"Memphis Spurs Country/Blues Merger," *Billboard*, LXXXI (March 29, 1969), p. 24.

Pugh, John. "Rise and Fall of Sun Records," *Country Music*, II (November 1973), pp. 26-32.
Sasfy, Joe. "Sunrise at Memphis," *Musician*, No. 88 (February 1986) pp. 96-100, 110.
Vernon, Paul. *The Sun Legend*. London: Steve Lane, 1969.

B. Biographical Studies

Cain, Robert. *Whole Lotta Shakin' Goin' On: Jerry Lee Lewis–The Rock Years, The Country Years, The Triumphs, and the Tragedies*. New York: Dial Press, 1981.
Clark, Alan. *Jerry Lee Lewis: The Ball of Fire*. West Covina, California: Alan Clark Productions, 1980.
Escott, Colin. *Jerry Lee Lewis: The Killer 1963-1968*. Bremen, West Germany: Bear Family Records, 1986.
Escott, Colin. *Jerry Lee Lewis: The Killer 1973-1977*. Bremen, West Germany: Bear Family Records, 1987.
Guterman, Jimmy. *Rockin' My Life Away: Listening to Jerry Lee Lewis*. Nashville, Tennessee: Rutledge Hill Press, 1991.
LeFebvre, Tania A. *Jerry Lee Lewis: The Killer's Story*. Paris, France: Horus Books, 1980.
Lewis, Myra, with Murray Silver, *Great Balls of Fire: The Uncensored Story of Jerry Lee Lewis*. New York: Quill Books, 1982.
Palmer, Robert. *Jerry Lee Lewis Rocks!* New York: Delilah Books, 1981.
Tosches, Nick. *Hellfire: The Jerry Lee Lewis Story*. New York: Dell Publishing Company, Inc., 1982.

C. Articles and Essays

Bolstad, Helen. "Jerry Lee Lewis: New Memphis Skyrocket," in *Legends of Sun Records*, compiled by Alan Clark (West Covina, California: Alan Lungstrum/ National Rock and Roll Archives, 1986), pp. 41-52.
Clark, Alan. "Jerry Lee Lewis," in *Legends of Sun Records–Number Two* (West Covina, California: Alan Lungstrum/National Rock and Roll Archives, 1992), pp. 58-67.
Clark, Alan. "Jerry Lee Lewis," in *Rock and Roll Legends–Number Two* (West Covina, California: Alan Lungstrum/National Rock and Roll Archives, 1987), pp. 52-56.
Clarke, Donald. "Jerry Lee Lewis," *The Penguin Encyclopedia of Popular Music* (New York: Viking Penguin, Inc., 1989), pp. 701-702.
Colman, Stuart. "Jerry Lee Lewis: The Killer Himself," in *They Kept on Rockin': The Giants of Rock 'n' Roll* (Poole, Dorset, England: Blandford Press, 1982), pp. 53-65.
Cook, Phil. "Jerry Lee Lewis," *Record Collector*, No. 17 (January 1981), pp. 13-19.

Cooper, B. Lee. "Jerry Lee Lewis and Little Richard: Career Parallels in the Lives of the Court Jesters of Rock 'n' Roll," *Music World and Record Digest*, No. 46 (May 23, 1979), p. 6.

Cooper, B. Lee. "Jerry Lee Lewis: Rock 'n' Roll's Living Legend," *Music World*, No. 90 (October 1981), pp. 28-36.

Doggett, Peter. "Jerry Lee Lewis: Killer Cuts," *Record Collector*, No. 146 (October 1991), pp. 90-93.

Dunsdon, Eric. "Another Place, Another Time . . ." *Now Dig This*, No. 87 (June 1990), p. 25.

Elson, Howard. "Jerry Lee Lewis," in *Early Rockers* (New York: Proteus Books, 1982), pp. 78-89.

Escott, Colin, and Martin Hawkins, "Jerry Lee Lewis" and "The Lewis Style," in *Sun Records: The Brief History of the Legendary Record Label* (New York: Quick Fox, 1980), pp 103-108 and 109-115.

Escott, Colin. "Jerry Lee Lewis: The Ferriday Wild Man," *Goldmine*, No. 234 (July 14, 1989), pp. 7-12.

Escott, Colin. "Jerry Lee Lewis: Huey P. Meaux and the 'Southern Roots' Sessions," *Goldmine*, No. 196 (January 29, 1988), pp. 38, 40.

Gambaccini, Paul. "Jerry Lee Lewis," in *Track Records: Profiles of 22 Rock Stars* (North Pomfret, Vermont: David and Charles, 1986), pp. 93-100.

Gollubier, Bruce. "Spotlight on Jerry Lee Lewis," *Rockin' 50s*, No. 21 (December 1989), pp. 8-16.

Grevatt, Ren. "Jerry Lee Lewis Is the Wildest of Them All!" *Melody Maker*, XXXIII (January 25, 1958), pp. 8-9.

Grissim, John. "Jerry Lee Lewis: Higher than Most . . . and Getting Higher," *Rolling Stone*, No. 66 (September 17, 1970), pp. 30-33.

Grissim, John. "Whole Lotta Shakin' at the D.J. Hop," in *Country Music: White Man's Blues* (New York: Paperback Library, 1970), pp. 271-296.

Guralnick, Peter. "Jerry Lee Lewis: The Greatest Rocker of Them All," *Fireball Mail*, XXII (January/February 1984), pp. 10-11.

Guralnick, Peter. "Jerry Lee Lewis: Hang up My Rock 'n' Roll Shoes," in *Feel Like Going Home: Portraits in Blues and Rock 'n' Roll* (New York: Outerbridge and Dienstfrey, 1971), pp. 146-162.

Hill, Randal C. "Jerry Lee Lewis," in *Legends of Sun Records*, compiled by Alan Clark (West Covina, California: Alan Lungstrum/National Rock and Roll Archives, 1986), pp. 32-40.

Hubner, John. "Jerry Lee Lewis," *Goldmine*, No. 62 (July 1981), pp. 23-25.

Humphrey, Mark. "Jerry Lee Lewis: Where The Lord and The Devil Both Have Their Way," *Esquire*, XCVII (June 1982), pp. 106-108.

Kinder, Bob. "Jerry Lee Lewis," *Record Exchanger*, No. 21 (1975), pp. 4-11.

Littleton, Bill. "Jerry Lee Lewis: There's Still 'A Whole Lotta Shakin' Goin' On'," *Country Style*, No. 69 (August 1981), pp. 28-31.

McAuliffe, Jon. "Jerry Lee Lewis: Another Place, Another Time–The Smash Years," *Goldmine*, No. 176 (April 24, 1987), p. 16.

McNutt, Randy. "Mr. Pumping Piano," in *We Wanna Boogie: An Illustrated History of the American Rockabilly Movement* (Fairfield, Ohio: Hamilton Hobby Press, 1988), pp. 103-105.

Miller, Jim. "Jerry Lee Lewis," in *The Rolling Stone Illustrated History of Rock 'n' Roll*, revised edition (New York: Random House/Rolling Stone Press Book, 1980), pp. 66-71.

Palmer, Robert. "The Devil and Jerry Lee Lewis," *Rolling Stone*. No. 306 (December 13, 1979), pp. 57-61.

Scott, Steve. "Jerry Lee Lewis," *Record Collector*, No. 41 (January 1983), pp. 20-26.

Seay, David. "The King and The Killer," in *Stairway to Heaven: The Spiritual Roots of Rock 'n' Roll from The King and Little Richard to Prince and Amy Grant* (New York: Ballantine Books, 1986), pp. 45-69.

Shaw, Arnold. "Jerry Lee Lewis Interview," in *The Rockin' 50's: The Decade that Transformed the Pop Music Scene* (New York: Hawthorn Books, 1974), pp. 190-193.

Silver, Jr., Murray M. "Jerry Lee Lewis Update: Dubs, Recent Discoveries, and Black Waxen Frisbees," *Goldmine*, No. 71 (April 1982), pp. 178-179.

Stambler, Irwin. "Jerry Lee Lewis," in *The Encyclopedia of Pop, Rock and Soul* (New York: St. Martin's Press, 1974), pp 306-308.

Tamarkin, Jeff. "Great Balls of Fire! Producer Adam Fields Talks About the New Jerry Lee Lewis Film Biography," *Goldmine*, No. 234 (July 14, 1989), pp. 16-20.

Tosches, Nick. "Behold a Shaking: Jerry Lee Lewis, 1953-1956," *Journal of Country Music*, IX (October 1981), pp. 4-11.

Tosches, Nick. "The Coming of Jerry Lee Lewis," *Journal of Country Music*, IX, No. 2 (1982), pp. 16-25.

Tosches, Nick. "Loud Covenants," in *Country: The Biggest Music in America* (New York: Dell Publishing Company, Inc., 1977), pp. 23-97.

Tosches, Nick. "Nashville Babylon–Loud Covenants: Jerry Lee Lewis, God's Garbage Man," *Creem*, IX (March 1978), pp. 48-51ff.

Tosches, Nick. "Jerry Lee Lewis: The Smash/Mercury Years," *Goldmine*, No. 112 (November 9, 1984), pp. 6-22.

Tosches, Nick. "Whole Lotta Shakin' Goin' On," *Goldmine*, No. 76 (September 1982), p. 19.

Tucker, Stephen R. "Pentecostalism and Popular Culture in the South: A Study of Four Musicians," *Journal of Popular Culture*, XVI (Winter 1982), pp. 68-80.

White, Cliff. "The Killer Speaks: An Interview," *New Kommotion*, No. 24 (1980), pp. 22-24.

White, Timothy. "Jerry Lee Lewis," in *Rock Lives: Profiles and Interviews* (New York: Henry Holt and Company, 1990), pp. 47-51.

White, Timothy. "Jerry Lee Lewis," in *Rock Stars* (New York: Stewart, Tabori, and Chang, 1984), pp. 66-71.

Williams, Bill. "Jerry Lee Lewis: Super Showman/Paradox," *Billboard*, LXXXV (March 31, 1973), pp. 39-46.

Woodford, Chris. "He Is What He Is!" *Now Dig This*, No. 82 (January 1990), p. 28.
Woodford, Chris. "Jerry Lee Lewis Meets the Press [May 1958]," *Now Dig This*, No. 62 (May 1988), pp. 12-13.
Woodford, Chris. "Kickin' Ass with The Killer," *Now Dig This*, No. 26 (May 1985), pp. 22-23.
Woodford, Chris. "*Still* the Greatest Live Show on Earth," *Now Dig This*, No. 50 (May 1987), pp. 9-10.
Woodford, Chris. "*Still* the Greatest Live Show on Earth," *Now Dig This*, No. 51 (June 1987), pp. 18-22.
Woodford, Chris. "The Tour that Never Was," *Now Dig This*, No. 87 (June 1990), pp. 24-25.

D. Interviews and Commentaries

Cain, Robert. "Steve Allen: An Interview," "Mickey Gilley: An Interview," "Sun Records Today: An Interview with Shelby Singleton," "Tom Jones and the 'Killer': An Interview," and "The Country Years: An Interview with Jerry Kennedy," in *Whole Lotta Shakin' Goin' On: Jerry Lee Lewis–The Rock Years, the Country Years, the Triumphs, and the Tragedies* (New York: Dial Press, 1981), pp. 61-69, 35-40, 103-108, 109-113, and 115-126.
Cajiao, Trevor. "Kenny Lovelace Interview," *Now Dig This*, No. 27 (June 1985), pp. 8-9.
Ferguson, Ben. "Speaking to The Killer: Jerry Lee Lewis Interview," *Paperback Writer*, I (July 1979), p. 8.
Forte, Dan. "Kenny Lovelace: Two Decades with Jerry Lee Lewis," *Guitar Players*, XVII (December 1983), pp. 80-82, 154.
Fugate, Bill and Jerry Lee Lewis, "Much Too Much," *Bop*, No. 1 (1982), pp. 32-37.
Kaval, Bill. "Exclusive Interview," *Music World and Record Digest*, No. 41 (May 16, 1979), p. 1.
Osborne, Jerry P. and Shelby Singleton, "Million Dollar Quartet!" in *Our Best to You–From Record Digest* (Prescott, Arizona: O'Sullivan, Woodside and Company, 1981), pp. 39-44.
Smith, Joe. "Jerry Lee Lewis," in *Off the Record: An Oral History of Popular Music* (New York: Warner Books, 1988), pp. 97-99.
Tosches, Nick. "Linda Gail Lewis," *Goldmine*, No. 67 (December 1981), p. 162.
White, Cliff. "The Killer Speaks: An Interview," *New Kommotion*, No. 24 (1980), pp. 22-24.

E. Book Reviews

Cocks, Jay. "A Few Rounds with The Killer," *Time*, CXXI (March 14, 1983) p. 98.
Cooper, B. Lee. "In Search of Jerry Lee Lewis," *JEMF Quarterly*, XVIII (Fall 1982/Winter 1983), pp. 192-193.
Cooper, B. Lee. "Review of *Whole Lotta Shakin' Goin' On: Jerry Lee Lewis Rocks* by Robert Palmer; *Hellfire: The Jerry Lee Lewis Story* by Nick Tosches; and

Great Balls of Fire: The Uncensored Story of Jerry Lee Lewis by Myra Lewis, with Murray Silver," *American Music*, III (Summer 1985), pp. 236-238.
Hilburn, Robert. "Review of Three Books About Jerry Lee Lewis," *Journal of Country Music*, IX, No. 2 (1982), pp. 126-129.
Hurst, Jack. "Child Bride Tells Jerry Lee's Story," *Detroit Free Press*, (July 4, 1982), pp. F1, 5.
Nelson, Paul. "'Hellfire': Devil's Music and Jerry Lee Lewis," *Rolling Stone*, No. 374 (July 22, 1982), p. 42.
Santelli, Robert. "Review of *Hellfire* by Nick Tosches," *Goldmine*, No. 75 (August 1982), p. 177.
Wolcott, James. "Review of *Hellfire* by Nick Tosches," *Esquire*, XCVII (July 1982), p. 120.
Yronwode, Catherine. "Review," *Bop*, No. 1 (1982), pp. 38-39.

F. Concert Reviews

Miller, Billy. "88 Keys of Fury: The Killer Slays New York!" *Kicks*, No. 2 (1979), pp. 43-44.
Palmer, Robert. "Jerry Lee's Shrine," *Rolling Stone*, No. 321 (July 10, 1980), p. 68.
Sandford, Paul. "Jerry Lee–Almost Back to Being Brilliant," *New Kommotion*, II (Spring 1977), p. 16.

G. Record Reviews

Cajiao, Trevor. " The Jerry Lee Lewis Boxing Match," *Now Dig This*, No. 79 (October 1989), pp. 22-25.
Cajiao, Trevor. "Lotsa' Killer," *Now Dig This*, No. 105 (December 1991), p. 15.
Cocks, Jay. "A Few Rounds with The Killer," *Time*, CXXI (March 14, 1983), p. 98.
Cooper, B. Lee. and James A. Creeth. "Present at the Creation: The Legend of Jerry Lee Lewis on Record, 1956-1963," *JEMF Quarterly*, XIX (Summer 1983), pp. 122-129.
Dodds, Harry. "Classic Cuts: Jerry Lee Lewis," *Now Dig This*, No. 99 (June 1991), pp. 18-19.
Escott, Colin. "Jerry Lee Lewis: Huey P. Meaux, and the 'Southern Roots' Sessions," *Goldmine*, No. 196 (January 29, 1988), pp. 38, 40.
Macon, Fry. "Think About It," *Wavelength*, No. 109 (November 1989), pp. 11-12.
Koda, Cub. "Time to Get Serious . . ." *Goldmine*, No. 265 (September 21, 1990), p. 34.
Koda, Cub. "200-Plus Sun Sides by The Killer Hizzownself," *Goldmine*, No. 131 (August 2, 1985), p. 60.
Komorowski, Adam. "Jerry Lee Lewis Sun Box," *New Kommotion*, No. 27 (1983), pp. 5-8.
Neale, Tony, Bill Humphreys, and Dave Oksanen, "Reviews and Previews–The Million Dollar Quartet," *Music World*, No. 84 (April 1981), pp. 56-58.
"Record Collector's Album of the Month–The Million Dollar Quartet (Charly/Sun 1006)," *Record Collector*, No. 25 (September 1981), pp. 50-51.

"Review of Jerry Lee Lewis–The Killer, 1963-1968 (Bear Family BFX 15210)," *Record Collector*, No. 88 (December 1986), pp. 53-54.

Tosches, Nick. "Review of Jerry Lee Lewis Album," *High Fidelity*, XXIX (June 1979), p. 109.

Vance, Joel. "Jerry Lee Lewis: Doing All He Can to Become a Legend in His Own Time," *Stereo Review*, XLV (July 1980), p. 71.

H. Discographies

Boer, Wim de. (comp.), *Breathless: The Jerry Lee Lewis Long Play Album Guide*, Best, Holland: De Witte Publications, 1983.

Cain, Robert. "Discography," in *Whole Lotta Shakin' Goin' On: Jerry Lee Lewis*, (New York: Dial Press, 1981), pp. 127-141.

Cook, Phil. "Jerry Lee Lewis U.K. Discography, 1957-67," *Record Collector*, No. 17 (January 1981), pp. 18-19.

Cooper, B. Lee. "The Charted 45 R.P.M. Hits of Jerry Lee Lewis, 1957-1980" and "Selected Discography of Jerry Lee Lewis Albums, 1958-1980," *Music World*, No. 90 (October 1981), pp. 32-34 and 34-36.

Escott, Colin, and Martin Hawkins (comps.), *Sun Records: The Discography*. Bremen, West Germany: Bear Family Records, 1987.

Gamblin, Barrie. "Jerry Lee Lewis–A Post-1970 Discography," *New Kommotion*, No. 6 (Summer 1974), pp. 22-23.

Gamblin, Barrie. "Jerry Lee Lewis, 1970-1974: Part 2," *New Kommotion*, No. 7 (Fall 1974), pp. 10-11.

Gamblin, Barrie. "Jerry Lee Lewis, 1970-1974: Part 3," *New Kommotion*, No. 8 (Winter 1975), pp. 8-9.

Gamblin, Barrie. "The Mercury Sessions: Jerry Lee Lewis Unreleased Masters," *Fireball Mail*, XXIII (July/August 1985), pp. 4-6.

Guterman, Jimmy. "The Records: A Selective Collection," in *Rockin' My Life Away: Listening to Jerry Lee Lewis* (Nashville, Tennessee: Rutledge Hill Press, 1991), pp. 209-215.

Kinder, Bob. "Jerry Lee Lewis Discography," *Record Exchanger*, No. 21 (1975), p. 11.

McAuliffe, Jon. "Jerry Lee Lewis: Another Place, Another Time–The Smash Years," *Goldmine*, No. 176 (April 24, 1987), p. 16.

Scott, Steve. "Jerry Lee Lewis Discography: The Sun Releases," *Record Collector*, No. 41 (January 1983), p. 26.

Tosches, Nick. "Jerry Lee Lewis: The Smash/Mercury Years–Part 2," *Goldmine*, No. 113 (November 23, 1984), pp. 30-38.

Tosches, Nick. "Session Recordings," *Goldmine*, No. 112 (November 9, 1984), pp. 6-22.

Umphred, Neal. "Jerry Lee Lewis U.S. Sun Records Discography and Price Guide," *Goldmine*, No. 234 (July 14, 1989), pp. 22-24.

Weize, Richard. (comp.), "A Preliminary Jerry Lee Lewis Discography," in *Jerry Lee Lewis: The Killer, 1963-1968* by Colin Escott (Bremen, West Germany: Bear Family Records, 1986), pp. 81-127.

Weize, Richard. (comp.), "A Preliminary Jerry Lee Lewis Discography," in *Jerry Lee Lewis: The Killer, 1969-1972* by Colin Escott (Bremen, West Germany: Bear Family Records, 1986), pp. 65-120.
Weize, Richard. (comp.), "A Preliminary Jerry Lee Lewis Discography (revised edition)," in *Jerry Lee Lewis: The Killer, 1973-1977* by Colin Escott (Bremen, West Germany: Bear Family Records, 1987), pp. 65-120.
"A Whole Lotta' Jerry Lee!" *Now Dig This*, No. 83 (February 1990), pp. 26-27.

BUDDY HOLLY

Thirty-five years after his death, Buddy Holly remains a legendary figure in the world of contemporary music. There have been many talented singers, songwriters, and musicians who have died unexpectedly–Eddie Cochran, Frankie Lymon, King Curtis, Clyde McPhatter, Bobby Darin, Jim Croce, Otis Redding, Jimi Hendrix, Janis Joplin, Jim Morrison, Elvis Presley, and John Lennon, just to name a few. However, it is particularly fascinating how continuing attention has focused on the compositions, the singing style, the instrumentation, and the recorded legacy of Charles Hardin Holly.

The details of the tragic death of one of rock's first legendary figures are well known. At 1:00 a.m. on the morning of February 3, 1959, a small private plane piloted by Roger Peterson crashed near Clear Lake, Iowa, while en route from Mason City, Iowa, to Fargo, North Dakota. The pilot and his three passengers–Ritchie Valens of Los Angeles, California; J. P. Richardson of Beaumont, Texas; and Buddy Holly of Lubbock, Texas–were all killed. The passengers were part of a touring pop-music show that had performed the previous evening at the Surf Ballroom in Clear Lake.

The young Valens, only 17 years old, had produced two major records by the time of his death: "Come on, Let's Go" and the two-sided Del-Fi hit "Donna"/"La Bamba." Richardson, at age 28, had been a disc jockey and program director at radio station KTRM in Beaumont before he emerged in 1958 as the "Big Bopper." He had hit the *Billboard* charts three times, with his Mercury-label tunes "Chantilly Lace," "Big Bopper's Wedding," and "Little Red Riding Hood." The 22-year-old Holly, who during a brief recording career had established himself as a creative force in pop music, was undeniably the headline performer. His unexpected death stunned the music world. The legacy of his 45-r.p.m. hits for Brunswick

("That'll Be the Day," "Oh, Boy!," "Maybe Baby," "Think It Over," and "Fool's Paradise") and for Coral ("Peggy Sue," "Rave On," and "Early in the Morning") was monumental. And after his death, three more Holly recordings on Coral–"Heartbreak," "It Doesn't Matter Anymore," and "Raining in My Heart"–reached *Billboard's* Hot 100 list. It was from this rich recording base, and because of his personal friendship with Holly, that Wichita Falls, Texas, disc jockey Snuff Garrett launched his special tribute to the young rock 'n' roll performer on the day of his passing. This piece of oral history, featuring Garrett as chief commentator, offers a personal and on-the-spot perspective that captures the emotional drama and the sense of loss that accompanied the death of Buddy Holly. It preserves a variety of Holly's early recordings, some familiar and some rare, between the rambling eulogy and personal reveries of the disc jockey; it is also a portrait of the American popular-music industry in a simpler time. The following text is a transcript of that program.

(*Snuff Garrett's "Tribute to Buddy Holly" begins with the playing of "Peggy Sue"*)

Garrett: Buddy Holly was one of the greatest guys in the world. This morning, we received a notice date-lined "Mason City, Iowa" that three rock 'n' roll singers who had just hit the big time had died in a plane crash in an Iowa farm field. Ritchie Valens, Buddy Holly, and J. P. "Big Bopper" Richardson were being flown in a private plane piloted by Roger Peterson, who was also killed, to a rock-and-roll concert in Fargo, North Dakota.[1]

The Big Bopper, after working for nine years at a radio station in Beaumont, Texas, as a disc jockey, had gained fame with a thing called "Chantilly Lace"–"a pretty face and a pony tail hanging down." Ritchie Valens, a 17-year-old guy, came on strong not too long ago out of Los Angeles with a smash hit called "Donna." The flip-side hit was "La Bamba." Now he'll never know the experience of being a really, really big star across the nation because he's dead.

Buddy Holly had his big taste of success with "Peggy Sue," "That'll Be the Day," "Maybe Baby," and a lot of 'em. Just recently, he released a brand new one called "It Doesn't Matter Anymore," which is probably going to hit the national charts in a couple of weeks. It's already a very big record in the Wichita Falls area. Buddy, it couldn't have missed. Nobody could sing rock 'n' roll any better. One of the greatest guys in the world. And all of a sudden, it's all ended in Mason City, Iowa. Ritchie Valens, one of the three guys who was killed, had this big hit of the present day. Most recording companies, when they go in to cut a record, will usually do four to six tunes during a recording session. Probably, Ritchie Valens has got maybe four or five or six more songs "in the can" (as they say in the trade). Maybe they got some more records; maybe they don't. Maybe they were going to have a recording session tomorrow with him. Just like Buddy.

We talked to Buddy's manager not long ago. You'll be hearing the interview with Norman Petty, Buddy Holly's manager, in a little while.[2] Buddy was due in New York next week for a recording date. Norman will tell you all about it in a little while. We also talked to The Crickets awhile ago in Lubbock. Contrary to what it said in the paper tonight, The Crickets were not in the bus that went ahead to the next engagement, while the other three fellows flew. They weren't even there. They were in Lubbock at that time. The Crickets were not on the tour. It was Buddy by himself; he just went on a weekend thing.[3]

They were all tore up about it in Lubbock, all the radio stations there, all the guys that Buddy had known for a long time. They remember him when he was laying brick. Buddy started out as a brick layer–just like anybody else. He loved to sing; used to sing in all kinds of different places. You often hear the story that he started out touring around that little Texas town [Lubbock] . That's just the way it was. He used to sing around town, but he didn't pick up much loot. He made more money as a brick contractor, and he bought his first big car with money from laying brick. He kept that same car until last year, too. They say that there's two things a rock 'n' roll singer buys first: a brand new Cadillac and a diamond ring. And I don't know a one that hasn't got both. Buddy wasn't like that. He was just another singer and swinger and had a good time. He had a lot of money and carried on. But he remembered his friends–that was the nice thing. He didn't just go big-hat and leave the group.

This is one of the songs that hit big all across the nation, and it stayed up on the charts for a long time, too. Like Buddy said about all of his records, they don't go right to the top of the charts like The Everly Brothers' tunes, but they make just as much money because they get into the number 50 or 60 position and they just stay there month after month, for about three or four months, and just keep piling in the old loot. That's what he said, just piling in the money month after month. This is one of Buddy's records that did it. Anybody who likes rock 'n' roll will like this one by The Crickets–"Maybe Baby."

(*Garrett plays "Maybe Baby"*)

Garrett: The chirpin' Crickets right there with "Maybe Baby." Buddy had a guy that helped him more than anyone else. His name was Norman Petty. Many older people used to dance to the music of The Norman Petty Trio, a great combo that had played a lot of club dates across the nation. The leader of that group was Buddy Holly's manager. And to give you an idea of what kind of money Buddy, Ritchie Valens, and J. P. Richardson make from their records, just Norman's 10% for being manager of The Crickets kept him living very mellow for quite awhile. I don't mean to say that he didn't earn his commission by any means. He lives and has his recording studio in Clovis, New Mexico. We talked earlier this afternoon on the phone.[4]

S.G.: Mr. Petty, this is Snuff Garrett at KSYD in Wichita Falls.
N.P.: How are you, Snuff?
S.G.: Fine, thank you. I've never met you personally, but everyone knew you in the recording industry as the maker and founder of The Crickets.
N.P.: You had a lot to do with their success, too, you know.
S.G.: Thank you very much. Buddy was a great guy.
N.P.: He was probably one of the finest young talents in America.
S.G.: That's true, Norman. It seems strange that he started out not doing too much around Lubbock, just trying to make music like 28,000 other boys did. But he was

lucky enough to make it. Of course, with your help. Have you gotten any additional word on what's happened up in Iowa?

N.P.: Well, Snuff, I received a call this morning from Indiana, from one of our radio-station friends, who said the only thing he had heard was that the private plane had crashed and that three fellows and the pilot had been killed.

S.G.: Yeah, Ritchie Valens and The Big Bopper.

N.G.: And Buddy and, I believe, the pilot, too.

S.G.: He played a show up there in Iowa last night, didn't he?

N.P.: Yes, and he was on his way to the next town for another show.

S.G.: Norman, how long had Buddy been married?

N.P.: Well, let's see–you caught me off guard with that question–not very long.

S.G.: About four months?

N.P.: Probably four or five months.[5]

S.G.: Is his wife still in New York?

N.P.: She's in New York.

S.G.: I'm certainly sorry about Buddy's death, and I'm very sorry to bother you at a time like this.

N.P.: Well, Snuff, sometimes things happen like this and there's nothing we can do to control them. We may question why things like this happen, of course, but there's always bound to be a reason somewhere.

S.G.: Norm, does Buddy have many more records in the can?

N.P.: I think he has two more that we did in New York.[6] Do you know the last tune we had?

S.G.: Paul Anka's tune?[7]

N.P.: Well, we have two others that were done at the same time. I probably have some here in the can in Clovis, too.

S.G.: Oh, I see.

N.P.: He was supposed to go in for another session next week.

S.G.: Oh, gosh.

N.P.: However, the ones that we did in New York and the ones that I have here are the only ones left now.

S.G.: I see. Will you put most of those out? I hope you will. I mean, his last songs?

N.P.: It depends, of course. There's bound to be some legal action concerning Buddy's estate, which we are not going to comment on.

S.G.: Yeah, that's true.

N.P.: I'm sure that the two that we did in New York will be out, though.

S.G.: Well, good. All right, Mr. Petty, thank you very much for talking to us. We certainly appreciate it.

N.P.: Thank you for calling, Snuff.

S.G.: Goodbye.

Garrett: That's Norman Petty, the manager of Buddy Holly and The Crickets. Buddy thought a million dollars' worth of Norman Petty. He felt that he owed him everything in the world for getting him started. Norman took care of all of Buddy's financial matters. He would invest Buddy's money; he wasn't going to let him be an overnight sensation and then a broke has-been. You know how a lot of the guys have two or three hit records and make a fortune, then pretty soon its all gone. Norman wasn't going to let that happen to Buddy.[8] Buddy had his money invested in several different business firms and record shops. He called me one day and talked about record shops. He said that he wanted to invest some of his money in something that wasn't going to be a here-today-and-gone-tomorrow deal. He liked the feeling of having money, and he intended to keep it.

I think that one of the greatest stories in the world is how The Crickets wrote "That'll Be the Day." Buddy's best friend in high school was Jerry Allison, the drummer for The Crickets. You'll hear Jerry in a little while. Jerry and Buddy went all through high school together and lived in Lubbock. Their families are still real good friends. Jerry liked to write songs. He had a girl in California, and he wrote a song one day for her. Of course, you've already heard it–"Peggy Sue." Jerry wrote the first draft of "Peggy Sue," and Buddy helped him with it.[9] It became a never-to-be-forgotten million seller. Not too long ago, we had "Buddy Holly Day" here at KSYD radio, and Buddy and the guys came down for a couple of days after their last trip to New York, when they were on *The Ed Sullivan Show.*

Jerry had gotten married only two days before that visit; she was [his] Peggy Sue. I only met Buddy's wife one time. His wife was real nice. Buddy died at only 22 years of age, leaving a bride of six months living in New York City. They were married on August 15, 1958, and her name was Maria Elena Santiago. She had been a receptionist, but Buddy told her to stop working because he had enough money to support them. She told him that she wanted to keep on working, though, since he's on the road so much. She worked at Southern Music Company in New York, which had published several of Buddy's hits. After six months, it's all gone, the whole thing.

As I was saying a while ago, there is a funny story behind the title of the first big hit The Crickets had. Jerry and Buddy went to see a show called *The Searchers*, with John Wayne. It was a typical cowboy show. All the way through the film somebody would say, "I'm gonna kill ya, John Wayne," and he would answer, "That'll be the day." Everything was "That'll be the day." After they left the show, Jerry said, "Let's write a song called 'That'll Be the Day' " and they did. That was pretty clever.

That was The Cricket's first big hit. It was one of Buddy's slow risers, too. This was one of the first times I met Buddy. This record had just come out, and I asked, "Buddy, what's the good side on this record?" He said, "Well, I'll tell you the side I like is 'That'll Be the Day,' but it'll never do anything. The other side is the side, the one we're really pushing to be a big hit–"I'm Looking For Someone to Love." Six months later, "That'll Be the Day" was the number one song across the nation.

Buddy was on his way after that. They worked like beavers with busted teeth. Last year, Buddy was only home nine days out of the whole year. The Crickets traveled 355 days, you know, doing shows every night, traveling; they even went to Australia. They were a big hit in England, too. And next year, they were going to go to Europe. Buddy told me how much fun they had on these tours, getting together with guys like The Everly Brothers, who were Buddy's closest friends. But it still gets kinda tiresome, just a bunch of guys rolling around the country together, playing shows night after night, working three hours each night and then getting off with nothing to do. You don't have time to meet too many people or to make good friends. They took up games like poker 'cause it would pass the time. They even got a teacher and took up fencing; *all* of them, The Everly Brothers and The Crickets. They bought those little white suits with face cages, and they'd fence in the hotel rooms after the shows. We tried to telephone The Everly Brothers today, but they were unavailable. I wanted to get them to comment on what they thought about Buddy. I'm sorry we couldn't find them; maybe we can tomorrow. Along with Buddy and Ritchie Valens was one more guy, a disc jockey only 28 years of age. It had taken him eight years to get to the top, but he had finally made it in a big way. He started out at the age of fifteen with a radio station in Beaumont, Texas. His name was J. P. Richardson. He tried to capitalize on a record fad of the time, "The Purple People Eater," by writing and singing "The Purple People Eater Meets the Witchdoctor."

(*Garrett plays "The Purple People Eater Meets the Witchdoctor"*)

Garrett: That was the Big Bopper's first record. Actually, that was the flip side of his first hit record. Then Mercury Records picked up the master. They apparently thought so much of "The Purple People Eater" that they wanted the rights to "The Purple People Eater Meets the Witchdoctor" by J. P. "Big Bopper" Richardson, too. They reissued the disc, and still nothing happened. All across the nation, jockeys listened to it, played it on their shows, and it just didn't sell. Then some disc jockey listened to the "B" side of the record. The flip-side of "Purple People Eater Meets the Witchdoctor" was "Chantilly Lace." The flip-side of his fad-following record went right to the top, and the "Big Bopper" was a star.

(*Garrett plays "Chantilly Lace"*)

Garrett: That was The Big Bopper, "Chantilly lace, a pretty face, and a ponytail hanging down," which became the saying all across the red-white-and-blue not too many months ago. And the Big Bopper brought it all into being.

This is a tribute to Buddy Holly. Buddy was one of the best friends I've ever had, one of the greatest guys in the world. He was killed this morning–early this morning or late last night–in a plane crash near Mason City, Iowa. Dead along with him are The Big Bopper and Ritchie Valens. If there's any song of Buddy's that you want to hear, I think we have just about everything he ever released here in our studio. I love to sit and listen to 'em. They're probably scratched because I've played them a million times. I don't play Buddy Holly records just because he's a friend of mine. I play them because they're good; they are good rock 'n' roll. So if you've got some of Buddy's records you want to hear, just call me at 723-0791 and I'll play it. That's all I can say–this is for him. Do it now.

If there's a song that shows Buddy's rock 'n' roll versatility, it's this next one. No one else can record his songs because nobody else can sing like Buddy. Here he sounds like he's crying, almost like a little girl crying. One of the guys teased Buddy about it, but he took it goodnaturedly. This shows one side of Buddy that no one else could copy.

(*Garrett plays "I'm Gonna Love You, Too"*)

Garrett: Buddy Holly right there, singing "I'm Gonna Love You, Too." We know its gonna go big. This is Buddy Holly plus ninety-seven violins just fiddling around on a song called "It's Raining in My Heart."

(*Garrett plays "Raining in My Heart"*)

Garrett: There's Charles Hardin Holly. Buddy Holly was only 22 years old. I'll never forget the last time I took the weekend off. Buddy had called me from Lubbock, and I flew over to see him. We went out to eat, he and Jerry Allison and me. When Buddy asked me how I was gonna get back to Wichita Falls, I said, "I don't know, take a bus or walk." He said, "We'll drive you back. We got nothing better to do; we'll drive you back. I want to take a trip anyway. We need to get out of town." I said that would be fine, but Jerry said we should wait a minute. He went over and bought a package of No-Doz and said, "Ya'll take these. We been up quite a while now, so we'll probably be getting sleepy." So I took a couple of the tablets, and Buddy took a couple, then Jerry put them back in his pocket. Then Buddy said, "Aren't you going to take any of these No-Doz Jerry?" "No, man, I'm going to sleep while ya'll drive." We thought that was pretty clever.

All the way back from Lubbock, Jerry slept in the back seat while Buddy and I talked. It was one of the greatest nights of my life.

Buddy was always tapping on stuff. I'd say a song title and he'd begin slapping the dash of his car, beating out the tune and singing it. My favorite Buddy Holly record–I'll play it for you in a minute–is called "Last Night." I think it's the best thing Buddy ever made. It was released on an album, and he never got too many requests for it, but I still think that it's the best thing he ever made. I bet he sang that 2,800 times between Lubbock and here that night. He sang it and sang it, and then I'd say, "Sing it again." And Jerry slept all the way through it.

Some very nice people have been callin' in telling us which Buddy Holly records they want to hear. This is what we call a wailer down here. This is where Buddy Holly really wails. Listen to the opening note.

(*Garrett plays "Rave On"*)

Garrett: That's the chirpin' Crickets right there, featuring big Buddy Holly doing "Rave On." I don't know if you recognized the band in the background or not, but it was a Wichita Falls group called "Big Beats." That was C. W. Kendall beating the tar out of the piano in the background. Buddy played a mean guitar, too. A lotta times on the road, you would see all the guys get together playing guitars. That's where they wrote most of their songs–on the road. The Everly Brothers even recorded one of Buddy Holly's songs.[10] Buddy also wrote a thing called "Words of Love," which The Diamonds made a big hit out of about two years ago.[11] Buddy wrote a lot of songs. It's sort of a trade-off thing among songwriters. Buddy has recorded Paul Anka songs several times. They thought very highly of each other, and on the road they depended on each other.

This is Jerry Allison, Buddy's drummer and very closest friend. We talked with Jerry by telephone about an hour-and-a-half ago.

S.G.: Hello there, how're you doing?
J.A.: Just fine.
S.G.: Listen, we heard about Buddy's death awhile ago–and very sorry to hear about it.
J.A.: I was awfully shocked.
S.G.: Listen, Jerry, he came through here and stopped on his way out.

J.A.: Well, Joe B. and I decided that we wanted to live here in the Southwest, but Buddy wanted to live in New York, so we weren't with him on this tour. We were in Lubbock at the time it happened.

S.G.: You will still play with The Crickets from now on, won't you?

J.A.: I don't know what we'll do now, Snuff.

S.G.: Don't know yet?

J.A.: I sure don't.

S.G.: I'm very sorry to hear it, Jerry. What about his wife? Have you talked to her yet?

J.A.: She's in New York now. She wasn't with him on the road. I have not talked with her, but she is supposed to be coming to Lubbock tomorrow.

S.G.: She is? Have they set the time of the funeral yet? I guess his mother and daddy will handle the details. He was just getting started and everything was just beginning to go his way.

J.A.: Everybody sure is sad about the whole thing.

Garrett: That was Jerry Allison, one of the chirpingest Crickets you'll ever hear. He and Buddy were very good friends. This is one of the first songs they did together. It's one of my favorites of all time, called "Last Night."

(*Garrett plays "Last Night"*)

Garrett: That's The Crickets chirping for you. A girl named Peggy Underwood just called from Bowie, and there was another call from Abilene. Please give us time to answer the phone if you want to hear something of Buddy's. We're gonna play whatever you request. It's the very, very least we can do. No one knows yet when the funeral will be held in Lubbock. It would be nice if people would send cards to the radio station in Lubbock, in care of Buddy Holly, and we'll see that they are sent to the proper address. Just send a card to let them know that the people will not forget Buddy Holly.

This was one of Buddy's biggest records. It was a weirdo that came out right after "That'll Be the Day." This song flipped nearly everybody, although I didn't particularly like it. It just caught on like wildfire. Here are The Crickets chirping "Oh, Boy!"

(*Garrett plays "Oh, Boy!"*)

Garrett: That reminds me of the time Buddy came in to the studio to cut intro tapes; I'm sure if you ever heard it, you'll never forget it. This is one he cut one time–crank up the station blurb: [Garrett plays tape recording of Buddy Holly] "This is Buddy Holly with The Crickets reminding you that this is KSYD Wichita Falls–the station that other stations listen to." That's telling 'em.

(*Garrett plays "Not Fade Away"*)

Garrett: Buddy Holly's mother was extremely proud of him. I don't know how old his folks are, but they're pretty old and they just have a small home in Lubbock. The first time I ever met them, I was with a good friend of Buddy's, Carey Hobbs. He was the first person that pushed Buddy's career and played his early records. Carey, Jerry, Buddy, and I were out together one night in Lubbock, and just after Buddy had returned from being on *The Ed Sullivan Show.* His mother was really proud of him. She was real nice and even called me once or twice to request records. Not just Buddy's songs, either. She said she listened to the radio all the time, just to hear Buddy's records. She had a long table with all of Buddy's albums on it, particularly the ones with his picture on the front of it. She had a picture of him and Ed Sullivan together and little personal mementos, along with pieces of sheet music with his picture on the front. She thought he was the living end. The night we went over to Mrs. Holly's–I was a disc jockey in Lubbock then and so was Carey–he was just going to change clothes so we could go out to eat. Well, she took Buddy off to another room and scolded him for not warning her that two radio stars were coming over to eat. She thought it was terrible that he hadn't called her and given her a chance to clean up the house or dust up or anything before we came over. She insisted that we eat there, but he told her we planned to go out and didn't want her going to all the trouble of preparing dinner for us. And Buddy returned all this love. He urged his dad, who was a painter and contractor, to retire, bought the family a brand new Chevrolet, and was in the process of building them a brand new home.

The last time I saw Buddy Holly was when I was in a marathon at the Merrick Motor Company, here in Wichita Falls, not too long ago. Buddy just showed up one night when he was on his way to New York with his wife. They were going up to New York, and he just walked in and stayed for 30 to 45 minutes. That was the last time I saw Buddy. I had a card from him last Christmas saying he's still in New York and wished he were back here, but that was the last time I saw him.

A lot of people will remember Buddy Holly because this is going to be one of his biggest hits ever. This is Buddy Holly's hit of tomorrow, "It Doesn't Matter Anymore."

(*Garrett plays "It Doesn't Matter Anymore"*)

Garrett: There's Buddy Holly singing "It Doesn't Matter Anymore."

This is one of The Crickets. His name is Joe Mauldin. I talked to Joe B. earlier this afternoon to see what they have decided to do with the group now.

S.G.: What have you heard?
J.M.: Just what we read in the papers and heard over the radio.
S.G.: I talked to Norman a while ago. Some friend of his called him from somewhere in North Dakota and said they didn't know too much about it. It said in the paper that ya'll were with him, so I thought that ya'll were with him.
J.M.: No, we weren't.
S.G.: Ya'll were in Clovis, weren't you?
J.M.: We came into Lubbock about ten last night.
S.G.: You did what?
J.M.: I said Jerry and I drove to Lubbock about ten last night. We were here when it happened.
B.G.: I'm sorry to hear it.
J.M.: Yeah, man. Me, too.
S.G.: What are ya'll going to do? Do you know?
J.M.: Like we told you earlier, it's up to Jerry.

Garrett: Both the guys are shook up, believe me. Jerry would serve as the comic of the group. Buddy came down in August to do the TV show with his cousin, and we were sitting around when I said, "Well, I really miss the guys." He said, "I do, too." So we called 'em on the phone and they flew down. We all went out to eat that night around the old campfire out there at The Wayfarer. Jerry brought his brand-new record with him, the one where he went by the name of "Ivan," and so it was played here for the first time in the nation.[12] The record was really great, and tonight Jerry said his next record was just released. You'll be hearing it anytime now. He was really shook up to hear about Buddy.

We'll play this for Buddy: "Little Baby, Baby Me." C. W. Kendall plays the piano.

(*Garrett plays "Little Baby, Baby Me"*)

Garrett: There you go, Charles Hardin Holly–Buddy Holly–and "Little Baby, Baby Me." Buddy was going to have a record company and a publishing company of his own and name it after the color of his Cadillac: taupe. He was looking around for artists for Taupe Records. No one knows where they got the name for The Crickets. They were just sitting around saying what are we going to call the name of our group–they wanted to think of something different–so they decided on The Crickets.[13] He named his record company the same way.

Here's Buddy Holly's "It's So Easy."

(*Garrett plays "It's So Easy"*)

Garrett: There you go, "It's So Easy," with the chirpin' Crickets. I'm sure everyone has heard by now about the death of Buddy Holly, along with J. P. "Big Bopper" Richardson and Ritchie Valens. These two guys shouldn't be forgotten either, but I'm sorry to say I didn't know them personally. I just knew Buddy Holly, the greatest guy in the world. And like we said earlier, if you want to make a contribution in Buddy's memory, just put it in an envelope–whatever you want: a dime, a quarter, a dollar or whatever–and mail it to Buddy Holly, care of KSYD Radio in Wichita Falls, Texas. We'll see that your donation goes to Muscular Dystrophy. We appreciate it.

Buddy had only been married for six months. I guess the funeral will be in Lubbock. I'm going to try to make it up to the funeral.

You can't say too much, just recall the times that you had fun with him and the things that he enjoyed talking about most. I asked him one time, "What's the greatest thrill that you've ever had?" He said, "I think the greatest thrill I ever had was playing the Palace Theatre last Christmas–not this last Christmas, the Christmas before that. I've never seen crowds like that. I had so much fun; I've never enjoyed playing to a crowd more than I had that Christmas." That was his greatest thrill, playing the Palace Theatre in New York along with all those top rock 'n' roll stars.[14]

Here's another one of his earlier records, a Little Richard tune.

(*Garrett plays "Send Me Some Lovin'"*)

Garrett: There you go, the chirpin' Crickets along with Buddy Holly, and the old Little Richard tune "Send Me Some Lovin'." Buddy thought Little Richard was a gas, and he was one of his favorites. Buddy used to talk about all the trips they'd made together and about how much fun Little Richard was to sing with on the show.

We appreciate KSYD letting us play all these records of Buddy Holly's. We do this because we enjoy it, and we're glad that you like 'em. Buddy Holly won't be forgotten. They've got some more of his records coming out. As long as I can find a way, we'll play them all. Rock 'n' roll singers come and go, but there's only gonna be one Buddy Holly, believe me, and you'll never find anybody else to sing like him. He's the greatest guy in the world. And if you can find time tonight, if you want to keep on calling in to keep on requesting Buddy's records, I don't think our station manager Jack Grady would mind a bit. I'm sure he'd be happy to play whatever you wanted to hear by Buddy 'cause we can't stop here, believe me. So I'll ask you once again before I go off the air to send whatever donation you can in an envelope to KSYD Radio, in care of Buddy Holly, Wichita Falls, Texas, and we'll give it to Muscular Dystrophy. Here's a number that Elvis Presley popularized by Buddy. He insisted that it would be on his first album of Taupe Records, he liked the song so much. Here's Buddy's version of "Ready Teddy."

(*Garrett plays "Ready Teddy"*)

BUDDY HOLLY NOTES

1. Actually, the next evening's performance was scheduled for Moorehead, Minnesota. Details of the ill-fated flight to Fargo, which is located just across the Red River from Moorehead, are provided in *Buddy Holly: His Life and Music*, by John Goldrosen (Bowling Green: Bowling Green University, 1975).

2. Although Petty had been Holly's manager since early 1957 and continued to serve as manager for two of The Crickets–Jerry Allison and Joe Mauldin–during 1959, Buddy had actually severed the managerial relationship with the Clovis, New Mexico, record producer during late October 1958. See Goldrosen, *Buddy Holly*, pp. 151-161.

3. The two original Crickets, Allison and Mauldin, were in Lubbock, but Holly's touring band–which consisted of Tommy Allsup on rhythm guitar, Waylon Jennings on bass, and Charlie Bunch on drums–was also billed as The Crickets. And rather than being just the "weekend thing" described by Garrett, the Clear Lake-to-Moorehead trip was part of a pre-planned, fully-sponsored three-week tour of Midwestern states–including Wisconsin, Iowa, and Minnesota. It was billed as "The Winter Dance Party." See Goldrosen, *Buddy Holly*, pp. 183-185.

4. Portions of the telephone conversations included in this transcript have appeared in the one-page article "February 3, 1959: The Day the Music Died." *Goldmine* No. 26 (May/June 1978): p. 26, written by William F. Griggs, the president of the Buddy Holly Memorial Society.

5. For information on Holly's marriage, see *Buddy Holly . . . A Biography in Words, Photographs, and Music*, by Elizabeth and Ralph Peer II (New York: Peer, 1972), p. 31.

6. Petty significantly underestimates the number of unreleased Holly songs at this point. For a detailed report on the extent of unissued studio masters, demos, and tapes by Holly as of February 1959, see Goldrosen, *Buddy Holly*, pp. 200-211.

7. The song referred to here is Anka's 1958 song "It Doesn't Matter Anymore," which was published by Spanka Music Corporation. See *Popular Music, 1950-1959–Volume I*, second edition, by Nat Shapiro (ed.) (New York: Adrian, 1967), p. 241.

8. The conflict over finances that ultimately prompted the dissolution of the Petty-Holly partnership is outlined in Goldrosen, *Buddy Holly*, pp. 151-161, 182-186, and 200-212.

9. John Goldrosen reports two other stories regarding the origin of the tune "Peggy Sue." One has Holly as the author of the music, with Petty as the source of the lyrics. Another has Holly doing both words and music, but agreeing to alter the song's original title, "Cindy Lou," to coincide with Allison's current romantic interest. See Goldrosen, *Buddy Holly*, pp. 94-95.

10. Goldrosen relates a humorous tale of Wesley Rose, The Everly Brothers' manager, refusing to accept the donation of two new songs–"Love Makes a Fool of You" and "Wishing"–that Holly wrote hoping that Don and Phil would record them. See *Buddy Holly*, p. 131.

11. This is an exaggeration. The Diamonds' version of "Words of Love" lasted only one week on *Billboard*'s Hot 100 chart during June 1957. See Joel Whitburn (comp.). *Top Pop Records, 1955-1972* (Menomonee: Record Research, 1973), p. 74.

12. Jerry "Ivan" Allison's recording of "Real Wild Child" lasted for five weeks on *Billboard*'s Hot 100 chart, peaking at number 68. See Whitburn, *Top Pop Records, 1955-1972*, p. 124. For a detailed account of the origin of this off-the-wall recording, see Goldrosen, *Buddy Holly*, pp. 113-114.

13. See Goldrosen, *Buddy Holly*, p. 70.

14. Jerry Allison also asserts that the high point in his performing career was the 12-day engagement at the New York Paramount (not Palace) Theatre under the direction of Alan Freed during the 1957 Christmas period. See Goldrosen, *Buddy Holly*, pp. 105-107.

BUDDY HOLLY REFERENCE SOURCES

Aquila, Richard. " 'Not Fade Away': Buddy Holly and the Making of an American Legend." *Journal of Popular Culture* XV (Spring 1982): pp. 75-80.

Beecher, John, and John Goldrosen. *Remembering Buddy*. London: Pavilion Books, 1987.

Bush, William J. "Buddy Holly: The Legend and Legacy." *Guitar Player* XVI (June 1982): pp. 64-66 ff.

Clark, Alan. *Buddy Holly and the Crickets*. West Covina, California: Alan Clark, 1979.

Colman, Stuart. "Buddy Holly: Reminiscing." In *They Kept on Rockin': The Giants of Rock 'n' Roll*. Poole, Dorset: Blandford, 1982.

Cott, Jonathan. "Buddy Holly." In *The Rolling Stone Illustrated History of Rock and Roll* (revised edition). Edited by Jim Miller. New York: Random House/Rolling Stone, 1980.

Dallas, Karl. "They Died Young." *The History of Rock*. 10 (1982): pp. 194-195.

Denisoff, R. Serge. "Waylon Jennings 'The Last Tour': A New Journalism Approach." *Journal of Popular Culture* XIII (Spring 1980): pp. 663-671.

Doggett, Peter. "Buddy Holly." *Record Collector*. 101 (January 1988): pp. 3-9.

Doggett, Peter. "Buddy Holly, 1936-1959." *Record Collector*. 114 (February 1989): pp. 37-40.

Elson, Howard. "Buddy Holly." In *Early Rockers*. New York: Proteus, 1982.

Flippo, Chet. "The Buddy Holly Story." *Rolling Stone* No. 274 (September 21, 1978): pp. 49-51.

Goldrosen, John. *Buddy Holly: His Life and Music*. Bowling Green: Bowling Green University, 1975.

Goldrosen, John. *The Buddy Holly Story*. New York: Quick Fox, 1979.

Griggs, Bill. " 'American Pie': Was It a Tribute to Buddy Holly? Was It a Protest Song?" *Rockin' 50s*. No. 20 (October 1989): pp. 22-23.

Griggs, Bill, and Jim Black (comps.). *Buddy Holly: A Collector's Guide*. Sheboygan, Wisconsin: Red Wax Publishing, 1983.

Griggs, Bill. "The Buddy Holly Legend: Separating Fact from Fiction." *DISCoveries*. I (January-February 1988): pp. 26-29.

Griggs, Bill. "An Interrupted Bus Trip: New Facts About Buddy Holly's Last Tour." *Goldmine*, No. 223 (February 10, 1989): p. 10.

Griggs, Bill. "Spotlight on February 3, 1959." *Rockin' 50s*. No. 16 (February 1989): pp. 6-14.

Goldrosen, John, and John Beecher. *Remembering Buddy: The Definite Biography of Buddy Holly*. New York: Penguin Books, 1986.

Harris, Brandon L. "The Norman Petty Chronicles." *Time Barrier Express* No. 27 (April-May 1980): pp. 55-64.

Harris, Brandon L. "A Texas Yankee in Queen Liz's Court." *Trouser Press* V (July 1978): pp. 34-37.

Holmes, John. "American Pie: The Adventures of Buddy Holly–The Early Days of Rock 'n' Roll." *Buddy: The Original Texas Music Magazine* IX (September 1981): pp. 13-14.

Ingman, John, and Brian Shepherd. "Buddy Holly Discography/Buddy Holly Sessions." *New Kommotion* No. 23 (1980): pp. 34-38.

King, Gary. "Buddy Holly–The Last Tour." *Music World* No. 82 (February 1981): pp. 8-15.

Laing, Dave. *Buddy Holly*. New York: MacMillan, 1971.

McAuliffe, Jon. "Those Fabulous Foreign Pressings: 'The Complete Buddy Holly.'" *Music World* No. 83 (March 1981): pp. 34-37.

McDonald, Gary. "Hey, Buddy, Can You Spare a Song? Looking for a Hit? Dig Through the Buddy Holly Catalog." *Buddy: The Original Texas Music Magazine* IX (September 1981): pp. 15-16.

Millar, Bill. "Bob Montgomery and His Buddies." *Goldmine*, No. 60 (May 1981): p. 169.

Peer, Elizabeth, and Ralph Peer II. *Buddy Holly . . . A Biography in Words, Photographs, and Music*. New York: Peer, 1972.

Peters, Richard. The Legend that Is Buddy Holly. London: Souvenir Press, 1990.

Scott, Steve. "Buddy Holly." *Record Collector*, No. 22 (June 1981): pp. 10-17.

Turner, Joan, and Allen Moline. "The Holly Magic." *Record Exchanger*, No. 5 (November/December 1970): p. 8.

Yronwode, Catherine. "Why the 'Complete Buddy Holly' Isn't Complete." *Music World* No. 89 (September 1981): pp. 44-46.

Chapter 20

Sports Heroes

Whoever wants to know the heart and mind of America had better learn baseball.

–Jacques Barzun (1954)

There are virtually no scholarly treatments of the connection between popular music and baseball.

–John D. Wells and James K. Skipper, Jr. (1988)

Some scholars have contended that the alliance between major league baseball and contemporary song is natural, productive, and highly popular.[1] This assertion seems reasonable. Consider the lament penned by Simon and Garfunkel in "Mrs. Robinson" (1968): "Where have you gone Joe DiMaggio? A nation turns its lonely eyes to you." Recall the debate between a sexually aroused teenage boy and his reluctant girlfriend in Meatloaf's "Paradise by the Dashboard Light" (1978). Or ponder John Fogerty's impassioned plea to play "Centerfield" (1985). Other popular songs featuring baseball themes include Bruce Springsteen's "Glory Days" (1985) and The Intruders' "(Love Is Like a) Baseball Game" (1968). Writers who champion the link between popular song and baseball note three primary reasons for the sport's thematic popularity: (1) baseball is celebrated

---

This essay, originally entitled "Where Have You Gone . . . Babe, Ty, Lou, Mickey, Willie, Duke, Pee Wee, and Joe DiMaggio? The Decline of Contemporary Baseball Heroes in American Popular Recordings," by B. Lee Cooper and Donald E. Walker, with the assistance of William L. Schurk, was presented at the annual meeting of The Midwest Popular Culture Association in East Lansing, Michigan, in October 1989. Reprint permission has been granted by the authors.

as a contest of wills within a well-defined game; (2) baseball provides a showcase for national heroes and fabled athletic achievements; and (3) baseball is a useful metaphor for both dating and sex.[2] Each of these justifications is illustrated in the five tunes cited above.

In truth, baseball is only a .180 hitter as a songwriter's game. It has seldom secured substantial links with commercially successful music. During the past three decades, in fact, the decline of baseball-related lyrical imagery is staggering. The *Billboard*-charted tunes of Simon and Garfunkel, Meatloaf, John Fogerty, Bruce Springsteen, and The Intruders are really anomalies to a dismal showing for contemporary baseball tunes. It's not that the music or lyrics are bad, or that creative efforts by contemporary singers and songwriters have ceased. Since 1960, baseball tunes have simply failed to attract substantial national interest. The record-buying public has ignored many humorous, inventive, interesting songs about post-1960 baseball. Singers like Joe Cocker, Terry Cashman, Billy Joel, and Steve Goodman have issued vibrant baseball-related songs that have been unable to achieve either *Cash Box* or *Billboard* Hot 100 listings. Granted, their tunes have been enjoyed by a limited number of listeners, their use of baseball imagery has continued to be ingenious, and their songs have even been featured on several "pre-game" or "post-game" television broadcasts. But these productions never become popular.

THE BASEBALL BUSINESS AND PUBLIC CYNICISM

In contrast to the recent decline (1960-1990) of songs having baseball-related themes, the halcyon decades for popular baseball tunes were the '20s, '30s '40s, and '50s. (This fact can be readily documented by examining sheet-music purchases rather than just sales of 78- or 45-r.p.m. records.[3]) To what particular historical events or public perceptions can this trend be attributed? Why are fewer artists extolling the exploits of modern baseball heroes? Why are metaphorical references to the national pastime so rare? Why are American cultural values now more easily expressed outside of the baseball scheme? This is a complex issue. But the key to understanding the shift in public sympathy is the decline of baseball mythology and the accompanying collapse of contemporary major-league heroes. This decline has prompted most post-1960 songwriters to rely on players, teams, and events of bygone summers for their imagery. Events of the past three decades–player strikes, free agency, the decline of team loyalty, charges of management racism, soaring ticket prices, personal indiscretions by players, salary-arbitration squabbles, reports of drug abuse, cheating, ruthless behavior by owners, and team relocations to the West Coast–have fueled 30 years of cynicism toward baseball. But it is the lack of genuine heroes (even Pete Rose, that throwback to Ty Cobb's and The Gashouse Gang's rough-and-tumble approach, was stigmatized by allegations of gambling) that makes modern baseball less attractive and less effective as a musical venue.[4]

Despite winning American League Pennants in 1960, 1961, 1962, 1963, 1964, 1976, 1977, 1978, and 1981 (with World Series Championships in 1961, 1962, 1977, and 1978 as well), the New York Yankee baseball dynasty tottered after 1965, and the image of classy, unruffled pinstripe heroes collapsed.[5] This diminution occurred because of George Steinbrenner's volatile ownership, Billy Martin's managerial histrionics, Mel Allen's 1964 dismissal, the retirements of Yankee legends Mickey Mantle, Whitey Ford, and Yogi Berra, and the transfer of local fan loyalty from the Yankees to the more lovable (although initially laughable) New York Mets. The hitting feats of Reggie Jackson, Dave Winfield, and Don Mattingly have even been marred by Steinbrenner's ceaseless carping and complaining. It is obvious that the golden age of Babe Ruth, Lou Gehrig, Lefty Grove, Bill Dickey, and Phil Rizzuto dominates popular memories much more than Roger Maris' 61 home runs or Reggie Jackson's World Series heroics.

Major-league expansion and the shifting of franchises among cities eroded the perception of baseball's stability, while also kindling cynicism about money-mongering club owners. It is undeniable that mobility created financial goldmines for several clubs, particularly Walter O'Malley's from-Brooklyn-to-Los Angeles Dodgers. But the anger of rejected fans in New York (Giants and Dodgers), in Milwaukee (Braves), in Washington (Senators), and elsewhere was an extremely high price to pay. Expansion has proved to be a high-stakes game in terms of attempted team relocations (St. Petersburg White Sox, 1988), damaging litigation (Seattle

Mariners, 1977), bankruptcy (Seattle Pilots, 1970), and regional frustration across the country. Meanwhile, many new baseball towns emerged in the United States and Canada–Minneapolis (1961), Houston (1962), Atlanta (1966), Oakland (1968), Montreal (1969), San Diego (1969), Seattle (1969), Dallas (1972), and Toronto (1977). Although more people were exposed to major-league play by this surge of expansion and mobility, many serious fans felt that the creation of intra-league games lessened the meaning of regular-season play. The World Series has remained only a distant dream for many cities that acquired teams during the post-1960 period. Fan loyalty, so stable from 1903 until the early '50s, was the ultimate sacrifice to geographical manipulation in baseball.

Free agency contributed further to the demise of team loyalty. It also increased fans' sense of sport as business rather than athletic competition. Curt Flood's unsuccessful anti-trust suit (1970-1972) and Jim "Catfish" Hunter's victorious contract dispute with Oakland A's owner Charles Finley (1974) paved the way for the free-agency ruling by a federal arbitrator in 1974. Dave McNally and Andy Messersmith were the initial beneficiaries of player freedom from the traditional reserve clause. By 1987 and 1988, two different arbitrators concluded that baseball owners were conspiring to limit free agency. Images of greed (among both players and owners) and front-office duplicity in baseball abound from 1970 to the present. But it has been the frequent reports of huge player incomes linked to salary arbitrations and long-term contracts that have caused many fans to question the daily motivation of "silver spoon" athletes. The imperious attitudes of players, especially those of average talent, in seeking spectacular raises through contract renegotiation have soured many blue-collar baseball supporters.

The big business-versus-labor union image of baseball in the '70s and '80s worsened due to umpire strikes (1970, 1978, 1979, and 1984), player strikes over pension contributions (1972), threatened salary arbitration (1973), free-agency issues (1981), and an owner's lockout (1976) during spring training in retaliation for a federal arbitrator's free-agency ruling. Individually, owners have further tarnished baseball's image of fairness. Examples abound. The high-handed behavior of Oakland owner Charles Finley in his dealings with Jim Hunter, Reggie Jackson, Ken Holtzman, Joe

Rudi, Rollie Fingers, and Vida Blue were publicly censored by both a federal arbitrator and baseball commissioner Bowie Kuhn. Oakland A's fans, of course, were dismayed and disgusted by the owner's dismantling of a world championship team (1972, 1973, and 1974) and the corresponding slide of the club to last place by 1977. Only Yankee owner George Steinbrenner looked more manipulative, more egocentric, more vindictive, and more outrageous than Finley. Steinbrenner has instigated two dozen pitching-coach changes and 17 managerial shifts since his purchase of The Bronx Bombers in 1973. The on-again/off-again services of Billy Martin as Yankee skipper were derisively portrayed in numerous television reports, comedy programs, and even in national beer commercials. Steinbrenner's running verbal warfare with Martin, Reggie Jackson, Dave Winfield, and numerous National League and American League umpires led to imposed fines and negative press coverage.

Fan nostalgia for legendary major-league heroes has proven to be nontransferable to contemporary performers, no matter how exceptional their performances. The giants of baseball lore–Babe Ruth, Ty Cobb, Bob Feller, Walter Johnson, and others–set remarkable single-game, annual, and lifetime standards. But even when several of these records were eclipsed, the new baseball heroes failed to achieve the same reverence accorded to their predecessors. In 1961, Roger Maris slugged 61 home runs to erase Ruth's single-season mark of 60 set in 1927; in 1962, Maury Wills stole 104 bases to best Cobb's record of 96 from 1915 (what's more, Lou Brock swiped 118 in 1974, and Rickey Henderson stole 130 in 1982); in 1974, Henry Aaron surpassed Ruth's career home-run mark of 714 (Aaron accumulated 755 homers by the end of his career); and in 1969 Steve Carlton struck out 19 batters to surpass Bob Feller's single-game mark of 18 set in 1938 (Tom Seaver also fanned 19 in 1970, as did Nolan Ryan in 1974; Roger Clemens struck out 20 in 1986). Although some unbreakable records persist–Joe DiMaggio's 56-game hitting streak from 1941, Ted Williams' .406 average from 1941, Cy Young' 511 major-league victories, and Johnny Vander Meer's two consecutive no-hit games in 1938–the luster of most new baseball records seems less captivating to fans than the memory of more historic achievements. Even Pete Rose's much-heralded 1985 overhauling of Ty Cobb's 4,191 lifetime hit mark has been tarnished by 1989 allegations that the Cincinnati star was an inveterate gambler.

It is the actions of contemporary players themselves–and the national publicity generated by their on-field antics and off-field scandalous behaviors–that have dramatically diminished the public perception of baseball heroes. Group actions such as strikes and boycotts are generally less harmful in fan's eyes than serious individual indiscretions. The initial kiss-and-tell baseball book was Jim Bouton's *Ball Four* (1970).[6] It reported numerous incidents of player drinking and drug use. Other literary exposés have followed. Although steroid use is relatively rare among baseball players, cocaine addictions and convictions have sidelined numerous major-league athletes during the past decade. Ferguson Jenkins, Alan Wiggins, Steve Howe, Vida Blue, Willie Wilson, Pasquel Perez, Chili Davis, and even New York Mets pitching ace Dwight Gooden were involved in cocaine-related incidents; Bob Welch and many other major leaguers enrolled in alcohol rehabilitation programs. Efforts by the Players Association and the Commissioner's Office have failed to halt the burgeoning drug problem in baseball.

Ethical lapses by team management and outright admissions of cheating by numerous ballplayers have deteriorated baseball's image for good sportsmanship, integrity, and character building.[7] Rumors of the illegal use of spitballs were common in the '40s and '50s. But open acknowledgments of ball and bat tampering soared during the '70s and '80s. Norm Cash and Dave Rader admitted that they frequently used illegally corked bats; Rick Honeycutt, Gaylord Perry, and Joe Niekro were suspened for scuffing, scraping, and doctoring baseballs. But more serious illegal activities by well-known ballplayers also occurred. In 1970, Denny McLain was suspended for his long-term involvement with professional gamblers; in 1985, he was convicted of racketeering, extortion, conspiracy, and drug trafficking. The Detroit Tigers' 30-game winner in 1968 slid from fame to infamy. In 1986, Dwight Gooden was charged with battery on a police officer, resisting arrest, and disorderly conduct. In 1988, Red Sox third-baseman and American League batting-champion Wade Boggs was charged by his long-time mistress Margo Adams with failure to support her and with negligence that supposedly contributed to ruining her acting career. This sex scandal continued into 1989 and shared the front pages with allegations that Cincinnati Reds manager Pete Rose had gambled on baseball games.[8] All of these embarrassing disclosures were greeted by the American public with dismay and disgust.

IMAGERY AND POPULAR NOSTALGIA

Released in 1989, the Rhino Records' anthology of *Baseball's Greatest Hits* clearly illustrated the pre-1960 nostalgia factor.[9] From the exquisite comedy of DeWolf Hopper's 1909 rendition of "Casey at the Bat" and Bud Abbott and Lou Costello's 1945 version of their "Who's on First" routine to the authentic tragedy of Lou Gehrig's 1939 "Farewell Speech," the early years of baseball sound immortal. But the heroes featured in these reissued songs are antiques to fans born in the '70s and '80s. The Rhino pressing eulogized "Joltin' Joe DiMaggio" (1941), "Say Hey (The Willie Mays Song)" (1954), and "I Love Mickey [Mantle]" (1956). References to the New York Giants/Brooklyn Dodgers rivalry of the '30s, '40s, and '50s echo in the grooves of "Van Lingle Mungo" (1981), "D-O-D-G-E-R-S Song (Oh, Really? No, O'Malley)" (1962), and a radio-broadcast excerpt entitled "Bobby Thomson's Shot Heard 'Round the World" (1951). Even Bill Slayback's "Move Over Babe (Here Comes Henry)" (1973)–a tribute to the mighty Ruth and Hammerin' Hank Aaron–sounds as nostalgic as Terry Cashman's "Willie, Mickey, and The Duke (Talkin' Baseball)" (1981), which is a tribute to Mays, Mantle, and Snider. Equally hindsighted, but much more humorous, are the lyrical images set forth by The Naturals, with Mel Allen, on "Baseball Dreams" (1985); Rockin' Ritchie Ray in "Baseball Card Lover" (1977); and Steve Goodman's "A Dying Cub Fan's Last Request" (1981). The other cuts on the album include two versions of "Take Me out to the Ballgame" by Doc and Merle Watson (1983) and by stylistic mimic Bruce Springstone (1982), The Intruders' metaphorical "(Love Is Like a) Baseball Game" (1968), and a profane 1976 interview with Tommy LaSorda concerning the home-run antics of Dave Kingman.

Baseball's Greatest Hits is a marvelous disc. It's a joyful audio romp through the exploits of Ty Cobb, Roy Campanella, and Sandy

Koufax. The song selection is profound and perverse, as are most Rhino collections. One can only hope that there will soon be volumes 2 and 3 to pick up such obvious omissions as Arthur Field's "Along Came Ruth" (1914), Chuck Berry's "Brown-Eyed Handsome Man" (1956), Joe Cocker's "Catfish" (1976), John Fogerty's "Centerfield" (1985), Terry Cashman's "Cooperstown (The Town Where Baseball Lives)" (1982), Buddy Johnson's "Did You See Jackie Robinson Hit that Ball?" (1949), Freddie Mitchell's instrumental "[Larry] Doby's Boogie" (1949), Little Milton's "Feel So Bad" (1967), Bruce Springsteen's "Glory Days" (1985), Little Jimmy Dickens' "He Knocked Me Right out of the Box" (1967), The Four Aces' "Heart" (1955), from *Damn Yankees*, Simon and Garfunkel's "Mrs. Robinson" (1968), Meatloaf's "Paradise by the Dashboard Light" (1978), and even Sister Sledge's Pittsburgh-Pirated tune "We Are Family" (1979). In addition, there are dozens and dozens of other hero-worship tunes lauding the exploits of Michael "King" Kelly, Ty Cobb, Stan Musial, and even Pete Rose, as well as a slew of Terry Cashman team-salute songs originally issued in 1981 and 1982.

CONCLUSION

Even Terry Cashman, the modern poet laureate of baseball, acknowledges that popular support for the contemporary game is deeply rooted in nostalgia. "Willie, Mickey, and The Duke" (1981) marks more than just a chronological break between legendary and contemporary baseball players. A *Sports Illustrated* writer recently noted, "Cashman's record began to be played on radio just about the time of that year's [1981] baseball strike. In fact, it received considerable air play and caught on quickly. Cashman says that's because it offered a nostalgic look at the game and some of its postwar heroes, a perfect contrast to the strike."[10] For the singer-songwriter himself, the success of his "Talkin' Baseball" song series was easily explained. Cashman declared, "People related to it. They longed for that time when they were young and baseball was played by men who loved to play the game and weren't making a million dollars a year."[11]

This same longing undergirds the motion-picture adaption of W. P. Kinsella's novel *Shoeless Joe* (1982). *Field of Dreams* (1989) takes the most tarnished figure from baseball's early years and places him amid a lustrous team of Hall of Fame superstars who play eternally for sheer joy. Shoeless Joe Jackson is thus totally exonerated by the grace of his love of the game.[12] We can only hope that a similar future interpretation awaits Denny McLain, Pete Rose, Wade Boggs, and other contemporary major-league offenders. In the meantime, public interest in baseball songs won't rebound until America's traditional heartland values once again become central to the game.

Finally, one must note that the myths of baseball, the statistics of baseball, the lore and history of baseball, and the wonderful old cards of baseball[13] are currently more powerful cultural commentators than commercial recordings about America's national pastime.[14] Baseball is a reasonable metaphor for The Intruders, a wonderful source of comic Chicago Cubs nostalgia for Steve Goodman, and a convenient source (prior to 1960) for untarnished sports stars and larger-than-life heroes. But the real music of baseball is still the crack of a wooden Louisville slugger, not the rattle of a rocker's snare drum. Popular records are not substitutes for the grand old game. Nevertheless, they do serve as valuable reminders of how truly influential pre-1960 baseball was in American culture.[15]

Recorded References: A Selected Discography of Baseball-Related Songs

- "Amazin' Willie Mays"
  (Perspective 5001)
  The King Odom Quartette (1954)

- "Babe Ruth, the Winner of Them All"
  (Heart and Soul)
  Cathy Lynn (1975)

- "The Ballad of Don Larsen"
  (TNT 9010)
  Red River Dave (1956)

- "The Ballad of Roberto Clemente"
  (BBB 233)
  Paul New (1973)

- "Ballad of Satchel Paige (Don't Look Back)"
  (Cain and Able 3118)
  Raynola Smith (1982)

- "The Bambino, The Clipper, and The Mick"
  (Lifesong 45097)
  Terry Cashman (1982)

- "Baseball (America's National Pastime)"
  (Lifesong 45087)
  The Mudville Nine (1981)

- "Baseball Ballet"
  (Lifesong 45117)
  Terry Cashman (1982)

- "Baseball Boogie"
  (King 4368)
  Mable Scott (1950)

- "Baseball Card Lover"
  (Rhino 004)
  Ritchie Ray (1977)

- "The Brooklyn Dodgers"
  (Leslie 918)
  Ralph Branca, Carl Furillo, and Erv Palica (1949)

- "Brown-Eyed Handsome Man"
  (Chess 1635)
  Chuck Berry (1956)

- "The Catfish Kid (The Ballad of Jim Hunter)"
  (Moon 6021)
  Big Tom White (1976)

- "Centerfield"
  (Warner Brothers 29053)
  John Fogerty (1985)

- "Charlie Hustle"
  (Nu-Sound 1030)
  Jim Wheeler (1974)

- "Chicago Cubs Song: Hey, Hey! Holy Mackerel!"
  (Universal 76936)
  The Len Dresslar Singers (1969)

- "Cincinnati's Red Machine"
  (Metrostar 45852)
  Terry Cashman (1985)

- "Cooperstown (The Town Where Baseball Lives)"
  (Lifesong 45117)
  Terry Cashman (1982)

- "Did You See Jackie Robinson Hit that Ball?"
  (RCA Victor 47-2990)
  Count Basie and His Orchestra (1949)

- "Doby at the Bat"
  (Abbey 3016)
  Fatman Humphries (1948)

- "Doby's Boogie"
  (Derby 713)
  Freddie Mitchell (1949)

- "D-O-D-G-E-R-S Song (Oh, Really? No, O'Malley)"
  (Reprise 1368)
  Danny Kaye (1962)

- "A Dying Cub Fan's Last Request"
  (Red Pajamas 1001)
  Steve Goodman (1981)

- "Feel So Bad"
  (Checker 1162)
  Little Milton (1967)

- "Glory Days"
  (Columbia 04924)
  Bruce Springsteen (1985)

- "He Knocked Me Right out of the Box"
  (Columbia 44162)
  Little Jimmy Dickens (1967)

- "Heart"
  (Decca 29476)
  The Four Aces (1955)

- "Hey Hank I Know You're Gonna Do It"
  (Capitol 3851)
  Nellie Briles (1974)

- "Homerun Willie"
  (Warner Brothers 8445)
  Larry Hosford (1977)

- "I Love Mickey"
  (Coral 61700)
  Mickey Mantle and Teresa Brewer (1956)

- "(I Used To Be a) Brooklyn Dodger"
  (Lifesong 1784)
  Dion (1978)

- "Joltin' Joe DiMaggio"
  (Columbia 38544)
  Les Brown and His Orchestra, featuring Betty Bonney (1941)

- "Let's Keep The Dodgers in Brooklyn"
  (Coral 61840)
  Phil Foster (1957)

- "(Love Is Like a) Baseball Game"
  (Gamble 217)
  The Intruders (1968)

- "The Man Called Bench"
  (High Spiral 287)
  Cliff Adams (1983)

- "Move Over Babe (Here Comes Henry)"
  (Karen K714)
  Bill Slayback (1973)

- "Mrs. Robinson"
  (Columbia 44511)
  Simon and Garfunkel (1968)

- "Myti Kaysi at the Bat"
  (Reprise 1370)
  Danny Kaye (1962)

- "New Baseball Boogie"
  (Savoy 5561)
  Brownie McGhee (1948)

- "Paradise by the Dashboard Light"
  (Epic 50588)
  Meatloaf (1978)

- "Pete's Hit Record"
  (Genius 4192)
  Gale Watson (1985)

- "Playing Catch with The Babe"
  (Thurman 82579)
  Jess DeMaine (1979)

- "Pine Tar Wars"
  (AFR 4233)
  C. W. McCall (1983)

- "The Pine Tarred Bat (The Ballad of George Brett)"
  (Longhorn 2004)
  Red River Dave (1983)

- "Please Jimmy Piersall"
  (G. C. 609)
  Jimmy Piersall and The Three Heartbreakers (1960)

- "Polish Baseball Power"
  (Michawake 1702)
  Sig Sakowicz (1970)

- "Reggie for Christmas"
  (Reel Dreams 1005)
  Hozay Smith and The Hammerhead (1982)

- "Robbie–Doby Boogie"
  (Savoy 5550)
  Brownie McGhee (1948)

- "Roberto's Gone"
  (Ace of Hearts 0476)
  Jim Owen (1973)

- "Safe at Home (A Tribute to Babe Ruth)"
  (Flint 1788)
  Tex Fletcher (1948)

- "Say Hey! (A Tribute to Willie Mays)"
  (Apollo 460)
  The Nite Riders (1954)

- "Say Hey, Willie Mays"
  (Coral 61238)
  Johnny Long (1954)

- "Say Hey (The Willie Mays Song)"
  (Epic 9066)
  Willie Mays and The Treniers (1954)

- "Seasons in the Sun (A Tribute to Mickey Mantle)"
  (Metrostar 45853)
  Terry Cashman (1985)

- "Stan The Man"
  (Norman 543)
  Marty Bronson (1963)

- "The Summer There Was No Baseball"
  (Home Run)
  Randy Haspel (1981)

- "Take Me out to the Ball Game"
  (MCA 65016)
  The Andrews Sisters and Dan Dailey (1949)

- "Take Me out to the Ball Game"
  (Churchill 7714)
  Harry Caray (1978)

- "Take Me out to the Ball Game"
  (Red Pajamas 1001)
  Steve Goodman (1983)

- "Take Me out to the Ball Game"
  (Clean Cuts 902)
  Bruce Springstone (1982)

- "Thanks Mister Banks"
  (Barking Gecko 10655)
  Roger Bain (1979)

- "That Last Home Run"
  (Spoonfull)
  Willie Dixon's Chicago Blues All Stars (1973)

- "There Must Be Something Inside (A Tribute to Pete Rose)"
  (Metrostar 45852)
  Terry Cashman (1985)

- "Those Cleveland Indians"
  (Bison 105)
  Lee Sullivan (1954)

- "Tony, The Killer, and Carew"
  (Lifesong 45114)
  Terry Cashman (1982)

- "Viva Fernando"
  (Domain 1019)
  The Gene Page Orchestra (1981)

- "Warren Spahn"
  (Armada 104)
  The Blackholes (1979)

- "We Are Family"
  (Cotillion 44251)
  Sister Sledge (1979)

- "Yankee Clipper"
  (RCA Victor 3552)
  Charlie Ventura and His Orchestra (1949)

- "Yaz's Last at Bat"
  (Lincoln 003)
  John Lincoln Wright and The Designated Hitters (1985)

NOTES

1. Don Johnson, "Baseball: The Songwriter's Game" (Mimeographed paper presented at the 1985 annual meeting of the Popular Culture Association of the South in Charleston, South Carolina) and John D. Wells and James K. Skipper, Jr., "The Songs of Summer: A Sociological Study of Songs About Baseball and The Play Element in Culture," *Popular Music and Society* XXII (Spring 1988): pp. 25-35.

2. *Ibid.* Also see Ronald F. Briley, "Where Have You Gone William Bendix? Baseball as a Symbol of American Values in World War II," *Studies in Popular Culture* VIII, No. 2 (1985): pp. 18-32; Kent Cartwright and Mary McElroy, "Malamud's 'The Natural' and the Appeal of Baseball in American Culture,"

Journal of American Culture VIII (Summer 1985): pp. 47-55; and Leverett T. Smith, Jr., "Ty Cobb, Babe Ruth, and the Changing Image of the Athletic Hero," in *Heroes of Popular Culture*, edited by Ray B. Browne, Marshall Fishwick, and Michael T. Marsden (Bowling Green: Bowling Green State University, 1972).

3. Joseph Petrarca, "Baseball Sheet Music," *Sheet Music Exchange* III (October 1985): pp. 9-15. Also see Michael G. Corenthal, "'Casey at the Bat': 1909 and 1929 Records," *Goldmine,* No. 149 (April 11, 1986): p. 83.

4. The authors doubt that baseball-records collector Michael Brown will subscribe to this thesis. For an examination of Brown's collecting activities, see Paul Richman, "Baseball's Greatest Hits!" *Sports Collectors Digest* (August 20, 1982): pp. 94-95ff.

5. Statistical information and historical material presented in this section has been drawn from the following sources: David Halberstam, *Summer of '49* (New York: William Morrow, 1989); Jim Hunter and Armen Keteyian, *Catfish* (New York: McGraw-Hill, 1988); Bill James (comp.), *Bill James Historical Baseball Abstract* (New York: Billard, 1986); Daniel Okrent and Harris Lewine (eds.), *The Ultimate Baseball Book* (Boston: Houghton Mifflin, 1979); Lawrence Ritter and Donald Honig, *The Image of Their Greatness* (New York: Crown, 1979); Curt Smith, *Voices of the Game* (South Bend: Diamond Communications, 1987); John Thorn and Pete Palmer, with David Reuter, *Total Baseball* (New York: Warner, 1989); and John Tullius, *I'd Rather Be a Yankee* (New York: Macmillan, 1986).

6. Jim Bouton, *Ball Four* (New York: Dell, 1970). Other revealing baseball exposés include: Bill Lee and Dick Lally, *The Wrong Stuff* (New York: Viking, 1984); Billy Martin and Peter Golenbock, *Number One* (New York: Delacorte, 1980); and Graig Nettles and Peter Golenbock, *Balls* (New York: G. P. Putnam's Sons, 1984).

7. Peter Gammons, "O.K., Drop that Emery Board," *Sports Illustrated* LXVII (August 17, 1987): pp. 34-36. Also see "The Big Story," *Sports Illustrated* LXXI (August 28, 1989): p. 15. This brief essay reports that a computer-accessed information service scanned 650 newspapers, magazines, and wire services to determine the most-written-about baseball topics of the 1980s. The discouraging results of this survey were: (a) drug abuse, (b) contract disputes and salary arbitrations, (c) player strikes, (d) on-the-field rule violations, including doctored bats and balls, (e) George Steinbrenner, (f) racism, (g) the Pete Rose gambling case, (h) Bo Jackson, (i) installation of lights in Wrigley field, (j) Pete Rose breaks Ty Cobb's hitting record, (k) Steve Garvey's womanizing activities, and (l) Wade Bogg's affair with Margo Adams.

8. Jill Lieber and Craig Neff, "The Case Against Pete Rose," *Sports Illustrated* LXXI (July 3, 1989): pp. 10-25. Also see E. M. Swift, "Facing the Music," *Sports Illustrated* LXX (March 6, 1989): pp. 38-41.

9. Baseball's Greatest Hits (R70710). Santa Monica: Rhino Records, 1989.

10. Jim Schottelkotte, "Terry Cashman Scores Hit After Hit As Big League Baseball's Balladist," *Sports Illustrated* LXII (April 15, 1985): pp. 9-10.

11. *Ibid:* p. 10.

12. W. P. Kinsella, *Shoeless Joe* (Boston: Houghton Mifflin, 1982). Also see David Ansen, "Baseball Diamonds Are Forever," *Newsweek* CXIII (April 24, 1989): pp. 72-73.

13. Susan Dillingham, "Playing Hardball in Card Design," *Insight* (April 10, 1989): pp. 44-45 and Murry R. Nelson, "Baseball Cards in the Classroom," *Social Education* XLV (May 1981): pp. 364-366.

14. Listen to the 1982 Lifesong records "Talkin' Baseball–National League" (LS 8137) and "Talkin' Baseball–American League" (LS 8136) by Terry Cashman for an attempt to unite nostalgia and contemporary elements of several baseball teams.

15. Additional examples of baseball, music, and American-culture studies are Dr. Demento, "Sportsmen as Music Makers: From Dugouts to Discs," *Wax Paper* II (July 29, 1977): pp. 11-13 and Gerard O'Connor, "Where Have You Gone Joe DiMaggio?" in *Heroes of Popular Culture*, edited by Ray B. Browne, Marshall Fishwick, and Marshall T. Marsden (Bowling Green: Bowling Green State University, 1972).

Chapter 21

Symptoms, Illnesses, and Medical Imagery

Bridging the gap between imagery and reality is a major challenge for media analysts. The examination of varying stereotypes–physical images, behavioral patterns, or general assumptions about thoughts and values–is of significant concern for many popular-culture scholars. For example, portrayals of black men and women on television and in motion pictures have garnered commentaries from numerous critics over the past 30 years.[1] Compared with racial or ethnic images, though, relatively few occupational or age-related stereotypes have been explored.[2]

In 1982, Philip and Beatrice Kalisch issued a brief report entitled "Nurses on Prime-Time Television." Linking today's video perspectives to tomorrow's professional well-being, the authors noted:

> Popular attitudes and assumptions about nurses and their contributions to a patient's welfare can determine to a large extent the future of nursing. Today some opinions held by the public have been derived directly from the image of nursing projected through television fiction over the past three decades. . . . The reality of contemporary nursing practice over the past 30 years has found little or no echo in the largely fictional world of television broadcasting. Over the past 15 years, the popular image of the nurse not only has failed to reflect changing professional conditions, but it has also assumed strong derogatory traits that undermine public confidence in and respect for the professional nurse.[3]

This essay was written by B. Lee Cooper and William L. Schurk for this anthology.

The chief concern of the Kalischs was that the medical profession was being degraded through continuous media misrepresentation. Stating their objections, they concluded:

> . . . television entertainment creators have paid insufficient attention to the depiction of nurses, using nurses far too often as background scenery for hospital-centered drama. When nurse characters have been singled out for attention, this attention has usually taken the form of delving into personal problems rather than professional concerns.[4]

Unlike television or motion pictures, popular recordings have rarely been scrutinized for occupational stereotypes.[5] During the late nineteenth and early twentieth centuries, many folk tunes detailed the lives of cowboys, coal miners, sailors, military men, railroad engineers, and other laborers. But post-1950 recordings have been less employment-oriented, despite obvious exceptions such as Tennessee Ernie Ford's "Sixteen Tons" (1955) and Dolly Parton's "9 to 5" (1980). Labor historian and folklore specialist Archie Green has recently launched an extensive oral history exploration of the subject in his audio anthology *Work's Many Voices.*[6] Ironically, there have been no published studies that concentrate on audio images of the medical world. Doctors, nurses, hospitals, and the entire health-care profession await the scrutiny of vinyl oral history.[7]

DOCTORS

Fueled by the fictional images of *Dr. Kildare*, *Ben Casey*, and *Marcus Welby, M.D.*, one might expect song lyrics to portray the physician as a kindly, middle-aged sage with selfless dedication to the needy.[8] Johnny Cash profiles "Old Doc Brown" (1960) as this kind of caring, community-oriented saint who cancels all of his patients' bills before he passes away in his sleep. But the stock images of medical practitioners in song lyrics is overwhelmingly unconventional. Weird Al Yankovic depicts an off-beat hospital intern who behaves "Like a Surgeon" (1985), "cuttin' for the very first time." A more direct character parody, though equally zany, is presented by Dickie Goodman in "Ben Crazy" (1962). And while Ray Charles recognized his own feelings of pain and emptiness, he declares, "I Don't Need No Doctor" (1966). This judgment, as illustrated later in this text, is quite common among disenchanted lovers. However, some singers acknowledge their concern about an experienced physician's learned perspective. Jan and Dean discuss the mortal danger encountered when trying to outrace a sportscar rival in "Dead Man's Curve"(1964). In a mocking vein, Lonnie Mack recites a doctor's earnest warning that his junk-food eating habits will eventually kill him. Nevertheless, the sugar-saturated "Oreo Cookie Blues" (1985) continue to dominate his life.

Although the general practitioner is the primary referent in most medical songs, it is the psychiatrist who is the non-speaking resource behind many, many lyrical situations.[9] Self-proclaimed insanity, or varying degrees of imbalanced behavior, are often documented by singers. The most severe case of self-identified paranoia is Napoleon XIV's emotionally unhinged "They're Coming to Take Me Away, Ha-Haaa!" (1966). One can feel the imminent arrival of a sanitarium crew in their white coats, and hear the strapping sound of the impending straitjacket. Another narrative, this one between a psychiatrist and his patient, features Rick Springfield explaining the emotional suffering caused by his public misrepresentation as "Bruce" (1984) Springsteen. Girlfriends, young male fans, and even his own mother reportedly contribute to Rick's growing mania.

The use of psychiatric terminology by amateur analysts and by lovesick persons is also prominent in song lyrics. Illustrations of these pseudo-clinical personality disorders include: The El Dorados' "At My Front Door (Crazy Little Mama)" (1955), Patsy Cline's "Crazy" (1961), Madonna's "Crazy for You" (1985), J. J. Cale's "Crazy Mama" (1972), Chilliwack's "Crazy Talk" (1974), Lindsey Buckingham's "Go Insane" (1984), Foreigner's "Head Games" (1979), Lou Rawls' "I Go Crazy" (1980), Jack Scott's "Insane" (1986), Michael Sembello's "Maniac" (1983), The Nighthawks' "Nervous Breakdown" (1979), The Rolling Stones' "19th Nervous Breakdown" (1966), Desmond Child and Rouge's "Our Love Is Insane" (1979), Black Sabbath's "Paranoid" (1970), Bobby Hendricks' "Psycho" (1960), Talking Heads' "Psycho Killer" (1978), The Alan Parson Project's "Psychobabble" (1982),

The Count Five's "Psychotic Reaction" (1966), Ivan's "Real Wild Child" (1958), and Paul Simon's "Still Crazy After All These Years" (1976).

The use of the title "Doctor" in contemporary lyrics often has less to do with medical training than with personal experience and expertise in love-making. Wolfman Jack, the gravel-voiced disc jockey, refers to his radio persona as "the doctor of love" in The Guess Who tune "Clap for The Wolf Man" (1974). Match-making aside, the skills of such non-medical doctors vary greatly. Personal vanity and the desire for a 300-pound woman drive Dr. Feelgood and The Interns to craft the self-congratulatory song "Doctor Feel-Good" (1962). But for Aretha Franklin, the reliable lover who is the center of her existence is the real "Doctor Feelgood" (1967). Awarding himself the title of "Doctor Brown" (1987), Buster Brown notes that he can cure any woman's ills. The delightfully wicked Buchanan Brothers make the same argument in "Medicine Man" (1969). Ignoring sexual activity, Roy Buchanan and The Doobie Brothers equate musical titillation and enthusiasm with physical and mental health. The introductory lines to "Dr. Rock and Roll" (1980) and "The Doctor" (1989) clearly portray this message.

SYMPTOMS AND ILLNESSES

Popular lyrics are bipolar in depicting symptoms and illnesses. That is, recorded commentaries are equally divided between real and symbolic (imagined or metaphorical) medical problems.[10] This is hardly an unexpected phenomenon. In literature, in motion pictures, and on television, the language of the American people is heavily spiced with references to the health of the body politic, special remedies or cures for social problems, public debates conducted in a feverish fashion, and hyperactive citizens. But it is the romantic impulse, particularly sexual attraction, that triggers the highest degree of medical imagery. As Peggy Lee asserts in "Fever" (1958), "chicks" were born to give men fever, whether measured in fahrenheit or centigrade.

Taja Sevelle declares "Love Is Contagious" (1987). While Robert Palmer asserts that a singular romantic commitment can result in a "Bad Case of Loving You" (1979), he also describes a young woman whose body aches and sweats because she is "Addicted to Love" (1986). What other symptoms are noted by the romantically afflicted? The king of rock 'n' roll describes his own condition as "All Shook Up" (1957); Elvis Presley also felt "Paralyzed" (1957) and became the victim of a sweet honey bee in "I Got Stung" (1958). Other claims of physical discomfort are registered by Ronnie Love in "Chills and Fever" (1961), by James Brown in "Cold Sweat" (1967), by Olivia Newton-John in "Heart Attack" (1982), by Bobby Hendricks in "Itchy Twitchy Feeling" (1958), by Diana Ross in "Love Hangover" (1976), by Robert Gordon in "Nervous" (1980), and by The Ohio Players in "Pain" (1971). The obvious conclusion that one can be "Injured in the Game of Love" (1985) is detailed by Donnie Iris.

From alapachia to alcoholism and from hypertension to headaches, popular recordings also depict a variety of genuine medical maladies. Roy Byrd, the famous Professor Longhair from New Orleans, laments a "Bald Head" (1950); Wynonie Harris charges his girl with having "Bloodshot Eyes" (1951) from over-imbibing; Huey Smith contends that he gets "High Blood Pressure" (1957) from his romantic relationships; and Allan Sherman complains of "Headaches" (1963). Self-abuse often results in physical debilitation. Behavior such as Motley Crue's "Smokin' in the Boys Room" (1985) and Commander Cody's "Smoke! Smoke! Smoke! (that Cigarette)" (1973) obviously ignores the Surgeon General's warnings about nicotine, lung cancer, and heart disease. The horrors of drug abuse are graphically described by Canned Heat in "Amphetamine Annie" (1968) and by Steppenwolf in "Snow Blind Friend" (1971). The sexually overactive "Sixty-Minute Man" (1951) lauded by The Dominoes is depicted as an exhausted lover four years later by The Checkers in "Can't Do Sixty No More" (1955). A similar state of physical decline brought on by indiscriminate sexual liaisons is described by Bobby Bland in "Goin' Down Slow" (1974).

Other more common pseudo-medical problems are defined by Huey Smith and The Clowns. They declare, "Would You Believe It (My Baby's Got a Cold)" (1984). Ray Pillow notes that nothing is more familiar to him that "Common Colds and Broken Hearts" (1966). Paul Simon describes "Allergies" (1984); The Coasters warn about "Poison Ivy" (1959); and Weird Al Yankovic expresses the discomfort of "Living with a Hernia" (1986). More mysterious ailments are depicted in Little Willie John's "Spasms" (1957), Huey Smith's "Rockin' Pneumonia and the Boogie Woogie Flu" (1957), and David Lindley's "Tu-Ber-Cu-Lucas and the Sinus Blues" (1981). The most blatant example of self-destructive tendencies leading to hospitalization is found in Nervous Norvus' homicidal driver, who is constantly arriving at the hospital for a "Transfusion" (1956).

MEDICINE

Psychology plays a major role in medical practice. A patient must have confidence in a physician in order to accept a diagnosis, to follow the doctor's advice, and to take the prescribed medicine.[11] Of course, not all dispensers of prescriptions are professional doctors. In cases where home remedies, patent medicines, or other brews, potions, or elixirs are suggested, the mindset of the injured party is a key element in determining the impact of the medication. Romantic shortcomings, ranging from lover's quarrels to infrequent dating opportunities, prompt searches for special cures in many popular songs. Sometimes, the solution to the personal problem is located without outside assistance, as in The Marvelettes' "You're My Remedy" (1964) or Ashford and Simpson's "Found a Cure" (1979). When extreme loneliness occurs, though, strange sources of aid are sometimes consulted. David Seville's "Witch Doctor" (1958) chants on behalf of a frustrated suitor, while the mysterious Madame Ruth conjures up a bottle of "Love Potion No. 9" (1959) for The Clovers. The patent medicines sold at tent show revivals[12] are alluded to in Neil Diamond's "Brother Love's Travelling Salvation Show" (1969) and more clearly defined in Ray Stevens' "Jeremiah Peabody's Poly Unsaturated Quick Dissolving Fast Acting Pleasant Tasting Green and Purple Pills" (1961).

It is fascinating to trace the use and abuse of medicine in contemporary lyrics. Whether a homemade salve like Roy Buchanan's "Goose Grease" (1987), a prescription for an oral contraceptive as in Loretta Lynn's "The Pill" (1975), or the potentially life-threatening uppers and downers described in The Rolling Stones' "Mother's Little Helper" (1966), care should be exercised in self-administered medication. The contemporary fascination with drugs is a frightening sidebar to a society that once spoke reverently of achieving better living through chemistry. The literary allusion to Lewis Carroll's fictional Alice is especially clear in The Jefferson Airplane's "White Rabbit" (1967). Grace Slick sings, "One pill makes you larger, and one pill makes you small. But the ones that Mother gives you don't do anything at all." Clearly, the distinction between throat lozenges, cough drops, aspirin, and other household medications and the more exotic mind-altering substances is exciting. It is also dangerous, as illustrated in anti-drug songs by Canned Heat, Steppenwolf, Jimi Hendrix, Paul Revere, and others.

The final paean to medicines is provided by Allan Sherman. In his parody of the early-twentieth-century song "Smiles," he champions the case for "Pills" (1965). Sherman sings:

> There are pills that make you happy,
> There are pills that make you blue,
> There are pills to kill your streptococi,
> There are pills to cure your cockeye, too . . .

Whether metaphorically or physically, relying on external remedies to improve health and to resolve immediate feelings of depression, frustration, and long-range blues or tension is a strange–and often dangerous–activity.

OTHER MEDICAL REFERENCES

Beyond doctors, illnesses, and medicines, popular recordings feature a variety of references to the medical world. Although a few of the images are realistic, most are based upon comedy routines, fictional characters from radio and television programs, or imagined commentaries by physicians, nurses, psychiatrists, and other health-care personnel.[13] Included in this are a variety of songs that use hospital jargon or medical-research terminology to define non-medical personal situations. Recordings that illustrate this latter approach are Cherrelle's "Artificial Heart" (1986), Randy Newman's "Back on My Feet Again" (1974), The Crows' "Call a

Doctor" (1972), Bloodrock's "D.O.A." (1985), The Oak Ridge Boys' "Doctor's Orders" (1982), and Kenny Rogers and The First Edition's "Just Dropped in (to See What Condition My Condition Was in)" (1968).

Composers of popular songs are likely to seize titles or lyric themes from any well-known literary or media source.[14] The influences of Mary Shelley and Robert Louis Stevenson are readily apparent in the mad-doctor stereotypes conjured up by The Edgar Winter Group's "Frankenstein" (1973) and Men at Work's "Dr. Heckyll and Mr. Jive" (1983). Motion pictures have also provided opportunities to link romantic songs with fictional physicians and to create mythical men of medical science who have startling powers.[15] Examples of these situations are Lara's theme from *Dr. Zhivago* ("Somewhere, My Love") (1966) by Ray Conniff and "Doctor Doolittle" (1967) by The Do Re Mi Children's Chorus. Such theme-related music carries over to televised medical series as well: Richard Chamberlain's "Theme from Dr. Casey" (1962), Charles Randolph Grean's "Marcus Welby, M.D." (1970), and The Afternoon Delights' "General Hospi-Tale" (1981).

Finally, there are several recordings that illustrate off-beat references to peculiar medical situations. George Thorogood's "Bad to the Bone" (1982) features a discussion by a maternity-ward nursing team about the unique nature of a newborn infant; Stevie Wonder recalls his childhood sexual experimentation of playing doctor and nurse in "I Wish" (1976); and Alice Cooper longs to ravish the sexy "Nurse Rozetta" (1978). In the realm of audio imitation of medical situations, two recordings stand out. The black humor of Weird Al Yankovic mimicking the noisy compression drones while he talks to "Mr. Frump in the Iron Lung" (1983) is unforgettable. And the powerful, repetitive, thumping rhythm generated by Huey Lewis and The News in "The Heart of Rock and Roll" (1984) is striking. The last level of medically related imagery stems from the rise of health, fitness, and wellness campaigns during the 1980s. Although the lyrics mix sexual attraction with pumping iron, dietary control, and health-club participation, the physiological improvement imagery is still obvious. Recordings in this genre are Olivia Newton-John's "Physical" (1982), Diana Ross' "Muscles"

(1982) and "Work that Body" (1982), and First Circle's "Workin' up a Sweat" (1987).

OBSERVATIONS AND CONCLUSIONS

After examining more than 500 contemporary recordings that feature medical imagery in their titles or lyrics, one is startled by the invisibility of modern medical science in popular music. This conclusion might seem peculiar, especially since it appears at the end of a lengthy report on medical images and metaphors. Yet it is the distinction between fact and fiction–between occupations and stereotypes–that fuels this invisibility claim. Just as many blacks object to the restricted, wooden images of African-Americans in many films and televisions shows, physicians and nurses should also be appalled by the one-dimensional portrayals in contemporary music.[16]

Perhaps it is unreasonable to expect the popular recording media, operating with only a three-minute communication format, to accurately depict the complex world of medicine. Similarly, it is probably not the responsibility of RCA, Columbia, or Warner Brothers Records to educate Americans about medical insurance, physician liabilities, recent research discoveries, abortion counseling, artificial insemination, RNA and DNA experimentation, medical ethics, and so on. Surely, no one would expect medical professionals to launch recording careers in order to provide knowledgeable, experienced insights into the day-to-day workings of clinics and hospitals, psychiatric wards, or intensive-care units. Clearly, though, songwriters and performers are severely flawed sources for informed imagery about medicine. Their ideas about the medical profession might be drawn from direct experience–receiving penicillin shots, physical examinations, maternity care, or emergency-room attention–but most lyricists seem to formulate their images of hospitals, doctors, psychiatrists, nurses, chaplains, and all medical-related activities from the media.[17] As illustrated throughout this study, it is motion pictures (like *One Flew Over the Cuckoo's Nest*, *M*A*S*H*, *Young Frankenstein*, and *Young Doctors in Love*), televised medical dramas (such as *Ben Casey*, *Marcus Welby, M.D.*, *St. Elsewhere*, *Nightingales*, *Heartbeat*, *General Hospital*, *Quincy*, *Trapper John, M.D.*, *Emergency!*, and *Medical Center*), and various popular print resources (including *Soap Opera Digest*, *National Enquirer*, *People Magazine*, and *TV Guide*) that fuel lyrical imaginations regarding medicine.[18]

What can be expected of future songs containing medical imagery? Not much will change. It would be safe to predict that: (1) chaplains will continue to be ignored as integral components of the health-care team; (2) nurses will continue to receive little recognition other than as fantasized sex objects; (3) hospitals will still be pictured as huge buildings peopled by faceless, nameless, white-jacketed doctors and operated in strict bureaucratic fashion; (4) special surgical techniques, research breakthroughs, and experimental treatment modes will either be totally ignored or mentioned only metaphorically; (5) sexual references will be rampant, but disguised in medical metaphors; (6) excellence in musical talent, sexual activity, athletic skill, and other non-medical pursuits will continue to be recognized by the authoritative label "doctor"; and (7) few, if any, complaints will be registered from medical professionals about the less-than-accurate portrayals of health-care personnel. The last prediction assumes that even in this litigious society, the tendency of all professionals to accept humor directed at their fields is quite well documented. Coupled with this stance is the prevalent public feeling that record lyrics are generally harmless entertainment. It is ironic that the so-called Washington Wives and their right-wing religious counterparts–who are so vehement about exposing the sexist, violent, and satanic portions of rock music–are apparently oblivious to the more subtle anti-intellectualism of popular lyrics.[19] The investigation of this latter trend must fall to those who genuinely support free speech, but who also fear that mediated knowledge is insufficient to promote the individual perception necessary for a truly democratic society.[20]

Recorded References: A Selected Discography

45-RPM Records

- "Addicted to Love"
  (Island 99570)
  Robert Palmer (1986)

- “Against Doctor’s Orders”
  (Arista 9830)
  Kenny G (1989)

- “All Shook Up”
  (RCA 47-6870)
  Elvis Presley (1957)

- “Allergies”
  (Warner Brothers 29453)
  Paul Simon (1983)

- “Artificial Heart”
  (Tabu 05901)
  Cherrelle (1986)

- “At My Front Door (Crazy Little Mama)”
  (Vee-Jay 147)
  The El Dorados (1955)

- “Bad Case of Loving You (Doctor, Doctor)”
  (Island 49016)
  Robert Palmer (1979)

- “Bad Medicine”
  (Mercury 59962)
  Bon Jovi (1988)

- “Bald Head”
  (Mercury 8175)
  Roy Byrd (1950)

- “Ben Casey”
  (Carlton 573)
  ValJean (1962)

- “Ben Crazy”
  (Diamond 119)
  Dickie Goodman (1962)

- "Bloodshot Eyes"
  (King 4461)
  Wynonie Harris (1951)

- "Brother Love's Travelling Salvation Show"
  (Uni 55109)
  Neil Diamond (1969)

- "Bruce"
  (Mercury 880405)
  Rick Springfield (1984)

- "Call a Doctor"
  (Legend 125)
  Jack Wakefield (1963)

- "Callin' Doctor Casey"
  (RCA 8054)
  John D. Loudermilk (1962)

- "Chills and Fever"
  (Dot 16144)
  Ronnie Love (1961)

- "Clap for The Wolfman"
  (RCA 0324)
  The Guess Who (1974)

- "Cold Sweat"
  (King 6110)
  James Brown (1967)

- "Common Colds and Broken Hearts"
  (Capitol 5597)
  Ray Pillow (1966)

- "Crazy"
  (Decca 31317)
  Patsy Cline (1961)

- "Crazy Mama"
  (Shelter 7314)
  J. J. Cale (1972)

- "Crazy Talk"
  (Sire 716)
  Chilliwack (1974)

- "D.O.A."
  (Capitol 3009)
  Bloodrock (1971)

- "Dead Man's Curve"
  (Liberty 55672)
  Jan and Dean (1964)

- "The Doctor"
  (Capitol 44376)
  The Doobie Brothers (1989)

- "The Doctor"
  (Jubilee 56211)
  Mary Wells (1968)

- "Dr. Ben Basey"
  (Tuba 8001)
  Mickey Shorr and The Cutups (1962)

- "Doctor! Doctor!"
  (Arista 9209)
  The Thompson Twins (1984)

- "Doctor Doolittle"
  (Kapp 864)
  The Do Re Mi Children's Chorus (1967)

- "Doctor Feel-Good"
  (Okeh 7144)
  Dr. Feelgood and The Interns (1962)

- "Doctor Feelgood"
  (Atlantic 2403)
  Aretha Franklin (1967)

- "Dr. Feelgood"
  (Elektra 69271)
  Motley Crue (1989)

- "Dr. Heckyll and Mr. Jive"
  (Columbia 04111)
  Men at Work (1983)

- "Dr. Jon (The Medicine Man)"
  (Abnak 127)
  Jon and Robin and The In Crowd (1968)

- "Dr. Kildare"
  (Carlton 573)
  ValJean (1962)

- "Doctor Love"
  (Trojan 256)
  John Holt (1976)

- "Dr. Love Power"
  (Hi 2302)
  Ann Peebles (1976)

- "Doctor My Eyes"
  (Asylum 11004)
  Jackson Browne (1972)

- "Doctor of Love"
  (Columbia 43372)
  Dr. Feelgood and The Interns (1965)

- "Doctor Oh Doctor (Massive Infusion)"
  (Acto 3237)
  The Electric Flag (1975)

- "Doctor Rock"
  (RCA 47-7275)
  The Wild Bees (1958)

- "Dr. Rock and Roll"
  (Paramount 155)
  Gary St. Clair (1972)

- "Doctor's Orders"
  (MCA 5294)
  The Oak Ridge Boys (1982)

- "Double Vision"
  (Atlantic 3514)
  Foreigner (1978)

- "Feelin' Alright"
  (Capitol 3095)
  Grand Funk Railroad (1971)

- "Fever"
  (Capitol 3998)
  Peggy Lee (1958)

- "Found a Cure"
  (Warner Brothers 8870)
  Ashford and Simpson (1979)

- "Frankenstein"
  (Epic 10967)
  The Edgar Winter Group (1973)

- "General Hospi-Tale"
  (MCA 51148)
  The Afternoon Delights (1981)

- "Go Insane"
  (Elektra 69714)
  Lindsey Buckingham (1984)

- "Go See the Doctor"
  (Jive 1041)
  Kool Moe Dee (1987)

- "Goin' Down Slow"
  (Dunhill 4379)
  Bobby Bland (1974)

- "Good Lovin'"
  (Atlantic 2321)
  The Young Rascals (1966)

- "Hanging on a Heart Attack"
  (Chrysalis 42996)
  Device (1986)

- "Heart Attack"
  (MCA 52100)
  Olivia Newton-John (1982)

- "The Heart of Rock and Roll"
  (Chrysalis 42782)
  Huey Lewis and The News (1984)

- "High Blood Pressure"
  (Ace 545)
  Huey (Piano) Smith and The Clowns (1957)

- "Hyperactive"
  (Island 99545)
  Robert Palmer (1986)

- "I Don't Need No Doctor"
  (ABCTRC 10865)
  Ray Charles (1966)

- "I Go Crazy"
  (Philadelphia International 8114)
  Lou Rawls (1980)

- "I Go Crazy"
  (Bang 733)
  Paul David (1978)

- "I Got Stung"
  (RCA 47-7410)
  Elvis Presley (1958)

- "I Love Them Nasty Cigarettes"
  (Chart 5112)
  Jim Nesbitt (1971)

- "I Want a New Drug"
  (Chrysalis 42766)
  Huey Lewis and The News (1984)

- "I Wish"
  (Tamia 54274)
  Stevie Wonder (1976)

- "Injured in the Game of Love"
  (HME 04734)
  Donnie Iris (1986)

- "Itchy Twitchy Feeling"
  (Sue 706)
  Bobby Hendricks (1958)

- "Jeremiah Peabody's Poly Unsaturated Quick Dissolving Fast Acting Pleasant Tasting Green and Purple Pills"
  (Mercury 71843)
  Ray Stevens (1961)

- "Junk Food Junkie"
  (Warner Brothers 8165)
  Larry Groce (1976)

- "Just Dropped in (to See What Condition My Condition Was In)"
  (Reprise 0655)
  Kenny Rogers and The First Edition (1968)

- "Lady Doctor"
  (Epic 10607)
  Johnny Robinson (1970)

- "Like a Surgeon"
  (Rock 'n' Roll 04937)
  Weird Al Yankovic (1985)

- "Love Is Contagious"
  (Reprise 28257)
  Taja Sevelle (1987)

- "Love Potion No. 9"
  (United Artists 180)
  The Clovers (1959)

- "Maniac"
  (Casablanca 812516)
  Michael Sembello (1983)

- "Marcus Welby, M.D."
  (Ranwood 872)
  Charles Randolph Grean (1970)

- "Medicine Man"
  (Event 3302)
  The Buchanan Brothers (1969)

- "Mother's Little Helper"
  (London 902)
  The Rolling Stones (1966)

- "Muscles"
  (RCA 13348)
  Diana Ross (1982)

- "19th Nervous Breakdown"
  (London 9823)
  The Rolling Stones (1966)

- "No Pain, No Gain"
  (MS. B. 4501)
  Betty Wright (1988)

- "Our Love Is Insane"
  (Capitol 4669)
  Desmond Child and Rouge (1979)

- "Papa's Medicine Show"
  (Hickory 1670)
  Leona Williams (1968)

- "Paralyzed"
  (RCA EPA-992)
  Elvis Presley (1957)

- "Paranoid"
  (Warner Brothers 7437)
  Black Sabbath (1970)

- "Physical"
  (MCA 51182)
  Olivia Newton-John (1982)

- "The Pill"
  (MCA 40358)
  Loretta Lynn (1975)

- "Poison Ivy"
  (Atco 6146)
  The Coasters (1959)

- "Psycho"
  (Sue 732)
  Bobby Hendricks (1960)

- "Psycho Killer"
  (Sire 1013)
  Talking Heads (1978)

- "Psychobabble"
  (Arista 1029)
  The Alan Parsons Project (1982)

- "Psychotic Reaction"
  (Double Shot 104)
  The Count Five (1966)

- "Real Wild Child"
  (Coral 62017)
  Ivan (1958)

- "Rockin' Pneumonia and the Boogie Woogie Flu"
  (Ace 530)
  Huey Smith and The Clowns (1957)

- "Sexual Healing"
  (Columbia 03302)
  Marvin Gaye (1983)

- "Sixty-Minute Man"
  (Federal 12022)
  The Dominoes (1951)

- "Smoke! Smoke! Smoke! (that Cigarette)"
  (Paramount 0216)
  Commander Cody (1973)

- "Smokin' in the Boy's Room"
  (Elektra 69625)
  Motley Crue (1985)

- "Snow Blind Friend"
  (Donhill 4269)
  Steppenwolf (1971)

- "Somewhere, My Love"
  (Columbia 43636)
  Ray Conniff and The Singers (1966)

- "Song from M*A*S*H"
  (Farr 007)
  The New Marketts (1976)

- "Still Crazy After All These Years"
  (Columbia 10332)
  Paul Simon (1976)

- "Theme from *Ben Casey*"
  (Carlton 573)
  ValJean (1962)

- "Theme from *Dr. Kildare* (Three Stars Will Shine Tonight)"
  (MG 13075)
  Richard Chamberlain (1962)

- "They're Coming to Take Me Away, Ha-Haaa!"
  (Warner Brothers 5831)
  Napoleon XIV (1966)

- "Transfusion"
  (Dot 15470)
  Nervous Norvus (1956)

- "White Rabbit"
  (RCA 9248)
  Jefferson Airplane (1967)

- "Witch Doctor"
  (Liberty 55132)
  David Seville (1958)

- "Workin' up a Sweat"
  (E.M.I. American 8384)
  First Circle (1987)

- "Work that Body"
  (RCA 13201)
  Diana Ross (1982)

- "(You're) Having My Baby"
  (United Artists 454)
  Paul Anka with Odia Coates (1974)

- "You're My Remedy"
  (Ramla 54097)
  The Marvelettes (1964)

33 1/3-rpm Record Cuts

- "Amphetamine Annie"
  (Liberty 7551)
  Canned Heat (1968)

- "Back on My Feet Again"
  (Warner Brothers 2193)
  Randy Newman (1974)

- "Bad to the Bone"
  (E.M.I. American 17076)
  George Thorogood and The Destroyers (1982)

- "The Boogie Disease"
  (Solid Smoke 8015)
  Billy Hancock and The Tennessee Rockets (1981)

- "Call a Doctor"
  (Roulette 114)
  The Crows (1972)

- "Doctor Brown"
  (Collectibles 5110)
  Buster Brown (1987)

- "Dr. Rock and Roll"
  (Waterhouse 12)
  Roy Buchanan (1980)

- "Goose Grease"
  (Alligator 4756)
  Roy Buchanan (1987)

- "Headaches"
  (Warner Brothers 1501)
  Allan Sherman (1963)

- "How Could You Do It to Me"
  (EveJim 1991)
  Little Joe Blue (1987)

- "I See Bones"
  (Warner Brothers 1501)
  Allan Sherman (1963)

- "Insane"
  (Charly CDX 12)
  Jack Scott (1986)

- "Living with a Hernia"
  (Rock 'n' Roll 40520)
  Weird Al Yankovic (1986)

- "Love Doctor"
  (Warner Brothers 2719)
  Millie Jackson (1973)

- "Mr. Frump in the Iron Lung"
  (Rock 'n' Roll 38679)
  Weird Al Yankovic (1983)

- "Nervous"
  (RCA 3523)
  Robert Gordon (1980)

- "Nervous Breakdown"
  (Adelphi 4125)
  The Nighthawks (1979)

- "Nurse Rozetta"
  (Warner Brothers 3263)
  Alice Cooper (1978)

- "Old Doc Brown"
  (Columbia 1464)
  Johnny Cash (1960)

- "Oreo Cookie Blues"
  (Alligator 4739)
  Lonnie Mack (1985)

- "Pills"
  (Warner Brothers 1569)
  Allan Sherman (1965)

- "Poison Ivy"
  (Atlantic 81885)
  The Nylons (1988)

- "Psycho"
  (Imperial 1546731)
  Huey (Piano) Smith and His Clowns (1983)

- "Rock and Roll Doctor"
  (Warner Brothers 2850)
  Cher (1975)

- "Serious as a Heart Attack"
  (Alligator 4742)
  Johnny Winter (1985)

- "Sickness and Disease"
  (A&M 4319)
  Fairport Convention (1971)

- "Source of Infection"
  (Warner Brothers 25732)
  Van Halen (1988)

- "Spasms"
  (King 603)
  Little Willie John (1957)

- "Teenage Nervous Breakdown"
  (Varrick 007)
  The Nighthawks (1983)

- "Tobacco"
  (RCA Victor LSP 3601)
  George Hamilton IV (1966)

- "Tu-Ber-Cu-Lucas and the Sinus Blues"
  (Asylum 5E-524)
  David Lindley (1981)

- "Would You Believe It (My Baby's Got a Cold)"
  (Ace CH 100)
  Huey (Piano) Smith and The Clowns (1984)

NOTES

1. Cherry A. McGee Banks, "A Content Analysis of the Treatment of Black Americans on Television," *Social Education* XLI (April 1977): pp. 336-339, 344; Donald Bogle, *Toms, Coons, Mulattoes, Mammies, and Bucks: An Interpretative History of Blacks in American Films* (New York: Viking, 1973); Melbourne S. Cummings, "The Changing Image of the Black Family on Television," *Journal of Popular Culture* XXII (Fall 1988): pp. 75-85; Betty Darden and James Bayton, "Self-Concept and Blacks' Assessment of Black Leading Roles in Motion Pictures and Television," *Journal of Applied Psychology* LXII (October 1977): pp. 620-623; Adelaide C. Culliver (ed.), *Black Images in Films: Stereotyping and Self-Perception as Viewed by Black Actresses* (Boston: Boston University, 1974); Lenworth Gunther, "Can Blacks Escape American Stereotypes?" *Encore* II (July 1973); pp. 39-46; George Hill, *Ebony Images: Black Americans and Television* (Carson: Daystar, 1985); Daniel J. Lab, *From Sambo to Superspade: The Black Experience in Motion Pictures* (Boston: Houghton Mifflin, 1975); J. Fred MacDonald, *Blacks and White TV: Afro-Americans in Television Since 1948* (Chicago: Nelson-Hall, 1983); Richard A. Maynard (ed.), *The Black Man on Film: Racial Stereo-typing* (Rochelle Park: Hayden, 1974); James P. Murray, *To Find an Image: Black Films from Uncle Tom to Superfly* (Indianapolis: Bobbs-Merrill, 1974); James R. Nesteby, *Black Images in American Film, 1896-1954* (Washington,

D.C.: University Press of America, 1982); Lindsay Paterson (ed.), *Black Film and Film-Makers: A Comprehensive Anthology from Stereotype to Superhero* (New York: Dodd, Mead, 1975); Nagueyalti Warren, "From Uncle Tom to Cliff Huxtable, Aunt Jemima to Aunt Nell: Images of Blacks in Film and the Television Industry," in *Images of Blacks in American Culture: A Reference Guide to Information Sources*, edited by Jessie Carney Smith (Westport: Greenwood, 1988); Mell Watkins, "Beyond the Pale," *Channels* I (April/May 1981): pp. 56-60; and Allen L. Woll and Randall M. Miller (eds.), *Ethnic And Racial Images in American Film and Television* (New York: Garland, 1987).

2. James A. Inciardi and Juliet L. Dee, "From The Keystone Cops to *Miami Vice*: Images of Policing in American Popular Culture," *Journal of Popular Culture* XXI (Fall 1987): pp. 84-102; Kathy Huffhines, "From *E.T.* to *Empire*: Steven Spielberg's Films Show a Changing View of Childhood," *Detroit [Michigan] Free Press* (December 13, 1987): pp. 1, 8H; and Penny Ward Moser, "Diagnosis: Drama–Off-Screen Doctors Add to Realistic TV Treatment," *Detroit [Michigan] Free Press* (February 2, 1988): pp. 1C, 3C.

3. Philip A. Kalisch and Beatrice J. Kalisch, "Nurses on Prime-Time Television," *American Journal of Nursing* (February 1982): p. 264.

4. *Ibid.*

5. Occupation-related images in songs are documented in Norm Cohen, *Long Steel Rail: The Railroad in American Folksong* (Urbana: University of Illinois, 1981); Charles W. Darling (comp.), *The New American Songster: Traditional Ballads and Songs of North America* (Lanham: University Press of America, 1983); and Philip S. Foner, *American Labor Songs of the Nineteenth Century* (Urbana: University of Illinois, 1975). For a thorough profile of job-related songs, see B. Lee Cooper, "Occupations, Materialism, and Workplaces" and "Poverty and Unemployment," in *A Resource Guide to Themes in Contemporary American Song Lyrics, 1950-1985* (Westport: Greenwood, 1986).

6. *Work's Many Voices–Volumes I and II* (JEMF 110/111), compiled by Archie Green (1986). Also see B. Lee Cooper, "Review of *Work's Many Voices*," *Popular Music and Society* XII (Spring 1988): pp. 77-79.

7. A preliminary investigation of this topic–entitled "The Image of the Medical Profession in Popular Song: A Selected List of Recordings"–was compiled by William L. Schurk on October 11, 1988. The most thorough analysis of a particular medical situation via popular song is featured on the 1977 Stash Records album *Jake Walk Blues* (St110). See Joel Vance, "Review of *Jake Walk Blues*," *Stereo Review* XL (June 1978): p. 116. The historical background of this epidemic is recounted in John P. Morgan and Thomas C. Tulloss, "The Jake Walk Blues: A Toxicologic Tragedy Mirrored in American Popular Music," *The Annals of Internal Medicine* LXXXV (December 1976): pp. 804-808.

8. "Through the Years with Dr. Kildare," *TV Guide* XXI (January 20, 1973): pp. 15-18; Richard Gehman, "Caseyitis," in *TV Guide: The First 25 Years*, edited by Jay S. Harris (New York: Simon and Schuster, 1978); and Michael R. Real, "Marcus Welby and the Medical Genre," in *Mass-Mediated Cultures* (Englewood Cliffs: Prentice-Hall, 1977).

9. Film-related images of psychiatrists and their theories are discussed in Irving Schneider, "Images of the Mind: Psychiatry in the Commercial Film," *American Journal of Psychiatry* CXXXIV (June 1977): pp. 613-620 and Leslie Y. Rabkin, "The Celluloid Couch: Psychiatrists in American Films," *Psychocultural Review* III (Spring 1979): pp. 73-89.

10. Susan Sontag, *Illness as Metaphor* (New York: Farrar, Straus, and Giroux, 1977).

11. Horace Newcomb, "Doctors and Lawyers: Counselors and Confessors," in *TV: The Most Popular Act* (Garden City: Doubleday, 1974).

12. Brooks McNamara, *Step Right up: An Illustrated History of the American Medicine Show* (Garden City: Doubleday, 1976).

13. For a full review of medical imagery in literature, film, and television, see Anne Hudson Jones, "Medicine and the Physician," in *Concise Histories of American Popular Culture*, edited by M. Thomas Inge (Westport: Greenwood, 1982). Also see Nancy Y. Hoffman, "The Doctor and the Detective Story," *Journal of the American Medical Association* CCXXIV (April 2, 1973): pp. 74-77 and E. R. Peschel (ed.), *Medicine and Literature* (New York: Neale Watson, 1980).

14. For a recent discussion of this media borrowing practice, see B. Lee Cooper, "Rhythm 'n' Rhymes: Character and Theme Images from Children's Literature in Contemporary Recordings, 1950-1985," *Popular Music and Society* XIII (Spring 1989): pp. 53-71.

15. Jack Spears, "The Doctor on the Screen," in *Hollywood: The Golden Era* (New York: Barnes, 1971) and Peter Roffman and Jim Purdy, "The Doctors," in *The Hollywood Social Problem Film: Madness, Despair, and Politics from the Depression to the Fifties* (Bloomington, IN: Indiana University, 1981).

16. Thelma Schorr, "Nursing's TV Image," *American Journal of Nursing* LXIII (October 1963): pp. 119-121; Michael J. Halberstam, "An M.D. Reviews Dr. Welby of TV," *New York Times Magazine* (January 17, 1972): pp. 12-13ff; Mary K. Wolfe and Gary Wolfe, "Metaphors of Madness: Popular Psychological Narratives," *Journal of Popular Culture* IX (Spring 1976): pp. 895-907; and Beatrice J. Kalisch, Philip A. Kalisch, and Mary McHugh, "A Content Analysis of Film Stereotypes of Nurses," *International Journal of Women's Studies* III (November/December 1980): pp. 531-558.

17. The dangers of oversimplifying complex scientific issues are discussed in B. Lee Cooper, "Information Services, Popular Culture, and the Librarian: Promoting a Contemporary Learning Perspective," *Drexel Library Quarterly* XVI (July 1980): pp. 24-42 and J. L. Heilbron and Daniel J. Kevles, "By Failing to Discuss the 'Civics' of Science and Technology, History Textbooks Distort the Past and Endanger the Future," *The Chronicle of Higher Education* XXXV (February 15, 1989): p. A48.

18. For a longitudinal perspective on the interaction of public perspective and audio-visual imagery, see Daniel J. Czitrom, *Media and the American Mind: From Morse to McLuhan* (Chapel Hill: University of North Carolina, 1982).

19. Parents' Music Resource Center, *Let's Talk Rock: A Primer for Parents* (Arlington: PMRC, 1986); Steve Lawhead, *Rock of this Age: The Real and Imag-*

ined Dangers of Rock Music (Downers Grove, IL: InterVarsity, 1987); Dan Peters and Steve Peters, with Cher Merrill, *Rock's Hidden Persuader: The Truth About Back Masking* (Minneapolis: Bethany House, 1985); and Dan Peters and Steve Peters, *The Peters Brothers Hit Rock's Bottom*, revised edition (North St. Paul: Truth About Rock, 1986). For an excellent, more objective overview of the criticism of rock music, see Linda Martin and Kerry Segrave, *Anti-Rock: The Opposition to Rock 'n' Roll* (Hamden: Archon, 1988).

20. Daniel C. Noel, "An Analytical and Technological Culture Revels in the 'Power of Myth,'" *The Chronicle of Higher Education* XXXV (February 15, 1989): p. B2; William Woodward, "History and Popular Culture . . . and Vice Versa," *Popular Culture Association Newsletter* XVI (February 1989): pp. 1-8; and Spencer R. Weart, "Learning How to Study Images as Potent Forces in Our History," *The Chronicle of Higher Education* XXXV (March 8, 1989): p. A44.

Chapter 22

Work Experiences

Work's Many Voices–Volumes I and II (JEMF 110/111), compiled by Archie Green. El Cerrito: John Edwards Memorial Forum (Arhoolie Records), 1987.

Under the subtitle "Songs of Work Reissued," labor historian Archie Green has assembled two albums containing 32 songs drawn from 45-rpm recordings produced between 1950 and 1985. Reportedly, *Work's Many Voices* will ultimately extend to ten volumes and will include 78-rpm discs dating back to the 1920s. The first two albums feature a diversity of little-known performers (Linda Gale Lewis, Tommy Riddle, Marcia Ball, and Pat Riley) singing in English, Spanish, and Cajun French; the selected songs are sung in varying styles (country, blues, folk, rockabilly, and pop) and were originally released on major (Mercury), minor (Republic), and independent (Ol' Podner) labels.

Green provides a fascinating glimpse at what he fondly refers to as "Laborlore." Examining the idiosyncratic, crazy-quilt pattern of oral history, the albums reveal the views of workers on all sorts of issues. In his liner notes, Green depicts his humanistic approach succinctly: "I view American workers, and their everyday tasks, through the lens of cultural and philosophical pluralism. Songs of labor are kaleidoscopic statements of identity–anger in neglect, shame in poverty, humor in situation, pride in skill, appreciation in custom, in custom, strength in numbers." Assembled with loving care and clearly documented by title, composer, recording artist, record number, city of

---

This review by B. Lee Cooper originally appeared in *Popular Music and Society* XII (Spring 1988): pp. 77-79. Reprint permission has been granted by the author and The Popular Press.

release, date, publisher, copyright, source, and playing time, the songs are delightful and revealing. The sagas of teachers ("Mind-worker"), cowboys ("Cowboy's Sweetheart"), mill workers ("Hard Times in a Cotton Mill"), transit drivers ("Cable Car Operator"), miners ("Trouble in Coal Country"), and heavy-machine operators ("Pan Man Jake") populate Green's vinyl salute to working folks. My personal favorites among the collected tunes include the son-to-his-father tribute "Working Class Hero," the tongue-in-cheek brag "Working Man," and Richard "Big Boy" Henry's critical open letter to Ronald Reagan entitled "Mr. President."

This audio historical resource has been carefully researched, neatly assembled, and thoughtfully documented. Yet why does it seem so antiquated–and so folksy? The answer is clear. The most popular, commercially successful work-theme songs of the past 35 years are inexplicably absent from Green's initial two volumes. How could one compile 45-rpm commentaries from the 1950-1985 period on coal miners, steel laborers, or automobile assembly-line employees without including Tennessee Ernie Ford's "Sixteen Tons" (1955), Jimmy Dean's "Big Bad John" (1961), Billy Joel's "Allentown" (1985), Bobby Bare's "Detroit City" (1963), and Albert King's "Cadillac Assembly Line" (1976)? Worse yet, how could popular laments of labor frustration–including Dolly Parton's "9 to 5" (1980), Johnny Paycheck's "Take this Job and Shove It" (1977), and Jim Croce's "Workin' at the Car Wash Blues" (1974)–have been overlooked? Hopefully, future volumes of *Work's Many Voices* will look to The Beatles, Chuck Berry, Mac Davis, Don Williams, Johnny Cash, Sugarloaf, The Rolling Stones, Roy Orbison, Harry Chapin, The Coasters, Huey Lewis and The News, Styx, Bob Seger and The Silver Bullet Band, Billy Joe Royal, Human League, and Jimmy Reed as sources of labor-related themes. Ethnicity issues and small-town work problems notwithstanding, the nature and meaning of urban labor situations–both white and blue collar, male and female, day and night shifts–deserve much more careful exploration and audio inclusion in Green's so-called "vocumentary."

Despite the potential educational value of selected recordings, there is a continuing legal conflict that often blunts the instructional use of songs. Although not explained by Green, this difficulty might be the source of many of his song omissions. Commercial recording companies, modern composers and lyricists, and several other forces within the vinyl business community have been slow to recognize–and often unwilling to support–the educational reproduction of previously released hit songs. Securing copyright permissions is undeniably mandatory. But few scholarly agencies or small record companies can afford the astronomical rates charged by those firms controlling rights to songs by Bob Dylan, Paul Simon, Willie Nelson, Gordon Lightfoot, Stevie Wonder, Neil Diamond, and others. Yet, it's these talented troubadours who are key public interpreters of many modern American workplaces. Green's groundbreaking compilation may begin to weaken this economic dam that is holding back a flood of key oral-history commentaries.

Contemporary recordings warrant student investigation and serious scholarly study. They are wonderful barometers of social and personal concerns. Archie Green has begun to dig into only one rich vein of the broad goldmine of recorded oral commentary. The JEMF label deserves praise for sponsoring such a worthwhile project. The next eight volumes in this series will expand upon the fine beginning of the first two. Teachers of labor history, American studies, ethno-musicology, and contemporary sociology should find these vinyl texts to be invaluable classroom resources.

Bibliography

Books

Albert, George, and Frank Hoffmann (comps.). 1984. *The Cash Box Country Singles Charts, 1958-1982*. Metuchen, NJ: Scarecrow Press.

Albert, George, and Frank Hoffmann (comps.). 1986. *The Cash Box Black Contemporary Singles Charts, 1960-1984*. Metuchen, NJ: Scarecrow Press.

Allen, Don (ed.). 1975. *The Electric Anthology: Probes into Mass Media and Popular Culture*. Dayton, OH: Pflaum Publishing.

Aquila, Richard. 1989. *That Old Time Rock and Roll: A Chronicle of an Era, 1954-1963*. New York, NY: Schirmer Books.

Bailey, Beth L. 1989. *From Front Porch to Back Seat: Courtship in Twentieth-Century America*. Baltimore, MD: Johns Hopkins University.

Bane, Michael. 1982. *White Boy Singin' the Blues: The Black Roots of White Rock*. New York, NY: Penguin Books.

Barnard, Stephen. 1989. *On the Radio: Music Radio in Britain*. Milton Keynes, England: Open University.

Belz, Carl. 1972. *The Story of Rock* (second edition). New York: Harper & Row.

Bennett, Tony, et al. (eds.). 1986. *Popular Culture and Social Relations*. Milton Keynes, England: Open University.

Benton, Mike. 1991. *The Illustrated History of Horror Comics*. Dallas: Taylor Publishing.

Berry, Jason, Jonathan Foose, and Tad Jones. 1986. *Up from the Cradle of Jazz*. Athens, GA: University of Georgia.

Betrock, Alan. (comp.). 1979. *Rock 'n' Roll Movie Posters*. Brooklyn: Shake Books.

Betrock, Alan. 1982. *Girl Groups: The Story of a Sound*. New York: Delilah Books.

Betrock, Alan. (ed.). 1988. *The Illustrated Price Guide to Scandal Magazines, 1952-1966*. Brooklyn: Shake Books.

Betrock, Alan. (ed.). 1989a. *Cult Exploitation Movie Posters, 1940-1973*. Brooklyn: Shake Books.

Betrock, Alan. (ed.). 1989b. *The Tabloid Poster Book, 1959-1969*. Brooklyn: Shake Books.

Betrock, Alan. (comp.). 1990. *Unseen America: The Greatest Cult Exploitation Magazines, 1950-1966*. Brooklyn: Shake Books.

Betrock, Alan. 1991. *Hitsville: The 100 Greatest Rock 'n' Roll Magazines, 1954-1968*. Brooklyn: Shake Books.

Bianco, David. (comp.). 1988. *Heat Wave: The Motown Fact Book*. Ann Arbor, MI: Pierian Press.

Bigsby, C. W. E. (ed.). 1976. *Approaches to Popular Culture*. Bowling Green, OH: Bowling Green State University.

Bloom, Allan. 1987. *The Closing of the American Mind*. New York: Simon and Schuster.

Bode, Carl. 1959. *The Anatomy of American Popular Culture, 1840-1861*. Berkeley: University of California.

Booth, Mark W. 1981. *The Experience of Song*. New Haven, CT: Yale University.

Booth, Mark W. (comp.). 1983. *American Popular Music: A Reference Guide*. Westport, CT: Greenwood Press.

Bottigheimer, Ruth B. (ed.). 1986. *Fairy Tales and Society: Illusion, Allusion, and Paradigm*. Philadelphia: University of Pennsylvania.

Brady, Barry. 1982. *Reelin' and Rockin': The Golden Age of Rock 'n' Roll Movies*. Australia: The Printing Place, Ltd.

Brake, Robert J. (ed.). 1975. *Communication in Popular Culture*. Bowling Green, OH: Bowling Green State University.

Bronson, Fred. 1988. *The Billboard Book of Number One Hits* (second edition). New York: Billboard Books.

Broven, John. 1974. *Walking to New Orleans: The Story of New Orleans Rhythm and Blues*. Bexhill-On-Sea, Sussex: Blues Unlimited.

Brown, Les. 1982. *Les Brown's Encyclopedia of Television* (second edition). New York: Zoetrope Press.

Browne, Ray B. (ed.). 1973. *Popular Culture and the Expanding Consciousness*. New York: John Wiley and Sons.

Browne, Ray B. 1989. *Against Academia: The History of the Popular Culture Association/American Culture Association and the Popular Culture Movement, 1967-1988*. Bowling Green, OH: Bowling Green State University.

Browne, Ray B., and Ronald J. Ambrosetti (eds.). 1972. *Popular Culture and Curricula*. Bowling Green, OH: Bowling Green State University.

Browne, Ray B., and Marshall Fishwick (eds.). 1978. *Icons of America*. Bowling Green, OH: Bowling Green State University.

Browne, Ray B., and Marshall W. Fishwick (comps.). 1983. *The Hero in Transition*. Bowling Green, OH: Bowling Green State University.

Browne, Ray B., and David Madden. 1972. *The Popular Culture Explosion: Experiencing Mass Media*. Dubuque, IA: William C. Brown Company.

Browne, Ray B., Marshall Fishwick, and Michael T. Marsden (eds.). 1972. *Heroes of Popular Culture*. Bowling Green, OH: Bowling Green State University.

Bruner, David, et al. 1974. *America Through the Looking Glass: A Historical Reader in Popular Culture*. Englewood Cliffs, NJ: Prentice-Hall.

Buhle, Paul (ed.). 1987. *Popular Culture in America*. Minneapolis: University of Minnesota.

Burns, Gary, and Robert J. Thompson (eds.). 1989. *Television Studies: Textual Analysis*. Westport, CT: Greenwood Press.

Busnar, Gene. 1979. *It's Rock 'n' Roll: A Musical History of the Fabulous Fifties*. New York: Wanderer Books.

Callahan, Mike. 1991. *A Guide to Oldies on Compact Disc*. Fairfax Station, VA: Both Sides Now Press.

Campbell, Joseph, with Bill Moyers. 1988. *The Power of Myth*. Garden City, NY: Doubleday.

Cantor, Louis. 1992. *Wheelin' on Beale*. New York: Pharos Books.

Cantor, Norman F., and Michael S. Werthman (eds.). 1968. *The History of Popular Culture* (two volumes). New York: MacMillan.

Carney, George O. (ed.). 1979. *The Sounds of People and Places: Readings in the Geography of American Folk and Popular Music*. Lanham, MD: University Press of America.

Castleman, Harry, and Walter J. Podrazik. 1982. *Watching TV: Four Decades of American Television*. New York: McGraw-Hill.

Cawelti, John. 1976. *Adventure, Mystery, and Romance: Formula Stories as Art and Popular Culture*. Chicago: University of Chicago.

Chapple, Steve, and Reebee Garofalo. 1977. *Rock 'n' Roll Is Here to Pay: The History and Politics of the Music Industry*. Chicago: Nelson-Hall, Inc.

Charters, Samuel B. 1963. *The Poetry of The Blues*. New York: Oak Publications.

Chase, Gilbert. 1987. *America's Music: From the Pilgrims to the Present* (revised third edition). Urbana, IL: University of Illinois.

Christensen, Robert, and Karen Christensen (comps.). 1988. *Christensen's Ultimate Movie, TV, and Rock 'n' Roll Directory* (third edition). San Diego: Cardiff-by-the-Sea Press.

Christgau, Robert. 1973. *Any Old Way You Choose It: Rock and Other Pop Music, 1967-1973*. Baltimore: Penguin Books.

Clark, Alan (comp.). 1987. *Rock and Roll in the Movies* (three volumes). West Covina, CA: Alan Lungstrum.

Clark, Alan (comp.). 1987. *Rock and Roll Memories* (two volumes). West Covina, CA: Alan Lungstrum.

Clarke, Donald (ed.). 1989. *The Penguin Encyclopedia of Popular Music*. New York: Viking Penguin Books.

Cohen, Norm (with music edited by David Cohen). 1981. *Long Steel Rail: The Railroad in American Folksong*. Urbana, IL: University of Illinois.

Cohen-Stratyner, Barbara (ed.). 1988. *Popular Music, 1900-1919: An Annotated Guide to American Popular Song*. Detroit: Gale Research.

Cohn, Nik. 1989. *Ball the Wall: Nik Cohn in the Age of Rock*. London: Picador Books.

Collins, Jim. 1989. *Uncommon Cultures: Popular Culture and Post-Modernism*. New York: Routledge, Chapman, and Hall.

Colman, Stuart. 1982. *They Kept on Rockin': The Giants of Rock 'n' Roll*. Poole, Dorset, England: Blandford Press.

Cooper, B. Lee. 1981. "Popular Music in the Social Studies Classroom: Audio Resources for Teachers" in *How To Do It*–Series II, No. 13. Washington, DC: National Council for Social Studies.

Cooper, B. Lee. 1982. *Images of American Society in Popular Music: A Guide to Reflective Teaching*. Chicago: Nelson-Hall, Inc.

Cooper, B. Lee. 1984. *The Popular Music Handbook: A Resource Guide for Teachers, Librarians, and Media Specialists*. Littleton, CO: Libraries Unlimited, Inc.

Cooper, B. Lee. 1986. *A Resource Guide to Themes in Contemporary American Song Lyrics, 1950-1985*. Westport, CT: Greenwood Press.

Cooper, B. Lee. 1991. *Popular Music Perspectives: Ideas, Themes, and Patterns in Contemporary Lyrics*. Bowling Green, OH: Bowling Green State University.

Cooper, B. Lee, and Wayne S. Haney. 1990a. *Response Recordings: An Answer Song Discography, 1950-1990*. Metuchen, NJ: Scarecrow Press.

Cooper, B. Lee, and Wayne S. Haney. 1990b *Rockabilly: A Bibliographic Resource Guide*. Metuchen, NJ: Scarecrow Press.

Corenthal, Michael G. 1986. *The Iconography of Recorded Sound, 1886-1986: One Hundred Years of Commercial Entertainment and Collecting Opportunity*. Milwaukee: Yesterday's Memories.

Cotten, Lee. 1989. *Shake, Rattle, and Roll–The Golden Age of American Rock 'n' Roll: Volume One, 1952-1955*. Ann Arbor, MI: Pierian Press.

Curtis, James M. 1987. *Rock "Eras": Interpretations of Music and Society, 1954-1984*. Bowling Green, OH: Bowling Green State University.

Dain, Phyllis, and John Y. Cole (eds.). 1990. *Libraries and Scholarly Communication in the United States: The Historical Dimension*. Westport, CT: Greenwood Press.

Daniels, Les, and John Peck. 1971. *Comix: A History of Comic Books in America*. New York: Outerbridge and Dienstfrey.

Dean, Roger, and David Howells (comps.). 1987. *The Ultimate Album Cover Album*. New York: Prentice-Hall.

Debenham, Warren (comp.). 1988. *Laughter on Record: A Comedy Discography*. Metuchen, NJ: Scarecrow Press.

DeCurtis, Anthony, and James Henke, with Holly George-Warren (eds.). 1992. *The Rolling Stone Illustrated History of Rock and Roll* (revised edition). New York: Random House.

Deer, Irving, and Harriet A. Deer (eds.). 1967. *The Popular Arts: A Critical Reader*. New York: Charles Scribner's Sons.

Del Rey, Lester. 1979. *The World of Science Fiction, 1926-1976: The History of a Subculture*. New York: Ballantine Books.

Dellar, Fred (comp.). 1981. *New Musical Express Guide to Rock Cinema*. Middlesex, England: Hamlyn Paperbacks.

Denisoff, R. Serge. 1983. *Sing a Song of Social Significance* (third edition). Bowling Green, OH: Bowling Green University.

Denisoff, R. Serge. 1991. *Inside MTV*. New Brunswick, NJ: Transaction Books.

Denisoff, R. Serge, and Richard A. Peterson (eds.). 1972. *The Sounds of Social Change: Studies in Popular Culture*. Chicago: Rand McNally.

Denisoff, R. Serge, with William L. Schurk. 1986. *Tarnished Gold: The Record Industry Revisited*. New Brunswick, NJ: Transaction Books.

Denisoff, R. Serge, and William D. Romanowski. 1991. *Risky Business: Rock in Film*. New Brunswick, NJ: Transaction Books.

Dennison, Sam. 1982. *Scandalize My Name: Black Imagery in American Popular Music*. New York: Garland Publishing.

Denselow, Robin. 1990. *When the Music's Over: The Story of Political Pop*. London, England: Faber and Faber.

DeTurk, Davia A., and A. Poulin, Jr., (eds.). 1967. *The American Folk Scene: Dimensions of the Folksong Revival*. New York: Dell Publishing.

DeWitt, Howard A. 1985. *Chuck Berry: Rock 'n' Roll Music* (second edition). Ann Arbor, MI: Pierian Press.

Doherty, Thomas. 1988. *Teenagers and Teenpics: The Juvenilization of American Movies in the 1950s*. Winchester, MA: Unwin Hyman Books.

Duxbury, Janell R. 1985. *Rockin' the Classics and Classicizin' the Rock: A Selectively Annotated Discography*. Westport, CT: Greenwood Press.

Dychtwald, Ken, and Joe Flower. 1990. *Age Wave*. New York: Bantam Books.

Ehrenstein, David, and Bill Reed. 1982. *Rock on Film*. New York: Delilah Books.

Eisen, Jonathan (ed.). 1969. *The Age of Rock: Sounds of the American Cultural Revolution*. New York: Vintage Books.

Eisen, Jonathan (ed.). 1970. *The Age of Rock–2: Sights and Sounds of the American Cultural Revolution*. New York: Vintage Books.

Eisen, Jonathan (ed.). 1971. *Twenty-Minute Fandangos and Forever Changes: A Rock Bazaar*. New York: Vintage Books.

Elias, Allen (ed.). 1992. *Popular Culture and Acquisitions*. Binghamton, NY: The Haworth Press.

Ellison, Mary. 1989. *Lyrical Protest: Black Music's Struggle Against Discrimination*. New York: Praeger Books.

Elrod, Bruce C. (comp.). 1985. *Your Hit Parade and American Top Ten Hits, 1958-1984* (third edition). White Rock, SC: B. Elrod.

Erlewine, Michael, and Scott Bultman (eds.). 1992. *All Music Guide*. San Francisco: Miller Freeman, Inc.

Evans, David. 1987. *Big Road Blues: Tradition and Creativity in the Folk Blues*. Jersey City, NJ: Da Capo Press.

Ewen, David. 1977. *All the Years of American Popular Music: A Comprehensive History*. Englewood Cliffs, NJ: Prentice-Hall.

Fallon, Eileen. 1984. *Words of Love: A Complete Guide to Romance Fiction*. New York: Garland Books.

Field, Carolyn W. (ed.). 1982. *Special Collections in Children's Literature*. Chicago: American Library Association.

Fieffer, Jules. 1965. *The Great Comic Book Heroes*. New York: Dial Press.

Fishwick, Marshall W. 1981. *Common Culture and the Great Tradition: The Case for Renewal*. Westport, CT: Greenwood Press.

Fishwick, Marshall W. 1985. *Seven Pillars of Popular Culture*. Westport, CT: Greenwood Press.

Fishwick, Marshall, and Ray B. Browne (eds.). 1970. *Icons of Popular Culture*. Bowling Green, OH: Bowling Green State University.

Fiske, John. 1989. *Reading the Popular*. Winchester, MA: Unwin Hyman.

Fiske, John. 1989. *Understanding Popular Culture*. Winchester, MA: Unwin Hyman.

Flanagan, Bill. 1987. *Written in My Soul: Conversations with Rock's Great Songwriters*. Chicago: Contemporary Books.

Fong-Torres, Ben (ed.). 1974. *The Rolling Stone Rock 'n' Roll Reader*. New York: Bantam Books.

Fong-Torres, Ben (comp.). 1976. *What's that Sound: The Contemporary Music Scene from the Pages of Rolling Stone*. Garden City, NY: Doubleday Anchor Books.

Fox, Ted. 1983. *Showtime at the Apollo*. New York: Holt, Rinehart, and Winston.

Fox, Ted. 1986. *In the Groove: The Men Behind the Music*. New York: St. Martin's Press.

Frith, Simon. 1981. *Sound Effects: Youth, Leisure, and the Politics of Rock 'n' Roll*. New York: Pantheon Books.

Frith, Simon (ed.). 1988. *Facing the Music*. New York: Pantheon Books.

Frith, Simon. 1988. *Music for Pleasure: Essays in the Sociology of Pop*. New York: Routledge, Chapman, and Hall.

Frith, Simon, and Andrew Goodwin (ed.). 1990. *On Record: Rock, Pop, and the Written Word*. New York: Pantheon Books.

Gaar, Gillian G. 1992. *She's a Rebel: The History of Women in Rock 'n' Roll*. Seattle: Seal Press.

Gans, Herbert J. 1974. *Popular Culture and High Culture: An Analysis and Evaluation of Taste*. New York: Basic Books.

Gardner, Carl (ed.). 1979. *Media, Politics, and Culture: A Socialist View*. Atlantic Highlands, NJ: Humanities Press.

Garon, Paul. 1975. *Blues and the Poetic Spirit*. London: Eddison Press.

Gart, Galen. 1986. *First Pressings–1948-1952: Rock History as Chronicled in Billboard Magazine* (two volumes). Milford, NH: Big Nickel Publications.

Gelt, Andrew L. (comp.). 1982. *Index to Alcohol, Drugs, and Intoxicants in Music*. Albuquerque: A. L. Gelt.

George, Nelson. 1983. *Top of the Charts–The Most Complete Listing Ever: The Top 10 Records and Albums for Every Week of Every Year from 1970*. Piscataway, NJ: New Century Publishers.

George, Nelson. 1985. *Where Did Our Love Go: The Rise and Fall of the Motown Sound*. New York: St. Martin's Press.

George, Nelson. 1988. *The Death of Rhythm and Blues*. New York: Pantheon Books.

Gillett, Charlie. 1983. *The Sound of the City: The Rise of Rock and Roll* (revised edition). New York: Pantheon Books.

Girgus, Sam. 1980. *The American Self: Myth, Popular Culture, and the American Ideology.* Albuquerque: University of New Mexico.

Giroux, Henry A., and Roger I. Simon. 1989. *Popular Culture: Schooling and Everyday Life*. Westport, CT: Bergin and Garvey.

Goldstein, Stewart, and Alan Jacobson. 1977. *Oldies but Goodies: The Rock 'n' Roll Years*. New York: Mason Charter.

Goodall, H. L. Jr. 1991. *Living in the Rock 'n' Roll Mystery: Reading Context, Self, and Others as Clues*. Carbondale, IL: Southern Illinois University.

Gordon, Lois, and Alan Gordon. 1987. *American Chronicle: Six Decades of American Life, 1920-1980*. New York: Atheneum Books.

Gordon, Mark, and Jack Nachbar (comps.). 1980. *Currents of Warm Life: Popular Culture in American Higher Education*. Bowling Green, OH: Bowling Green State University.

Goulart, Ron. 1986. *Great History of Comic Books*. Chicago: Contemporary Books.

Govenar, Alan. 1988. *Meeting the Blues: The Rise of the Texas Sound*. Dallas: Taylor Publishing.

Gowans, Alan. 1981. *Learning to See: Historical Perspectives on Modern Popular/Commercial Arts*. Bowling Green, OH: Bowling Green State University.

Gray, Michael H. (comp.). *Bibliography of Discographies–Volume Three: Popular Music*. New York: R. R. Bowker.

Green, Jeff (comp.). 1986. *The 1987 Green Book: Songs Classified by Subject*. Altadena, CA: Professional Desk Reference.

Greenfield, Patricia Marks. 1984. *Mind and Media: The Effects of Television, Video Games, and Computers*. Cambridge: Harvard University.

Greenfield, Thomas Allen. 1989. *Radio: A Reference Guide*. Westport, CT: Greenwood Press.

Gregory, Hugh. 1991. *Soul Music A-Z*. London: Blandford Press.

Greig, Charlotte. 1989. *Will You Still Love Me Tomorrow: Girl Groups from the '50s On. . .* London: Virago Press.

Gribin, Anthony J., and Matthew M. Schiff. 1992. *Doo-Wop: The Forgotten Third of Rock 'n' Roll*. Iola, WI: Krause Publications.

Grissim, John. 1970. *Country Music: White Man's Blues*. New York: Paperback Library.

Grixti, Joseph. 1989. *Terrors of Uncertainty: The Cultural Contexts of Horror Fiction*. London: Routledge Books.

Groia, Philip. 1984. *They All Sang on the Corner: A Second Look at New York City's Rhythm and Blues Vocal Groups* (revised edition). West Hempstead, NY: Phillie Dee Enterprises.

Grun, Bernard. 1982. *The Timetables of History: A Horizontal Linkage of People and Events*. (new, updated edition). New York: Touchstone Books.

Grushkin, Paul D. 1987. *The Art of Rock: Posters from Presley to Punk*. New York: Abbeville Press.

Guralnick, Peter. 1971. *Feel Like Going Home: Portraits in Blues and Rock 'n' Roll*. New York: Outerbridge and Dienstfrey.

Guralnick, Peter. 1979. *Lost Highway: Journeys and Arrivals of American Musicians*. Boston: David R. Godine.

Guralnick, Peter. 1986. *Sweet Soul Music: Rhythm and Blues and the Southern Dream of Freedom*. New York: Harper & Row.

Hall, Charles J. (comp.). 1989a. *A Nineteenth-Century Musical Chronicle: Events, 1800-1899*. Westport, CT: Greenwood Press.

Hall, Charles J. (comp.). 1989b. *A Twentieth-Century Musical Chronicle: Events, 1900-1988*. Westport, CT: Greenwood Press.

Hall, Stuart, and Paddy Whannel. 1964. *The Popular Arts: A Critical Guide to the Mass Media*. New York: Pantheon Books.

Hamm, Charles. 1979. *Yesterdays: Popular Song in America*. New York: W. W. Norton.

Hamm, Charles. 1983. *Music in the New World*. New York: W. W. Norton.

Hamm, Charles, Bruno Nettl, and Ronald Byrnside. 1975. *Contemporary Music and Music Cultures*. Englewood Cliffs, NJ: Prentice-Hall.

Hammel, William M. (ed.). 1972. *The Popular Arts in America: A Reader*. New York: Harcourt Brace Jovanovich.

Hampton, Wayne. 1986. *Guerrilla Minstrels: John Lennon, Joe Hill, Woody Guthrie, and Bob Dylan*. Knoxville, TN: University of Tennessee.

Hanel, Ed (comp.). 1983. *The Essential Guide to Rock Books*. London: Omnibus Books.

Hannusch, Jeff (a.k.a. Almost Slim). 1985. *I Hear You Knockin': The Sound of New Orleans Rhythm and Blues*. Ville Platte, LA: Swallow Publications.

Haralambos, Michael. 1975. *Right On: From Blues to Soul in Black America*. New York: Drake Publishers.

Hardison, O. B. Jr. 1989. *Disappearing Through the Skylight: Culture and Technology in the Twentieth Century*. New York: Viking/Penguin Books.

Hardy, Phil, and Dave Laing (comps.). 1977. *Encyclopedia of Rock, 1955-1975*. London: Aquarius Books.

Hardy, Phil, and Dave Laing. 1990. *The Faber Companion to 20th-Century Music*. London: Faber and Faber.

Harris, Sheldon (comp.). 1979. *Blues Who's Who: A Biographical Dictionary of Blues Singers*. New Rochelle, NY: Arlington House.

Hatch, David and Stephen Millward. 1987. *From Blues to Rock: An Analytical History of Pop Music*. Manchester, England: Manchester University.

Havlice, Patricia Pate (comp.). 1975. *Popular Song Index*. Metuchen, NJ: Scarecrow Press.

Havlice, Patricia Pate (comp.). 1978. *Popular Song Index–First Supplement*. Metuchen, NJ: Scarecrow Press.

Havlice, Patricia Pate (comp.). 1984. *Popular Song Index–Second Supplement*. Metuchen, NJ: Scarecrow Press.

Havlice, Patricia Pate (comp.). 1989. *Popular Song Index–Third Supplement*. Metuchen, NJ: Scarecrow Press.

Heilbut, Tony. 1985. *The Gospel Sound: Good News and Bad Times* (revised edition). New York: Limelight Editions.

Hendler, Herb. 1983. *Year by Year in the Rock Era: Events and Conditions Shaping the Rock Generations that Reshaped America*. Westport, CT: Greenwood Press.

Herbst, Peter (ed.). 1981. *The Rolling Stone Interviews: Talking with the Legends of Rock and Roll, 1967-1980*. New York: St. Martin's Press/Rolling Stone Press.

Heylin, Clinton. 1992. *The Penguin Book of Rock and Roll Writing*. New York: Penguin Books.

Hibbard, Don J., and Carol Kaleialoha. 1983. *The Role of Rock.* Englewood Cliffs, NJ: Prentice-Hall.

Hirsch, Paul, and James W. Carey (eds.). 1978. *Communication and Culture: Humanistic Models in Research.* Beverly Hills: Sage Publications.

Hirshey, Gerri. 1984. *Nowhere to Run: The Story of Soul Music.* New York: Times Books.

Hoare, Ian, Tony Cummings, Clive Anderson, and Simon Frith. 1976. *The Soul Book.* New York: Dell Publishing.

Hoffmann, Frank. 1981. *The Literature of Rock, 1954-1978.* Metuchen, NJ: Scarecrow Press.

Hoffmann, Frank (comp.). 1983. *The Cashbox Singles Charts, 1950-1981.* Metuchen, NJ: Scarecrow Press.

Hoffmann, Frank (comp.). 1984. *Popular Culture and Libraries.* Hamden, CT: Library Professional Publications/Shoe String Press.

Hoffmann, Frank (comp.). 1989. *Intellectual Freedom and Censorship: An Annotated Bibliography.* Metuchen, NJ: Scarecrow Press. Co

Hoffmann, Frank W., and William G. Bailey. 1990. *Arts & Entertainment Fads.* Binghamton, NY: Haworth Press.

Hoffmann, Frank, and B. Lee Cooper. 1986. *The Literature of Rock II, 1979-1983* (two volumes). Metuchen, NJ: Scarecrow Press.

Hoffmann, Frank, and B. Lee Cooper. In press. *The Literature of Rock III, 1984-1990.* Metuchen, NJ: Scarecrow Press.

Hoffmann, Frank, and George Albert, with Lee Ann Hoffmann (comps.). 1987. *The Cash Box Album Charts, 1975-1985.* Metuchen, NJ: Scarecrow Press.

Hoffmann, Frank, and George Albert, with Lee Ann Hoffmann (comps.). 1988. *The Cash Box Album Charts, 1955-1974.* Metuchen, NJ: Scarecrow Press.

Horn, David (comp.). 1977. *The Literature of American Music in Books and Folk Music Collections: A Fully Annotated Bibliography.* Metuchen, NJ: Scarecrow Press.

Horn, David, with Richard Jackson (comps.). 1988. *The Literature of American Music in Books and Folk Music Collections: A Fully Annotated Bibliography, Supplement One.* Metuchen, NJ: Scarecrow Press.

Huebel, Harry Russell (ed.). 1972. *Things in the Driver's Seat: Readings in Popular Culture*. Chicago: Rand McNally.

Hughes, Winifred. 1980. *The Maniac in the Cellar: Sensational Novels of the 1860s*. Princeton: Princeton University.

Huyssen, Andreas. 1986. *After The Great Divide: Modernism, Mass Culture, and Post-Modernism*. Bloomington, IN: Indiana University.

Inge, M. Thomas (ed.). 1982. *Concise Histories of American Popular Culture*. Westport, CT: Greenwood Press.

Inge, M. Thomas (ed.). 1988. *Handbook of American Popular Literature*. Westport, CT: Greenwood Press.

Inge, M. Thomas (ed.). 1989. *Handbook of American Culture* (second edition, revised and enlarged–three volumes). Westport, CT: Greenwood Press.

Inge, M. Thomas. 1990. *Comics as Culture*. Jackson, MS: University of Mississippi.

Iwaschkin, Roman (comp.). 1986. *Popular Music: A Reference Guide*. New York: Garland Publishing.

Jackson, John A. 1991. *Big Beat Heat: Alan Freed and the Early Years of Rock and Roll*. New York: Schirmer.

Jacobs, Will, and Gerald Jones. 1985. *The Comic Book Heroes: From the Silver Age to the Present*. New York: Crown Books.

Jancik, Wayne. 1990. *The Billboard Book of One-Hit Wonders*. New York: Billboard Books/Watson-Guptill Publications.

Jenkinson, Philip, and Alan Warner. 1974. *Celluloid Rock: Twenty Years of Movie Rock*. London: Lorrimer Publishing.

Jowett, Garth, and James M. Linton. 1989. *Movies as Mass Communication* (second edition). Newbury Park, CA: Sage Publications.

Kaiser, Charles. 1988. *1968 in America: Music, Politics, Chaos, Counterculture, and the Shaping of a Generation*. New York: Weldenfeld and Nicolson.

Kaplan, E. Ann. 1987. *Rocking Around the Clock: Music Television, Postmodernism, and Consumer Culture*. New York: Methuen.

Kawin, Bruce F. 1972. *Telling It Again and Again: Repetition in Literature and Film*. Ithaca, NY: Cornell University.

Kell, Charles. 1966. *Urban Blues*. Chicago: University of Chicago.

Kemp, Edward C. 1978. *Manuscript Solicitation for Libraries, Special Collections, Museums, and Archives*. Littleton, CO: Libraries Unlimited.

Kiefer, Kit (ed.). 1991. *They Called It Rock: The Goldmine Oral History of Rock 'n' Roll, 1950-1970*. Iola, WI: Krause Publications.

King, Stephen. 1981. *Danse Macabre*. New York: Everest House.

Kingman, Daniel. 1990. *American Music: A Panorama* (second edition). New York: Schirmer Books.

Kingsbury, Paul, and Alan Axelrod (eds.). 1988. *Country: The Music and the Musicians*. New York: Abbeville Press.

Krummel, D. W. 1987. *Bibliographical Handbook of American Music*. Urbana, IL: University of Illinois.

LaForse, Martin W., and James A. Drake. 1981. *Popular Culture and American Life: Selected Topics in the Study of American Popular Culture*. Chicago: Nelson-Hall, Inc.

Lance, David (ed.). 1983. *Sound Archives: A Guide to Their Establishment and Development*. London: International Association of Sound Archives.

Landau, Jon. 1972. *It's Too Late to Stop Now: A Rock and Roll Journal*. San Francisco: Straight Arrow Books.

Landrum, Larry N. 1982. *American Popular Culture: A Guide to Information Sources*. Detroit: Gale Research.

Larkin, Colin (ed.). 1993. *The Guinness Encyclopedia of Popular Music* (four volumes). Enfield, Middlesex, England: Guinness Superlatives, Ltd.

Larson, Gary. 1989. *The PreHistory of the Far Side: A 10th Anniversary Exhibit*. Kansas City: Andrews and McMeel.

Lasch, Christopher. 1979. *The Culture of Narcissism: American Life in an Age of Diminishing Expectations*. New York: Warner Books.

Lax, Roger, and Frederick Smith (comps.). 1989. *The Great Song Thesaurus* (updated edition). New York: Oxford University.

Lazell, Barry, with Dafydd Rees and Luke Crampton (eds.). 1989. *Rock Movers and Shakers: An A to Z of the People Who Made Rock Happen*. New York: Billboard Publications.

Lehnus, Donald J. 1982. *Angels to Zeppelins: A Guide to the Persons, Objects, Topics, and Themes on United States Postage Stamps, 1847-1980*. Westport, CT: Greenwood Press.

Leppert, Richard, and Susan McClary (eds.). 1987. *Music and Society: The Politics of Composition, Performance, and Reception.* Cambridge, England: Cambridge University.

Levine, Lawrence W. 1977. *Black Culture and Black Consciousness: Afro-American Folk Thought from Slavery to Freedom.* New York: Oxford University.

Levine, Lawrence W. 1988. *Highbrow/Lowbrow: The Emergence of Cultural Hierarchy in America.* Cambridge, MA: Harvard University.

Lewis, George H. (ed.). 1972. *Side-Saddle on the Golden Calf: Social Structure and Popular Culture in America.* Pacific Palisades, CA: Goodyear Publishing.

Lewis, Peter M., and Jerry Booth. 1989. *The Invisible Medium: Public, Commercial, and Community Radio*. London: MacMillan Books.

Lindsay, Joe (edited by Peter Bukoski and Marc Grobman). 1990. *Picture Discs of the World Price Guide: International Reference Book for Picture Records, 1923-1989*. Scottsdale, AZ: BIOdisc Publications.

Lipsitz, George. 1981. *Class Culture in Cold War America: A Rainbow at Midnight*. Brooklyn: J.F. Bergin Publishers, Inc.

Lipsitz, George. 1990. *Time Passages: Collective Memory and American Popular Culture*. Minneapolis: University of Minnesota.

Lohof, Bruce A. 1982. *American Commonplace: Essays on the Popular Culture of the United States*. Bowling Green, OH: Bowling Green State University.

London, Herbert I. 1984. *Closing the Circle: A Cultural History of the Rock Revolution*. Chicago: Nelson-Hall, Inc.

Luciano, Patrick. 1987. *Them or Us: Archetypal Interpretations of Fifties Alien Invasion Films*. Bloomington: Indiana University.

Lull, James (ed.). 1992. *Popular Music and Communication* (second edition). Newbury Park, CA: Sage Publications.

Lydon, Michael, and Ellen Mandel. 1980. *Boogie Lightning: How Music Became Electric* (second edition). New York: Da Capo Press.

Lydon, Michael. 1971. *Rock Folk: Portraits from the Rock 'n' Roll Pantheon*. New York: Dial Press.

MacCabe, Collin (ed.). 1986. *High Theory/Low Culture: Analyzing Popular Television and Film*. New York: St. Martin's Press.

MacDonald, J. Fred. 1979. *Don't Touch that Dial! Radio Programming in American Life from 1920 to 1960*. Chicago: Nelson-Hall, Inc.

MacDonald, J. Fred. 1983. *Black and White TV: Afro-Americans in Television Since 1948*. Chicago: Nelson-Hall, Inc.

MacDonald, J. Fred. 1985. *Television and the Red Menace: The Video Road to Vietnam*. New York: F. A. Praeger.

MacDonald, J. Fred. 1986. *Who Shot the Sheriff? The Rise and Fall of the Television Western*. Westport, CT: Greenwood Press.

Macken, Bob, Peter Fornatale, and Bill Ayres. 1980. *The Rock Music Source Book*. Garden City, NY: Doubleday.

Makower, Joel. 1989. *Woodstock: The Oral History*. Garden City, NY: Tilden Press Books/Doubleday.

Malone, Bill C. 1979. *Southern Music/American Music*. Lexington: University of Kentucky.

Malone, Bill C. 1985. *Country Music U.S.A.* (revised edition). Austin: University of Texas.

Maltby, Richard (ed.). 1989. *Dreams for Sale: Popular Culture in the Twentieth Century*. London: Harrap Press.

Marc, David. 1984. *Demographic Vistas: Television in American Culture*. Philadelphia: University of Pennsylvania

Marc, David. 1989. *Comic Visions: Television Comedy and American Culture*. Boston: Unwin Hyman.

Marcus, Greil (ed.). 1979. *Stranded: Rock and Roll for a Desert Island*. New York: Alfred A. Knopf.

Marcus, Greil. 1990. *Mystery Train: Images of America in Rock 'n' Roll Music* (third edition). New York: Plume/Penguin Books.

Marsden, Michael T., John G. Nachbar, and Sam L. Groff, Jr. (eds.). 1982. *Movies as Artifacts: Cultural Criticism of Popular Film*. Chicago: Nelson-Hall, Inc.

Marsh, Dave. 1985. *Sun City: The Making of the Record*. New York: Penguin Books.

Marsh, Dave, with Lee Ballinger, Sandra Choron, Wendy Smith, and Daviel Wolff. 1985. *The First Rock and Roll Confidential*

Report: Inside the Real World of Rock and Roll. New York: Pantheon Books.

Martin, George (ed.). 1983. *Making Music: The Guide to Writing, Performing, and Recording*. London: Pan Books.

Mayo, Edith (ed.). 1984. *American Material Culture: The Shape of Things Around Us*. Bowling Green, OH: Bowling Green State University.

McKee, Margaret, and Fred Chisenhall. 1981. *Beale Black and Blue: Life and Music on Black America's Main Street*. Baton Rouge: Louisiana University.

McNutt, Randy. 1987. *We Wanna Boogie: An Illustrated History of the American Rockabilly Movement*. Fairfield, OH: Hamilton Hobby Press.

McRobbie, Angela (ed.). 1989. *Zoot Suits and Second-Hand Dresses: An Anthology of Fashion and Music*. Winchester, MA: Unwin Hyman.

Meeker, David. 1982. *Jazz in the Movies* (revised edition). New York: Da Capo Press.

Meeth, L. R., and Dean S. Gregory (comps.). 1981. *Directory of Teaching Innovations in History.* Arlington, VA: Studies in Higher Education.

Melhuish, Martin. 1983. *Heart of Gold: 30 Years of Canadian Pop Music*. Toronto: Canadian Broadcasting Corporation.

Mellers, Wilfrid. 1986. *Angels of the Night: Popular Female Singers of Our Time*. New York: Basil Blackwell.

Middleton, Richard. 1972. *Pop Music and The Blues: A Study of the Relationship and Its Significance*. London: Victor Gollancz.

Middleton, Richard. 1989. *Studying Popular Music*. Milton Keynes, England: Open University.

Middleton, Richard, and David Horn (eds.). 1981. *Popular Music 1: Folk or Popular? Distinctions, Influences, Continuities*. Cambridge, England: Cambridge University.

Middleton, Richard, and David Horn (eds.). 1982. *Popular Music 2: Theory and Method*. Cambridge, England: Cambridge University.

Middleton, Richard, and David Horn (eds.). 1983. *Popular Music 3: Producers and Markets*. Cambridge, England: Cambridge University.

Middleton, Richard, and David Horn (eds.). 1984. *Popular Music 4: Performers and Audiences*. Cambridge, England: Cambridge University.

Miles, Daniel J., Betty T. Miles, and Martin J. Miles (comps.). 1973. *The Miles Chart Display of Popular Music, Volume I: Top 100, 1955-1970*. Boulder, CO: Convex Industries.

Miles, Daniel J., Betty T. Miles, and Martin J. Miles (comps.). 1977. *The Miles Chart Display of Popular Music, Volume II: Top 100, 1971-1975*. New York: Arno Press.

Miller, Jim (ed.). 1980. *The Rolling Stone Illustrated History of Rock and Roll*, (revised edition). New York: Random House/Rolling Stone Press.

Miller, Mark Crispin. 1988. *Boxed In: The Culture of TV.* Evanston, IL: Northwestern University.

Moore, MacDonald Smith. 1985. *Yankee Blues: Musical Culture and American Identity.* Bloomington: Indiana University.

Morrison, Joan, and Robert Morrison, 1987. *From Camelot to Kent State: The Sixties Experience in the Words of Those Who Lived It.* New York: Quadrangle/Times Books.

Morse, David. 1971. *Motown and the Arrival of Black Music*. New York: Collier Books.

Morthland, John. 1984. *The Best of Country Music: A Critical and Historical Guide to the 750 Greatest Albums*. Garden City, NY: Dolphin/Doubleday.

Mukerji, Chandra, and Michael Schudson (eds.). 1991. *Rethinking Popular Culture: Contemporary Perspectives in Cultural Studies*. Berkeley: University of California.

Murdoch, Brian. 1990. *Fighting Songs and Warring Words: Popular Lyrics of Two World Wars*. London: Routledge Publishing.

Murrells, Joseph. 1986. *Million-Selling Records from the 1900s to the 1980s: An Illustrated Directory.* London: Batsford Press.

Music/Records/200: Billboard's July 4, 1976, Spotlight on America. 1976. New York: Billboard Publications.

Mussell, Kay. 1984. *Fantasy and Reconciliation: Contemporary Formulas of Women's Romance Fiction.* Westport, CT: Greenwood Press.

Nachbar, Jack, Deborah Weiser, and John L. Wright (comps.). 1978. *The Popular Culture Reader*. Bowling Green, OH: Bowling Green State University.

Naha, Ed (comp.). 1978. *Lillian Roxon's Rock Encyclopedia* (revised edition). New York: Grosset and Dunlap.

Naisbitt, John. 1984. *Megatrends: The New Directions Transforming Our Lives*. New York: Warner Books.

Newman, Mark. 1988. *Entrepreneurs of Profit and Pride: From Black Appeal to Radio Soul*. New York: Praeger Books.

Nite, Norm N. (comp.). 1982. *Rock On: The Illustrated Encyclopedia of Rock 'n' Roll–Volume One: The Solid Gold Years* (revised edition). New York: Harper & Row.

Nite, Norm N. (comp.). 1984. *Rock On: The Illustrated Encyclopedia of Rock 'n' Roll–Volume Two: The Years of Change* (revised edition). New York: Harper & Row.

Nite, Norm N. (comp.). 1985. *Rock On: The Illustrated Encyclopedia of Rock 'n' Roll–Volume Three: The Video Revolution*. New York: Harper & Row.

Nite, Norm N. (comp.). 1989. *Rock On Almanac: The First Four Decades of Rock 'n' Roll–A Chronology*. New York: Harper & Row.

Nugent, Stephen, and Charlie Gillett (comps.). 1976. *Rock Almanac: Top Twenty American and British Singles and Albums of the '50's, '60's, and '70's.* Garden City, NY: Anchor Press/Doubleday.

Nye, Russell. 1970. *The Unembarrassed Muse: The Popular Arts in America*. New York: Dial Press.

Nye, Russell B. (ed.) 1972. *New Dimensions in Popular Culture*. Bowling Green, OH: Bowling Green State University.

Oakley, Giles. 1978. *The Devil's Music: A History of The Blues*. New York: Harcourt Brace Jovanovich.

Obst, Lynda R. (ed.). 1977. *The Sixties: The Decade Remembered Now, by the People Who Lived It Then*. New York: Random House/Rolling Stone Press.

Ochs, Michael. 1984. *Rock Archives: A Photographic Journey Through the First Two Decades of Rock and Roll*. Garden City, New York: Doubleday.

Oliver, Paul. 1972. *The Meaning of the Blues*. New York: Collier Books.

Oliver, Paul (ed.). 1989. *The Blackwell Guide to Blues Records*. Cambridge, MA: Basil Blackwell.

Opie, Iona, and Moire Tatem (eds.). 1989. *A Dictionary of Superstitions*. New York: Oxford University.

Orman, John. 1984. *The Politics of Rock Music*. Chicago: Nelson-Hall, Inc.

Osborne, Jerry, and Bruce Hamilton (comps.). 1980. *Blues/Rhythm and Blues/Soul: Original Record Collectors Price Guide*. Phoenix: O'Sullivan, Woodside and Company.

Osborne, Jerry (comp.). 1979. *Our Best to You–From Record Digest*. Prescott, AZ: Record Digest.

Osborne, Jerry (comp.). 1981. *Soundtracks and Original Cast Recordings Price Guide*. Phoenix: O'Sullivan, Woodside and Company.

Palmer, Robert. 1978. *Baby, That Was Rock and Roll: The Legendary Leiber and Stoller*. New York: Harcourt Brace Jovanovich.

Palmer, Robert. 1981. *Deep Blues*. New York: Viking Press.

Palmer, William J. 1987. *The Films of the Seventies: A Social History*. Metuchen, NJ: Scarecrow Press.

Panati, Charles. 1991. *Panati's Parade of Fads, Follies, and Manias: The Origins of Our Most Cherished Obsessions*. New York: HarperCollins.

Pareles, Jon, and Patricia Romanowski (eds.). 1983. *The Rolling Stone Encyclopedia of Rock and Roll*. New York: Rolling Stone Press/Summit Books.

Pattillo, Craig W. 1990. *TV Theme Soundtrack Directory and Discography with Cover Versions*. Portland, OR: Braemar Books.

Pavletich, Aida. 1980. *Sirens of Song: The Popular Female Vocalist in America*. New York: Da Capo Press.

Pavlow, Al (comp.). 1983. *Big Al Pavlow's The R&B Book: A Disc-History of Rhythm and Blues*. Providence: Music House Publishing.

Paxton, John, and Sheila Fairfield (comps.). 1984. *Chronology of Culture: A Chronology of Literature, Dramatic Arts, Music, Architecture, Three-Dimensional Art, and Visual Arts from 3,000 B.C. to the Present*. New York: Van Nostrand Reinhold.

Peretti, Burton W. 1992. *The Creation of Jazz: Music, Race, and Culture in Urban America*. Urbana, IL: University of Illinois Press.

Philbin, Marianne (ed.). 1983. *Give Peace a Chance: Music and the Struggle for Peace*. Chicago: Chicago Review Press.

Pichaske, David. 1979. *A Generation in Motion: Popular Music and Culture in the Sixties*. New York: Schirmer Books.

Pichaske, David. 1981a. *Beowulf to Beatles and Beyond: The Varieties of Poetry*. New York: Macmillan.

Pichaske, David. 1981b. *The Poetry of Rock: The Golden Years*. Peoria, IL: Ellis Press.

Pielke, Robert G. 1986. *You Say You Want a Revolution: Rock Music in American Culture*. Chicago: Nelson-Hall, Inc.

Podell, Janet (ed.). 1987. *Rock Music in America*. New York: H. W. Wilson.

Pollock, Bruce. 1975. *In Their Own Words: Twenty Successful Song Writers Tell How They Write Their Songs*. New York: Collier Books.

Pollock, Bruce. 1981. *When Rock Was Young: A Nostalgic Review of the Top 40 Era*. New York: Holt, Rinehart, and Winston.

Pollock, Bruce. 1983. *When the Music Mattered: Rock in the 1960s*. New York: Holt, Rinehart, and Winston.

Pollock, Bruce (ed.). 1986a. *Popular Music, 1980-1984–Volume 9*. Detroit: Gale Research.

Pollock, Bruce (ed.). 1986b. *Popular Music 1985–Volume 10*. Detroit: Gale Research.

Pollock, Bruce (ed.). 1987. *Popular Music 1986–Volume 11*. Detroit: Gale Research.

Pollock, Bruce (ed.). 1988. *Popular Music, 1987–Volume 12*. Detroit: Gale Research.

Porter, Dennis. 1981. *The Pursuit of Crime: Art and Ideology in Detective Fiction*. New Haven, CT: Yale University.

Potter, David M. 1954. *People of Plenty: Economic Abundance and the American Character*. Chicago: University of Chicago.

Powers, Richard G. 1983. *G-Men: Hoover's FBI in American Popular Culture*. Carbondale, IL: Southern Illinois University.

Prakel, David. 1987. *Rock 'n' Roll on Compact Disc: A Critical Guide to the Best Recordings*. New York: Harmony Books.

Pratt, Ray. 1990. *Rhythm and Resistance: Explorations in the Political Uses of Popular Music*. Westport, CT: Praeger.

Pruter, Robert. 1991. *Chicago Soul*. Champaigne-Urbana, IL: University of Illinois Press.

Quirin, Jim, and Barry Cohen (comps.). 1987. *Chartmasters' Rock 100: An Authoritative Ranking of the 100 Most Popular Songs for Each Year, 1956 Through 1986* (supplements for 1987, 1988, etc, are also available). Covington, LA: Chartmasters.

Rachlin, Harvey (comp.). 1981. *The Encyclopedia of the Music Business*. New York: Harper & Row.

Rader, Barbara H., and Howard G. Zettler (eds.). 1988. *The Sleuth and the Scholar: Origins, Evolution, and Current Trends in Detective Fiction*. Westport, CT: Greenwood Press.

Ramsdell, Kristin. 1987. *Happily Ever After: A Guide to Reading Interest in Romance Fiction*. Littleton, CO: Libraries Unlimited.

Redd, Lawrence N. 1974. *Rock Is Rhythm and Blues: The Impact of Mass Media*. East Lansing, MI: Michigan State University.

Reich, Charles A. 1970. *The Greening of America*. New York: Random House.

Reid, Robert. 1971. *Music and Social Problems: A Poster Series*. Portland, ME: J. Weston Walch.

Rimler, Walter. 1984. *Not Fade Away: A Comparison of Jazz Age with Rock-Era Pop Song Composers*. Ann Arbor, MI: Pierian Press.

Rissover, Fredric, and David C. Birch (eds.). 1983. *Mass Media and the Popular Arts* (third edition). New York: McGraw-Hill.

Robbins, Ira A. (ed.). 1985. *The New Trouser Press Record Guide* (second edition). New York: Charles Scribner's Sons.

Robinson, Red, and Peggy Hodgins. 1983. *Rockbound: Rock 'n' Roll Encounters, 1955-1969*. Surrey, Canada: Hancock House.

Rodnitzky, Jerome L. 1976. *Minstrels of the Dawn: The Folk-Protest Singer as a Cultural Hero*. Chicago: Nelson-Hall, Inc.

Rogers, Jimmie N. 1983. *The Country Music Message: All About Lovin' and Livin'*. Englewood Cliffs, NJ: Prentice-Hall.

Rollin, Roger B. (comp.). 1973. *Hero/Anti-Hero*. New York: McGraw-Hill.

Rollin, Roger (ed.). 1989. *The Americanization of the Global Village: Essays in Comparative Popular Culture*. Bowling Green, OH: Bowling Green State University.

Rollins, Peter C. (ed.). 1983. *Hollywood as the Historian: American Film in a Cultural Context*. Lexington, KY: University Press of Kentucky.

Rooney, John F. Jr., Wilbur Zelinsky, and Dean R. Louder (general editors). 1982. *This Remarkable Continent: An Atlas of United States and Canadian Society and Cultures*. College Station, TX: For the Society for the North American Cultural Survey by Texas A&M University.

Romanowski, Patricia (ed.). 1983. *Rolling Stone Rock Almanac: The Chronicles of Rock and Roll*. New York: Collier Books.

Root, Robert L. Jr. 1987. *The Rhetoric of Popular Culture: Advertising, Advocacy, and Entertainment*. Westport, CT: Greenwood Press.

Rose, Brian (ed.). 1985. *TV Genres: A Handbook and Reference Guide*. Westport, CT: Greenwood Press.

Rosenberg, Betty. 1986. *Genreflecting: A Guide to Reading Interest in Genre Fiction* (second edition). Littleton, CO: Libraries Unlimited.

Roszak, Theodore. 1969. *The Making of a Counter Culture: Reflections on the Technocratic Society and Its Youthful Opposition*. Garden City, NY: Doubleday Anchor Books.

Rowe, Mike. 1981. *Chicago Blues: The City and the Music*. New York: Da Capo Press.

Roxon, Lillian. 1969. *Lillian Roxon's Rock Encyclopedia*. New York: Universal Library/Grosset and Dunlap.

Ruppli, Michel (comp.). 1979. *Atlantic Records: A Discography* (four volumes). Westport, CT: Greenwood Press.

Ruppli, Michel (comp.). 1983. *The Chess Labels: A Discography* (two volumes). Westport, CT: Greenwood Press.

Ruppli, Michel (comp.). 1985. *The King Labels: A Discography* (two volumes). Westport, CT: Greenwood Press.

Ruppli, Michel (comp.). 1991. *The Aladdin/Imperial Labels: A Discography*. Westport, CT: Greenwood Press.

Ryan, John. 1985. *The Production of Culture in the Music Industry: The ASCAP-BMI Controversy.* Lanham, MD: University of America.

Sandahl, Linda J. (comp.). 1987. *Rock Films: A Viewer's Guide to Three Decades of Musicals, Concerts, Documentaries, and Soundtracks, 1955-1986.* New York: Facts on File.

Sander, Ellen. 1973. *Trips: Rock Life in the Sixties.* New York: Charles Scribner's Sons.

Sanjek, Russell. 1988. *American Popular Music and Its Business–The First Four Hundred Years: Volume Three, 1900-1984.* New York: Oxford University.

Santelli, Robert. 1985. *Sixties Rock: A Listener's Guide.* Chicago: Contemporary Books.

Sarlin, Bob. 1973. *Turn It Up (I Can't Hear the Words): The Best of the New Singer/Song Writers.* New York: Simon and Schuster.

Savage, William W., Jr. 1990. *Comic Books and America, 1945-1954.* Norman, OK: University of Oklahoma.

Savage, William W. Jr. 1982. *Singing Cowboys and All That Jazz: A Short History of Popular Music in Oklahoma.* Norman, OK: University of Oklahoma.

Sayres, Sohnya, Anders Stephanson, Stanley Aronowitz, and Fredric Jameson (eds.). 1985. *The '60s Without Apology.* Minneapolis: University of Minnesota.

Schaffner, Nicholas. 1982. *The British Invasion: From the First Wave to the New Wave.* New York: McGraw-Hill.

Schatz, Thomas. 1981. *Hollywood Genres: Formulas, Filmmaking, and the Studio System.* Philadelphia: Temple University.

Scheurer, Timothy E. (ed.). 1989a. *American Popular Music–Volume One: The 19th Century and Tin Pan Alley.* Bowling Green, OH: Bowling Green State University.

Scheurer, Timothy E. (ed.). 1989b. *American Popular Music–Volume Two: The Age of Rock.* Bowling Green, OH: Bowling Green State University.

Scheurer, Timothy E. 1991. *Born in the U.S.A.: The Myth of America in Popular Music from Colonial Times to the Present.* Jackson, MS: University Press of Mississippi.

Schroeder, Fred E. H. 1977. *Outlaw Aesthetics: Arts and the Public Mind.* Bowling Green, OH: Bowling Green State University.

Schroeder, Fred E. H. 1980. *5000 Years of Popular Culture*. Bowling Green, OH: Bowling Green State University.

Schroeder, Fred E. H. (ed.). 1981. *Twentieth-Century Popular Culture in Museums and Libraries*. Bowling Green, OH: Bowling Green State University.

Schultze, Quentin J., Roy M. Anker, James D. Batt, William D. Romanowski, John W. Worst, and Lambert Zuidervaart. 1991. *Dancing in the Dark: Youth, Popular Culture, and the Electronic Media*. Grand Rapids, MI: William B. Eerdmans Publishing.

Scott, Frank. et al. (comps.). 1991. *The Down Home Guide to the Blues*. Chicago: A Cappella Books.

Scott, John Anthony. 1983. *The Ballad of America: The History of the United States in Song and Story.* Carbondale, IL: Southern Illinois University.

Scott, Randall W. 1990. *Comics Librarianship: A Handbook.* Jefferson, NC: McFarland.

Sculatti, Gene, and Davin Seay. 1985. *San Francisco Nights: The Psychedelic Music Trip, 1965-1968*. New York: St. Martin's Press.

Seeger, Pete, and Bob Reiser. 1985. *Carry It On: A History in Song and Pictures of the Working Men and Women of America*. New York: Simon and Schuster.

Shannon, Bob, and John Javna. 1986. *Behind the Hits: Inside Stories of Classic Pop and Rock and Roll.* New York: Warner Books.

Shapiro, Nat, and Bruce Pollock (comps.). 1985. *Popular Music, 1920-1979–A Revised Compilation* (three volumes). Detroit: Gale Research.

Shaw, Arnold. 1974. *The Rockin' 50s*. New York: Hawthorn Books.

Shaw, Arnold. 1978. *Honkers and Shouters: The Golden Years of Rhythm and Blues*. New York: Collier Books.

Shaw, Arnold. 1986. *Black Popular Music in America: From the Spirituals, Minstrels, and Ragtimes to Soul, Disco, and Hip-Hop*. New York: Schirmer Books.

Shore, Michael (comp.). 1987. *Music Video: A Consumer's Guide*. New York: Ballantine Books.

Silvani, Lou. 1992. *Collecting Rare Records*. Bronx, NY: Times Square Records.

Silber, Irwin (ed.). 1971. *Songs America Voted By.* Harrisburg, PA: Stackpole Books.

Simels, Steve. 1985. *Gender Chameleons: Androgeny in Rock 'n' Roll.* New York: Arbor House.

Sitton, Thad, George L. Mehaffy, and O. L. David, Jr. 1983. *Oral History: A Guide for Teachers (and Others).* Austin: University of Texas.

Small, Christopher. 1987. *Music of the Common Tongue: Survival and Celebration in Afro-American Music.* New York: River-Run Press.

Smith, Henry Nash (ed.). 1967. *Popular Culture and Industrialism, 1865-1890.* Garden City, NY: Anchor Books.

Smith, Joe (edited by Mitchell Fink). 1988. *Off the Record: An Oral History of Popular Music.* New York: Warner Books.

Smith, Wes. 1989. *The Pied Pipers of Rock 'n' Roll: Radio DeeJays of the '50s and '60s.* Marietta, GA: Longstreet Press.

Sontag, Susan. 1966. *Against Interpretation.* New York: Dell Publishing.

Spignesi, Stephen J. 1991. *The Shape under the Sheet: The Complete Stephen King Encyclopedia.* Ann Arbor, MI: Popular Culture, Ink.

Stacy, Jan, and Ryder Syvertsen. 1984. *Rockin' Reels: An Illustrated History of Rock and Roll Movies.* Chicago: Contemporary Books.

Stambler, Irwin (comp.). 1989. *Encyclopedia of Pop, Rock, and Soul* (revised edition). New York: St. Martin's Press.

Stanley, John. 1988. *Revenge of the Creature Features Movie Guide: An A to Z Encyclopedia to the Cinema of the Fantastic* (third revised edition). Pacifica, CA: Creatures at Large Press.

Stecheson, Anthony, and Anne (comps.). 1961. *The Stecheson Classified Song Directory.* Hollywood: Music Industry Press.

Stecheson, Anthony, and Anne Stecheson (comps.). 1978. *The Supplement to the Stecheson Classified Song Directory.* Hollywood: Music Industry Press.

Stidom, Larry (comp.). 1986. *Izatso?! Larry Stidom's Rock 'n' Roll Trivia Fact Book.* Indianapolis: L. Stidom.

Street John. 1986. *Rebel Rock: The Politics of Popular Music.* New York: Basil Blackwell.

Stuessy, Joe. 1990. *Rock and Roll: Its History and Stylistic Development*. Englewood Cliffs, NJ: Prentice-Hall.

Szatmary, David P. 1991. *Rockin' in Time: A Social History of Rock and Roll*, (second edition). Englewood Cliffs, NJ: Prentice-Hall.

Taylor, Paul (comp.). 1985. *Popular Music Since 1955: A Critical Guide to the Literature*. New York: Mansell Publishing.

Tebbel, John, and Mary Ellen Zuckerman. 1991. *The Magazine in America, 1741-1990*. New York: Oxford University.

Tharpe, Jac L. (ed.). 1979. *Elvis: Images and Fancies*. Jackson, MS: University of Mississippi.

Thomas, James L. (ed.). 1982. *Nonprint in the Secondary Curriculum: Readings for Reference*. Littleton, CO: Libraries Unlimited.

Titon, Jeff Todd. 1977. *Early Downhome Blues: A Musical and Cultural Analysis*. Urbana, IL: University of Illinois.

Tobler, John (ed.). 1991. *Who's Who in Rock and Roll*. New York: Crescent Books.

Tosches, Nick. 1984. *Unsung Heroes of Rock 'n' Roll: The Birth of Rock 'n' Roll in the Dark and Wild Years Before Elvis*. New York: Charles Scribner's Sons.

Tosches, Nick. 1985. *Country: Living Legends and Dying Metaphors in America's Biggest Music* (revised edition). New York: Charles Scribner's Sons.

Tudor, Dean (comp.). 1983. *Popular Music: An Annotated Guide to Recordings*. Littleton, CO: Libraries Unlimited.

Twitchell, James B. 1989. *Preposterous Violence: Fables of Aggression in Modern Culture*. New York: Oxford University.

Umphred, Neal (comp.). 1992. *Goldmine's Rock 'n' Roll 45 R.P.M. Record Price Guide* (second edition). Iola, WI: Krause Publications.

Urdang, Laurence (ed.). 1981. *The Timetables of History*. New York: Touchstone/Simon and Schuster.

Van Der Merwe, Peter. 1989. *Origins of the Popular Style: The Antecedents of Twentieth-Century Popular Music*. Oxford, England: Clarendon Press.

Vassal, Jacques. 1976. *Electric Children: Roots and Branches of Modern Folkrock*. New York: Taplinger Publishing.

Ventura, Michael. 1985. *Shadow Dancing in the U.S.A.* Los Angeles: Jeremy P. Tarcher.

Vulliamy, Graham, and Edward Lee. 1982a. *Popular Music: A Teacher's Guide*. London: Routledge and Kegan Paul.

Vulliamy, Graham, and Edward Lee. 1982b. *Pop, Rock, and Ethnic Music in School*. Cambridge, England: Cambridge University.

Wade, Dorothy, and Justine Picardie. 1990. *Music Man: Ahmet Ertegon, Atlantic Records, and the Triumph of Rock 'n' Roll*. New York: W.W. Norton.

Walker, Donald E., and B. Lee Cooper. In press. *Baseball and American Culture: A Bibliographic Guide for Teachers and Librarians*. Jefferson, NC: McFarland.

Waller, Gregory A. (ed.). 1987. *American Horrors: Essays on the Modern American Horror Film*. Urbana, IL: University of Illinois.

Ward, Alan. 1990. *A Manual of Sound Archive Administration*. Aldershot, England: Gower Publishing.

Ward, Ed, Geoffrey Stokes, and Ken Tucker. 1986. *Rock of Ages: The Rolling Stone History of Rock and Roll*. New York: Rolling Stone Press/Summit Books.

Warren, Bill. 1982. *Keep Watching the Skies! American Science Fiction Movies of the Fifties: Volume One, 1950-1957*. Jefferson, NC: McFarland.

Welding, Pete, and Toby Byron (eds.). 1991. *Bluesland: Portraits of Twelve Major American Blues Masters*. New York: Dutton/Penguin Books.

Wenzel, Lynn, and Carol J. Binkowski. 1989. *I Hear America Singing: A Nostalgic Tour of Popular Sheet Music*. New York: Crown Publishers.

Westcott, Steven D. (comp.). 1985. *A Comprehensive Bibliography of Music for Film and Television*. Detroit: Information Coordinators.

Whetmore, Edward Jay. 1987. *Mediamerica: Form, Content, and Consequence of Mass Communication* (third edition). Belmont, CA: Wadsworth Publishing.

Whitburn, Joel (comp.). 1982. *Bubbling Under the Hot 100, 1959-1981*. Menomonee Falls, WI: Record Research.

Whitburn, Joel (comp.). 1987a. *The Billboard Book of Top 40 Albums: The Complete Chart Guide to Every Album in the Top 40 Since 1955*. New York: Billboard Books.

Whitburn, Joel (comp.). 1987b. *The Billboard Book of Top 40 Hits* (third edition). New York: Billboard Books.

Whitburn, Joel (comp.). 1987c. *Pop Singles Annual, 1955-1986.* Menomonee Falls, WI: Record Research.

Whitburn, Joel (comp.). 1988a. *Billboard's Top 10 Charts: A Week-by-Week History of the Hottest of the Hot 100, 1958-1988.* Menomonee Falls, WI: Record Research.

Whitburn, Joel (comp.). 1988b. *Billboard's Top 3,000+, 1955-1987: A Ranking of Every Top 10 Hit of the Rock Era.* Menomonee Falls, WI: Record Research.

Whitburn, Joel (comp.). 1988c. *Music and Video Yearbook 1987.* Menomonee Falls, WI: Record Research.

Whitburn, Joel (comp.). 1988d. *Top Rhythm and Blues Singles, 1942-1988.* Menomonee Falls, WI: Record Research.

Whitburn, Joel (comp.). 1989a. *Music and Video Yearbook 1988.* Menomonee Falls, WI: Record Research.

Whitburn, Joel (comp.). 1989b. *Top Country Singles, 1944-1988.* Menomonee Falls, WI: Record Research.

Whitburn, Joel (comp.). 1990a. *Daily #1 Hits: A Day-by-Day Listing of the #1 Pop Records of the Past Fifty Years, 1940-1989.* Menomonee Falls, WI: Record Research.

Whitburn, Joel (comp.). 1990b. *Music and Video Yearbook 1989.* Menomonee Falls, WI: Record Research.

Whitcomb, Ian. 1972. *After the Ball: Pop Music from Rag to Rock.* Baltimore, MD: Penguin Books.

Whitcomb, Ian. 1982. *Whole Lotta Shakin': A Rock 'n' Roll Scrapbook.* London: Arrow Books.

Whitcomb, Ian. 1983. *Rock Odyssey: A Musician's Guide to the Sixties.* Garden City, NY: Dolphin Books.

White, David Manning, and John Pendleton (eds.). 1977. *Popular Culture: Mirror of American Life.* Del Mar, CA: Publisher's.

White, Timothy. 1984. *Rock Stars.* New York: Stewart, Tabori, and Chang.

White, Timothy. 1990. *Rock Lives: Profiles and Interviews.* New York: Henry Holt.

Wicke, Peter. 1990. *Rock Music: Culture, Aesthetics, and Sociology.* New York: Cambridge University.

Wiegand, Wayne A. (ed.). 1978. *Popular Culture and the Library: Current Issues Symposium II*. Lexington, KY: College of Library Science at the University of Kentucky.
Williamson, Judith. 1986. *Consuming Passions: The Dynamics of Popular Culture*. New York: Marion Boyars Books.
Wilson, Charles R., and William Feris (eds.). 1989. *Encyclopedia of Southern Culture*. Chapel Hill, NC: University of North Carolina.
Winks, Robin W. 1988. *Detective Fiction: A Collection of Critical Essays*. Woodstock, VT: Foul Plays Countryman Press.
Winks, Robin W. 1969. *The Historian as Detective: Essays as Evidence*. New York: Harper & Row.
Winks, Robin W. 1982. *Modus Operandi: An Excursion into Detective Fiction*. Boston: David R. Godine.
Witek, Joseph. 1989. *Comic Books as History: The Narrative Art of Jack Jackson, Art Spiegelman, and Harvey Pekar*. Jackson, MS: University Press of Mississippi.
Wright, Gene. 1986. *Horrorshows: The A-to-Z of Horror in Film, TV, Radio and Theater*. New York: Facts On File.
Wright, Will. 1975. *Sixguns and Society: A Structural Study of the Western*. Berkeley: University of California.
Yorke, Ritchie. 1971. *Axes, Chops, and Hot Licks: The Canadian Rock Music Scene*. Edmonton: M. G. Hurtig.
Zalkind, Ronald (comp.). 1980. *Contemporary Music Almanac 1980/81*. New York: Schirmer Books.

Articles

Anderson, T. J., and Lois Fields Anderson. 1988. "Images of Blacks in Instrumental Music and Song." *Images of Blacks in American Culture: A Reference Guide to Information Sources*, edited by Jessie Carney Smith. Westport, CT: Greenwood Press, pp. 119-137.
Auslander, H. Ben. 1981. "'If Ya Wanna End War and Stuff, You Gotta Sing Loud': A Survey of Vietnam-Related Protest Music." *Journal of American Culture*, IV September, pp. 108-113.
Aydelotte, William O. 1967. "The Detective Story as a Historical Source." *The Popular Arts: A Critical Reader*, edited by Irving

Deer and Harriet A. Deer. New York: Charles Scribner's Sons, pp. 132-153.

Bailey, Anne Lowrey. 1988. "Scholars at Mississippi Center Preserve and Promote the Culture of the South." *Chronicle of Higher Education*, XXXIV August 3, pp. A4, A6.

Baker, Glenn A. 1981. "Recording the Right." *Goldmine*. No. 66 November, pp. 176-178.

Baker, Glenn A. 1982. "Rock's Angry Voice." *Goldmine*, No. 75 July, pp. 10-11.

Barol, Bill. 1988. "The Eighties Are Over." *Newsweek*, CXI January 4, pp. 40-48.

Bell, Michael J. 1989. "The Study of Popular Culture." *Handbook of American Culture–Volume Three* (second edition, revised and enlarged), edited by M. Thomas Inge. Westport, CT: Greenwood Press, pp. 1459-1484.

Blosser, Betsy J., and Gretchen Lagana. 1989. "Popular Culture in the Rare Book Room and Special Collections Department." *Journal of Popular Culture*, XXIII Fall, pp. 125-137.

Bold, Rudolph. 1980. "Trash in the Library." *Library Journal*, CV May 15, pp. 1138-1189.

Bowman, Elsa M. 1989. "The Relationship of Music and Popular Culture in Schooling." *Perspectives of New Music*, XXVII Winter, pp. 118-123.

Brooks, Tim. 1983. "ARSC: Association for Recorded Sound Collections–An Unusual Organization." *Goldmine*, No. 81 February 1983, pp. 22-23.

Brooks, Tim. 1990. "Review of *Pop Memories* by Joel Whitburn." *ARSC Journal*, XXI Spring, pp. 134-141.

Brown, Richard C. 1974. "Postage Stamps and American Women: Stamping Out Discrimination in the Mails." *Social Education*, XXXVIII January, pp. 20-23.

Browne, Ray B. 1972a. "Popular Culture: Notes Toward a Definition." *Side-Saddle on the Golden Calf: Social Structure and Popular Culture in America*, edited by George H. Lewis. Pacific Palisades, CA: Goodyear Publishing, pp. 5-13.

Browne, Ray B. 1972b. "The Uses of Popular Culture in the Teaching of American History." *Social Education*, XXXVI January, pp. 49-53.

Browne, Ray B. 1978. "Popular Culture–The World Around Us." *The Popular Culture Reader,* edited by Jack Nachbar, Deborah Weiser, and John L. Wright. Bowling Green, OH: Bowling Green University, pp. 12-18.

Browne, Ray B. 1980. "Libraries at the Crossroads: A Perspective on Libraries and Culture." *Drexel Library Quarterly*, XVI July, pp. 12-23.

Browne, Ray B. 1984. "Popular Culture as the New Humanities." *Journal of Popular Culture*, XVII Spring, pp. 1-8.

Browne, Ray B. 1987. "Popular Culture: Medicine for Illiteracy and Associated Educational Ills." *Journal of Popular Culture*, XXI Winter, pp. 1-15.

Browne, Ray B. 1989. "Redefining Literature." *Journal of Popular Culture*, XXIII Winter, pp. 11-21.

Burns, Gary. 1983. "Trends in Lyrics in the Annual Top Twenty Songs in the United States, 1963-1972." *Popular Music and Society*, IX, pp. 25-39.

Burns, Gary. 1988. "Film and Popular Music." *Film and the Arts in Symbiosis: A Resource Guide*, edited by Gary R. Edgerton, Westport, CT: Greenwood Press, pp. 217-242.

Burchart, Ronald E., and B. Lee Cooper. 1987. "Perceptions of Education in the Lyrics of American Popular Music, 1950-1980." *American Music*, V Fall, pp. 271-281.

Carey, James T. 1969. "Changing Courtship Patterns in the Popular Song." *American Journal of Sociology*, LXXIV May, pp. 720-731.

Carney, George O. 1982. "Music and Dance." *This Remarkable Continent: An Atlas of United States and Canadian Society and Cultures*, edited by John F. Rooney, Jr., Wilbur Zelinsky, and Dean R. Louder. College Station, TX: For the Society for the North American Cultural Survey by Texas A&M University, pp. 234-253.

Cawelti, John G. 1976. "Popular Culture's Coming-of-Age." *Journal of Aesthetic Education*, X July-October, pp. 165-182.

Chenoweth, Lawrence. 1981. "The Rhetoric of Hope and Despair: A Study of the Jimi Hendrix Experience and the Jefferson Airplane." *American Quarterly*, XXIII Spring, pp. 25-45.

Chilcoat, George W., Laurence I. Seidman, Sheldon Brown, and B. Lee Cooper. 1985. "Study U.S. History Through Songs." *Social Education*, XLIX October, pp. 579-603.

Christianson, Nora D. 1949. "Teaching American History Through It's Period Music." *Social Studies*, XL April, pp. 156-165.

Clarke, Jack A. 1973. "Popular Culture in Libraries." *College and Research Libraries*, XXXIV May, pp. 216-217.

Cobb, James M. 1982. "From Muskogee to Luckenbach: Country Music and the Southernization of America." *Journal of Popular Music*, XVI Winter, pp. 81-91.

Cohn, William H. 1977. "Popular Culture and Social History." *Journal of Popular Culture*, XI Summer, pp. 167-179.

Cole, Richard. 1971. "Top Songs of the Sixties: A Content Analysis of Popular Lyrics." *American Behavioral Scientist*, XIV January-February, pp. 389-400.

Collison, Michele. 1988. "Today's Students Flock to Courses About 1960's." *Chronicle of Higher Education*, XXXIV May, pp. 33A, 34A.

Combs, James. 1984. "Popular Culture and American Politics." *Polpop: Politics and Popular Culture in America*. Bowling Green, OH: Bowling Green State University Popular Press, pp. 3-20.

Cooper, B. Lee. 1973. "Examining Social Change Through Contemporary History: An Audio Media Proposal." *The History Teacher*, VI August, pp. 523-534.

Cooper, B. Lee. 1974. "Popular Music and Academic Enrichment in the Residence Hall." *NASPA Journal*, XI Winter, pp. 50-57.

Cooper, B. Lee. 1975. "Rock Music and Religious Education: A Proposed Synthesis." *Religious Education*, LXX May-June, pp. 289-299.

Cooper, B. Lee. 1976a. "Exploring the Future Through Popular Music." *Media and Methods*, XII April, pp. 32-35ff.

Cooper, B. Lee. 1976b. "Futurescope." *Audiovisual Instruction*, XXI January, pp. 42-48.

Cooper, B. Lee. 1976c. "Teaching American History Through Popular Music," *AHA* (American Historical Association) *Newsletter*, XIV October, pp. 3-5.

Cooper, B. Lee. 1976-77. "Bob Dylan, Isaac Asimov, and Social Problems: Non-Traditional Materials for Reflective Teaching." *International Journal of Instructional Media*, IV No. 1, pp. 105-115.

Cooper, B. Lee. 1977. "Folk History, Alternative History, and Future History." *Teaching History: A Journal of Methods*, II Spring, pp. 58-62.

Cooper, B. Lee. 1977-78. "Constructing Popular Culture Biographies: History Instruction Through Literary and Audio Resources." *International Journal of Instructional Media*, V, pp. 357-369.

Cooper, B. Lee. 1978a. "The Image of the Outsider in Contemporary Lyrics." *Journal of Popular Culture*, XII Summer, pp. 168-178.

Cooper, B. Lee. 1978b. "Record Revivals as Barometers of Social Change: The Historical Use of Contemporary Audio Resources." *JEMF Quarterly*, XIV Spring, pp. 38-44.

Cooper, B. Lee. 1978c. "A Science Fiction Perspective on Contemporary Issues." *Dayton, Ohio: An Occasion Paper of the Ohio Council for the Social Studies*, 16 pp.

Cooper, B. Lee. 1978-79. "Searching for Personal Identity in the Social Studies: Male and Female Perspectives in Contemporary Lyrics." *International Journal of Instructional Media*, VI, pp. 351-360.

Cooper, B. Lee. 1979a. "Beyond Lois Lane and Wonder Woman: Exploring Images of Women Through Science Fiction." *Library-College Experimenter*, V November, pp. 7-15.

Cooper, B. Lee. 1979b. "Images of the Future in Popular Music: Lyrical Comments on Tomorrow." *Ideas for Teaching Gifted Students: Social Studies*, edited by Jackie Mallis. Austin: Multi Media Arts, pp. 97-108.

Cooper, B. Lee. 1979c. "Rock Discographies: Exploring the Iceberg's Tip." *JEMF Quarterly*, XV Summer, pp. 115-120.

Cooper, B. Lee. 1979d. "Social Change, Popular Music, and the Teacher." *Ideas for Teaching Gifted Students: Social Studies*, edited by Jackie Mallis. Austin: Multi Media Arts, pp. 9-19.

Cooper, B. Lee. 1979e. "The Song Revival Revolution of the Seventies: Tapping the Musical Roots of Rock." *Goldmine*, No. 42 November, p. 126.

Cooper, B. Lee. 1980a. "Discographies of Contemporary Music, 1965-1980: A Selected Bibliography." *Popular Music and Society*, VII Fall, pp. 253-269.

Cooper, B. Lee. 1980b. "Les McCann, Elvis Presley, Linda Ronstadt, and Buddy Holly: Focusing on the Lives of Contemporary Singers." *Social Education*, XLIV March, pp. 217-221.

Cooper, B. Lee. 1980c. "Popular Music: An Untapped Resource. . ." *Ideas for Teaching Gifted Students: Music*, edited by Jackie Mallis. Austin: Multi Media Arts, pp. 179-189.

Cooper, B. Lee. 1980d. "Rock Discographies Revisited." *JEMF Quarterly*, XVI Summer, pp. 89-94.

Cooper, B. Lee. 1980-81. "Sounds of the City: Popular Music Perspectives on Urban Life." *International Journal of Instructional Media*, VIII, pp. 241-254.

Cooper, B. Lee. 1981a. "Audio Images of the City." *Social Studies*, LXXII May-June, pp. 129-136.

Cooper, B. Lee. 1981b. "Examining a Decade of Rock Bibliographies, 1970-1979." *JEMF Quarterly*, XVII Summer, pp. 95-101.

Cooper, B. Lee. 1981c. "An Opening Day Collection of Popular Recordings: Searching for Discographic Standards." *Twentieth-Century Popular Culture in Museums and Libraries*, edited by Fred E. H. Schroeder. Bowling Green, OH: Bowling Green University, pp. 228-255.

Cooper, B. Lee. 1982a. "Huntin' for Discs with Wild Bill: William L. Schurk–Sound Recordings Archivist." *ARSC Journal*, XIV No. 3, pp. 9-19.

Cooper, B. Lee. 1982b. "Popular Music: A Creative Teaching Resource." *Nonprint in the Secondary Curriculum: Readings for Reference*, edited by James L. Thomas. Littleton, CO: Libraries Unlimited, pp. 78-87.

Cooper, B. Lee. 1982-83a. "Popular Music in the Classroom: A Bibliography of Teaching Techniques and Instructional Resources." *International Journal of Instructional Media*, X No. 1, pp. 71-87.

Cooper, B. Lee. 1982-83b. "Shifting Images of Transportation Technology and American Society in Railroad Songs, 1920-1980." *International Journal of Instructional Media*, X, pp. 131-146.

Cooper, B. Lee. 1983-84. "Just Let Me Hear Some of That . . ." Discographies of Fifty Classic Rock-Era Performers." *JEMF Quarterly*, No. 74 Fall-Winter, pp. 100-116.

Cooper, B. Lee. 1984a. "Dr. Rock on Little Richard: Speculating on a Long-Awaited Biography." *Record Profile Magazine*, No. 4 February-March, pp. 21-22, 25.

Cooper, B. Lee. 1984b. "Foreword." *Popular Culture and Libraries*, compiled by Frank W. Hoffmann. Hamden, CT: Library Professional Publications/Shoe String Press, pp. viii-xv.

Cooper, B. Lee. 1984c. "'It's a Wonder I Can Think at All': Vinyl Images of American Public Education, 1950-1980." *Popular Music and Society*, IX No. 4, pp. 47-65.

Cooper, B. Lee. 1986a. "Race Relations." *A Resource Guide to Themes in Contemporary American Song Lyrics, 1950-1985*. Westport, CT: Greenwood Press, pp. 213-222.

Cooper, B. Lee. 1986b. "Sequel Songs and Response Recordings: The Answer Record in Modern American Music, 1950-1985." *International Journal of Instructional Media*, XIII No. 3, pp. 227-239.

Cooper, B. Lee. 1987a. "Political Protest Movements and Social Trends Depicted in American Popular Music, 1960-1985: A Chronological Guide to Recorded Resources." *International Journal of Instructional Media*, XIV No. 2, pp. 147-160.

Cooper, B. Lee. 1987b. "Recorded Resources for Teaching the History of Contemporary Music, 1950-1985: A Discography of Musical Styles and Recording Artists." *International Journal of Instructional Media*, XIV No. 1, pp. 63-81.

Cooper, B. Lee. 1987c. "Response Recordings as Creative Repetition: Answer Songs and Pop Parodies in Contemporary American Music." *OneTwoThreeFour: A Rock 'n' Roll Quarterly*, No. 4, pp. 79-87.

Cooper, B. Lee. 1988. "Bear Cats, Chipmunks, and Slip-In Mules: The Answer Song in Contemporary American Recordings, 1950-1985." *Popular Music and Society*, XII Fall, pp. 57-77.

Cooper, B. Lee. 1989a. "Creating an Audio Chronology: Utilizing Popular Recordings to Illustrate Ideas and Events in American History, 1965-1987." *International Journal of Instructional Media*, XVI No. 2, pp. 167-179.

Cooper, B. Lee. 1989b. "Popular Records as Oral Evidence: Creating an Audio Time Line to Examine American History, 1955-1987." *Social Education*, LIII January, pp. 34-40.

Cooper, B. Lee. 1989c. "Promoting Social Change Through Audio Repetition: Black Musicians as Creators and Revivalists, 1953-1978." *Tracking: Popular Music Studies*, II Winter, pp. 26-46.

Cooper, B. Lee. 1990a. "Christmas Songs as American Cultural History: Audio Resources for Classroom Investigation." *Social Education*, LIV October, pp. 374-379.

Cooper, B. Lee. 1990b. "Dancing: The Perfect Educational Metaphor." *Institute for Educational Management/Management Development Program Newsletter*, VI Spring-Summer, p. 5.

Cooper, B. Lee. 1992. "Popular Songs, Military Conflicts, and Public Perceptions of the United States at War." *Social Education*, LVI March, pp. 160-168.

Cooper, B. Lee. In press. "American Popular Music and the Myth of U.S. Military Morality." *Journal of American Culture*.

Cooper, B. Lee, and Larry S. Haverkos. 1972. "Using Popular Music in Social Studies Instruction." *Audiovisual Instruction*, XVII November, pp. 86-88.

Cooper, B. Lee, and Larry S. Haverkos. 1977. "An Error in Punctuation." *Stellar 3: Science Fiction Stories*, edited by Judy-Lynn del Rey. New York: Ballantine Books, pp. 108-115.

Cooper, B. Lee, and Verdan D. Traylor. 1979. "Establishing Rock Standards: The Practice of Record Revivals in Contemporary Music, 1953-1977." *Goldmine*, No. 36 May, pp. 37-38.

Cooper, B. Lee, Frank W. Hoffmann, and William L. Schurk. 1983-84. "A Guide to Popular Music Periodicals of the Rock Era, 1953-1983." *International Journal of Instructional Media*, XI No. 4, pp. 369-381.

Cooper, B. Lee, and William L. Schurk. 1987a. "Audio Feasts for The Junk Food Junkie: An Investigation of Popular Recordings Featuring Food-Related Themes, 1950-1985." *Shipherd's Record*, VII Summer, pp. 5-6.

Cooper, B. Lee, Simon Frith, Bernhard Hefele, Frank Hoffmann, David Horn, Toru Mitsui, Robert Springer, and Erzsebet Szeverenyl (comps.). 1987b. "Booklist." *Popular Music*, VI October, pp. 361-385.

Cooper, B. Lee, Simon Frith, Bernhard Hefele, Frank Hoffmann, David Horn, Toru Mitsui, Paul Oliver, Stan Rijuen, and Robert

Springer (comps.). 1988. "Booklist." *Popular Music*, VII October, pp. 357-371.

Cooper, B. Lee, Bernhard Hefele, Frank Hoffmann, David Horn, Toru Mitsui, and Robert Springer (comps.). 1989. "Booklist." *Popular Music*, VII October, pp. 335-347.

Cooper, B. Lee, and Larry S. Haverkos. 1990. "Total Recall." *Garfield Lake Review*, pp. 15-18.

Cooper, B. Lee, and Donald Walker, with assistance from William L. Schurk. 1991. "The Decline of Contemporary Heroes in American Popular Recordings." *Popular Music and Society*, XV Summer, pp. 49-58.

Coughlin, Ellen K. 1983. "From the Great Society to the Me Decade: A Minority View of the '60s and '70s." *The Chronicle of Higher Education*, XXVI June 1, pp. 29-30.

Denisoff, R. Serge. 1969. "Folk-Rock: Folk Music, Protest, or Commercialism?" *Journal of Popular Culture*, III Fall, pp. 214-230.

Denisoff, R. Serge. 1970. "Protest Songs: Those on the Top Forty and Those on the Streets." *American Quarterly*, XXII Winter, pp. 807-823.

Denisoff, R. Serge. 1972. "A Short Note on Studying Popular Culture." *Popular Culture Methods*, I August, pp. 2-5.

Denisoff, R. Serge. 1973. "The Evolution of Pop Music Broadcasting, 1920-1972." *Popular Music and Society*, II Spring, pp. 202-226.

Denisoff, R. Serge, and Mark H. Levine. 1971. "The Popular Protest Song: The Case of 'Eve of Destruction'." *Public Opinion Quarterly*, XXXV Spring, pp. 117-122.

Denisoff, R. Serge, and Richard A. Peterson. 1972. "Theories of Culture, Music, and Society." *The Sounds of Social Change: Studies in Popular Culture*. Chicago: Rand McNally, pp. 1-12.

Denisoff, R. Serge, and David Fandray. 1977. "'Hey, Hey Woody Guthrie I Wrote You a Song': The Political Side of Bob Dylan." *Popular Music and Society*, V, pp. 31-42.

Denisoff, R. Serge, and John Briges. 1981. "The Battered and Neglected Orphan: Popular Music Research and Books." *Popular Music and Society*, VIII, pp. 43-59.

Denisoff, R. Serge, and Mark H. Levine. 1989. "The One-Dimensional Approach to Popular Music: A Research Note." *American Popular Music–Volume One: The 19th Century and Tin Pan Alley*, edited by Timothy E. Scheurer, Bowling Green, OH: Bowling Green State University, pp. 9-15.

Desruisseaux, Paul. 1983. "A Scholar Teaches History of Rock-and-Roll–and, in the Process, the Country's." *Chronicle of Higher Education*, XXVI April 20, pp. 5-6.

Dimaggio, Paul. 1977. "Market Structure, The Creative Process, and Popular Culture: Toward an Organizational Reinterpretation of Mass-Culture Theory." *Journal of Popular Culture*, XI Fall, pp. 436-450.

Dimaggio, Paul, Richard A. Peterson, and Jack Esco, Jr. 1972. "Country Music: Ballad of the Silent Majority." *The Sounds of Social Change: Studies in Popular Culture*, edited by R. Serge Denisoff and Richard A. Peterson. Chicago: Rand McNally, pp. 38-55.

Dudley, Bruce. 1978. "Comic Books and Rock 'n' Roll: The Artifacts of Our Society." *At Bowling Green: News for Alumni*, VIII February, pp. 3-7.

Duxbury, Janell R. 1988. "Shakespeare Meets the Backbeat: Literary Allusion in Rock Music." *Popular Music and Society*, XII Fall, pp. 19-23.

Ellis, Allen, and Doug Highsmith, 1990. "Popular Culture and Libraries." *College and Research Library News*, LI May, pp. 410-413.

Ellison, Mary. 1986. "War–It's Nothing But a Heartbreak: Attitudes to War in Black Lyrics." *Popular Music and Society*, X No. 4, pp. 29-42.

Ferrandino, Joe. 1972. "Rock Culture and the Development of Social Consciousness." *Side-Saddle on the Golden Calf: Social Structure and Popular Culture in America*, edited by George H. Lewis. Pacific Palisades, CA: Goodyear Publishing, pp. 263-290.

Fiedler, Leslie. 1975. "Towards a Definition of Popular Culture." *Superculture: American Popular Culture and Europe*, edited by C.W. E. Bigsby. Bowling Green, OH: Bowling Green State University, pp. 28-42.

Fiore, Jannette. 1980. "Popular Culture and the Academic Library: The Nye Collection." *Drexel Library Quarterly*, XVI July, pp. 53-64.

Floyd, Samuel A. 1990. "Center for Black Music Research–Columbia College Chicago." *Sonneck Society Bulletin*, XVI Spring, pp. 3-6.

Fluck, Winfried. 1987. "Popular Culture as a Mode of Socialization: A Theory About the Social Functions of Popular Cultural Forms." *Journal of Popular Culture*, XXI Winter, pp. 31-46.

Franklin, Frances. 1988. "He Hopes to Fill Historical Silence with Music." *Battle Creek* [Michigan] *Enquirer*, June 19, p. 3A.

Friedlander, Paul. 1988. "The Rock Window: A Systematic Approach to an Understanding of Rock Music." *Tracking: Popular Music Studies*, I Spring, pp. 42-51.

Frith, Simon. 1981. "'The Magic That Can Set You Free': The Ideology of Folk and the Myth of the Rock Community." *Popular Music I: Folk or Popular? Distinctions, Influences, Continuities*, edited by Richard Middleton and David Horn. Cambridge, England: Cambridge University, pp. 159-168.

Frith, Simon. 1983. "Rock Biography: Essay Review." *Popular Music 3: Producers and Markets*, edited by Richard Middleton and David Horn. Cambridge, England: Cambridge University, pp. 271-277.

Fryer, Paul. 1981. "Can You Blame the Colored Man?: The Topical Song in Black American Popular Music." *Popular Music and Society*, VIII, pp. 19-31.

Garofalo, Reebee. 1986. "Rocking Against Racism in Massachusetts." *OneTwoThreeFour: A Rock 'n' Roll Quarterly*, No. 3 Autumn, pp. 75-85.

Garofalo, Reebee, and Steve Chapple. 1978. "From ASCAP to Alan Freed: The Pre-History of Rock 'n' Roll." *Popular Music and Society*, VI, pp. 72-80.

Glenn, William H. 1983. "Postage Stamps Enhance the Teaching of Social Studies." *Social Studies*, LXXIV March-April, pp. 70-75.

Goodfriend, James. 1976. "A Calendar of American Music." *Stereo Review*, XXXVII July, pp. 64-69.

Greeley, Andrew. 1988. "Agon and Empathos: A Challenge to Popular Culture." *Popular Culture Association Newsletter*, XV April, pp. 2-5.

Gritzner, Charles F. 1978. "Country Music: A Reflection of Popular Culture." *Journal of Popular Culture*, XI Fall, pp. 857-864.

Grossberg, Lawrence. 1984. "Another Boring Day in Paradise: Rock and Roll and the Empowerment of Everyday Life." *Popular Music 4: Performers and Audiences*, edited by Richard Middleton and David Horn. Cambridge, England: Cambridge University, pp. 225-258.

Gulon, David. 1982. "Booster Songs: Musical Manifestations of Civic Pride in American Towns and Cities." *Journal of American Culture*, V Summer, pp. 56-61.

Guralnick, Peter. 1989. "My Back Pages: What Motivates a Music Critic?" *Musician*, No. 126 April, pp. 27-34, 89.

Hamm, Charles. 1975. "Changing Patterns in Society and Music: The U.S. Since World War II." *Contemporary Music and Music Cultures*, compiled by Charles E. Hamm, Bruno Nettl, and Ronald Byrnside. Englewood Cliffs, NJ: Prentice-Hall, pp. 35-70.

Harmon, James E. 1972. "Meaning in Rock Music: Notes Toward a Theory of Communication." *Popular Music and Society*, II Fall, pp. 18-32.

Harmon, James E. 1982. "The New Music and Counter-Culture Values." *Youth and Society*, IV September, pp. 61-82.

Heckman, Don. 1970. "Black Music and White America." *Black America*, edited by John F. Szwed. New York: Basic Books, pp. 158-170.

Henderson, Floyd M. 1974. "The Image of New York City in American Popular Music of 1890-1970." *New York Folklore Quarterly*, XXX December, pp. 267-278.

Hesbacher, Peter, and Les Waffen. 1982. "War Recordings: Incidence and Change, 1940-1980." *Popular Music and Society*, VIII, pp. 77-101.

Hey, Kenneth R. 1977. "I Feel a Change Comin' On: The Counter-Cultural Image of the South in Southern Rock 'n' Roll." *Popular Music and Society*, V, pp. 93-99.

Hilsabech, Steven A. 1984. "The Blackboard Bumble: Popular Culture and Recent Challenges to the American High School." *Journal of Popular Culture*, XVIII Winter, pp. 25-30.

Hirsch, Paul M. 1971. "Sociological Approaches to the Pop Music Phenomenon." *American Behavioral Scientist*, XIV January-February, pp. 371-388.

Hirsch, Paul, John Robinson, Elizabeth Keogh Taylor, and Stephen B. Withey. 1972. "The Changing Popular Song: An Historical Overview." *Popular Music and Society,* I Winter, pp. 83-93.

"The History Teacher: 'Piano Man' Joel Lights a Fire in the Nation's Classrooms." 1990. *Lansing* [Michigan] *State Journal,* January 21, pp. 1f.

Hoffmann, Paul Dennis. 1985. "Rock and Roll and J.F.K.: A Study of Thematic Changes in Rock and Roll Lyrics Since the Assassination of John F. Kennedy." *Popular Music and Society,* X No. 2, pp. 59-79.

Horton, Donald. 1957. "The Dialogue of Courtship in Popular Songs." *American Journal of Sociology,* LXII May, pp. 569-578.

Huffmann, James R., and Julie L. Huffmann. 1987. "Sexism and Cultural Lag: The Rise of the Jailbait Song, 1955-1985." *Journal of Popular Culture,* XXI Fall, pp. 65-83.

Hugunin, Marc. 1979. "ASCAP, BMI, and the Democratization of American Popular Music." *Popular Music and Society,* VII, pp. 8-17.

Kamin, Jonathan. 1974. "Parallels in the Social Reactions to Jazz and Rock." *Journal of Jazz Studies,* II December, pp. 95-125.

Kamin, Jonathan. 1972. "Taking the Roll out of Rock 'n' Roll: Reverse Acculturation." *Popular Music and Society,* II Fall, pp. 1-17.

Kamin, Jonathan. 1975. "The White R&B Audience and the Music Industry, 1952-1956." *Popular Music and Society,* IV, pp. 170-187.

Keetz, Frank. 1976. "Nostalgia, History, and Postcards." *Social Education,* XL January, pp. 19-25.

Kelly, William P. 1981. "Running on Empty: Reimaging Rock and Roll." *Journal of American Culture,* IV Winter, pp. 152-159.

Kelm, Rebecca Sturm. 1990. "The Lack of Access to Back Issues of the Weekly Tabloids: Does It Matter?" *Journal of Popular Culture,* XXIII Spring, pp. 45-50.

King, Florence. 1974. "Rednecks, White Socks, and Blue-Ribbon Fear: The Nashville Sound of Discontent." *Harper's Magazine,* CCXLIX July, pp. 30-34.

Knupp, Ralph E. 1981. "A Time for Every Purpose Under Heaven: Rhetorical Dimensions of Protest Music." *Southern Speech Communication Journal,* XLVI Summer, pp. 377-389.

Lawrence, John Shelton. 1978. "A Critical Analysis of Roger B. Rollin's 'Against Evaluation.'" *Journal of Popular Culture*, XII Summer, pp. 99-112.

Lees, Gene. 1968. "1918-1968: From *Over There* to *Kill for Peace*." *High Fidelity*, XVIII November, pp. 56-60.

Lees, Gene. 1978. "War Songs: Bathos and Acquiescence." *High Fidelity*, XXVIII December, pp. 41-44.

Lees, Gene. 1979. "War Songs II: Music Goes AWOL." *High Fidelity*, XXIX January, pp. 20-22.

Levine, Mark H., and Thomas J. Harig. 1975. "The Role of Rock: A Review and Critique of Alternative Perspectives on the Impact of Rock Music." *Popular Music and Society*, IV, pp. 195-207.

Lewis George H. 1973. "Social Protest and Self-Awareness in Black Popular Music." *Popular Music and Society*, II Summer, pp. 327-333.

Lewis, George H. 1976. "Country Music Lyrics." *Journal of Communication*, XXVI Autumn, pp. 37-40.

Lewis, George H. 1979. "The Sociology of Popular Music: A Selected and Annotated Bibliography." *Popular Music and Society*, VII, pp. 57-68.

Lewis, George H. 1981. "Commercial and Colonial Stimuli: Cross-Cultural Creation of Popular Culture." *Journal of Popular Culture*, XV Fall, pp. 142-156.

Lewis, George H. 1982. "Between Consciousness and Existence: Popular Culture and the Sociological Imagination." *Journal of Popular Culture*, XV Spring, pp. 81-92.

Lewis, George H. 1986. "Uncertain Truths: The Promotion of Popular Culture." *Journal of Popular Culture*, XX Winter, pp. 31-44.

Lewis, James R. 1987. "Adam and Eve on Madison Avenue: Symbolic Inversion in Popular Culture." *Studies in Popular Culture*, X No. 1, pp. 74-82.

Litoff, Judy Barrett, and David C. Smith. 1990. "'Will He Get My Letter?" Popular Portrayals of Mail and Morale During World War II." *Journal of Popular Culture*, XXIII Spring, pp. 21-43.

Lund, Jens. 1972a. "Country Music Goes to War: Songs for the Red-Blooded American." *Popular Music and Society*, I Summer, pp. 210-230.

Lund, Jens. 1972b. "Fundamentalism, Racism, and Political Reaction in Country Music." *Sounds of Social Change: Studies in Popular Culture*, edited by R. Serge Denisoff and Richard A. Peterson. Chicago: Rand McNally, pp. 79-91.

Lund, Jens, and R. Serge Denisoff. 1971. "The Folk Music Revival and the Counter Culture." *Journal of American Folklore*, LXXXIV October/December, pp. 394-405.

Lunstrum, John P., and Donald O. Schneider. 1969. "Commercial Television in the Teaching of the Social Studies." *Social Education*, XXXIII February, pp. 154-160.

Marcus, Greil. 1976. "Rock Films." *The Rolling Stone Illustrated History of Rock and Roll*, edited by Jim Miller. New York: Random House, pp. 350-357.

Maultsby, Portia K. 1983. "Soul Music: Its Sociological and Political Significance in American Popular Culture." *Journal of Popular Culture*, XVII Fall, pp. 51-65.

McCarthy, John D., Richard A. Peterson, and William L. Yancey. 1977. "Singing Along with the Silent Majority." *Popular Culture: Mirror of American Life*, edited by David Manning White and John Pendleton. Del Mar, CA: Publisher's, pp. 169-173.

McClary, Susan, and Robert Walser. 1990. "Start Making Sense! Musicology Wrestles with Rock." *On Record: Rock, Pop, and the Written Word*. New York: Pantheon Books, pp. 277-292.

McCourt, Tom. 1983. "Bright Lights, Big City: A Brief History of Rhythm and Blues, 1945-1957." *Popular Music and Society*, IX, pp. 1-18.

McDonald, James R. 1985. "Popular Music and Gender Studies: A Research Priority." *JEMF Quarterly*, XXI Spring-Summer, pp. 59-62.

McMullen, Haynes, and Jay E. Daily. 1984. "Teaching the Use of Popular Materials in a Library School." *Popular Culture and Libraries*, compiled by Frank W. Hoffmann. Hamden, CT: Library Profession Publications/Shoe String Press, pp. 41-52.

Miller, Lloyd, and James K. Skipper, Jr. 1968. "Sounds of Protest: Jazz and the Militant Avant-Garde." *Approaches to Deviance: Theories, Concepts, and Research Findings*, edited by Mark Lefton, James K. Skipper, Jr., and Charles H. McCaghy. New York: Appleton-Century-Crofts, pp. 129-140.

Miller, Richard E. 1987. "The Music of Our Sphere: Apocalyptic Visions in Popular Music of the Eighties." *Popular Music and Society*, XI No. 3 Fall, pp. 75-90.

Mistichelli, Judith A., and Christine Roysdon. 1981. "Technology in American Culture: Current Publications." *Journal of American Culture*, IV Fall, pp. 185-196.

Mohrmann, G. P., and F. Eugene Scott. 1976. "Popular Music and World War II: The Rhetoric of Continuation." *Quarterly Journal of Speech*, LXII February, pp. 145-156.

Monaghan, Peter. 1989. "Icons of Popular Culture are Grist for Historian's Research." *Chronicle of Higher Education*, XXXVI September 13, p. 3A.

Mooney, Hughson F. 1972. "Popular Music Since the 1920's: The Significance of Shifting Taste." *Popular Music and Society*, I Spring, pp. 129-143.

Mooney, Hughson F. 1974. "Just Before Rock: Pop Music 1950-1953 Reconsidered." *Popular Music and Society*, III, pp. 65-108.

Mooney, Hughson F. 1980a. "Commercial 'Country' Music in the 1970s: Some Special and Historical Perspectives." *Popular Music and Society*, VII pp. 208-213.

Mooney, Hughson F. 1980b. "Twilight of the Age of Aquarius? Popular Music in the 1970s." *Popular Music and Society*, VII, pp. 182-198.

Mooney, Hughson F. 1988. "Years of Strain and Stress: 1917-1929 in the Whitburn Record Charts." *Popular Music and Society*, XII Summer, pp. 1-20.

Moran, Barbara B. 1981. "Popular Culture and its Challenge to the Academic Library." *Twentieth-Century Popular Culture in Museums and Libraries*, edited by Fred E. H. Schroeder. Bowling Green, OH: Bowling Green University, pp. 179-186.

Moran, Barbara B. 1983. "The Popular Culture Collection Quandry: A Survey of Faculty Needs." *Collection Building*, Spring, pp. 13-17.

Moran, Barbara B. 1985. "Popular Culture and Library Education." *Journal of Education for Library and Information Science*, XXVI Summer.

Morgan, John P., and Thomas C. Tulloss. 1976. "The Jake Walk Blues: A Toxicologic Tragedy Mirrored in American Popular Music." *Annals of Internal Medicine*, LXXXV December, pp. 804-808.

Morse, David E. 1969. "Avant-Rock in the Classroom." *English Journal*, LVIII February, pp. 196-200ff.

Myers, Robert. 1990. "There Are Right Reasons and Wrong Reasons for Studying Rock." *Chronicle of Higher Education*, XXXVI February 14, pp. 2B, 3B.

Nye, Russel B. 1981. "Eight Ways of Looking at an Amusement Park." *Journal of Popular Culture*, XV Summer, pp. 63-75.

Oldfield, Paul. 1989. "After Subversion: Pop Culture and Power," *Zoot Suits and Second-Hand Dresses: An Anthology of Fashion and Music*, edited by Angela McRobbie. Boston: Unwin Hyman Books, pp. 256-266.

Paul, Angus. 1987. "New Research Center in Chicago Strives to Preserve and Promote the Legacy of Black Music." *Chronicle of Higher Education*, XXXIII January 28, pp. 6-7, 10.

Peterson, Richard A. 1971. "Taking Popular Music Too Seriously." *Journal of Popular Culture*, IV Winter, pp. 590-594.

Peterson, Richard A. 1973. "The Unnatural History of Rock Festivals: An Instance of Media Facilitation." *Popular Music and Society*, II Winter, pp. 97-123.

Peterson, Richard A. 1977. "Where the Two Cultures Meet: Popular Culture." *Journal of Popular Culture*, XI Fall, pp. 385-400.

Peterson, Richard A. 1978a. "Disco!" *The Chronicle Review*, XVIII October, 2. pp. 26R, 27R.

Peterson, Richard A. 1978b. "The Production of Cultural Change: The Case of Contemporary Country Music." *Social Research*, XLV Summer, pp. 292-314.

Peterson, Richard A. 1989. "Five Constraints on the Production of Culture: Law, Technology, Market, Organizational Structure, and Occupational Careers." *American Popular Music–Volume One: The 19th Century and Tin Pan Alley*, edited by Timothy E. Scheurer. Bowling Green, OH: Bowling Green State University, pp. 16-27.

Peterson, Richard A., and David G. Berger. 1975. "Cycles in Symbol Production: The Case of Popular Music." *American Sociological Review*, XL April, pp. 158-173.

Pickens, Donald K. 1981. "The Historical Images in Republican Campaign Songs, 1860-1900." *Journal of Popular Culture*, XV Winter, 165-174.

Plasketes, George M., and Julie Grace Plasketes. 1987. "From Woodstock Nation to Pepsi Generation: Reflections on Rock Culture and the State of Music, 1969 to the Present." *Popular Music and Society*, XI Spring, pp. 25-52.

Politis, John. 1983. "Rock Music's Place in the Library." *Drexel Library Quarterly*, XIX Winter, pp. 78-92.

Postol, Todd. 1985. "Reinterpreting the Fifties: Changing Views of a 'Dull' Decade." *Journal of American Culture*, VIII Summer, pp. 39-45.

Prager, Bud. 1980. "Rock 'n' Roll: Neglected Giant." *Billboard*. January 26, p. 18.

Pratt, Ray. 1989. "Popular Music, Free Space, and the Quest for Community." *Popular Music and Society*, XIII Winter, pp. 59-76.

Prechter, Robert R. 1985a. "Elvis, Frankenstein, and Andy Warhol: Using Pop Culture to Forecast the Stock Market." *Barron's*, LXV September 9, pp. 6-7ff.

Prechter, Robert R. 1985b. "Popular Culture and the Stock Market." *The Elliott Wave Theorist*, August 22, pp. 1-20.

Prosser, H. L. 1983. "Teaching Sociology with the Martian Chronicles." *Social Education*, XLVII March, pp. 212-215ff.

Raasch, Chuck. 1988. "'50s Seem Nifty in '80s: But Nostalgia Neglects Reality of Cold War Era." *Battle Creek* [Michigan] *Enquirer*, June 9, pp. 1B, 2B.

Reinartz, Kay. 1975. "The Paper Doll: Images of American Women in Popular Songs." *Women: A Feminist Perspective*, edited by Jo Freeman. Palo Alto, CA: Mayfield Publishing, pp. 293-308.

Rice, Ronald E. 1980. "The Content of Popular Recordings." *Popular Music and Society*, VII, pp. 140-158.

Robinson, John P., Robert Pilskaln, and Paul Hirsch. 1976. "Protest Rock and Drugs." *Journal of Communication*, XXVI Autumn, pp. 125-136.

Rodger, Jonathan. 1972. "Back to the '50s." *Newsweek*, LXXX October 16, pp. 78-82.

Rodnitzky, Jerome. 1971. "The Decline of Contemporary Protest Music." *Popular Music and Society*, I Fall, pp. 44-50.

Rodnitzky, Jerome. 1988. "Also Born in the U.S.A.: Bob Dylan's Outlaw Heroes and the Real Bob Dylan." *Popular Music and Society*, XII Summer, pp. 37-43.

Rollin, Roger B. 1970. "Beowulf to Batman: The Epic Hero and Pop Culture." *College English*, XXXI February, pp. 431-449.

Rollin, Roger B. 1975. "Against Evaluation: The Role of the Critic of Popular Culture." *Journal of Popular Culture*, IX Fall, pp. 355-365.

Rollin, Roger B. 1976. "Trash Gratia Artis: Popular Culture as Literature." *Intellect*, December, pp. 191-194.

Rollin, Roger B. 1978. "Son of 'Against Evaluation': Reply to John Shelton Lawrence." *Journal of Popular Culture*, XII Summer, pp. 113-117.

Rollin, Roger B. 1980. "TV Heroes and the Denial of Death." *Prospects: An Annual of American Cultural Studies–Volume Five*, edited by Jack Salzman. New York: Burt Franklin, pp. 457-466.

Rollin, Roger B. 1983. "The Lone Ranger and Lenny Skutnik: The Hero as Popular Culture." *The Hero in Transition*, edited by Ray B. Browne and Marshall W. Fishwick. Bowling Green, OH: Bowling Green University, pp. 14-45.

Rollin, Roger B. 1989a. "On Comparative Popular Culture, American Style." *The Americanization of the Global Village: Essays in Comparative Popular Culture*. Bowling Green, OH: Bowling Green University, pp. 1-10.

Rollin, Roger B. 1989b. "Popular Culture–The Essential Humanity." *The Comparatist*, XIII May, pp. 98-108.

Rollin, Roger B. 1989c. "'Words, Words, Words . . .': On Redefining 'Literature.'" *Journal of Popular Culture*, XXIII Winter, pp. 1-10.

Romanowski, William D., and R. Serge Denisoff. 1987. "Money for Nothin' and the Charts for Free: Rock and the Movies." *Journal of Popular Culture*, XXI Winter, pp. 63-78.

Root, Robert L. Jr. 1986. "A Listener's Guide to the Rhetoric of Popular Music." *Journal of Popular Culture*, XX Summer, pp. 15-26.

Root, Robert L. Jr. 1987. "The Nature of Popular Culture." *The Rhetorics of Popular Culture: Advertising, Advocacy, and Entertainment*. Westport, CT: Greenwood Press, pp. 3-12.

Rosenstone, Richard A. 1969. "'The Times They Are A 'Changin'': The Music of Protest." *The Annals of the American Academy of Political and Social Science*, CCCLXXXI March, pp. 131-144.

Ryant, Carl. 1982. "Oral History as Popular Culture." *Journal of Popular Culture*, XV Spring, pp. 60-66.

Schilling, James Von. 1981. "Records and the Record Industry." *Handbook of American Popular Culture–Volume Three*, edited by M. Thomas Inge. Westport, CT: Greenwood Press, pp. 385-411.

Schroeder, Fred E. H. 1977. "The Discovery of Popular Culture Before Printing." *Journal of Popular Culture*, XI Winter, pp. 629-640.

Schroeder, Fred E. H. 1980. "Studying Popular Culture in the Public Library: Suggestions for Cooperative Programs." *Drexel Library Quarterly*, XVI July, pp. 65-72.

Schroeder, Fred E. H. 1981. "How to Acquire, Access, Catalog, and Research a Popular Culture Collection for Your Museum of History, Technology, or Art for $97 per Year." *Twentieth-Century Popular Culture in Museums and Libraries*. Bowling Green, OH: Bowling Green University, pp. 77-83.

Schroeder, Fred E. H. 1989. "Extra-Academic Agents For Cultural Literacy in America." *Journal of American Culture*, XII Spring, pp. 17-23.

Schurk, William L. 1980. "Popular Culture and Libraries: A Practical Perspective." *Drexel Library Quarterly*, XVI July, pp. 43-52.

Seidman, Laurence I. 1973. "Teaching about the American Revolution Through Its Folk Songs." *Social Education*, XXXVIII November, pp. 654-664.

Seidman, Laurence I. 1976. "'Get on the Raft with Taft' and Other Musical Treats." *Social Education*, XL October, pp. 436-437.

Seidman, Laurence I. 1985. "Folksongs: Magic in Your Classroom." *Social Education*, XLIX October, pp. 580-587.

Sewell, Robert G. 1984. "Trash or Treasure: Pop Fiction in Academic and Research Libraries." *College and Research Libraries*, XLV November, pp. 450-461.

Shulins, Nancy. 1984. "Pop Culture: 'What Water Is to Fish'–It Is the World We Live in." *The [Columbia, South Carolina] State*, March 18, pp. 1E, 7E.

Simels, Steve. 1980. "The All-Star No Nukes Concerts: Three Discs of Delicious Music." *Stereo Review*, XLIV March, pp. 88-91.

Singleton, Gregory H. 1977. "Popular Culture or the Culture of the Populace?" *Journal of Popular Culture*, XI Summer, pp. 254-266.

Skaggs, David Curtis. 1978. "Postage Stamps as Icons." *Icons of America*, edited by Ray B. Browne and Marshall Fishwick. Bowling Green, OH: Bowling Green State University, pp. 198-208.

Skaggs, David Curtis, and Larry Dean Wills. 1977. "Don't Stamp on Me: Postage Stamps as a Teaching Device." *Social Education*, XLI November-December, pp. 626-629.

Smith, Jeff. 1985. "The Sixties Revisited: Reflections on the Meaning of the Movement." *The Cresset*, XLVIII January, pp. 13-19.

Snook, Lee Ann. 1988. "Stuff 'n' Such: Popular Culture Experts Tell Who Saves What, and Why." *At B.G.*, XVIII Summer, pp. 10-12.

Sontag, Susan. 1965. "The Imagination of Disaster." *Commentary*, XL October, pp. 42-48.

Stevenson, Gordon. 1975a. "Race Records: Victims of Benign Neglect in Libraries." *Wilson Library Bulletin*, L November, pp. 224-232.

Stevenson, Gordon. 1975b. "Sound Recordings." *Advances in Librarianship–Volume Five*, edited by Melvin J. Voight and Michael H. Harris. New York: Academic Press, pp. 279-320.

Stevenson, Gordon. 1977a. "Popular Culture and the Public Library." *Advances in Librarianship–Volume Seven*, edited by Melvin J. Voight and Michael H. Harris. New York: Academic Press, pp. 177-229.

Stevenson, Gordon. 1977b. "Popular Culture Studies and Library Education." *Journal of Education for Librarianship*, XV April, pp. 235-250.

Stevenson, Gordon. 1977c. "The Wayward Scholar: Resources and Research in Popular Culture." *Library Trends*, XXV April, pp. 779-818.

Stevenson, Gordon. 1978. "Popular Culture and the Academic Librarian." *Popular Culture and the Library: Current Issues Symposium II* edited by Wayne A. Wiegand. Lexington, KY: University of Kentucky, pp. 28-51.

Stidom, Larry. 1985. "A Few Political and Topical Records from Years Past." *Goldmine*, No. 126 May 24, p. 28.

Tamarkin, Jeff. 1988. "White House Funnies: Presidential Satire Records." *Goldmine*, No. 217 November 18, pp. 26-27, 83-85.

Tamke, Susan S. 1977. "Oral History and Popular Culture: A Method for the Study of the Experience of Culture." *Journal of Popular Culture*, XI Summer, pp. 267-279.

Thorpe, Peter. 1970. "I'm Movin' On: The Escape Theme in Country and Western Music." *Western Humanities Review*, XXIV Autumn, pp. 307-318.

Tosches, Nick. 1984. "What That Was: A Chronology of the Coming of Rock 'n' Roll." *Unsung Heroes of Rock 'n' Roll: The Birth of Rock 'n' Roll in the Dark and Wild Years Before Elvis*. New York: Charles Scribner's Sons, pp. 147-168.

Turner, Thomas N. 1979. "Using Popular Culture in the Social Studies." *How To Do It Series*, Series Two, No. 9. Washington, DC: National Council for the Social Studies.

Ventura, Michael. 1987a. "Hear That Long Snake Moan: The Voodoo Origins of Rock and Roll Culture." *The Whole Earth Review*, No. 54 Spring, pp. 28-45.

Ventura, Michael. 1987b. "Hear That Long Snake Moan–Part Two." *The Whole Earth Review*, No. 55 Summer, pp. 82-93.

Waffen, Les, and Peter Hesbacher. 1981. "War Songs: Hit Recordings During the Vietnam Period." *ARSC Journal*, XIII No. 2, pp. 4-18.

Wells, John. 1978. "Bent Out of Shape from Society's Pliers: A Sociological Study of the Grotesque in the Songs of Bob Dylan." *Popular Music and Society*, VI, pp. 27-38.

Whitburn, Joel. 1986. "Chronology of Milestones in Popular Music/Recording History, 1877-1954." *Pop Memories, 1890-1950: The History of American Popular Music*. Menomonee Falls, WI: Record Research, pp. 11-17.

Wiegand, Wayne A. 1979. "Popular Culture: A New Frontier for Academic Libraries." *Journal of Academic Librarianship*, V September, pp. 200-204.

Wiegand, Wayne A. 1980. "Taste Cultures and Librarians: A Position Paper." *Drexel Library Quarterly*, XVI July, pp. 1-11.
Wiegand, Wayne A. 1981. "The Academic Library's Responsibility to the Resource Needs of the Popular Culture Community." *Twentieth-Century Popular Culture in Museums and Libraries*, edited by Fred E. H. Schroeder. Bowling Green, OH: Bowling Green State University, pp. 189-198.
Winkler, Karen J. 1983. "The Study of Popular Culture: Thriving in a Back-to Basics Era." *The Chronicle of Higher Education*, XXVI June 29, p. 9.
Winkler, Karen J. 1985. "Television and Film Ignored Vietnam Until the Late 1960s, Scholars Argue." *The Chronicle of Higher Education*, XXXI November 20, pp. 5, 9.
Wolfe, Charles. 1978. "Nuclear Country: The Atomic Bomb in Country Music." *Journal of Country Music*, VI January, pp. 4-22.
Wolfe, Tom. 1976. "The 'Me' Decade and the Third Great Awakening." *New York Times Magazine*, August 23, pp. 26-40.
Woodward, William. 1988a. "America as a Culture (I): Some Emerging Lines of Analysis." *Journal of American Culture*, XI Spring, pp. 1-16.
Woodward, William. 1988b. "America as a Culture (II): A Fourfold Heritage." *Journal of American Culture*, XI Spring, pp. 17-32.

Unpublished Materials

Bailey, Robert T. 1979. "A Study of the Effect of Popular Music on Achievement in and Attitude Toward Contemporary United States History." MEd Thesis, West Georgia College.
Berger, David G. 1966. "The Unchanging Popular Tune Lyric, 1910-1955." PhD Dissertation, Columbia University.
Burns, Gary. 1981. "Utopia and Dystopia in Popular Song Lyrics: Rhetorical Visions in the United States, 1963-1972." PhD Dissertation, Northwestern University.
Butchart, Ronald E., and B. Lee Cooper. 1981. "'Teacher, Leave Them Kids Alone!': Perceptions of Schooling and Education in American Popular Music." Mimeographed paper presented at the Annual Convention of The American Education Studies Association.

Cantor, Louis. 1978. "Bob Dylan and the Protest Movement of the 1960s: The Electronic Medium Is the Apocalyptic Message." Mimeographed paper presented at the 8th National Convention of The Popular Culture Association.

Cooper, B. Lee. 1981. "Popular Music and American History: Exploring Unusual Audio Teaching Resources." Mimeographed paper presented at the 24th Annual Missouri Valley History Conference.

Cooper, B. Lee. 1985a. "Hello, Baby . . . Yeah, This Is the Big Bopper Speakin': Perspectives on Communications Media in Contemporary Lyrics." Mimeographed paper presented at the 7th National Convention of The American Culture Association.

Cooper, B. Lee. 1985b. "Yes Bearcat, I'll Save the Last Dance for You: Answer Songs and Sequel Tunes in American Popular Music, 1950-1985." Mimeographed paper presented at the 8th Annual Convention of The American Culture Association.

Cooper, B. Lee. 1988a. "I'm a Hog for You Baby: Problems of Thematic Classification in Popular Music." Mimeographed paper presented at the Annual Convention of The Music Library Association.

Cooper, B. Lee. 1988b. "Little Red Riding Hood Meets Sam The Sham and The Pharoahs: A Selected Discography of Popular Recordings Featuring Nursery Rhyme and Fairy Tale Themes, 1950-1985." Mimeographed paper presented at the Annual Convention of The Association of Recorded Sound Collections.

Cooper, B. Lee. 1989. "The Historian as a Freelance Writer." Mimeographed paper presented at the Duquesne History Forum.

DeWitt, Howard A. 1977. "Using Popular History in the American Survey: Rock and Roll as an Expression of American Culture in the 1950s." Mimeographed paper presented at the 7th Annual Convention of The Popular Culture Association.

Emblidge, David Murray. 1973. "A Dialogue of Energy: Rock Music and Cultural Change." PhD Dissertation, University of Minnesota.

Fuchsman, Kenneth A. 1983. "Deliver Me from the Days of Old: Lyrical Themes in 1950s Rock and Roll." Mimeographed paper presented at the 13th National Convention of The Popular Culture Association.

Fuchsman, Kenneth A. 1984. "Between the Garden and the Devil's Bargain: The 1960s Counter Culture in Rock Music." Mimeographed paper presented at the 6th National Convention of The American Culture Association.

Harmon, James Elmer. 1971. "The New Music and the American Youth Subculture." PhD Dissertation, United States International University.

Johnson, Mary Jane Carle. 1978. "Rock Music as a Reflector of Social Attitudes Among Youth of the 1960s." PhD Dissertation, St. Louis University.

Kamin, Jonathan. 1976. "Rhythm and Blues in White America: Rock and Roll as Acculturation and Perceptual Learning." PhD Dissertation, Princeton University.

Keesing, Hugo. 1972. "Youth in Transition: A Content Analysis of Two Decades of Popular Music." PhD Dissertation, Adelphi University.

Keesing, Hugo. 1978. "Culture in the Grooves: American History at 78, 45 and 33 1/3 r.p.m." Mimeographed paper presented at the 8th National Convention of The Popular Culture Association.

Keesing, Hugo. 1979. "Pop Goes to War: The Music of World War II and Vietnam." Mimeographed paper presented at the 9th National Convention of The Popular Culture Association.

Keesing, Hugo. 1983. "Popular Recordings and the American Presidency: From John F. Kennedy to Ronald Reagan." Mimeographed paper presented at the 13th National Convention of The Popular Culture Association.

Keesing, Hugo. 1987. "Recorded Music and the Vietnam War: The First 25 Years." Mimeographed paper presented at the 17th National Convention of The Popular Culture Association.

Petterson, James. 1977. "Using Popular Music to Teach Topics in American History Since 1950 for High School Students." MSEd, University of Southern California.

Reading, Joseph D. 1980. "Tears of Rage: A History, Theory, and Criticism of Rock Song and Social Conflict Rhetoric, 1965-1970." PhD Dissertation, University of Oregon.

Redd, Lawrence N. 1971. "The Impact of Radio, Motion Pictures, and Blues on Rock and Roll Music." MA Thesis, Michigan State University.

Schnell, James. 1985. "No Nukes: Music as a Form of Countercultural Communication." Mimeographed paper presented at the 15th National Convention of The Popular Culture Association.

Slater, Thomas J. 1982. "Rock Music, Youth, and Society: The Uses of Rock Music in the Movies, 1955-1981." Mimeographed paper presented at the 12th National Convention of The Popular Culture Association.

Wanzenried, John Werner. 1974. "Extentional and Intentional Orientations of Rock and Roll Song Lyrics, 1955-1972: A Content Analysis." PhD Dissertation, University of Nebraska.

Weller, Donald J. 1971. "Rock Music: Its Role and Political Significance as a Channel of Communication." PhD Dissertation, University of Hawaii.

Index